# Debates in Modern Philosophy

"There have now been three generations of analytical philosophers who have studied the early modern period from Descartes to Kant. This collection spans all three, exhibiting the excellence of scholarship and philosophy found in this tradition. It also illustrates some of the changes in position and in approach that have occurred in the analytical tradition. We also see in this collection how the analytical study of modern philosophy has come to recognize that analytical philosophy itself, earlier in its history, tended to overestimate the extent to which it had made progress over the philosophers of the seventeenth and eighteenth centuries. There is a lot to be learned from reading this book both about the philosophy of the early modern period and the philosophy of the twentieth and twenty-first centuries."

Allen Wood, Stanford University

"*Debates in Modern Philosophy* is an extremely useful collection. The exchanges here are accessible and provocative, and show just how philosophically productive debate over the interpretation of historical texts can be. The model of one commentator directly engaging the interpretation of another works well, giving students concrete illustrations of reasoned interpretive disagreement and a sense of what is at stake in the construction and assessment of rival readings of historical texts. The topics are well chosen, providing both a representative sample of key issues in modern epistemology and metaphysics, and a range of texts that are ripe for further analysis and debate in the classroom."

Tom Holden, University of California Santa Barbara

*Debates in Modern Philosophy: Essential Readings and Contemporary Responses* provides an in-depth, engaging introduction to important issues in modern philosophy. It presents 13 key interpretive debates to students, and ranges in coverage from Descartes' *Meditations* to Kant's *Critique of Pure Reason*.

Debates include:

Did Descartes have a developed and consistent view about how the mind interacts with the body?
Was Leibniz an idealist, or did he believe in corporeal substances?
What is Locke's theory of personal identity?
Could there be a Berkeleian metaphysics without God?
Did Hume believe in causal powers?
What is Kant's transcendental idealism?

Each of the thirteen debates consists of a well known article or book chapter from a living philosopher, followed by a new response from a different scholar, specially commissioned for this volume. Every debate is prefaced by an introduction written for those coming upon the debates for the first time and followed by an annotated list for further reading. The volume starts with an introduction that explains the importance and relevance of the modern period and its key debates to philosophy and ends with a glossary that covers terms from both the modern period and the study of the history of philosophy in general.

*Debates in Modern Philosophy* will help students evaluate different interpretations of key texts from modern philosophy, and provide a model for constructing their own positions in these debates.

**Stewart Duncan** is Associate Professor of Philosophy at the University of Florida.

**Antonia LoLordo** is Associate Professor of Philosophy at the University of Virginia.

---

### About the Series

### Key Debates in the History of Philosophy

New students to the history of philosophy risk equating a summary of an important philosopher as the final word on that thinker. Lost in the introductions and primers to the great philosophers are the complexities and range of competing interpretations that result from close readings of the primary texts. Unlike any other undergraduate introduction in this field, **Key Debates in the History of Philosophy** are designed to lead students back to the classic works so that they may better understand what's at stake in these competing viewpoints. Each volume in the series contains 10 to 15 interpretive issues, or sections, with two chapters included in each section. The first chapter is a re-printed well known journal article or book chapter. The second chapter either takes to task or builds upon the argument in the first article and is written by a different scholar especially for the volume. The result is a new kind of introduction—one that enables students to understand philosophy's history as a still-living debate, rather than a string of unearthed truths from the past.

### Volumes in the Series

*Debates in Modern Philosophy: Essential Readings and Contemporary Responses*
Edited by Stewart Duncan and Antonia LoLordo

*Debates in Medieval Philosophy: Essential Readings and Contemporary Responses*
Edited by Jeffrey Hause

# Debates in Modern Philosophy

## Essential Readings and Contemporary Responses

Edited by
Stewart Duncan and Antonia LoLordo

Routledge
Taylor & Francis Group

NEW YORK AND LONDON

First published 2013
byRoutledge
711 Third Avenue, New York, NY 10017

Simultaneously published in the UK
by Routledge
2 Park Square, Milton Park, Abingdon, Oxon OX14 4RN

*Routledge is an imprint of the Taylor & Francis Group, an informa business*

*Library of Congress Cataloging in Publication Data*
    Debates in modern philosophy / edited by
    Stewart Duncan and Antonia LoLordo.
    p. cm.—(Key debates in the history of philosophy)
    Includes bibliographical references (p. ) and index.
    1. Philosophy, Modern.  I. Duncan, Stewart.
    II LoLordo, Antonia, 1972–
    B790.D43 2013
    190—dc23
    2012022526

ISBN: 978–0–415–88797–7 (hbk)
IBSN: 978–0–415–88798–4 (pbk)

Typeset in Minion
by Swales & Willis Ltd, Exeter, Devon

Certified Sourcing
www.sfiprogram.org
SFI-00453

Printed and bound in the United States of America
by Edwards Brothers, Inc.

# Contents

# Contributors

**Lucy Allais** is Senior Lecturer at the University of Sussex and Professor at the University of the Witwatersrand. She is the author of numerous articles on Kant and on the nature of forgiveness and punishment.

**Helen Beebee** is Samuel Hall Professor of Philosophy at the University of Manchester. She is the author of *Hume on Causation* (Routledge, 2006) and the co-editor of the *Oxford Handbook of Causation* (with Chris Hitchcock and Peter Menzies: Oxford, 2009).

**Deborah Brown** is Associate Professor at the University of Queensland and Associate Dean of the Faculty of Arts. She is the author of *Descartes and the Passionate Mind* (Cambridge, 2006) as well as numerous articles.

**Emily Carson** is Associate Professor at McGill University and serves as an Executive Editor for the *Canadian Journal of Philosophy*. She is the author of numerous papers on Kant and on early modern philosophy and mathematics.

**Lisa Downing** is Professor at Ohio State University. She is the author of articles on Berkeley, Descartes, Locke, Malebranche and others.

**Stewart Duncan** is Associate Professor at the University of Florida. As well as editing this book, he is the author of articles on Cavendish, Hobbes, Leibniz, More, and Toland.

**Sukjae Lee** is Associate Professor at Seoul National University. He is the author of articles on Leibniz, Malebranche, and Scotus.

**Martin Lin** is Associate Professor at Rutgers University. He is the author of a number of articles on Lebniz and Spinoza.

**Antonia Lolordo** is Associate Professor at the University of Virginia. She is the author of *Pierre Gassendi and the Birth of Early Modern Philosophy* (Cambridge, 2007) and *Locke's Moral Man* (Oxford, 2012).

**Brandon Look** is Professor of Philosophy at the University of Kentucky. He is the author of *Leibniz and the 'vinculum substantiale'* (Franz Steiner Verlag, 1999) and editor of the *Continuum Companion to Leibniz* (Continuum, 2011).

**Yitzhak Melamed** is Associate Professor at Johns Hopkins. He is the author of *Spinoza's Metaphysics of Substance and Thought* (Oxford, 2012), and of several articles on Spinoza and Descartes. He is co-editor of *Spinoza's Theological-Political Treatise* (with Michael Rosenthal: Cambridge, 2010), *Spinoza and German Idealism* (with Eckart Föstrer; Cambridge 2012) and the editor of *The Young Spinoza* (Oxford: Forthcoming).

**Peter Millican** is University Reader at Oxford. He is the author of *Reading Hume on Human Understanding* (Oxford, 2002) and numerous papers.

**Lex Newman** is Associate Professor at the University of Utah. He is the editor of *The Cambridge Companion to Locke's* Essay (Cambridge, 2007) and numerous papers on Descartes and Locke.

**Tom Stoneham** is Head of Department and Professor of Philosophy at the University of York. He is the author of *Berkeley's World: An Examnation of the the Three Dialogues* (Oxford, 2002) and numerous articles.

**Matthew Stuart** is Professor of Philosophy at Bowdoin College. He is the author of *Locke's Metaphysics* (Oxford, 2013) and of articles on Locke and Descartes.

# Introduction

## Why Is This Called *Modern* Philosophy?

This book discusses the views of various European philosophers of the seventeenth and eighteenth centuries. That may not seem terribly modern. René Descartes, the philosopher discussed in Chapters 1 and 2, was writing in the 1630s and 1640s. Even the most recent figure discussed, Immanuel Kant, died in 1804. By many standards, that was a long time ago. So why is the work of Descartes, Kant, and their contemporaries called *modern* philosophy?

In one way this puzzle has a trivial answer. 'Modern' is being used here to describe a long period of time, and to contrast it with other long periods of time. So modern philosophy is not the philosophy of the 2010s as contrasted with the philosophy of the 1990s, or even the 1950s. Rather it's the philosophy of the 1600s and onwards, as opposed to ancient and medieval philosophy. Classes on ancient philosophy typically focus on the work of Plato and Aristotle, who lived in the fourth century BCE. Famous medieval philosophers include Thomas Aquinas, John Duns Scotus, and William Ockham, who lived in the thirteenth and fourteenth centuries. Compared to Plato or Ockham, Descartes and Kant are relatively recent authors.

But there's a more interesting answer too. Many people have thought that certain seventeenth- and eighteenth-century philosophers were doing something new—something radically different from what their ancient and medieval predecessors were doing. One might question whether this is really true. But certainly many seventeenth- and eighteenth-century philosophers themselves thought that they were doing something different and new.

Descartes, in his *Discourse on the Method*, praised previous philosophers, saying that philosophy "has been cultivated for many centuries by the most excellent minds" (AT 6.8, CSM 1.114–15). But he also said that those excellent minds had not made much progress: "there is still no point in it [philosophy] which is not disputed and hence doubtful" (AT 6.8, CSM 1.115). And he set out a new method for investigating the world, free from the "defects" of previous methods, that would let him construct his own, new, better system in metaphysics, the sciences, and even ethics (AT 6.18, CSM 1.120).

No doubt some of this was a matter of exaggeration, indeed of advertising. But Descartes and many of his contemporaries—Thomas Hobbes, for instance—did see themselves as engaged in a new project in philosophy and the sciences, which somehow contained a new way of explaining how the world worked. So what was this new project? And what, if anything, did all these modern philosophers have in common?

Two themes emerge when you read what Descartes and Hobbes say about their new philosophies. First, they think that earlier philosophers, particularly so-called Scholastic Aristotelians—medieval European philosophers who were influenced by Aristotle—were mistaken about many issues, and that the new, modern way is better. (They say nicer things about Aristotle himself, and about some other previous philosophers.) This view was shared by many of the modern philosophers, but not all of them. Among the next generation, for instance, Gottfried Leibniz argued that there was more good in the work of Scholastic Aristotelians than moderns like Descartes and Hobbes had realized. Second, they think that mathematics has been far more successful than philosophy at achieving consensus and finding certainty, and that it would be good if philosophy could somehow emulate this success. Mathematical learning, says Hobbes, "is free from controversies and dispute," but elsewhere "there is nothing not disputable" (Hobbes 1994, 19). And Descartes too notes, "mathematicians alone have been able to find any demonstrations" (AT 6.19, CSM 1.120).

The more you read about modern philosophy, the more you will discover people who have grand historical stories about what was going on. So you might read about the Scientific Revolution, the Enlightenment (or various Enlightenments), mechanism replacing Aristotelianism, or the conflict between empiricism and rationalism (or British Empiricism and Continental Rationalism). Indeed, several modern philosophers had their own views as to what the overarching story of modern philosophy was. Both Pierre Bayle and David Hume characterized modern philosophy as a view about the unreality of "colours, sounds, tastes, smells, heat and cold."[1] Hume's contemporary Thomas Reid thought an important part of the history of modern philosophy could be told in terms of different theories about the nature of ideas. Kant meanwhile gave Hume a pivotal role in his history of modern philosophy: "Since the Essays of *Locke* and *Leibniz*, or rather since the origin of metaphysics as far as history reaches, nothing has ever happened which could have been more decisive to its fate than the attack made upon it by *David Hume*" (Kant 1997, 7).

A great deal has been said about such narratives of modern philosophy. Even those with the most supporters have opponents. And because they're broad and general, they omit many details, and can easily mislead the unwary.[2] Instead of discussing general narratives at length, this book focuses on debates about smaller issues, about the interpretation of particular views of particular philosophers. So the questions asked are not questions like 'should we think about modern philosophy in terms of rationalism and empiricism?' nor even like 'was Hume an empiricist?' but more like 'what exactly did Hume believe about causation?'

However, the last part of the book deals with a related question: how should we study the history of philosophy? Some historians of philosophy engage with their subjects in roughly the same way contemporary philosophers engage with each other, analyzing, criticizing, and building on their arguments. They may think that the main reason to read historical philosophers is that their views are closer to the truth, at least on the issue at hand, than contemporary views. Other historians think of themselves as primarily trying to understand past philosophers, putting their views into a broader context to see how their problems, assumptions, and even conceptual schemes differ from our own. Such historians typically think that the history of philosophy is valuable in itself, like history in general. But they may also think that learning from past philosophers requires contextualizing their views so that we avoid projecting our own assumptions back on to the past. Part XIII's chapters by Daniel Garber and Martin Lin describe two different approaches to the history of philosophy.

## Galileo, Newton, and the Mechanical Philosophy

For modern philosophers, there was no clear dividing line between philosophy and science. Many of them pursued the project of 'natural philosophy'—a project that produced such diverse works as Isaac Newton's *Mathematical Principles of Natural Philosophy* and Leibniz's *Discourse on Metaphysics*. Seventeenth-century natural philosophy was extremely diverse: people's opinions differed about the aims, methodology, and conceptual vocabulary of science as well as about particular scientific theories. But all the philosophers we discuss were influenced by the research program known as "mechanism," or the "mechanical philosophy," which attempted to explain all the behavior of the material world in terms of the size, shape, and motion of tiny bits of matter. This research program is elegantly described in Robert Boyle's manifesto, *Considerations About the Excellency and Grounds of the Mechanical Hypothesis* (Boyle 1979, 138–54).

Why did the mechanical philosophy emerge in the seventeenth century, rather than earlier or later? One answer is that mechanism is what emerged when two quite different currents of thought happened to come together: the Galilean science of motion and the revival of ancient atomism. When we think of Galileo, we typically think of his defense of the Copernican view that the sun is the center of the solar system and the earth revolves around it. This conflicted with the official view of the Catholic Church that the earth was the center of the solar system, and because of this conflict Galileo was confined to house arrest and his books were banned. Our modern philosophers—most of whom were devoutly religious, many of whom were Catholics—would have seen this as a mistake by the church rather than evidence of a fundamental conflict between science and religion.

The relation between philosophy and religion in this period is complicated. We'll see a number of interpretive debates concerning the role of God and religion in philosophical systems. These debates involve a wide variety of questions. In the *Meditations* Descartes gives an argument for God's existence that is supposed to show that he can be certain that his clear and distinct thoughts are true. Many critics have believed that Descartes' argument is circular. The chapters by Harry Frankfurt and Lex Newman in Part I of this volume discuss this alleged circularity. Another of our debates is about the role of God in Berkeley's metaphysics. Berkeley was an idealist, believing that the world ultimately contains nothing but minds and their ideas. Within this system, God's role as an all-powerful, all-perceiving mind is clearly important. But just how important it is—and precisely what that role is—may be harder to see. The chapters by Margaret Atherton and Tom Stoneham in Part VIII discuss this issue. Part X's discussion of Hume's argument against knowledge of miracles, by John Earman and Peter Millican, is also about the role of God in philosophy, but in a rather different way. Hume argues that the testimony of others is never good enough evidence for us to believe that a miracle has happened. This view appears to have drastic consequences for the foundations of Christianity, the religion of the vast majority of Hume's audience.

Galileo said, "Philosophy is written in this all-encompassing book that is constantly open before our eyes, that is the universe . . . It is written in mathematical language."[3] This alludes to the notion that we can learn about God in two ways: by reading the book of revelation, i.e. the Bible, or by reading the book of nature, i.e. doing science. But it also marks an important shift in how people conceived of science. In comparison with the science of today—or even the science of the eighteenth century—Aristotelian philosophy was mainly qualitative rather than quantitative. Thus, emphasizing the search for mathematical laws of nature was a major change in strategy. And it went along with a major change in focus. Galileo began with the science of motion, studying inanimate objects; Aristotelians had typically focused on—and been most successful in explaining—the behavior of living beings.

A central thesis of Aristotelianism was that dogs, trees, stones, and all other physical objects are composites of *matter* and *form*. For example, think of a piece of clay. The clay cannot exist without having some form or shape, whether that form is the form of a statue or just a misshapen lump. But the form cannot exist on its own either: it doesn't make sense to have a statue or a lump that's not made out of anything. This example is a bit misleading. A piece of clay isn't really matter without form: there's already some form in it that makes it clay rather than sand or wine. And form needn't be literally shape: the form of a dog is what determines its growth and behavior, not just its shape. But the example does give a sense of what the Aristotelians meant by form and matter.

Philosophers who viewed themselves as modern opponents of Aristotle often denied the existence of forms, and tried to explain the behavior of physical objects by matter alone, which they typically thought of as composed of *atoms* or *corpuscles*. Atomists thought that the material world was made out of small, indivisible particles.[4] Their non-atomist mechanist contemporaries didn't believe there were any genuine indivisibles, but still thought that material things could be explained by thinking about the structures and interactions of small particles which they called 'corpuscles' (from the Latin *corpusculum,* 'little body').

Those philosophers who wanted to explain the physical world in terms of matter alone all thought, unlike the Aristotelians, that matter had properties. But they disagreed about what the properties of matter were and whether all matter has the same properties. Some chemists, for instance, argued that there were three or even five kinds of matter: salt, sulfur, mercury, and, perhaps, earth and water as well. Other philosophers thought of the parts of matter as homogeneous, differing only in size, shape, and motion. Each of these three properties is readily quantifiable, which makes it easy to describe matter in mathematical terms. Hence this version of corpuscularianism combined well with the Galilean science of motion, creating the mechanical philosophy.

Not all the philosophers discussed below *accepted* mechanism, but all were influenced by it in one way or another. Many key issues in modern philosophy arose because people recognized problem areas in mechanism and tried to figure out how to deal with them. Three of these problem areas are relevant to the debates discussed below: causation, the place of the human mind in nature, and what's called the problem of individuation.

First, causation. Aristotelians thought of matter as passive and form as active: they thought that forms caused all change. Their opponents who denied the existence of forms worried about the source of activity in the material world. These worries led to such differing views as Malebranche's 'occasionalist' claim that God is the only genuine cause and Hume's reductive analysis of causation. The notion that only God can really cause things is a strange one to most ears, but it was undoubtedly an important and influential view. The chapters by Walter Ott and Sukjae Lee in Part IV discuss it.

The notion of causation is discussed again, in a very different way, in Part III on Spinoza. In his chapter, Michael Della Rocca argues that Spinoza thinks that many important notions, including causation, should be understood in terms of intelligibility. Thus, "for *a* to cause *b* is nothing more than for *a* to make *b* intelligible, for *a* to explain *b*" (Della Rocca 2008a, 8). Yitzhak Melamed, in his chapter, objects to the claim that causation and other notions can all simply be reduced to intelligibility.

Hume also wrote about causation. Many readers have thought that, in his view, what we think of as causal connections are really just contingent regularities. Certainly, Hume denies that there is a 'necessary connection' between cause and effect: although as a matter of fact lightning causes thunder, the world could have been set up differently, so that lightning caused the sound of bells ringing. The chapters by Galen Strawson and Helen Beebee in Part IX discuss how we should understand Hume's claims about causation.

A second problem area within mechanism was the human mind. Many modern philosophers found it incomprehensible for the human mind to be just one more piece of matter. The tradition of Christian philosophy, and the established churches of the time, insisted that humans survive bodily death. To many philosophers, this was best explained by positing an immaterial, immortal soul. Moreover, it seemed inconceivable to philosophers—who thought that the only properties of matter were size, shape, and motion—that matter could think. Descartes famously made the mind an immaterial substance completely separate from the body, raising the problem of how mind and body could interact. Descartes tried to explain this in his correspondence with Princess Elisabeth of Bohemia, but readers from Elisabeth on have wondered whether he really had a good explanation. The chapters by Daniel Garber and Deborah Brown in Part II address this issue.

A third problem area within mechanism concerned what philosophers call 'individuation.' Matter is divisible into tiny parts; the bodies we interact with are composites. So, mechanists wondered, what makes it true that an animal is *one* thing, while something like an army or a flock of sheep—also a structured collection of parts—is many? This is a problem that Leibniz struggled with for decades, and it's often thought that even after he adopted the view that at the fundamental level reality is composed only of 'monads'—indivisible, immaterial, mind-like atoms—he still struggled to come up with a good explanation of the obvious fact that some parts of the world we experience are unified individuals and others are not. Leibniz's views about this are taken up by Glenn Hartz and Brandon Look in the chapters in Part V.

Locke also struggled with problems about individuation, and he too tried to explain an obvious fact—that animals and humans exist for years, although their properties change dramatically over time. You've existed since infancy, but your body is not composed of the same matter as your infant body, and you don't have the same thoughts. So what makes it true that you are the same person as that infant? Locke's answer to this question is the subject of Part VII, where Matthew Stuart responds to a chapter by William Alston and Jonathan Bennett.

Despite philosophical puzzles such as these, the mechanist project persisted throughout the second half of the seventeenth century, and even beyond. However, the notion that the world could be completely explained by the motions of small parts pushing on each other, like a giant piece of clockwork, came to have increasingly many scientific problems. In particular, Newton's views about gravity, which seemed inescapably to involve action at a distance, posed a great threat to the mechanist approach.

If Galileo was a hero for the first generation of modern philosophers, Newton played a similar role for later generations. Hume, for instance, said that he aspired to do for the human mind what Newton had done for the natural world.[5] Several parts of this book discuss how Newtonian physics affected modern philosophy. In the *Essay*'s introductory Epistle to the Reader, Locke lists four writers whose achievements he cannot hope to match: his fellow physician Thomas Sydenham, the experimental scientist Robert Boyle, the mathematician Christiaan Huygens, and "the incomparable Mr. Newton." In Part VI, Edwin McCann and Lisa Downing address Locke's attachment to mechanism and what happened to his philosophy as he gradually became aware of the problems Newtonian physics posed for mechanism.

Kant's philosophical system was partly an attempt to show that Newtonian physics was certain and necessarily true. Part of what this involved was showing how we could have certain, *a priori* knowledge of the properties of space—properties that are appealed to in both Euclidean geometry and Newtonian physics. Kant concluded that the space we experience, and indeed the whole world we experience, is a world of mere appearances, not the world of things in themselves. The chapters in Part XI by James van Cleve and Emily Carson discuss Kant's famous 'argument from geometry,' intended to show how *a priori* knowledge is possible. In Part XII, the chapters by Rae Langton and Lucy Allais discuss the contrast between appearances and things in themselves that is central to Kant's metaphysics.

## The Broader Context

It is easy to think of people like Descartes and Kant as just names attached to philosophical positions. But these historical figures were, of course, real people, who lived in particular places and times, survived and even participated in political and religious upheaval, learned various true and false things in the course of their education, talked to others about their work, and so on. Without trying to give biographies or explain the history of seventeenth- and eighteenth-century Europe, this section sketches some of the context in which the now-famous modern philosophers lived.

Few of them were professional academics. Of the philosophers discussed in this book, only Kant spent his whole career in a university. That said, Locke did spend some time teaching at Oxford, although without a great deal of enthusiasm; Hume was twice a candidate to be a professor and was rejected both times, perhaps because of his alleged atheism; and both Spinoza and Leibniz turned down offers of university positions.

Descartes, the first philosopher we'll discuss, was educated in the famous Jesuit school at La Flèche and studied law at the University of Poitiers. But after that, he didn't become a lawyer or a professor. Instead, he joined the army, serving in Prince Maurice of Nassau's army from 1618 to 1619, and then spent a decade traveling around Europe on his own before finally settling in Amsterdam in 1630.

Amsterdam was an important city for intellectuals because books could be published there without the sort of official approval from government or church required in other countries. Descartes published his *Meditations* in Amsterdam, avoiding official scrutiny. And he spent most of his working life in the Netherlands, remaining there until he moved to Sweden in 1649 to tutor Queen Christina. He took this job to help popularize Cartesianism, not for the money; unlike the rest of our philosophers, Descartes came from a wealthy enough family that finding a job was never a necessity.

During his time in the Netherlands, Descartes met and then corresponded with Princess Elisabeth of Bohemia, one of a number of early modern royal and aristocratic women interested in philosophy.[6] Although she was the daughter of someone who was (briefly) king of Bohemia, which is now part of the Czech Republic, Elisabeth was living in Holland. She was there because of the Thirty Years' War, a complicated and protracted conflict that originated in disputes between Catholics and Protestants, but also embodied the struggle for European supremacy between the French Bourbon monarchy and the Hapsburgs who ruled both Spain and Austria. Elisabeth came from a family of intellectual women: her sister, Electress Sophie of Hanover (mother of George I of England) talked and corresponded with Leibniz about many philosophical and other subjects, as did Sophie's daughter, who would become Queen Sophie Charlotte of Prussia. One fascinating part of Elisabeth's correspondence with Descartes contains his attempts to console Elisabeth about her brother's conversion to Catholicism—something that Descartes, who was a Catholic himself, would not have seen as a bad thing.

Benedict Spinoza came from a very different background than Descartes, but he too benefited from the greater freedoms of the Dutch Republic. His family, then the Espinosas, had come to Amsterdam as refugees. They had been part of a large Spanish and Portuguese Jewish community that had at times flourished and at other times been persecuted under Islamic rule. But when Ferdinand and Isabella finally completed the Catholic *Reconquista* of Spain in 1492, they expelled the entire Jewish population—many of whom, like the Espinosas, fled to Portugal only to be driven from there a generation later.

Spinoza himself was born and grew up in Amsterdam, where he was educated in the Portuguese-Jewish community's Talmud Torah school, and later worked in his family's business. But in 1656 he was excommunicated by his congregation, presumably because of early versions of the views he would later publish. Spinoza's views about the existence of God and the immortality of the soul were, to say the least, highly unorthodox, as were his views about scriptural interpretation. As the years passed, Spinoza acquired a broader reputation for atheism, becoming a hero of the radical wing of the Enlightenment and a villain for mainstream thought.

Despite the free intellectual life of Amsterdam, Paris was still in many respects the intellectual capital of seventeenth-century Europe. In the first half of the seventeenth century, many of the most prominent modern philosophers were in contact with the Parisian monk Marin Mersenne, who acted as a sort of middleman for correspondents throughout Europe. Among those correspondents were Descartes and his critics Thomas Hobbes and Pierre Gassendi: Mersenne had the unenviable task of keeping the peace between some very ill-tempered philosophers. The so-called Mersenne circle was very much aware of Galileo's work. Their discussions, and books such as Mersenne's 1634 *Galileo's Mechanics*, contributed a good deal to the growing awareness of Galileo's work.

Later in the century, Paris remained an important intellectual center. It was the home of the French Cartesian philosopher Nicolas Malebranche. He may well be currently the least famous of the philosophers discussed in this book, but his contemporary Pierre Bayle (himself an enormously prominent figure whose work is now little read) described him as "the premier philosopher of our age" (Schmaltz 2009).

While Malebranche was a Parisian by birth as well as education, others made considerable effort to get to this important city. An important part of Leibniz's early intellectual career was the time he spent in Paris in the 1670s. Leibniz was very much impressed by Paris: "One finds here, in all branches of knowledge, the most knowledgeable men of the age, and one needs much work and a little determination to establish a reputation here."[7] Leibniz only spent a few years in Paris though, and for much of his life lived and worked in Hanover. "I am not," he complained at one point "in a great city like Paris or London, where there are plenty of learned men from whom one can benefit and even receive assistance . . . here one scarcely finds anyone to talk to."[8] Thus for Leibniz, as for many other intellectuals of the time, correspondence was an incredibly important part of his intellectual life. Long before people were complaining about having too much email, Leibniz was at one point said to have a hundred unanswered letters—not because he was lazy, but because he was constantly corresponding with a great many people about a great many things. That was despite the great difficulties of correspondence at the time. Before the nineteenth century there weren't really organized national postal systems, so sending letters wasn't just a matter of buying a stamp and walking to the mailbox. And letters traveled slowly too, just as people did, in an unmechanized age. It's probably no coincidence that Paris, Amsterdam, and London, the three capitals of the seventeenth-century Republic of Letters, are within a few hundred miles of each other. Europeans could and did write to people in China at this time, but such long distance communication was a very slow affair.

For all the importance of correspondence and the difficulty of travel, many prominent philosophers did move around Europe. Locke, for instance, lived in Paris for a time and went into exile in Holland. The late seventeenth century was a tumultuous time in England. The country had suffered a bloody civil war, during which the king, Charles I, was executed in 1649. From 1653 to his death in 1658, Oliver Cromwell was lord protector, the head of state. The English monarchy was restored in 1660; Charles II became king, followed by his Catholic brother James II (who was also James VII of Scotland). Many Englishmen—including Locke's patron the Earl of Shaftesbury, as well as Locke himself—found the prospect of a Catholic succession unacceptable. When these feelings became too well known, Shaftesbury and Locke fled the country. They returned when the throne was handed over to the Dutch William of Orange and his wife Mary in the swift coup known as the Glorious Revolution, which was partly the result of Shaftesbury's machinations.

The Scot David Hume also had several connections to France. In the 1730s Hume lived in La Flèche, the town where Descartes had studied a century before. In the 1740s, he was part of a military expedition against the French, as secretary to Lieutenant-General James St Clair. And in the 1760s he lived in Paris as secretary to Lord Hertford, the British Ambassador.

Many of our philosophers were interested in places outside Europe. Leibniz was fascinated with China and its written language, because it could be read equally well by groups of people who couldn't understand each others' spoken words. He envisaged in this a way of healing the linguistic divisions of Europe, just as he sought a way to reconcile the Catholic and Protestant churches. He was also fascinated with Egypt, although that fascination took the more sinister form of trying to persuade Louis XIV of France to invade it. But the only one of our philosophers who ever actually left Europe was Berkeley, who spent three years in Rhode Island, working at his project of starting a college on Bermuda. Ultimately, however, Berkeley's project failed and he eventually returned to Ireland, where he was made Bishop of Cloyne in 1734.

In contrast to the traveling Berkeley, Kant's life was firmly anchored to his hometown, the East Prussian city of Königsberg. It's easy to think of Kant, like Leibniz, as a German philosopher. But neither of them actually lived in a country called Germany. There were many German states at the time, but no unified nation until the nineteenth century. Kant lived in Prussia (a place with its own complex history and shifting boundaries) and Leibniz lived in Hanover, in the Principality of Calenberg. And while Hanover is in what we now think of as Germany, Königsberg is now the Russian city of Kaliningrad.

Discussing the scientific context in which our philosophers wrote often helps us understand why they chose the topics they did. Knowing something about their lives can also help us understand them. We typically read the modern philosophers (except for Locke, Berkeley, and Hume) translated into contemporary English. This makes it easy to forget that in reading something like Descartes' *Meditations*, you are really reading a text from a foreign culture, regardless of your own cultural heritage. Thus, you should expect it to be difficult to figure out what it really means.

When you begin reading about the history of philosophy, it's easy to assume that there has to be one right answer to every question, one correct interpretation. But this just isn't true. There are lots of wrong answers and silly interpretations—but there's hardly ever just one clear right answer. Instead, there are usually several plausible interpretations, each with its own advantages and disadvantages. In the chapters that follow, you will see various examples of how interpretive debates work.

## Notes

1. Hume's discussion is in the *Treatise of Human Nature*'s chapter 'Of the modern philosophy' (T 1.4.4.3). Bayle's discussion is in Note B to the article "Pyrrho" in his Historical and Critical Dictionary (Bayle 1991, 197).
2. See e.g. Loeb 1981.
3. Galileo, *The Assayer*, §7.1 (Galileo 2008, 183).
4. 'Atom' means 'indivisible' in Greek, so the term 'atom' originally referred to indivisible particles, whatever their nature, rather than the things we call atoms today.
5. Before Newton "determined the laws and forces, by which the revolutions of the planets are governed and directed" (E 1.15), Hume said, astronomers had had to content themselves with merely describing the motion of the planets without explaining it. He hoped for "equal success in [his] enquiries concerning the mental powers and economy" (E 1.15) by discovering the laws of thought—'principles of association' which he compares to the laws governing gravitational attraction (T 1.1.4.6).
6. See O'Neill 1998 for more on the role of women in early modern philosophy.
7. This is from a letter Leibniz wrote to Duke Johann Friedrich in January 1675 (Antognazza 2009, 139).
8. From a letter Leibniz wrote to Thomas Burnett of Kemnay in March 1696 (Antognazza 2009, 196).

# Timeline

| Year | Births and Deaths | Books | Events |
|------|-------------------|-------|--------|
| 1564 | Death of Calvin | | |
| 1588 | Mersenne born | | Spanish Armada |
| 1596 | Descartes born | | |
| 1597 | | Suárez's *Metaphysical Disputations* | |
| 1598 | | | Edict of Nantes grants rights to French Protestants |
| 1600 | | | British East India Company established |
| 1603 | | | James VI of Scotland becomes James I of England |
| 1607 | | | First permanent English colony founded at Jamestown, VA |
| 1608 | | | Quebec City founded |
| 1610 | | Galileo's *Starry Messenger* | |
| 1616 | | | Condemnation of Galileo; Death of Shakespeare |
| 1618 | Elisabeth of Bohemia born | | Start of Thirty Years' War |

| | | | |
|---|---|---|---|
| 1619 | | | Elisabeth's father (Frederick V, Elector Palatine) becomes King of Bohemia; first African slaves brought to America |
| 1620 | | Bacon's *Great Instauration* | Elisabeth's father deposed; Mayflower arrives |
| 1621 | | Burton's *Anatomy of Melancholy* | |
| 1624 | | | Richelieu becomes first minister of France |
| 1625 | | Grotius' *On the Law of War and Peace* | |
| 1626 | | | Dutch found New Amsterdam |
| 1632 | Spinoza born | Galileo's *Dialogue on the Two Chief World Systems* | |
| 1637 | | Descartes' *Discourse on the Method* | |
| 1638 | Malebranche born | Galileo's *Two New Sciences* | |
| 1641 | | Descartes' *Meditations* | |
| 1643 | | Elisabeth begins to correspond with Descartes | Torricelli invents barometer |
| 1644 | | Descartes's *Principles of Philosophy* | |
| 1646 | Leibniz born | | |
| 1648 | Death of Mersenne | | End of Thirty Years' War |
| 1649 | | | Execution of Charles I |
| 1650 | Death of Descartes | | |
| 1651 | | Hobbes's *Leviathan* | |
| 1652 | | | Dutch found Cape Town, South Africa |
| 1658 | | Gassendi's *Syntagma Philosophicum* | Death of Oliver Cromwell |
| 1660 | | | Charles II restored as King of England |
| 1663 | | Boyle's *Considerations touching the Usefulness of Experimental Natural Philosophy* | |
| 1665 | | Hooke's *Micrographia* | New Amsterdam captured by English, becomes New York |
| 1666 | | | Great Fire of London |
| 1674 | | Malebranche's *Search After Truth* | |
| 1677 | Death of Spinoza | Spinoza's *Ethics* | |

| Year | Births and Deaths | Books | Events |
|------|-------------------|-------|--------|
| 1679 | Death of Hobbes | | |
| 1680 | Death of Elisabeth of Bohemia | | |
| 1685 | Berkeley born | | Edict of Nantes revoked |
| 1686 | | Leibniz's *Discourse on Metaphysics* | |
| 1687 | | Newton's *Mathematical Principles of Natural Philosophy* | |
| 1688 | | | William and Mary become rulers of England |
| 1689 | | Locke's *Two Treatises* and *Essay Concerning Human Understanding* | |
| 1697 | | Bayle's *Dictionary* | |
| 1704 | Death of Locke | | |
| 1706 | Death of Bayle | | |
| 1707 | | | Acts of Union of Scotland and England |
| 1710 | | Berkeley's *Principles of Human Understanding* | |
| 1711 | Hume born | | |
| 1712 | | Wolff's 'German Logic' (*Rational Thoughts on the Powers of the Human Understanding and their Correct Employment in the Cognition of the Truth*) | |
| 1713 | | Berkeley's *Three Dialogues* | |
| 1714 | | | End of the War of Spanish Succession |
| 1715 | Death of Malebranche | | Jacobite rising of 1715 |
| 1716 | Death of Leibniz | | |
| 1718 | | | New Orleans founded |
| 1719 | | Wolff's 'German Metaphysics' (*Rational Thoughts on God, the World and the Soul of Man, and on All Things Whatsoever*) | |

| | | | |
|---|---|---|---|
| 1720 | | | South Sea Bubble causes financial crash in Britain |
| 1721 | | | Christian missions banned in China |
| 1724 | Kant born | | |
| 1739 | | Hume's *Treatise of Human Nature* | John Wesley forms Methodist Society |
| 1745 | | | Jacobite rising of 1745 |
| 1748 | | Hume's *Enquiry Concerning Human Understanding* | |
| 1751 | | Hume's *Enquiry Concerning the Principles of Morals*; first volume of the *Encyclopédie* | |
| 1753 | Death of Berkeley | | |
| 1755 | | | Lisbon earthquake |
| 1759 | | Adam Smith's *Theory of Moral Sentiments*; Voltaire's *Candide*; Sterne's *Tristram Shandy* | |
| 1762 | | Rousseau's *Social Contract* | |
| 1763 | | Bayes' "Essay towards solving a problem in the doctrine of chances" | |
| 1764 | | Reid's *Inquiry into the Human Mind* | |
| 1776 | Death of Hume | Smith's *Wealth of Nations*; Volume 1 of Gibbon's *Decline and Fall* | American Revolution |
| 1781 | | Kant's *Critique of Pure Reason* (first, or 'A', edition) | |
| 1787 | | Kant's *Critique of Pure Reason* (second, or 'B', edition) | |
| 1788 | | | First British convicts shipped to Botany Bay, Australia |
| 1789 | | Bentham's *Introduction to the Principles of Morals and Legislation* | French Revolution; Washington becomes first US president |
| 1790 | | Burke's *Reflections on the Revolution in France* | |
| 1791 | | Boswell's *Life of Johnson*; Paine's *Rights of Man* | |
| 1792 | | Wollstonecraft's *A Vindication of the Rights of Women* | |

| Year | Births and Deaths | Books | Events |
|------|-------------------|-------|--------|
| 1793 | | | Execution of Louis XVI of France |
| 1798 | | | Napoleon's invasion of Egypt |
| 1800 | | | Alessandro Volta invents electric cell |
| 1803 | | | Louisiana Purchase |
| 1804 | Death of Kant | | Napoleon crowned Emperor of the French; Lewis and Clark head west |
| 1806 | | | Lewis and Clark return to St Louis |
| 1807 | | Hegel's *Phenomenology of Spirit* | Britain abolishes slave trade (but not slavery); invention of streetlights (gas lamps) in London |

## Editors' note

We have edited each of the thirteen previously published papers in various ways. We've standardized spelling, punctuation, and citation format. We've also shortened most of the previously published papers. Deleted material in the body of the paper is marked by ellipses (. . .), and deleted footnotes aren't marked at all. We've also added some footnotes, marked as 'Editors' note', to explain technical terms and the like.

# PART I

# The Cartesian Circle

# Editors' Introduction

René Descartes probably thought of himself first and foremost as a mathematician. He invented analytic geometry and used it to solve problems in physics, optics, and meteorology. But he also wanted to prove that his mathematics describes the world we live in. This motivated his most famous work, the *Meditations*. In the *Meditations*, Descartes doubts all his previous beliefs and starts from scratch, accepting only what is most certain. By using this method he finds that his most certain beliefs involve mathematics, physics, God, and the immaterial human soul. But many readers have worried that Cartesian doubt is too strong. Once you doubt everything, how can you ever hope to find any certain knowledge?

Descartes' answer is that we are created by an all-powerful, non-deceiving God. Thus, whatever we clearly and distinctly perceive is true. On hearing Descartes' answer, it's natural to ask how he knows that God exists. Many readers have thought that Descartes' argument for God's existence relies on clear and distinct perception. But this, they think, makes his theory blatantly circular.

Several of Descartes' early readers expressed this worry. Descartes responded with annoyance that such readers had completely misunderstood him. But where exactly have we gone wrong if we see the *Meditations* as circular? Scholars in the twentieth and twenty-first centuries have offered numerous suggestions.

One famous suggestion is due to Anthony Kenny, who argues that God's veracity is used to justify the belief that whatever we clearly and distinctly perceive is true—but *not* to justify particular clear and distinct perceptions. In Chapter 1 Harry Frankfurt argues that Kenny's solution fails. Indeed, *any* solution that assumes that Descartes is trying to find the truth will fail. Instead, we should just read Descartes as trying to show that beliefs based on reason are consistent. This is not as modest a goal as you might think. Even if this is all Descartes is trying to do, he is still trying to prove that we could never find any reason to doubt his mathematical physics or the existence of God and the immaterial soul.

In Chapter 2 Lex Newman objects that there's plenty of textual evidence that Descartes cares about truth—and none that he only cares about consistency. Newman goes on to argue for a new way of avoiding the circle. The key element of his intriguing suggestion is that by the end of the Fifth Meditation, if you've meditated properly, you will not be able to conceive of the existence of an evil demon or the non-existence of God.

## A Note on References

Descartes' writings are cited by volume and page number in the standard, original-language edition edited by Adam and Tannery ('AT'). Whenever possible, we also cite a volume and page number in the standard English translation by Cottingham, Stoothoff, and Murdoch ('CSM'). We give CSM references even when the author is using her own translation.

## Further Reading

- Harry Frankfurt (1970). *Demons, Dreamers, and Madmen.*
- Alan Gewirth (1941). "The Cartesian Circle."
- Anthony Kenny (1968). *Descartes: A Study of His Philosophy.*
- Louis Loeb (1992). "The Cartesian Circle."

## CHAPTER 1

# Descartes on the Consistency of Reason

## HARRY G. FRANKFURT

In one of the most central and familiar lines of argument of the *Meditations*, Descartes professes to perceive the following propositions clearly and distinctly: an omnipotent and benevolent deity exists; the existence of this deity entails that men cannot be subject to irretrievable deception, as they would be if they could ever have clear and distinct perceptions of what is false; whatever we perceive clearly and distinctly must, accordingly, be true. The apparent aim of the argument these propositions comprise is to establish that clear and distinct perception is unimpeachably reliable—that whatever we perceive clearly and distinctly is true.

How could Descartes have hoped to make any progress whatever in the direction of this goal, by means of an argument whose steps, as he himself acknowledges, are justified by nothing other than clear and distinct perception itself? The movement of his thought here seems egregiously circular. From an initial assumption that clear and distinct perceptions *are* reliable, which alone appears to enable him to regard each step of the argument as legitimate, Descartes proceeds to the final conclusion that it is justifiable to rely on such perceptions. It is no wonder that this piece of reasoning has puzzled and frustrated so many of his readers. It gives the strong impression of being utterly worthless, since the acceptability of its conclusion seems to be taken for granted throughout its construction.

Circular arguments are not formally fallacious. On the contrary, they are necessarily valid. Circularity in argument, after all, is essentially a matter of deriving a proposition from itself; and one is always entitled to do that. The troublesome question with respect to Descartes's argument is not whether it can be valid, but how it can have any point. Repeating at the end of a train of reasoning something which was assumed at its start is not a formal error in logic, but it appears to be quite a gross error in strategy. To say the least, it can hardly amount to a very productive demonstration of anything that needs to be proved.

Why does Descartes's argument arouse so much interest? No doubt part of the explanation is provided by considerations of charity, reinforced by the piety one tends to feel toward a great ancestor. The argument is at first glance a very bad one; yet Descartes is manifestly a very good philosopher. It is natural, and perhaps only decent, to wonder if the argument may not somehow turn out to be, if not altogether sound and fruitful, at least a little better than it looks.

Not that we ought to be incredulous at finding a flaw in the reasoning of one of the giants of our intellectual tradition. In fact this is very much to be expected. So far as I know, at any rate, there is not one really cogent and definitive argument of any consequence in the entire history of philosophy.[1] The best philosophers—that is, the most interesting and stimulating ones—have generally preferred to devote their energies to more important things than polishing away every trace of uncertainty or equivocation in the arguments they have contrived as vehicles for their insights. The contemporary mania in certain circles for absolute rigor and perfect clarity, regardless of any specific need, succeeds on the whole just in making philosophy a bore. Still, mistakes as blatant as the one Descartes appears to have made are not so common even among the greatest thinkers. The evidence of disorder in his thought understandably constitutes, for his interpreters, a provocative challenge.

This may not suffice to persuade those without a special interest in Descartes to take his argument seriously. Surely only a dedicated antiquarian could interest himself, they may feel, in reasoning which is concerned with such quaint concepts as "clear and distinct perception" and "divine benevolence." The former smacks too much of notions like, "self-evidence" and "intuition," which are now regarded by sophisticates as thoroughly discredited. As for the latter, there are natural qualms not only as to whether the idea of God can be permitted to play an essential role in philosophy. It has always been a question, even while Descartes was alive, whether what he says about God gives an authentic account of his own convictions. Despite his explicit professions of Roman Catholicism, and substantial evidence of his piety, Descartes's theological views have always aroused the darkest suspicions.[2] He has been mistrusted on this score, in fact, by practically everyone. The Catholics accused him of being a Protestant, the Protestants thought he was an atheist, and the atheists have tended to speculate that he was a hypocrite. It is not only the viability and pertinence of his problematic argument, then, which are uncertain. Descartes's very sincerity in promulgating it is under a cloud.

Considering just what is at stake in Descartes' concern with clear and distinct perception will help to identify more fully the source of the fascination his argument evokes. In brief, an attempt to establish the infallibility of clear and distinct perception as a guide to truth amounts to a defense of the authority of human reason. This is because clear and distinct perception conveys, to whatever propositions we clearly and distinctly perceive, the most impeccable credentials reason can provide. Moreover, since there is no appeal from reason to any superior natural source of knowledge, we can possess no natural basis for correcting a belief in what we have clearly and distinctly perceived. We can do no better in the formation of our judgments, accordingly, than to rely upon such perceptions. They constitute the best testimony of our highest faculty. If we will not or cannot be satisfied by that, then we must give up hoping to satisfy ourselves at all. By the same token, any error into which we might be led by clear and distinct perception would be altogether ineradicable and beyond redemption by reason.

What is it, exactly, for a person to perceive something clearly and distinctly? It consists in his recognizing that the evidence he has for some proposition, or his basis in experience for accepting the proposition, is logically definitive and complete. He perceives clearly and distinctly that $p$ when he sees that his evidence or basis for accepting $p$ is conclusive, in the sense that it is consistent and that no body of evidence which would warrant rejecting or doubting $p$ is logically compatible with the evidence or basis he already has. Given the evidence or basis for $p$ that he already has, in other words, he need not fear that the addition to it of further evidence will require him to change his mind.

A person who attentively grasps the rigorous connection of the premises and the conclusion of a valid argument, for example, perceives clearly and distinctly that the conclusion must be true if the premises are true. He apprehends that there is no gap between the evidence affirmed by the premises and the conclusion for which the premises cite evidence, into which opposing considerations might enter. Sensory experience itself may provide, as reason may recognize, a similarly complete and conclusive basis for a belief. Someone who feels a pain may perceive clearly and distinctly that he feels a pain; that is, he may understand that his feeling provides him with a conclusive basis for accepting the proposition that he has that feeling.

*Every* experience, indeed, provides a conclusive basis for the acceptance of *some* proposition; for every experience, there is some proposition that fits it perfectly—a proposition that captures the experience without asserting more than it warrants, and thus without leaving anything uncertainly awaiting confirmation by further experience. It is not only necessary truths like those of logic and mathematics, then, which can be perceived clearly and distinctly. Logically contingent propositions may also be objects of clear and distinct perception.

Descartes is sometimes thought to have advocated a kind of lunatic apriorism, according to which a person might spin all of philosophy and all of science out of his own head without ever needing to turn to perceptual data. This was by no means Descartes's view. He does, to be sure, deny that sense perception is in itself an adequate source of certainty. We cannot attain certainty even about perceptual matters, he insists, if we rely exclusively upon the senses. But he does not go on to maintain that we do not need the senses at all. Although genuine knowledge can be acquired only with the use of reason, not all of it is to be acquired by the use of reason alone. Clear and distinct perception, which consists in recognizing that a proposition and the basis for accepting it are perfectly matched, requires logical analysis and rational insight. Our acquaintance with the basis for accepting the proposition in question may well have its origin, however, in sensory experience.

In arguing for the reliability of clear and distinct perception, Descartes is attempting to establish the reliability of reason itself—that is, of our perceptions of logical relationships. How does this task come to present itself as one which needs to be undertaken? Exactly what question about reason does Descartes think must be asked, and in what way does he believe he can reasonably go about trying to answer it? The mere formulation of questions like these reveals how natural it is that Descartes's argument should have, at the very least, an appearance of circularity. Anyone who sets out to defend reason faces what seems to be an unavoidable and disastrous dilemma. How is he to escape having his defense turn out to be either circular or gratuitous? On the one hand, he may try to develop rationally compelling arguments in behalf of reason. But in that case he will certainly be told—as Descartes has been told by innumerable critics—that his procedure begs the very question he has set out to answer. On the other hand, he may offer in support of reason considerations of some nonrational sort, whose effect is in one way or another independent of their demonstrative value. In that case he may not need to worry about being charged with circularity, but he will find that few philosophers are interested in listening to him. What he says will rightly be dismissed by everyone who is committed to rationality.

Despite this, however, it is difficult to believe that we must be altogether silent when a question is raised about the credentials of reason. Surely there is *something* worthwhile to say concerning whether reason merits our trust? There must be *something* reason can offer in its own behalf, without being guilty of plain violations of the conditions of substantive argument. Descartes's treatment of these matters is philosophically intriguing, because it purports to cope with a serious question about the legitimacy of reason. One wonders just what question this can be, and what useful response to it could possibly be made.

Let us consider Anthony Kenny's proposal concerning what question about reason Descartes thought it both necessary to ask and possible to answer.[3] Kenny calls attention to the fact that it may be sensible for a person to entertain a general doubt concerning his own beliefs, without questioning any of those beliefs in particular. We have all discovered, at one time or another, that opinions we have been holding are incorrect; and it is likely that some of our present opinions are also false. It is reasonable to acknowledge this, Kenny suggests, even though doing so involves a certain inconsistency—the inconsistency of believing $p$ and $q$ and $r$ (our current opinions) while at the same time believing that either $p$ is false or $q$ is false or $r$ is false. Now Kenny claims that Descartes's doubt about reason is similar to this doubt—he calls it "omega doubt"—which a person may have concerning his own beliefs. Descartes does not, that is to say, mistrust any particular clear and distinct perception. What he questions is only the general proposition that everything perceived clearly and distinctly is true. In Kenny's judgment, this distinction illuminates the problem with which Descartes is contending, and makes it clear that the argument by which Descartes purports to solve the problem is not circular.

Before proceeding to evaluate Kenny's interpretation, it is important to understand what Descartes takes to be the relation between perceiving a proposition clearly and distinctly and assenting to it. Descartes maintains that when our perception of a proposition is clear and distinct, we have no choice but to give the proposition our assent. He insists not merely that we *should* not, but that we *cannot* doubt what we are actually perceiving clearly and distinctly. It may well be possible for us to doubt the very same thing at another time, when we are not having a clear and distinct perception of it. But while we are in the midst of perceiving it clearly and distinctly, we simply cannot withhold our assent. Doubt and belief, as Descartes conceives them, are functions of the will; and the will is irresistibly constrained when the perceptions of reason are clear and distinct. When reason is fully satisfied, in other words, assent follows necessarily.[4]

Kenny proposes to construe Descartes's procedure in the problematic argument as follows. Descartes perceives each of its premises clearly and distinctly, and hence he believes each of them to be true. These beliefs are entirely accounted for by the irresistibility of what is clearly and distinctly perceived. Descartes cannot help believing the premises of the argument, in virtue of his perceptions; and his believing the premises does not depend in any way upon his assuming the argument's conclusion that whatever is perceived clearly and distinctly is true. He can reach that conclusion, accordingly, by means of an argument in which its truth is not assumed. Thus, Kenny says,

> it is . . . clear why there is no circle in Descartes's argument. The clear and distinct perceptions used in the proof of God's existence are perceptions of particular propositions. . . . The veracity of God is used to establish not any particular clear and distinct perception, but the general proposition that whatever I clearly and distinctly perceive is true.[5]

The point of this interpretation is that the acceptance of the premises of Descartes's argument does not require legitimation by knowledge that the argument's conclusion is true. Assent to the premises is assured by their being clearly and distinctly perceived. It requires no epistemological warrant at all, since clear and distinct perception carries assent with it in any case.

For my own part, I cannot see in what way this interpretation can help to resolve the problem of circularity. If Descartes is to establish the unimpeachable truth of his conclusion, as Kenny supposes he intends to do, he must provide premises for it whose truth is reliably guaranteed; and it must be possible for him, if he is to avoid begging the question, to provide this guarantee for the premises without relying upon the assumption that the conclusion is true. What Kenny's approach can explain, however, is only how Descartes might come, without assuming the truth of his argument's conclusion, to believe that each of its premises is true. The question of whether the premises are true—and hence, of whether they establish that the conclusion is true—will then remain, even though it cannot be raised while the premises are being clearly and distinctly perceived. The answer to this question will depend, moreover, upon whether what leads Descartes to believe the premises is a reliable guide to truth. But what leads Descartes to believe the premises of his argument is, of course, just that he perceives them clearly and distinctly. And whether the fact that he thus perceives them entails that they are true, plainly depends upon nothing else than whether the conclusion of the argument is true or false. How, then, does the argument as Kenny understands it avoid circularity?

It is Kenny's claim that Descartes never doubts the truth of particular clearly and distinctly perceived propositions. Now Descartes does believe that there are certain propositions which can never be doubted, because they cannot be considered at all without being perceived clearly and distinctly and hence without assent to them being constrained.[6] The very fact that he especially considers propositions of this kind, however, makes it clear that he thinks *some* propositions are of a different kind. A person can doubt the latter even after he has perceived them clearly and distinctly, whenever the evidence that supports the clear and distinct perception of them is absent from his mind. Then he may remember perceiving *p* clearly and distinctly, and at the same time wonder whether *p* is true. Doubts can be raised, accordingly, about the value of particular clear and distinct perceptions; though not, to be sure, while the perceptions are actually occurring.

Such doubts do not concern whether there is as much evidence for the proposition in question as reason demands. To remember that the proposition was once perceived clearly and distinctly is precisely to remember that there is logically conclusive evidence for it. What the doubt concerns is whether logically conclusive evidence is compatible with the falsity of the proposition supported by that evidence. It is not a doubt concerning whether the reasons for believing something are as solid as they might be. It concerns whether reasons of even the most solid kind possible are good enough. In other words, it is a doubt about reason itself. Descartes's question is this: what basis is there for accepting what we clearly and distinctly perceive *besides* the irresistible conviction which having a clear and distinct perception arouses? I shall explain this question further later on.

Descartes cannot help believing the premises of his argument while he clearly and distinctly perceives them. But when he is not in the midst of clear and distinct perception of those premises, and therefore not irresistibly constrained to believe them, he may well wonder whether they are true or whether his having once perceived them clearly and distinctly is in fact compatible with their falsity. When he looks back over his argument, he can say no more than that certain premises, of whose truth he was at one time entirely convinced, lead to the conclusion that anything with the sort of warrant those premises had at that time is true. But whether the premises are actually true, and whether the conclusion to which they lead is consequenly true, are still quite open questions. Open, that is, unless we assume that the sort of warrant the premises had—namely, that of being clearly and distinctly perceived—means that they must be true. If we assume this, however, we beg the question.

In my opinion, it is hopeless to approach Descartes's argument with the presumption that its point is to provide a demonstration that its conclusion is true. This presumption has, I concede, a very high initial plausibility. But if we start with it, we are bound to discover both that the argument is patently circular and that its circularity is fatal to its purpose. Now what other way of construing the argument is there? If Descartes's aim is not the normal one of demonstrating that his conclusion is true, what can his aim be? I suggest that his primary aim is to display the connection between the premises of his argument and its conclusion. The argument is not designed to demonstrate that its conclusion is true, in other words, but to show that a correct exercise of reason leads us to it.

The argument terminates in the clear and distinct perception that whatever is clearly and distinctly perceived is true; and Descartes reaches this perception by means of other clear and distinct perceptions, which comprise the argument's earlier steps. That reason leads in this way to the principle that what reason endorses is true, is something Descartes can establish without claiming either that the conclusion of his argument is true or that its premises are true. What is necessary is only that he should clearly and distinctly perceive the premises, and that he should also perceive clearly and distinctly that the conclusion follows from them. There is plainly no circularity in such a procedure. It remains to make clear, however, what point it can have.

In this connection, it is pertinent to recall that before Descartes undertakes to evaluate the evidence of reason—that is, before formulating and attempting to validate the principle that whatever is perceived clearly and distinctly is true—he conducts, in Meditation I, an exhaustive critique of the evidence that the senses provide. The general outcome of his investigation into the reliability of sense perception is, of course, that the evidence of the senses is not good enough. Now it is both extremely natural and entirely reasonable to suppose that, having reached this outcome with respect to sensory evidence, the question Descartes then thinks it essential to ask about reason is the *same* question he has just finished asking and answering about the senses. As he turns from a consideration of the one kind of evidence to a consideration of the other, he can hardly avoid wondering whether the latter is capable of passing the test the former has failed. It is a compelling supposition, then, that the doubts Descartes will try to allay concerning reason must be analogous to the doubts he has been unable to allay concerning the senses.

Descartes's skeptical conclusion concerning the senses is based essentially upon the following consideration. Even if someone has the best sort of evidence the senses can provide for a belief, it is still possible that the senses will subsequently provide him with equally good evidence against the belief. However strong his sensory evidence for a proposition may be, Descartes finds, it is possible that he may acquire additional sensory evidence of opposite import. Anyone who relies merely upon his senses, then, runs the risk that they will betray him. For it is always possible that, having provided him with evidence of their best sort in favor of some belief, they will subsequently provide him with equally good evidence against it.

In other words, Descartes's fear about the senses is that their best testimony may be inconsistent. And if the senses do provide a person with conflicting testimony of what is, by their own measurement, equal weight—some during a dream, for example, and some while the person is awake—he will not be able *by using his senses* to decide which of this evidence to accept and which to reject. The senses cannot yield certainty, in short, because they are capable of permitting conflicts of evidence which they cannot themselves resolve.

When Descartes undertakes to evaluate the testimony of clear and distinct perception, he *must* consider the risk of being similarly betrayed by reason. The question he is committed to asking about reason is, in other words, whether it is possible that one clear and distinct perception should contradict another in the way that one sensory perception may contradict another. The best evidence reason provides cannot be good enough if beliefs based upon it may be contradicted by evidence which is equally good, anymore than beliefs based solely upon sensory considerations are acceptable once it is recognized that they may be contradicted by beliefs with equally strong sensory support. Descartes has concluded that having the best evidence the senses alone can provide—that is, evidence acquired under conditions that seem to the senses to be ideal for accurate perception—is not good enough. When he considers the value of reason, he needs to know whether *its* best evidence leaves open the possibility of encountering the same sort of dilemma to which he has found that a reliance on sensory evidence may lead.

Once we understand that it was this question about reason which Descartes was led to ask, we can also understand more exactly what value he supposed his answer to it would possess. The problem he faced was to rebut the skeptical contention that reliance upon reason may give rise to inconsistencies which reason cannot resolve, in the same way that reliance upon the senses may lead to inconsistencies which cannot be resolved by sensory testimony. Now the skeptic's position concerning this matter is, according to Descartes, tantamount to the claim that human reason is not the product of a benevolent deity. Remember that in Descartes's view we cannot *help* believing what we are perceiving clearly and distinctly. If our clear and distinct perceptions should conflict, therefore, we would find that reason had betrayed us, by constraining us to give our assent to one proposition and then to give it to another proposition inconsistent with the first. Thus reason would lead us unavoidably into contradiction, from which we could escape only by abandoning the use of reason altogether. For we have no other faculty superior to reason, which we might invoke in an effort to resolve a conflict generated by reason itself.

This would imply a corruption in our nature so deep and so hopeless that it cannot be intended by a benevolent creator. The assumption that we are creatures of a benevolent creator is compatible with the fact that we are flawed, and hence that we are susceptible to doubt and to error. But it could not be God's intention that we be condemned to incompatible beliefs without any recourse short of giving up the use of reason, as we would be if the results of reason's best work might be inconsistent. Only on the assumption that reason has some origin other than in God, then, is there a basis for fearing that the set of clear and distinct perceptions is incoherent.

But is this assumption reasonable? Is it really conceivable, in other words, that we are not creatures of a deity who is both omnipotent and benevolent? Is the supposition that we have a different origin than that a logically coherent one? It is only if this supposition is indeed coherent that the position of the skeptic is viable—that is, only if it is reasonable to suppose that we might have originated through the malicious work of a demon, or by chance, or from a blind succession of causes. Otherwise the skeptic is committed to a self-contradictory proposition, and his claim against reason is therefore one which it is not reasonable to credit.

Descartes's strategy is to show that the assumption required by the position of the skeptic is in fact not a reasonable one at all. In effect, the skeptic's argument must have the form of a reductio ad absurdum: if we rely upon reason we are led to the conclusion that reason is, or may be, unworthy of reliance. The skeptic has no alternative to this mode of argument; the only plausible line he can take is, after all, that his skeptical conclusion is one for which there are good reasons. What Descartes undertakes is to rebut this reductio by showing that reason does not, as the skeptic maintains, lead us to conclude that the circumstances of our origin are compatible with the radical deceitfulness of reason. Rather, he attempts to show, it leads us to the conclusion that God exists. Since we perceive clearly and distinctly that we are products of benevolent omnipotence, he claims, the opposite supposition—upon the coherence of which the skeptic's case depends—is logically inconceivable. It cannot be reasonable, therefore, to entertain fundamental doubts concerning reason.

The value to Descartes of his proof that God exists is not that it establishes as a fact that there is a benevolent and omnipotent being to whom we owe our existence and our nature. Descartes could not purport to demonstrate that this is a fact without begging the question of whether the premises of his argument are true. But he does not need to suppose that the premises of his argument for God's existence are true, in order to achieve the aim to which the argument is devoted. He needs only to make the point that he clearly and distinctly perceives both the premises and that the proposition that God exists follows from them. This is sufficient, because it means that if a person relies upon reason he is led to a conclusion which excludes the possibility that there is a demon (or that human existence is a product of chance, or whatever). The point of the argument is, in other words, that skepticism about reason is not reasonable; for reason leads to a judgment incompatible with the assumption upon which skepticism depends. The outcome of a reliance upon reason is the discovery of a reason for being confident that the best reasons—those provided by clear and distinct perception—will not conflict with one another. The reductio of which the skeptic warned does not materialize. What develops is, on the contrary, a conclusion which entails that the position of the skeptic involves a contradiction.

There is, however, a further question. Given that reason is reliable, in the sense that it does not betray itself by providing reasons for doubting its own reliability, is the testimony of reason a sufficient proof against what may be called "absolute" error? Even though reasons of the best kind provide a certainty with which no other reasons of that kind will interfere, is it not possible that we may achieve this certainty concerning something which is in fact false? A set of propositions may be consistent, after all, without any of them being true. Is it proper to conclude from the fact that judgments based upon clear and distinct perception form a consistent set, then, not only that it is safe for us to accept such judgments without fearing that we will later have to doubt them, but also that they are in the fullest sense true?

Descartes's argument appears to do nothing to show that what is perceived clearly and distinctly corresponds with reality. Even if it succeeds in establishing that propositions which are clearly and distinctly perceived cohere with each other, in other words, it seems to leave open the possibility that none of those propositions is true. And yet Descartes does claim to establish, of course, that what is clearly and distinctly perceived is true.

At one time I believed it appropriate to deal with this difficulty by ascribing to Descartes a coherence theory of truth. If he did conceive truth in terms of coherence, then the problem disappears: showing that what is clearly and distinctly perceived satisfies the condition of coherence is, in that case, the same as showing that it is true. I now think, however, that it was a mistake on my part to suggest that Descartes entertained a coherence conception of truth. The fact is that there is no textual evidence to support that suggestion; on the contrary, whenever Descartes gives an explicit account of truth he explains it unequivocally as correspondence with reality. It might still be possible to claim that Descartes is committed to conceiving truth in terms of coherence, even if he does not appreciate that he is. Even this claim now strikes me as unwarranted, however, since it may be that there are other ways—philosophically as plausible as a coherence theory of truth—of coping with the problem at issue.

Descartes was deeply preoccupied with certainty—with finding beliefs he could trust without qualification or reserve. He was above all concerned to determine what it was reasonable for him to regard as altogether unshakeable and permanent—that is, immune to any legitimate fear that he would someday discover it necessary to recant his adherence to it. It is unclear in what way, if at all, he worked through the relation between this ambition and the desire for truth. My present view of the matter is that he may never have thought through the implications of his defense of reason sufficiently to become fully aware of the question about truth to which it leads, and that he actually provides no clear or readily visible answer to that question.

There are plain indications, however, that Descartes was aware of the possibility that what satisfies the demand for certainty may not satisfy the conditions of truth. In his "Reply to Objections II" he says:

> What is it to us if someone should feign that the very thing of whose truth we are so firmly persuaded appears false to the eyes of God or of the Angels and that hence, speaking absolutely, it is false? Why should we concern ourselves with this absolute falsity, since we by no means believe in it or even have the least suspicion of it? For we are supposing a belief or a conviction so strong that nothing can remove it, and this conviction is in every respect the same as perfect certitude.
>
> [AT 7:145; HR 2:41]

In this passage, Descartes explicitly acknowledges the possibility that what is certain may not be true "speaking absolutely," and he makes it clear that certainty takes priority over absolute truth in his conception of the goals of inquiry.

It is sometimes suggested that Descartes does not really concede the possibility that there is a discrepancy between the certain and the absolutely true. The fact that someone might "feign" that such a discrepancy exists, it is argued, in no way implies that such a discrepancy is possible; rather, Descartes's use of the word "feign" indicates that he takes what he is describing to be only a pretense. But Descartes's response to whoever is doing the feigning is not to argue or to assert, that this person is proposing something inconceivable or known not to be the case. Descartes responds, not by denying the genuineness of the possibility "feigned," but by denying its pertinence to his interests. This shows that in his view the possession of certainty and the possession of absolute truth are not the same. The first suffices for his purposes, he insists, regardless of the presence or absence of the second.

Descartes may appear here to be denying what he is elsewhere at pains to assert, concerning the implications of God's benevolence. For if we have been created in such a way that what we find certain is absolutely false, then it may seem that our Creator is after all deceptive. But this is incorrect. Assuming that we recognize the limitations of our faculties, what we are condemned to by the possibility that absolute truth and certainty may diverge is not error, but only a certain sort of ignorance. Now to be sure, condemning someone to ignorance may do him serious injury. For us knowingly to suffer the ignorance in question here, however, is not incompatible with divine benevolence. Descartes's view is that God may have created us in such a way that we must in certain respects remain inescapably in the dark. To keep someone in the dark is to harm him, however, only if he cannot get along in the dark. Since our darkness is compatible with our possession of perfect certitude, which ensures that we need never stumble, it involves no harm to us.

Suppose that Descartes does show without circularity that reason leads to the conclusion that God exists and that whatever is perceived clearly and distinctly is true. How do we know that reason does not also lead to the conclusions that there is no God, that instead there is an omnipotent demon, and that what is clearly and distinctly perceived may well be false? That is, how do we know that reason does not lead in contrary directions? If it did, of course, that would mean that reason is hopelessly unreliable and inconsistent. But since it is precisely the reliability and consistency of reason that is at issue, it would seem that the opposite cannot be taken for granted. This suggests that Descartes's reasoning is ultimately circular after all. For it appears that his argument that what is perceived clearly and distinctly is true, while not circular in itself, serves its purpose only on the question-begging assumption that it is not possible to develop an equally good argument leading to a conclusion which contradicts the conclusion Descartes purports to derive.

It is useful to recognize, in this connection, that a difficulty very much like this one can be raised with equal point about any effort to demonstrate consistency. When we discover a proof that a certain logical calculus is consistent, how do we know that it is not also possible to find a proof that the calculus is inconsistent? Our knowledge of the existence of the first proof does not justify denying the possibility that the second exists, unless we assume that our inquiry cannot lead to contradictory results.

The precise value and import of consistency proofs, particularly in an unlimited context such as the one in which Descartes operates, are difficult to specify exactly. It might perhaps be desirable, instead of construing his argument as an attempt to prove the consistency of reason, to understand Descartes as attempting just to establish that there is no reasonable ground for doubting that reason is consistent. The skeptic might then persist in maintaining that a reductio ad absurdum of the supposition that reason is reliable can be found, whatever Descartes's success in showing that it is not found along the route followed in the *Meditations*. Unless the sceptic actually produces the destructive argument with which he threatens reason, however, his threat remains an idle or capricious one. There is no reason to credit it or to find it disturbing. As long as the skeptic provides no good reason for his mistrust of reason, it is reasonable to ignore him. Descartes can reasonably continue to rely upon reason, which he has shown to confirm its own reliability, since no reason for fearing that reason might also betray itself remains.

## Notes

1. This is no more than a rather provocative formulation of the familiar observation that philosophical theories are never conclusively demonstrated, and that philosophy is not a cumulative discipline. One may well wonder why philosophers continue to seek to prove their doctrines, since historical precedent suggests overwhelmingly that they will fail. On the other hand, argument plainly does have an integral role in philosophy. If its role is not probative, what is it?
2. For some of this evidence, see H. Gouhier, *La pensée réligieuse de Descartes* (Paris, 1972), pp. 11–12.
3. Anthony Kenny, "The Cartesian Circle and the Eternal Truths," *Journal of Philosophy* 67 (1970): 685–700.
4. "Our. mind is of such a nature," Descartes says, "that it cannot refuse to assent to what it apprehends clearly" (letter to Regius, 24 May 1640; AT 3:64; see also *Principles* I. 43). Descartes does not elaborate or attempt to justify this claim, and I do not propose to explore its basis here. I will say, however, that I find it plausible. It is at any rate no less plausible than the similar doctrine, whose plausibility is perhaps more readily apparent, that a person cannot simultaneously assent to incompatible propositions *while* fully aware of and attending to their incompatibility.
5. Kenny, "Cartesian Circle," p. 690.
6. Cf. AT 7:146; HR 2:42. Kenny mistakenly believes that propositions like "2 + 3 = 5" belong to this class. No such proposition appears in any of Descartes's lists of examples, and Descartes makes it clear in the First Meditation that simple arithmetic propositions can be doubted.

## CHAPTER 2

# Frankfurt and the Cartesian Circle

## LEX NEWMAN

Famously, Descartes contemplates the possibility of an evil genius—that a being "of the utmost power and cunning has employed all his energies in order to deceive me" (AT 7.22, CSM 2.15). This is the Evil Genius Doubt (hereafter, EGD). With everything seeming doubtful, the meditator proposes to investigate EGD further:

> [A]s soon as the opportunity arises I must examine whether there is a God, and, if there is, whether he can be a deceiver. For if I do not know this, it seems that I can never be quite certain about anything else.
>
> (AT 7.36, CSM 2.25)

The examination into "whether there is a God" commences an effort to *argue* out of the skeptical problem. The broader argument unfolds in two main steps. The first comprises the Third Meditation arguments for the existence of an all-perfect creator—God—a being who "cannot be a deceiver" (AT 7.52, CSM 2.35). The second comprises the Fourth Meditation derivation of the truth rule: "if, whenever I have to make a judgment, I restrain my will so that it extends to what the intellect clearly and distinctly reveals, and no further, then it is quite impossible for me to go wrong" (AT 7.62, CSM 2.43). (I'll refer to this as the C&D Rule.) Having thus established a divine guarantee of the C&D Rule, the meditator goes on in the closing paragraphs of the Fifth Meditation to celebrate having finally *solved* the skeptical problem.

The broader argument has seemed, to many readers, to unfold as a circle with these arcs:

Arc 1: The conclusion *that a non-deceiving God exists* is derived from premises that are clearly and distinctly perceived.

Arc 2: The conclusion *that whatever is clearly and distinctly perceived is true* (i.e. the C&D Rule) is derived from the conclusion that a non-deceiving God exists.

This is the so-called Cartesian Circle. In the broader argument, Descartes restricts himself to clear and distinct premises because of their epistemic value. In so doing, he seems thereby to presuppose what the broader argument is intended to establish—the C&D Rule.

What should we make of the charge of circularity? An influential interpretation popularized by Anthony Kenny seeks to vindicate Descartes. Harry Frankfurt's interpretation amounts to a re-indictment, while presenting an innovative understanding of Descartes' philosophical aims. Because key elements of Kenny's interpretation are common in the secondary literature, Frankfurt's analysis has far-reaching implications.

In what follows, I first sketch Kenny's interpretation, then clarify Frankfurt's critique of Kenny along with Frankfurt's own interpretation. Lastly I propose a solution to the remaining problems, building on insights from both interpretations.

## Kenny's Interpretation

Some interpretations avoid circularity by limiting EGD's scope. Accordingly, Descartes identifies an epistemically privileged class of indubitable, basic truths—immune to doubt—to serve as premises in his arguments. Because knowledge of them doesn't depend on a divine guarantee of the C&D Rule, the broader argument is not circular.[1]

Kenny thinks a different solution is needed, because *no propositions* start off immune to doubt. His account allows that clearly and distinctly perceived propositions have an epistemically privileged status, but even they are vulnerable to EGD. Part of what makes them epistemically impressive is that they compel our assent. Call this the Involuntary Assent Thesis:

> Involuntary Assent Thesis: While attending clearly and distinctly to a proposition, we cannot avoid giving our assent.

Importantly, the thesis doesn't fully block EGD, because involuntary assent occurs only *during* moments of clarity and distinctness:

> Admittedly my nature is such that so long as I perceive something very clearly and distinctly I cannot but believe it to be true. But my nature

is also such that I cannot fix my mental vision continually on the same thing, so as to keep perceiving it clearly . . .

(AT 7.69, CSM 2.48; cf. AT 3.64, CSM 3.147; AT 7.36, CSM 2.36; AT 7.65, CSM 2.45; and AT 8a.9, CSM 1.196–197)

*While* attending clearly and distinctly, EGD is powerless. Doubt can occur only after one's mental vision is diverted.

The manner in which EGD occurs depends on whether the dubious proposition is a *conclusion* or is instead *self-evident*. With conclusions, the doubt is straightforward:

There are other truths which are perceived very clearly by our intellect so long as we attend to the arguments on which our knowledge of them depends; and we are therefore incapable of doubting them during this time. But we may forget the arguments in question and later remember simply the conclusions which were deduced from them.

(AT 7.146, CSM 2.104)

Such conclusions are vulnerable to EGD unless the person has fully assimilated Descartes' theistic solution to doubt. With self-evident cases, the doubt is not so straightforward. It may be *impossible* to think of the proposition without perceiving it clearly and distinctly:

Now some of these perceptions are so transparently clear and at the same time so simple that we cannot ever think of them without believing them to be true. The fact that I exist so long as I am thinking, or that what is done cannot be undone, are examples of truths in respect of which we manifestly possess this kind of certainty. For we cannot doubt them unless we think of them; but we cannot think of them without at the same time believing they are true . . . that is, we can never doubt them.

(AT 7.145, CSM 2.104)

This last passage brings to the fore a textual tension about whether *all* truths are subject to doubt. *Prima facie*, the passage clarifies that some truths are inherently immune to doubt. Other passages, however, suggest that knowledge of God is a prerequisite to having any further indubitable knowledge. For example, Descartes writes that unless it be settled "whether there is a God, and, if there is, whether he can be a deceiver," then it seems we "can never be quite certain about anything else" (AT 7.36, CSM 2.25). And again: "I see that the certainty of *all other things* depends on this [knowledge of the true God], so that without it *nothing* can ever be perfectly known" (AT 7.69, CSM 2.48; italics added).

Kenny resolves the tension by distinguishing two senses of indubitability— one at the first-order, another at the second-order:

Take the proposition "What's done cannot be undone." If I explicitly think of this proposition, Descartes says, I cannot at that moment doubt it, that is, I cannot help judging that it is true. However, though I cannot doubt this proposition while my mind's eye is on it, I can, as it were, turn away from it and doubt it in a roundabout manner. I can refer to it under some [second-order] general heading, such as "what seems to me most obvious"; and I can raise the whole question whether everything that seems to me most obvious may not in fact be false. I cannot, while explicitly thinking of it, believe it to be false or even suspend judgment about its truth. But until I know that I was made by a veracious God, I can wonder whether my whole intellectual faculty may not be radically deceptive—including that feature of it that is its inability to entertain first-order doubt about metaphysical axioms of this kind.

(Kenny 1968, 183f)

The Involuntary Assent Thesis only entails first-order indubitability, leaving room for doubt when we're thinking about propositions indirectly, at the second-order. But in seeking *full* indubitability, Descartes requires that we overcome EGD even when applied in this indirect, second-order way. This interpretation explains well the following Third Meditation passage wherein simple, self-evident truths are undermined by EGD:

But what about when I was considering something very simple and straightforward in arithmetic or geometry, for example that two and three added together make five, and so on? Did I not see at least these things clearly enough to affirm their truth? Indeed, the only reason for my *later* judgment that they were open to doubt was that it occurred to me that perhaps some God could have given me a nature such that I was deceived even in matters which seemed most evident. And whenever my preconceived belief in the supreme power of God comes to mind, I cannot but admit that it would be easy for him, if he so desired, to bring it about that I go wrong even in those matters which I think I see utterly clearly with my mind's eye. Yet *when I turn to the things themselves* which I think I perceive very clearly, I am so convinced by them that I spontaneously declare: let whoever can do so deceive me, he will never bring it about that I am nothing, so long as I continue to think I am something; or make it true at some future time that I have never existed, since it is now true that I exist; or bring it about that two and three added together are more or less than five, or anything of this kind in which I see a manifest contradiction.

(AT 7.36, CSM 2.25; italics added)[2]

With *every* proposition subject to EGD, how does Kenny's Descartes avoid circularity? Circularity arises only if the premises are believed *because* of presupposing the ultimate conclusion—the C&D Rule. Yet Descartes holds that particular premises are initially believed only because of the Involuntary Assent Thesis. That thesis doesn't entail the general result that whatever is clearly and distinctly perceived is *true*; it entails only that the particular proposition thus perceived *can't but be believed*—i.e. *while* thus perceived. Therefore, the broader argument is not circular, whatever other flaws it may contain. As Kenny writes:

> It is by now clear why there is no circle in Descartes's argument. The clear and distinct perceptions used in the proof of God's existence are perceptions of particular propositions . . . The veracity of God is used to establish not any particular clear and distinct perception, but the general proposition that whatever I clearly and distinctly perceive is true.
>
> (Kenny 1970, 690)

## Frankfurt's Interpretation

My exposition of Frankfurt unfolds in four main parts: 1) why Frankfurt thinks Kenny's interpretation doesn't remove the circularity; 2) Frankfurt's coherence interpretation; 3) a subtler circle that still remains; 4) Frankfurt's star witness for his coherence interpretation.

### Why Kenny's Interpretation Doesn't Avoid Circularity

In Frankfurt's view, Kenny's interpretation doesn't avoid circularity. Kenny explains how the meditator can believe the premises of the broader argument without presupposing the C&D Rule, but *not* how those premises give rise to a fully indubitable grand conclusion:

> For my own part, I cannot see in what way this interpretation can help to resolve the problem of circularity. If Descartes is to establish the unimpeachable truth of his conclusion, as Kenny supposes he intends to do, he must provide premises for it whose truth is reliably guaranteed; and it must be possible for him, if he is to avoid begging the question, to provide this guarantee for the premises without relying upon the assumption that the conclusion is true. What Kenny's approach can explain, however, is only how Descartes might come, without assuming the truth of his argument's conclusion, to believe that each of its premises is true. The question of whether the premises are true—and hence, of whether they establish that the conclusion is true—will then remain, even though it cannot be raised while the premises are being clearly and distinctly perceived . . . But what leads Descartes to believe the premises of his argument is, of course, just that he perceives them clearly and distinctly.

And whether the fact that he thus perceives them entails that they are true, plainly depends upon nothing else than whether the conclusion of the argument is true or false. How, then, does the argument as Kenny understands it avoid circularity?

(see p. 10 above)

Kenny's Descartes draws a *fully* indubitable conclusion—i.e. at the first- and second-order—*based* on premises that are only first-order indubitable. As Frankfurt contends, if the truth of the premises remains in doubt, then so does the truth of the conclusion. That is, Kenny's Descartes can sustain an indubitably true conclusion—his C&D Rule—only if he's already *presupposed* that result in his premises.

*Frankfurt's Coherence Interpretation*

Frankfurt thinks the underlying problem with Kenny-style interpretations runs deeper than the particulars of Kenny's account. Any interpretation whereby Descartes seeks to establish the *truth* of clear and distinct perception will inevitably generate circularity. Frankfurt thinks a very different interpretation is needed, one that doesn't take absolute *truth* as the goal:

> Now what other way of construing the argument is there? If Descartes's aim is not the normal one of demonstrating that his conclusion is true, what can his aim be? I suggest that his primary aim is to display the connection between the premises of his argument and its conclusion. The argument is not designed to demonstrate that its conclusion is true, in other words, but to show that a correct exercise of reason leads us to it.
> The argument terminates in the clear and distinct perception that whatever is clearly and distinctly perceived is true; and Descartes reaches this perception by means of other clear and distinct perceptions, which comprise the argument's earlier steps. That reason leads in this way to the principle that what reason endorses is true, is something Descartes can establish without claiming either that the conclusion of his argument is true or that its premises are true. What is necessary is only that he should clearly and distinctly perceive the premises, and that he should also perceive clearly and distinctly that the conclusion follows from them. There is plainly no circularity in such a procedure.

(see p. 11 above)

On this interpretation, absolute truth is not within our cognitive grasp: we can establish neither the falsehood of EGD, nor the truth of the C&D Rule. What *is* within our grasp is to begin with clear and distinct premises and then show that, from them, it *follows* that there's a God who guarantees the C&D Rule. If Descartes brackets questions about the *truth-value* of what is clearly and distinctly perceived, the Cartesian Circle is avoided.

Although concerns about truth are off the table, the account nonetheless offers epistemic comfort. Our best judgments, as far as reason can discern, are those grounded in clear and distinct perception—making judgments on this basis "is what the faculty of reason does when it is at its best" (Frankfurt 1970, 156). The account therefore entails that, from our best starting point, Descartes establishes that there are *no* consistent reasons for accepting EGD, though there *are* consistent reasons for trusting clear and distinct perception. This is the point of Descartes' arguments for God and the C&D Rule:

> The point of Descartes's validation of reason is that if reason is properly employed—that is, if we give assent only to what we clearly and distinctly perceive—we are not led to doubt that reason is reliable . . . The crux of Descartes's validation of reason is not so much the discovery that a benign deity exists, but that reason leads to the conclusion that such a deity exists.
>
> (Frankfurt 1970, 176)

Helping support the interpretation, Frankfurt develops a unique reading of First Meditation doubts. Accordingly, Descartes' sensory doubts concern *consistency*: "Even if someone has the best sort of evidence the senses can provide for a belief, it is still possible that the senses will subsequently provide him with equally good evidence against that belief" (see p. 12 above). Likewise, for Descartes' doubts about our clear and distinct judgments:

> When Descartes undertakes to evaluate the testimony of clear and distinct perception, he *must* consider the risk of being similarly betrayed by reason. The question he is committed to asking about reason is, in other words, whether it is possible that one clear and distinct perception should contradict another in the way that one sensory perception may contradict another.
>
> (see p. 12 above)

Doubts about the consistency of reason cut deeper than doubts about the consistency of the senses. We can employ our faculty of reason to help resolve inconsistent sensory reports. But "we have no other faculty superior to reason, which we might invoke in an effort to resolve a conflict generated by reason itself" (1978, 35 see p. 13 above). Descartes introduces his theistic framework to deal with the consistency of reason. His novel idea is to argue that our best rational efforts logically support the conclusion that our best rational efforts are logically consistent: it is "an attempt to show that there are no good reasons for believing that reason is unreliable—that the mistrust of reason is not supported by reason and that it is accordingly irrational" (Frankfurt 1970, 175).

If indeed Descartes is unconcerned with truth, Frankfurt must explain why Descartes often writes *as if* concerned—for example, the broader project is framed as an argument for a criterion of *truth*. In his 1970 book, Frankfurt suggests that we understand such texts in light of a *coherence* theory of truth: "The conception of truth involved in his question about the truth of what is clearly and distinctly perceived is, in other words, a conception of *coherence* rather than of *correspondence*" (Frankfurt 1970, 170). His 1978 paper acknowledges, however, that the coherentist reading—about *truth*—is not, after all, a plausible interpretation:

> I now think, however, that it was a mistake on my part to suggest that Descartes entertained a coherence conception of truth. The fact is that there is no textual evidence to support that suggestion; on the contrary, whenever Descartes gives an explicit account of truth he explains it unequivocally as correspondence with reality.
>
> (see p. 15 above)

Frankfurt admits to having no fully satisfying explanation of why Descartes writes *as if* interested in truth (as correspondence): "My present view of the matter is that he may never have thought through the implications of his defense of reason sufficiently to become fully aware of the question about truth to which it leads" (see p. 16 above). Though he abandons a coherentist reading on the narrow issue of truth, Frankfurt nonetheless maintains that the *best* interpretation of Descartes' broader aims is his coherence reading—namely, that Descartes' broader goal is the consistency of reason.

*A Subtler Circle that Still Remains*

Frankfurt's account offers a surprise twist. Even on the truth-free interpretation, Descartes' argument generates circularity:

> Suppose that Descartes does show without circularity that reason leads to the conclusion that God exists and that whatever is perceived clearly and distinctly is true. How do we know that reason does not also lead to the conclusions that there is no God, that instead there is an omnipotent demon, and that what is clearly and distinctly perceived may well be false? That is, how do we know that reason does not lead in contrary directions? If it did, of course, that would mean that reason is hopelessly unreliable and inconsistent. But since it is precisely the reliability and consistency of reason that is at issue, it would seem that the opposite cannot be taken for granted. This suggests that Descartes's reasoning is ultimately circular after all. For it appears that his argument that what is perceived clearly and distinctly is true, while not circular in itself, serves its purpose only on the question-begging assumption that it is not possible to develop an

equally good argument leading to a conclusion which contradicts the conclusion Descartes purports to derive.

(see p. 16 above)

We're back to the very worry that the theistic framework was intended to resolve. On Frankfurt's own interpretation, Descartes' theistic proofs are designed to establish the consistency of reason; yet, those very proofs *presuppose* the consistency of reason.

In the final analysis, not even Frankfurt's interpretation exonerates Descartes from circularity. Frankfurt thinks the underlying problem so intractable that no project *could* avoid it:

> It is useful to recognize, in this connection, that a difficulty very much like this one can be raised with equal point about any effort to demonstrate consistency. When we discover a proof that a certain logical calculus is consistent, how do we know that it is not also possible to find a proof that the calculus is inconsistent? Our knowledge of the existence of the first proof does not justify denying the possibility that the second exists, unless we assume that our inquiry cannot lead to contradictory results.

(see p. 16 above)

### *The Star Witness for the Coherence Interpretation*

Standing by his account—as the *best* interpretation—Frankfurt cites a passage from the Second Replies as his star witness. While rebutting an objection about whether he's really proven God is no deceiver, Descartes writes (under the heading "*Fourthly*"):

> What is it to us that someone may feign that the perception whose truth we are so firmly convinced of may appear false to God or an angel, so that it is, absolutely speaking, false? Why should this alleged "absolute falsity" bother us, since we neither believe in it nor have even the smallest suspicion of it? For the supposition that we are making here is of a conviction so firm that it is quite incapable of being destroyed; and such a conviction is clearly the same as the most perfect certainty.

> (AT 7.145, CSM 1.103)

Frankfurt understands this "absolute falsity" passage as follows:

> In this passage, Descartes explicitly acknowledges the possibility that what is certain may not be true "speaking absolutely," and he makes it clear that certainty takes priority over absolute truth in his conception of the goals of inquiry.

(see p. 15 above; cf. Frankfurt 1970, 179)

Thus understood, the passage confirms the central claim of Frankfurt's interpretation: that Descartes aims at showing not that his conclusions are *true*, but that they *follow* from clear and distinct premises.

Note that what Descartes actually writes in the "absolute falsity" passage is rather different from Frankfurt's gloss. Descartes contemplates the scenario wherein someone may *feign* that God "is, absolutely speaking," a deceiver; Descartes does not contemplate this as an *actual possibility*. Frankfurt acknowledges the objection, offering this reply:

> Descartes's response to whoever is doing the feigning *is not to argue or to assert that this person is proposing something inconceivable* or known not to be the case. Descartes responds, not by denying the genuineness of the possibility "feigned," but by denying its pertinence to his interests. This shows that in his view the possession of certainty and the possession of absolute truth are not the same.
>
> (see pp. 15–16 above; italics added)

Evidently, Frankfurt thinks it would be a problem for the interpretation were the deceiving-God scenario inconceivable. He thinks Descartes makes no such claim.

But this narrative contradicts the text. Descartes *does* claim that the deceiving-God scenario is inconceivable—in the same Second Replies passage ("*Fourthly*"), immediately before the "absolute falsity" remarks:

> [O]nce we have become aware that God exists it is necessary for us to imagine that he is a deceiver if we wish to cast doubt on what we clearly and distinctly perceive. And since *it is impossible to imagine that he is a deceiver*, whatever we clearly and distinctly perceive must be completely accepted as true and certain.
>
> (AT 7.144, CSM 2.103; italics added)

This isn't an isolated remark. In an open letter (May 1643), Descartes writes that we know of the "true God," who's no deceiver, "from the fact that it implies a conceptual contradiction—that is, it cannot be conceived" (AT 8b.60, CSM 3.222). (We'll consider further such claims, in Section 3.) On Frankfurt's interpretation, Descartes should be making weaker, truth-neutral claims—e.g. that the deceiving-God scenario is *inconsistent* with clear and distinct premises.

How should we interpret the "absolute falsity" passage, if not Frankfurt's way? Consider an alternative. The passage says Descartes isn't bothered by the suggestion that his judgments about God are, absolutely speaking, false: "Why should this alleged 'absolute falsity' bother us?" On Frankfurt's reading, Descartes isn't bothered because the suggestion isn't *pertinent*—he's

interested in consistency, not truth. On the alternative reading, he isn't bothered precisely because the suggestion is inconceivable: "since *it is impossible to imagine that he is a deceiver,* whatever we clearly and distinctly perceive must be completely accepted as true and certain."[3] Descartes thinks
that—prior to careful reflection—it *is* possible to imagine God as a deceiver;
after careful reflection, this is *impossible.* As I'll now argue, *this* feature of Descartes' account explains why circularity worries finally dissolve.

## Rethinking Descartes' Final Solution to the Skeptical Problem

We've seen Descartes making strong epistemic claims about God—that "it is
impossible to imagine that he is a deceiver," that "it cannot be conceived." Neither Kenny's interpretation, nor Frankfurt's, contemplates an epistemic result
stronger than that the existence of a non-deceiving God is a *conclusion*—i.e.
based on inference. I want now to argue that clear texts support the stronger
result and that that result explains why Descartes thinks he finally overcomes
EGD, with *full* indubitability—without circularity.[4]

Descartes waits till the end of the Fifth Meditation to announce his victory
over EGD. Why wait? What does that meditation contribute? Largely unno-
ticed in the literature is an important Fifth Meditation theme concerning an
epistemic benefit of repeated meditation? Accordingly, innate truths initially
apprehended only via inference might come to be apprehended *self-evidently*—
a theme arising just prior to the announcement that EGD has been overcome:

> Some of the things I clearly and distinctly perceive are obvious to every-
> one, while others are discovered only by those who look more closely and
> investigate more carefully; but once they have been discovered, the latter
> are judged to be just as certain as the former. In the case of a right-angled
> triangle, for example, the fact that the square on the hypotenuse is equal
> to the square on the other two sides is not so readily apparent as the fact
> that the hypotenuse subtends the largest angle; but once one has seen it,
> one believes it just as strongly. But as regards God, if I were not over-
> whelmed by preconceived opinions, and if the images of things perceived
> by the senses did not besiege my thought on every side, I would certainly
> acknowledge him sooner and more easily than anything else. For what
> is more self-evident than the fact that the Supreme Being exists, or that
> God, to whose essence alone existence belongs, exists?
>
> (AT 7.68f, CSM 2.47)

In a parallel context (Second Replies), Descartes adds:

> I ask my readers to spend a great deal of time and effort on contemplating
> the nature of the supremely perfect being. Above all they should reflect on

the fact that . . . the idea of God contains not only possible but wholly necessary existence. This alone, without a formal argument, will make them realize that God exists; and this will eventually be just as self-evident [*per se notum*] to them as the fact that the number two is even or that three is odd, and so on.

(AT 7.163f, CSM 2.115)

The claim that truths about God *become* self-evident—and that EGD becomes inconceivable—raises interesting philosophical questions worthy of consideration. For our purposes let's *grant* it, focusing on this question: How is this supposed to help solve the skeptical problem while avoiding circularity?

Before answering this, let's review the skeptical problem—where Kenny's interpretation leaves it. By the end of the Fourth Meditation, the meditator can *work up* the premises of the broader argument, attending to them all at once. *While* thus attending, he clearly and distinctly perceives the conclusion and cannot doubt it. With Kenny, let's grant that certainty about these premises is based in the Involuntary Assent Thesis. With Frankfurt, let's grant that—to avoid circularity—the resulting conclusion is as dubitable as these premises. At this juncture, the conclusion can be doubted by attending to *it*, without also attending to its supporting premises.

Now, let's add that Descartes' conclusions about God have become self-evident. This might seem not to help, because, as noted above (p. 21), the Third Meditation meditator doubts even self-evident propositions. However, this doubting ability dissolves once the doubting hypothesis itself becomes *self-evidently contradictory*: the doubting procedure involves imagining a scenario—EGD—that's now *unimaginable*!

I suggest that propositions about God come to have a *cogito*-like status.[5] When trying to doubt *my* existence, I immediately (i.e. self-evidently) apprehend that I must exist in order to be attempting the doubt. Similarly, when trying to doubt *God's* existence, or benevolence, or the like, I immediately apprehend that "the idea of God contains not only possible but wholly necessary existence"; that "it is impossible to imagine that he is a deceiver"; that "it cannot be conceived."

Interestingly, the factors rendering EGD inconceivable serve to dissolve also the worry about circularity. Circularity arises when the intended result of an argument is presupposed in the steps of the argument. On Frankfurt's objection, Kenny's interpretation generates circularity *if* Descartes purports to deduce an indubitable conclusion: such a conclusion *follows* only if the indubitability of clarity and distinctness is presupposed in the premises. On my interpretation, Descartes does *not* purport to deduce an indubitable conclusion *based* on premises. Rather, his conclusions remain dubitable as long as they function epistemically *as* conclusions—i.e. as long as the meditator's certainty about them is based on premises. Indubitability emerges as the possibility of formulating EGD dissolves, namely, when those conclusions come to stand on their own, as self-evident truths. At that juncture, the epistemic status of the now-discarded premises becomes irrelevant. Descartes' claims about God are not based on circular arguments, because they are no longer based on arguments.

## Notes

1. For a fuller discussion of such interpretations, see Newman 1999 and Newman 2010.
2. Importantly, the continuation of this passage has Descartes making the claim we've called special attention to—that unless it be settled "whether there is a God, and, if there is, whether he can be a deceiver" then it seems we "can never be quite certain about anything else."
3. In Descartes' view, the problem with his critic's suggestion is not that it's impertinent, but that it reveals the critic to have missed one of the main points of his *Meditations*—as if the critic were still stuck in First Meditation doubts. It is in *this* context that Descartes' "absolute falsity" remarks are made. See the Second Replies, CSM 2:103, AT 7:144f.
4. Here, I am drawing on an interpretation I have published elsewhere (Nelson and Newman, 1999).
5. I develop this suggestion in Newman 2010.

# PART II

# Descartes on Mind-Body Interaction

# Editors' Introduction

In the *Meditations*, Descartes tries to prove that the human mind or soul is an immaterial substance distinct from the human body. Princess Elisabeth of Bohemia wrote to Descartes with an objection that many later readers are sympathetic to. If mind and body are two distinct substances with nothing in common, how can they affect each other? We all know by our own experience that mind and body *do* interact. So if Descartes' theory makes interaction impossible, then his theory must be false.

In his response to Elisabeth, Descartes says far more about mind-body interaction than in his published work. But the theory outlined in his letters to Elisabeth is puzzling, and in these two chapters Daniel Garber and Deborah Brown offer two different interpretations of that theory—and two different accounts of its implications for the rest of Descartes' system.

Elisabeth is worried about interaction in general. But she also points out a reason why interaction is a *special* problem for Descartes. In Descartes' physics, which is founded on the claim that the essence of body is extension, causation requires contact. But clearly, an immaterial mind cannot come into contact with anything! Descartes responds by claiming that we have two different 'primitive notions' of causation: one for body-body causation and one for mind-body causation. This is not something he says in his published work and it raises all sorts of questions about how he understands causation in general.

Causation is a major topic for philosophers in the seventeenth century, just as it's a major topic for philosophers today. Descartes, like many early modern philosophers, believes that the world depends causally on God at each moment, not just at the instant of creation. In other words, God must perform some activity at each moment to 'conserve' the world or keep it in existence. Some later Cartesians derived the occasionalist view that God is the *only* genuine cause from this, and some readers have suggested that Descartes is or should be committed to occasionalism as well (see Part IV for more about occasionalism). These larger issues about causation lurk in the background of the disagreement between Garber and Brown.

## A Note on References

Descartes' writings are cited by volume and page number in the standard original-language edition edited by Adam and Tannery ('AT'). Whenever possible, we also cite a volume and page number in the standard English translation by Cottingham, Stoothoff, and Murdoch ('CSM'). Note that we give CSM references even when the author is using her own translation.

## Further Reading

- Lilli Alanen (2003). *Descartes's Concept of Mind.*
- Deborah Brown (2006). *Descartes and the Passionate Mind.*
- Janet Broughton and Ruth Mattern (1978). "Reinterpreting Descartes on the notion of the union of mind and body."
- Daisie Radner (1971). "Descartes' notion of the union of mind and body."
- Tad Schmaltz (2007). *Descartes on Causation.*
- Lisa Shapiro (2007). *The Correspondence between Princess Elisabeth of Bohemia and René Descartes.*

## CHAPTER 3

# Understanding Interaction: What Descartes Should Have Told Elisabeth

### DANIEL GARBER

A typical textbook account of the philosophy of mind in the seventeenth century goes something like this. Descartes believed in two kinds of stuff, mental stuff and material stuff, substances distinct in nature that go together to constitute a single human being. But Descartes also took it for granted that these two substances were capable of genuine causal interaction, that minds can cause bodily events, and that bodies can cause mental events, i.e., that acts of will can genuinely cause changes in the state of the human body, and that the state of the sensory organs and the brain can cause sensation and imagination in the mind. But, the story goes, Descartes went astray here and vastly underestimated the philosophical problems inherent in his position. Descartes, it is claimed, repressed, or even worse, simply ignored the central question his position raises: How is it even possible that an immaterial substance, like the mind, could conceivably act on an extended substance like the human body? According to the standard account, later philosophers recognized the inherent unintelligibility of Descartes' position and started one of the largest cottage industries in the history of philosophy, the attempt to provide satisfactory solutions to the mind-body problem, intelligible accounts of how mental and physical events are related to one another. Realizing the unintelligibility of the doctrine of causal interactionism, this cottage industry produced such noteworthy products as occasionalism, dual-aspect theory, pre-established harmony, and so on, all in the attempt to fill in the gap in Descartes' dualist program.[1]

This general outline can (and has) been challenged; the actual history of philosophy is much richer than any of its rationalized reconstructions.

Sympathetic commentators usually call attention to an important pair of letters that Descartes wrote to the Princess Elisabeth in 1643,[2] where Descartes
takes up just this question, the intelligibility of mind-body interaction, and
offers a philosophically interesting and sophisticated account of why he thinks
that the notion of mind-body interaction is perfectly intelligible on its own
terms, and why it neither needs nor admits of clarification.[3]

Now, the letters to Elisabeth are carefully thought out responses to the very
questions that troubled later philosophers about Descartes' view, and as such,
they deserve careful study. But there is a curious difficulty in using these letters
as the key to Descartes' position. No one seems to have noticed that Descartes
is just not *entitled* to the answer he gives Elisabeth; despite Descartes' clear
endorsement, the answer he gives Elisabeth is blatantly inconsistent with other
well entrenched aspects of the Cartesian system.

The defense of this claim will be the central task of this essay. I shall begin
with an exposition of the account Descartes gives of mind-body interaction in
the letters he wrote to Elisabeth in May and June of 1643, letters that form the
first line of defense for Descartes' interactionism among those commentators
who are committed to defending Descartes' position. After a short digression
on a curious analogy Descartes makes between his position and the Scholastic
account of heaviness and free fall, I shall examine Descartes' answer to Elisabeth
in some detail, and argue that it is inconsistent with the foundations Descartes
gives to his theory of motion. Finally, I shall attempt to sketch out an answer
that Descartes *could* have given to Elisabeth in 1643, an answer that seems both
philosophically interesting, and consistent with the rest of his writings.

Before entering into the argument proper, though, I would like to make
a few prefatory remarks concerning the issues I intend to take up, and the
issues I don't. The issue that I intend to focus on is that of the *intelligibility*
of mind-body interaction. The issue is, admittedly, a fuzzy one, as fuzzy as
the notion of intelligibility itself. But historically speaking, it is an important one, as the reaction of Descartes' contemporaries and successors shows.
To make the question a bit more precise, I shall construe it, as Descartes
and his contemporaries often seemed to do, as the problem of whether the
notion of mind-body interaction is somehow intelligible on its own terms,
or whether its intelligibility requires an explication, analogy, or analysis in
terms of some other distinct variety of causal interaction, itself more basic,
or, at least, better understood. To be more precise still, given the promi-
nence of the notion of impact in the then modish mechanistic world view,
the question of the intelligibility of mind-body interaction quickly becomes
a question of whether mind-body interaction can be understood without
somehow relating it to the way in which bodies cause changes in one another
through impact.[4] The question of intelligibility should be distinguished from
the closely related question of whether or not the mind and body do, as a
matter of fact, *actually* interact with one another. Though Descartes and his

correspndents and critics often link the two questions for obvious reasons, they are really somewhat independent. One can hold that despite the intelligibility of mind-body interaction, minds and bodies do not, as a matter of fact, interact with one another. Philosophically, some reason must be given over and above the bare intelligibility of interactionism for adopting that position. Descartes does have an answer to this question, and an interesting one: It is experience, he claims, "the surest and plainest everyday experience,"[5] as he writes to Arnauld, that convinces us of the truth of interactionism. But as important as this question is, it will not interest me here. My concern will be with bare intelligibility.

Even more specifically, my main focus will be the bare intelligibility of the causal link in only one direction. Descartes' interactionism has two aspects: the mental causation of bodily events (volition) and the bodily causation of mental events (sensation and imagination). While both aspects are important, I shall be concerned mainly with the former, mind-body rather than body-mind causation. In part this is to narrow the range of the discussion. But more important, the account of body-body causation that, I shall argue, runs through Descartes' writings on physics makes it, to my mind at least, virtually impossible to understand how he conceived of body-mind causation. The reasons for this will become clearer as the argument progresses, I hope, and I shall point them out when the time comes. But this is an issue that I would like to sidestep in this essay.

And finally, there is one last issue I would like to sidestep. It will become apparent that mind-body interaction is closely connected with the question of the *unio substantial*, as Descartes called it, the substantial or real union between the mind and body. As a consequence of this doctrine, strictly speaking, one should not talk about a *causal interaction* between two different things, a mind and a body; one should talk about the *causal explanation* of certain behavior or states of a *single thing, the* mind-body union, in terms of mental acts of will or the physical states of the body.[6] But while I recognize that an understanding of Descartes' doctrine of the *unio substantiale* is important to a full understanding of Descartes' position on sensation and voluntary action, I shall try as much as possible to avoid this tangled issue. And, consequently, I shall follow Descartes' usual practice, and that of his correspondents, and consider the problem as one of making intelligible the *interaction* between two substances.

## I. The Doctrine of the Three Primitive Notions

Any attempt to come to terms with Descartes' thought on mind-body interaction must begin with a few short letters exchanged between Descartes and the Princess Elisabeth, the most explicit discussion of the problems raised by Descartes' interactionism in the corpus of his writings. The exchange begins with a question Elisabeth raises. She asks Descartes to explain:

how the mind of a human being can determine the bodily spirits [i.e., the fluids in the nerves, muscles, etc.] in producing voluntary actions, being only a thinking substance. For it appears that all determination of movement is produced by the pushing of the thing being moved, by the manner in which it is pushed by that which moves it, or else by the qualification and figure of the surface of the latter. Contact is required for the first two conditions, and extension for the third. [But] you entirely exclude the latter from the notion you have of the body, and the former seems incompatible with an immaterial thing.[7]

Or, as Elisabeth put the question when, unsatisfied with Descartes' first answer, she wrote for further clarification:

And I admit that it would be easier for me to concede matter and extension to the mind than it would be for me to concede the capacity to move a body and be moved by one to an immaterial thing.[8]

The problem Elisabeth has is an obvious and understandable one; she finds it impossible to conceive of how a non-extended mind can cause changes in an extended body. On the other hand, she finds the mechanist's conception of how one body can change the motion of another body at least reasonably unproblematic. There appears to be no mystery for Elisabeth with the phenomenon of impact that constitutes the basic concept in a mechanist physics like Descartes' own. What she seeks is some connection between the two domains, a way of understanding the seemingly incomprehensible mechanism of mind-body interaction in terms of the relatively more intelligible phenomenon of body-body interaction.

Descartes' reply is reasonably clear. Put briefly, Descartes denies that the mechanical explanation of change in terms of impact is relevant to the question as to how mind acts on the body. The claim is that we have a special notion in terms of which we understand mind-body interaction, a notion distinct from the notions in terms of which we understand things that pertain to the mind or to the body taken separately. Descartes argues as follows in his first reply to Elisabeth:

First I observe that there are in us certain primitive notions which are, as it were, the originals on the pattern of which we form all of our other thoughts.... First, there are the most general ones, such as being, number, and duration.... Then, as regards body in particular, we have only the notion of extension, which entails the notions of shape and motion; as regards mind in particular, we have only the notion of thought, which includes the conceptions of the intellect and the inclinations of the will. Finally, as regards the mind and body together, we have only the notion of their union, on which depends our notion of the mind's power to move the body, and the body's power to act on the mind and cause sensations and passions. I observe next that all human science consists solely in clearly distinguishing these notions and attaching each of them to the things to which it applies. For if we try to solve a problem by means of a notion that does not apply, we cannot help going wrong. Similarly, we go wrong if we try to explain one of these notions by another, for since they are primitive notions, each of them can only be understood by itself. The use of our senses has made the notions of extension, shape, and movement more familiar to us than the others; and the main cause of our errors is that we commonly want to use these notions to explain matters to which they do not apply. For instance, we try to use our imagination . . . to conceive the way in which the mind moves the body after the manner in which one body is moved by another. . . . So I think that we have hitherto confounded the notion of the mind's power [*force*] to act on the body with the power one body has to act on another.[9]

Descartes' full answer to Elisabeth is what might be called the doctrine of the three primitive notions. General notions aside, we have within us three basic ideas, that of mind, that of body, and that of their union. Each is separate, each is distinct, and each has its own domain of application; each is per se intelligible, and cannot be explained in terms of other primitive notions. Elisabeth's mistake is that of trying to explain one notion, that of mind-body interaction, which pertains to the primitive notion of the union of mind and body, in terms of impact, which pertains to another primitive notion, that of extension or body, something that is neither necessary, since each notion is per se intelligible, nor possible, since the notions are completely distinct. Mind-body interaction can be grasped only by grasping the unity of mind and body. Since the primitive notion of mind-body units is made "familiar and easy to us" only through the senses, Descartes recommends that the young Princess *abstain* from philosophy, and re-enter everyday life.[10] We *have* a notion that is per se intelligible in terms of which to understand interaction, and if anyone, like Elisabeth (or Arnauld, or Gassendi, or More, or Reguis . . .) fails to see this, it must be because their minds are confused and cluttered. What is called for is a bit of therapy, not argument or explanation. Go about your daily life, and you will find the appropriate notion, just as the unreflective man in the street does.

This is how Descartes tries to explain himself. It can, admittedly, look somewhat suspicious, as if Descartes is simply declining to deal with a serious problem, claiming to understand something that is just unintelligible. Worse than that, Descartes looks as if he is patronizing the sincere but penetrating young Princess who, many later readers have judged, actually got the better of the older and more distinguished Descartes in this exchange.

But I don't think that this is fair. I agree with Descartes' sympathetic commentators in seeing Descartes as offering a philosophically sophisticated answer to Elisabeth's serious question. The doctrine of the three primitive notions is an interesting and not implausible claim about what is going on in the mind, about our native endowments. It is, furthermore, a claim that coheres well with the epistemology and account of our mental faculties that Descartes already worked out in the unpublished *Regulae* and the then recently published *Meditations*.

Descartes' answer is a philosophically serious answer. While it may not ultimately hold up under philosophical scrutiny (what answer to what problem, alas, has?), it cannot be dismissed as begging the question or patronizing the questioner. On this much I agree with a number of friends of Descartes'. But the defense of the intelligibility of Cartesian interactionism cannot end here. For the answer Descartes gave to Elisabeth, while interesting and, perhaps, defensible, is flawed in an important way; it is, I claim, *not* the answer that should have been offered by the author of *Le Monde* and the *Principia*.

## II. The Heaviness Analogy

Before making good on my claim, though, I would like to digress for a few pages, and point out one comparison that Descartes *does* think illuminates the account of mind-body interaction, a comparison that involves the Scholastic account of free fall or heaviness. In part, I want to deal with an obvious question that this raises: How is this comparison different from the one that Elisabeth suggests? How is the use of this comparison consistent with Descartes' apparent claim that comparisons can be of no use in illuminating mind-body interaction? But in addition to dealing with these questions, I want to point out something that this discussion of Descartes' suggests, a way of looking at Descartes' conception of mind-body interaction that will be helpful in understanding the account of that notion that, I shall argue, better suits Descartes' system than the one he offered.

On the Scholastic account of heaviness, at least as Descartes understood it, the heavy body is impelled to the center of the earth by the *real quality* of heaviness, something distinct from the body itself, something incorporeal.[11] This account, which Descartes thinks is intelligible and generally understood,[12] can be helpful in getting his correspondents to understand his conception of mind-body union and interaction. Thus, Descartes writes to Elisabeth:

> When we suppose that heaviness is a real quality of which all we know is that it has the power [*force*] to move the body that possesses it towards the center of the earth, we find no difficulty in conceiving how it moves the body or how it is united to it. We do not suppose that the production of this motion takes place by a real contact between two surfaces, because

we experience in ourselves that we have a specific notion to conceive it by. I think that we misuse this notion when we apply it to heaviness, which as I hope to show in my physics [i.e., the yet to be published *Principia Philosophiae*], is not anything really distinct from body; but it was given us for the purpose of conceiving the manner in which the mind moves the body.[13]

It is important here to appreciate the difference between the analogy that Descartes appeals to, and the comparison Elisabeth makes between mind-body and body-body interaction, a comparison that Descartes rejects. Descartes' criticism of Elisabeth is that she is attempting to understand *one* primitive notion in terms of *another*, something that can only lead to grief. But the situation is altogether different with the Scholastic analogy to which Descartes appeals. As Descartes claimed in his reply to the Sixth Objections, in a passage to which he calls Elisabeth's attention, the common idea of heaviness, the idea the Scholastics and the common man and the idea that Descartes himself had in his naive and sense-bound youth, is, in fact, *derived* from the idea we have of mind. Descartes writes:

The chief sign that my idea of heaviness was derived from that which I had of the mind is that I though that heaviness carried bodies toward the center of the earth as if it contained some cognizance [*cognitio*] of this center within it. For it could not act as it did without such cognizance, nor can there be any such cognizance except in the mind.[14]

Thus, Descartes can claim, as he did to Elisabeth in the passage I quoted earlier, our notion of how the real quality of heaviness acts on the body to which it is attached must be derived from the notion we have of how the mind acts on the body. Now, since Descartes assumed that his readers were conversant with the Scholastic account of heaviness, he thought that he could use this familiar doctrine to call his skeptical reader's attention to the notion of mind-body union and interaction, and point out that, despite their claims of not being able to conceive how an incorporeal mind could act on an extended body, they really do have the notion in question. This is what he explained to Arnauld, to whom he offered the same analogy in 1648, five years after the letters to Elisabeth:

So, it is no harder for us to understand how the mind moves the body than it is for them [i.e., the Scholastics] to understand how such heaviness moves a stone downwards.[15]

Whether or not this explanatory device was successful,[16] it is clear that Descartes is entitled to use it. Unlike the comparison Elisabeth presses, the comparison between mind-body causation and mechanical causation, in Descartes' comparison there is no real analogy, no comparison between two *different* notions. Rather, Descartes claims, there is an *identity*: The *same* notion, that of mind-body union and interaction is at issue in both contexts. Only in one of those contexts it is misapplied.

This is all a fairly straightforward and unproblematic exposition of what Descartes was up to, of why Descartes thought the analogy drawn from Scholastic science was helpful, and, unlike the analogy Elisabeth tries to draw from mechanist science, unproblematic. But I would like to point out an interesting aspect of Descartes' use of the heaviness analogy. The account that Descartes gives of the Scholastic theory of heaviness makes the primitive notion of mind-body unity and the correlative notion of mind-body interaction *conceptually basic* in an extremely interesting sense. Descartes' claim is that the Scholastic scientist is just projecting his innately given conception of his own composite nature onto the inanimate world;[17] *unless* the Scholastic scientist had this primitive notion pertaining to the union of mind and body, he couldn't understand the explanations he gives of phenomena in the inanimate world. That is, as Descartes understands it, our comprehension of Scholastic explanations in terms of substantial forms and real qualities is *parasitic* on the notions we have of mind-body unity and interaction. The notion we have of the interaction between mind and body is a kind of *paradigm notion*, a notion that is intelligible on its own terms (i.e., through the closely related notion of mind-body unity), but one in terms of which at least some other seemingly distinct varieties of causal explanation are intelligible. Two things are worth noting about this paradigm. For one, it should be pointed out that though mind-body interaction is a paradigm with respect to Scholastic explanations, Descartes is unambiguous in thinking that Scholastic explanations in terms of forms and qualities are *bad* explanations. The Scholastic projection of mind and mental activity onto the material world is an *illicit* projection, in Descartes' judgment. And second, and more important, it should be noted that although mind-body interaction is *a* paradigm for causal explanation, it is not the *only* paradigm, it is not universally applicable. There are, Descartes seems to claim in his reply to Elisabeth, *some* causal explanations, those that involve the mechanical interactions of bodies with one another, that *cannot* be understood through our understanding of mind-body interaction; our understanding of voluntary action in animate beings can no more clarify mechanical explanations than vice versa. Or so, in any case, Descartes tells Elisabeth.

### III. Motion, Impact, and God

Let us return now to the main thread of my argument. In section I I presented Descartes' answer to Elisabeth's worries about the intelligibility of mind-body interaction. However, I suggested there that there is something radically wrong with the answer that Descartes gave Elisabeth; it is an answer, I claim, that goes against some of Descartes' most deeply held beliefs about the foundations of physics. Now I must make clear just what I have in mind.

I would like to begin by focusing in on the comparison Elisabeth attempts to draw between mind-body interaction and body-body inter-action, i.e., impact. Elisabeth finds body-body interaction perfectly intelligible. What she is asking Descartes, in effect, is to explain the one in terms of the other; she wants Descartes to explain how a nonextended and incorporeal mind can *literally* make contact with and impel an extended body. Descartes' answer is to say that body-body and mind-body interaction are both intelligible, but on their own terms, that each must be comprehended through its own primitive notion, body-body interaction through the notion of extension, and mind-body interaction through the notion of the unity of mind and body.

Let us examine these claims of Descartes'. Since we are dealing with claims that relate to primitive notions and the notions that derive from, are comprehended through, fall under, etc., these primitive notions, we must first inquire into how it is that the primitive notions are related to the less primitive notions that fall under them. Descartes, if you remember, characterizes the relation as follows:

> First I observe that there are in us certain primitive notions which are, as it were the originals [*comme des originaux*] on the pattern of which [*sur le patron desquels*] we form all of our other thoughts [*connoissances*].[18]

Descartes is none too clear in this passage. But at very least, I think that Descartes means to say that if a given idea Q falls under a primitive notion P, then having P is in some sense necessary for having Q, and that no primitive notion distinct from P is necessary for having Q. P is the original of and pattern for Q in at least this minimal sense.

The problem I see with Descartes' answer to Elisabeth relates to the claims that he seems to make about precisely what ideas fall under the primitive notions he enumerates. Now, it is tempting to suppose mat the real problem must arise in connecting mind-body interaction to the primitive notion of mind-body unity that Descartes claims we have, to suppose that Descartes' answer must break down there if it breaks down anywhere at all. But this is not what worries me. Although Descartes' conception of mind-body unity has its obscurities, I am reasonably confident that one can concoct a plausible account of mind-body unity that makes comprehensible just why Descartes saw mind-body interaction as falling under the primitive notion of mind-body unity.[19]

I certainly concede that working out this account may involve Descartes in some unforeseen difficulties. But be that as it may, the obvious problems lie not with unity and interaction, but with the prima facie more plausible account of the idea of body-body interaction as it relates to the primitive notion of extension. Descartes' answer *seems* to suggest that impact, body-body interaction falls under the primitive notion of extension. But does it?

In answering Elisabeth, Descartes gives only two examples of ideas that derive from the primitive notion of body: shape, and motion. It is clear why shape is included there. Shape is a *mode* of extension, in Descartes' technical vocabulary.[20] And it is plausible to suppose that we cannot have an idea of a mode, like shape, without having an idea of the kind of substance of which it is a mode, i.e., extended substance, and that no *other idea* is required for us to be able to have an idea of shape. That is, the idea of shape falls under the primitive notion of extension in the appropriate sense.

The same case can be made for the idea of motion. Though there are some complexities here, Descartes was clear in considering motion to be a mode of body, a mode of extension, just like shape. Descartes wrote in his *Principia* in offering a formal definition of the notion of motion:

> If we consider how motion must be understood . . . in accordance with the truth of the matter, we must say that it is the translation [*translatio*] of one part of matter, or of one body from the vicinity of those bodies which immediately touch it and which are regarded as being at rest, into the vicinity of others. . . . And I say strictly speaking that it is a mode [of body], not something substantial, just as shape is a mode of a thing with shape, and rest is a mode of a thing at rest.[21]

Similarly, Descartes wrote to Henry More:

> The translation that I call motion is a thing of no less entity than shape: It is a mode in a body.[22]

Consequently, one can say that motion is understood through the primitive notion of extension in roughly the same way as shape is.[23]

But, it should he noted, Elisabeth's question *didn't* deal with motion per se. The comparison she is attempting to press is not a comparison between mind-body interaction and *motion*, i.e., the translation a body undergoes with respect to other bodies, but between the way in which a *mind* can cause motion in bodies, and the way in which *bodies* can cause motion in other bodies. That is, the comparison is not between interaction and motion, but between two purported ways of *causing* motion. And while motion itself may be a mode of body, something comprehended through the notion of extension, change in motion and its causes are something altogether different.

Now, how *are* we to understand body-body interaction, the way in which one body can change the speed or direction of another body's motion through impact? Elisabeth takes this to be intelligible in and of itself and to be in need of no further explanation. And although Descartes *seems* to concur with this in his answer to her, quite a different answer emerges from his more careful writings on physics from early to late. A way into Descartes' position is through the question: What are the laws that govern the behavior and interaction of bodies, and why do bodies obey the laws they do? One might, as some of Descartes' contemporaries tried to do, answer this question either through empirical studies[24] or through an analysis of the nature of body and motion.[25] But for Descartes, the laws that govern bodies in motion and impact must derive from the *causes* of motion.

But what *are* the causes of motion for Descartes? He answers this question in very general terms in a letter to More that I quoted earlier. Descartes writes:

> The translation which I call motion is a thing of no less entity than shape: it is a mode in body. The force causing motion [*vis . . . mouens*] may be that of God Himself conserving the same amount of translation in matter as He put in it the first moment of creation; or it may be that of a created substance, like our mind; or of any other thing to which He gave the force to move a body.[26]

The causes of motion, then, are God, or minds.[27] Now, the mental causation of motion is something of great importance to Descartes, as we have seen already. But in physics, it is the *divine* causation of motion that is mostly at issue. And it is from an understanding of how God causes motion that the laws of motion are derived.

Descartes begins his discussion of the causes of motion and the laws it obeys with the following statement:

> After having considered the nature of motion, we must consider its cause, and that is twofold: first, indeed the universal and primary cause, which is the general cause of all motions in the world; and then the particular cause, by which it happens that individual parts of matter acquire motions which they did not have before. And it seems obvious to me that the general cause in question is nothing else but God Himself.[28]

The distinction between the universal and particular causes that Descartes announces here makes it look as if he is dealing with a distinction between a prime-mover God who is the first cause, setting the world in motion, and other corporeal causes; which result in the world changing from moment to moment. But this is not the picture at all. The universal and general cause, God, not only sets the world in motion, but *preserves* motion in the world; the secondary causes to which Descartes refers, as it turns out, are not causes of motion over and above God, but rather three laws in accordance with which God Himself preserves motion in the world from moment to moment.

In order to understand just how this works, we must remember that for Descartes, the world must be preserved from moment to moment by God, if it is not to pass out of existence. But since preservation and creation are the same tiling, Descartes argues, this is to say that God must continually re-create the world for it to persist.[29] So, Descartes' God is not merely the prime mover; He is the general cause of motion insofar as it is His continual activity, His changing of the relative places of bodies from moment to moment while keeping them in existence that *constitutes* motion in the world.[30] Consequently, the laws that bodies in motion obey must derive from the way in which God continuously re-creates the world. And this, indeed, is just how Descartes derives those laws. The first general principle Descartes notes is his famous conservation of motion law. This law is derived from the immutability of God. Descartes argues that:

> We must understand God to be perfect not only insofar as He is immutable, but also insofar as He works with the greatest constancy and immutability. . . . Whence it follows that it is most consistent with reason that we think that from this alone, that God moved the parts of matter in different ways when He first created them, and now conserves all that matter in the same way and for the same reason. He created it before, that He would also conserve the same amount of motion in it always.[31]

This is Descartes' "master law" of motion. But the secondary laws are also derived, as the master law was, from God's activity. Descartes writes:

> And from this same immutability of God, certain rules or laws of nature can be understood, which are secondary and particular causes of the different motions which we notice in individual bodies.[32]

The dependence of the first two of the secondary laws on God's immutability as a cause of motion is evident. These laws, the so-called Cartesian laws of inertia (laws of persistence would be more accurate) mandate that certain states in bodies, the state of motion itself in the first law, and the state of moving in a particular direction in the second, persist. These follow directly from the immutability of God, who, Descartes writes, "preserves motion precisely as it is in that very moment of time in which he conserves it."[33]

The third law, the law dealing with impact and the way in which one body can change the state of another body, is somewhat more difficult. In order to continue to argument, Descartes must argue that the *immutability* of God requires that He *change* the motion of a given body under certain circumstances, when, for example, it is hit by another body of appropriate size and speed (force of going on). And this, indeed, is how Descartes argues. The intuition is this. The fact that there is no space devoid of body,[34] together with the fact that God created a world of bodies in motion[35] entails that if God is to pre-serve motion in the world, as His immutability requires, He *must change* the motion of at least some bodies as they encounter one another. Thus Descartes writes in the *Principia*, in defense of his law of impact:

> All places are filled with body, and at the same time the motion of every body is rectilinear in tendency; so clearly, when God first created the world, He must not only have assigned various motions to its parts, but also have caused their mutual impulses and the transference of motion from one to another; and since He now preserves motion by the same activity and according to the same laws, as when He created it, he does not preserve it as a constant inherent property of given pieces of matter, but as something passing from one piece to another as they collide. Thus the very fact that creatures are continually changing argues for the immu-tability of God.[36]

Descartes' reasoning here is hardly a model of clarity and distinctness. But at least this much is clear: For Descartes, impact and the changes in bodily motion that result from impact are nothing but the changes that *God* must make in re-creating the world from moment to moment in order to accommodate the motion of bodies to one another. Strictly speaking, *bodies* in motion are *not* real causes of change in impact, it would appear; motion transferred, motion begun, and motion ended in impact must derive from God himself, shuffling bodies about as part of the process of "conserving the same amount of trans-lation in matter as He put in it the first moment of creation," as he wrote to More.[37]

(Here, by the way, is the reason why body-mind causality must be problem-atic for Descartes, as I suggested earlier. The picture one gets from the physics is one of inert matter being shuffled around from moment to moment by an active God and, from time to time, by active incorporeal minds. But given the inertness of matter on this picture, in what sense can one say that the body can cause changes in mental stuff?)

The discussion of the last few pages has taken us a bit out of our way. I started with the claim that Descartes *seems* to make to Elisabeth, that body-body causa-tion must be understood through the primitive notion of-extension. I claimed that while this may be true of motion *simpliciter* which is, indeed, a mode of body, the case of body-body interaction or impact is more complex, at least as analyzed in Descartes' writings on physics. An account of impact led us from motion *simpliciter* to its causes, to God and the way in which He acts on the world in shuffling bodies about from moment to moment. So, it seems, a full understanding of body-body interaction requires that we understand not only motion, a mode of extension, but the way in which God acts on the world. But under which of Descartes' three primitive notions does *this* fit?

Descartes never takes this question up in quite those terms. But a very similar question does arise in the all too brief correspondence with More at the end of Descartes' life. One of More's deepest criticisms of Descartes concerns the doctrine that the essence of material substance is extension. More argues that material substance is not mere extension, but *tangble* or *impenetrable* extended stuff. As part of his attack, More makes the claim that spirits and even *God* are extended.[38] In the case of God, More argues:

> Now, the reason why I judge that God is, in His way, extended is that He is omnipresent and intimately fills the whole machine of the universe and each of its individual parts. For how could He imprint motion on matter, which He once did, and which He actually does now, according to you [i.e., Descartes], unless He now as it were touches the matter of the universe, or at least once did? . . . God is thus in His way extended, and consequently, God is an extended thing.[39]

Descartes' answers to More's general attack are quite interesting, and bear interesting relations to his responses to Elisabeth's general worries about how incorporeal substances can move extended bodies.[40] But most interesting is his answer as to how we can conceive of a nonextended God as being able to act on an extended world. Descartes writes:

> It is no disgrace to a philosopher to believe that God can move a body, without regarding God as corporeal; it is no more of a disgrace to Him to think the same of other incorporeal substances. Of course I do not think that any mode of action [*modus agendi*] belongs univocally to both God and creatures, but I must confess that the only ideal I can find in my mind to represent the way [*modus*] in which God or an angel can move matter is the one which shows me the way in which I am conscious I can move my own body by my own thought.[41]

This comes as close as one could like to answering my question. The way God acts upon the world in sustaining motion and rearranging bodies in impact must, it seems, be derived from the conception I have of how I act upon my body; it, too, must be derived from the primitive notion of the unity of mind and body. Descartes' answer to Elisabeth, thus, cannot have been the *correct* answer, the answer that he should have given, on his own principles. Body-body interaction is *not* fully intelligible under the primitive notion of extension. A full undstanding of bodies in impact, of how one body can alter the motion of another, requires that we understand how God acts on the world. And this, in turn, requires that we be familiar with the way our minds act upon our bodies. So, if there is something wrong with the comparison mat Elisabeth tries to draw between mind-body and body-body interactions, it cannot be what Descartes says it is; it cannot be an illicit intermingling of discrete primitive notions. For the *same* primitive notion is ultimately involved with *both*.

## IV. What Descartes Should Have Told Elisabeth

The argument of the previous section undermines Descartes' answer to Elisabeth. Elisabeth's attempt to understand interaction through impact is *not* wrong for the reason Descartes says it is; Elisabeth is *not* confusing concepts that fall under different primitive notions. This much is clear. But the most interesting question still remains to be faced: how does this observation affect the claim for which Descartes is trying to argue? In responding to Elisabeth, Descartes is attempting to establish that mind-body interaction is per se intelligible, or, at least, intelligible through the closely related notion of mind-body unity, and that Elisabeth's attempt to connect mind-body interaction with body-body interaction is neither possible nor needed. I have shown that the argument he offers for these claims through the doctrine of the three primitive notions is not, on Descartes' own terms, correct. But what becomes of the claims themselves? Ironically enough, I think that my Cartesian refutation of Descartes' actual response to Elisabeth, if anything, *strengthens* his position. The considerations concerning motion and impact drawn from Descartes' writings on the foundations of physics suggest a line of defense for the claims in question which is more consistent with the rest of his works than the one he offered to Elisabeth, and which is, I think, philosophically stronger than the one he actually used. I should point out here that I make no claim that Descartes ever used, or even saw tile argument that I will try to develop in this section. All I claim is that it is an argument he *could* have used, and perhaps, *should* have used.

Let me begin setting out this new and improved answer to Elisabeth by recalling the earlier discussion of the analogy that Descartes appeals to in explaining his position, the analogy with the Scholastic account of heaviness: I pointed out that what allows Descartes to use that analogy is his claim that in this case we are not dealing with two different notions, but only one. The claim is that the Scholastic account of heaviness is comprehensible because it involves a projection of our composite nature onto the inanimate world. The real quality of heaviness is thought of as a kind of mind, united to the heavy body in just the way that the human mind is united to the human body, and, it is claimed, we conceive of heaviness acting on the heavy body in drawing it to the center of the earth in just the way we conceive of the mind acting on the body. Thus, the Scholastic mode of explanation is parasitic on the idea we have of mind-body interaction in the sense that if we didn't understand how minds acted on animate bodies, then we wouldn't understand how forms or qualities act in inanimate bodies. Furthermore, one can, perhaps, say that the notion we have of mind-body interaction is a paradigm notion with respect to the

Scholastic account of heaviness, and, more generally, with respect to all Scholastic explanations in terms of form and quality, insofar as our understanding of these modes of explanation involves a projection of our notion of mind-body interaction onto the world of inanimate things.

The discussion of motion and impact suggests that something similar can be said about the relation between mind-body interaction and the mechanical conception of explanation in terms of impact. Now, it is true that the notion of mind-body interaction is not a paradigm notion with respect to impact in quite the same way as it is with regard to the Scholastic conception of heaviness. While the notion of mind-body interaction does enter into a *full* understanding of interaction, it is not a *simple* projection of our composite nature onto the inanimate world, as the Scholastic theory is. The notion of mind-body interaction enters in at only the deepest level of analysis of the notion of impact, when we attempt to understand how God, the first and continuing cause of motion in the world, the real cause for the changes in the motion of bodies in impact, can act upon the material world. Consequently, impact cannot be used as Descartes tries to use the Scholastic theory of heaviness, to call attention to the idea of interaction he claims we all have. But, the notion we have of impact *is* like the notion we have of the Scholastics' account of heaviness in an important respect. Elisabeth, like most of her contemporaries, at least those sympathetic to the new mechanist science, took impact to be per se intelligible, in fact, the very model of intelligibility. What Descartes' analyses of motion and its laws purport to show is that this is not so. A full understanding of motion in the material world requires reference to God and His action on the material world, and through this, requires reference to our mind's action on our bodies. In this way we can say that the notion of impact, like the Scholastic notion of heaviness, is parasitic on the notion we have of mind-body interaction; for impact as for the Scholastics' heaviness, mind-body interaction is a notion without which the notion of body-body interaction is, strictly speaking, unintelligible, despite appearances to the contrary. And though mind-body interaction is not paradigmatic in the easy and obvious way that it is with respect to Scholastic science, a full understanding of body-body interaction requires an appeal to the way our minds can move our bodies.

This suggests an interesting line of defense for Descartes' position on the intelligibility of mind-body interaction. Mind-body interaction seems to be, for Descartes, a paradigm for both mechanist and Scholastic causal explanation. Since there were the two main competitors at the time, we can say that, for Descartes, mind-body interaction is the paradigm for *all* causal explanation, it is that in terms of which *all* other causal interaction must be understood. And in this there lies a defense for the intelligibility of interaction altogether different from the one, based on the doctrine of the three primitive notions, that he offered to Elisabeth. Mind-body interaction must be basic and intelligible on its own terms since if it were not, then *no* other kind of causal explanation would be intelligible at all; to challenge the intelligibility of mind-body interaction is to challenge the entire enterprise of causal explanation. Furthermore, we *cannot give* a simpler or more easily understood account of causal interaction than mind-body interaction because *there are no more basic or more inherently intelligible ways of explaining the behavior of anything open to us.* We cannot appeal to analogies with impact to clarify mind-body interaction, as Elisabeth does, not because of any confusion of primitive notions, but because we *must* work the other way: body-body interaction must ultimately be understood through the notion we have of the way in which the mind acts on the body.

I should repeat that, despite suggestions of a position like this in the writings on motion, Descartes never said anything like this, to the best of my knowledge. But it is a philosophically interesting answer, one that is open to him and, I think, more consistent with his conception of causal interaction in the physical world than the account that he actually offered. It is, I think, the way of understanding interaction that Descartes *should* have offered Elisabeth.

## Notes

1. This standard account dates back to the seventeenth century. For an account of this reading in the texts of Spinoza, Leibniz, and Malebranche, see, e.g., Jean Lapone, *Le Rationalisme de Descartes* (Paris, 1950), pp. 220–25. Richard Watson discusses similar themes in lesser known Cartesians of the late seventeenth century in his book, *The Downfall of Cartesianism* (The Hague, 1966). The claim that interaction is the scandal of Descartes' philosophy is still commonplace in the standard commentaries. See, e.g., Anthony Kenny, *Descartes* (New York, 1968), pp. 222–26; and Bernard Williams, *Descartes* (New York, 1978), pp. 287–88.

2. Descartes to Elisabeth, 21 May 1643, AT III 663–68; Descartes to Elisabeth, 28 June 1643, AT III 690–95.

3. For instances of this more sophisticated reading, see, e.g., Jean Laporte, op. cit., pp. 220–54; Henri Gouhier, *La Pensée Métaphysique de Descartes* (Paris, 1962), pp. 321–44; and Robert Richardson, "The 'Scandal' of the Cartesian Interactionism," *Mind* 91 (1982).

4. There are, of course, other ways in which the question of the intelligibility of mind-body interaction could be raised. One could take it to be a question about how interaction can be reconciled with certain commonsense notions about causality, in particular with the so called "reality principle" (the cause must, in some sense, contain everything that is in the effect), or with the intuition that causal relations can only hold among things that are sufficiently similar. On this question see, e.g., Richard A. Watson, op. cit., passim, but especially pp. 33–36; Louis Loeb, *From Descartes to Hume* (Ithaca, 1981), pp. 134–43; and chapters I and II of Eileen O'Neill's unpublished Ph.D. dissertation, *Mind and Mechanism* (Princeton, 1983). Another kind of incoherence involves the question as to how mind-body interaction can be reconciled with a law-governed conception of the material world like Descartes'. On this question see, e.g., Louis Loeb, op. cit., pp. 143–48, and Daniel Garber, "Mind, Body, and the Laws of Nature in Descartes and Leibniz," *Midwest Studies in Philosophy* 8 (1983).

5. Descartes for [Arnauld], 29 July 1648, AT V 222.

6. For an account of the substantial union of mind and body and some aspects of its relation to the problem of interaction, see, e.g., Geneviève Rodis-Lewis, *L'Oeuvre de Descartes* (Paris, 1971), vol. I, pp. 351–65, and the numerous references cited there; and Henri Gouhier, op. cit.

7. Elisabeth to Descartes, 6/16 May 1643, AT III 661.

8. Elisabeth to Descartes, 10/20 June 1643, AT III 685. Other contemporary critics and correspondents made the same point to Descartes. See, e.g., Gassendi's remarks in his *Fifth Objections*, AT VII 341; Arnauld to Descartes [July 1648], AT V 215; More to Descartes, 11 December 1648, AT V 238–39.

9. Descartes to Elisabeth, 21 May 1643, AT III 665–66. See also Descartes to Elisabeth, 28, June 1643, AT III 691–92; and Pr I 48.

10. This is the general theme of the letter, Descartes to Elisabeth, 28 June 1643, AT III 690–95.

11. For an account of the Scholastic theory of form and quality as Descartes understood it, and one of his principal lines of attack against it, see Etienne Gilson's classical essay, "De la critique des formes substantielles au doute méthodique" in his *Etudes sur le rôle de la pensée médiévale dans la formation du système cartésian* (Paris, 1930), pp. 141–90.

12. At least he *usually* concedes this. Descartes takes a different position in his letter to Regius, January 1642, AT III 506, 507.

13. Descartes to Elisabeth, 21 May 1643, AT III 667–68. Descartes uses similar comparisons in other writings as well. See, e.g., Descartes to Hyperaspistes, August 1641, AT III 424; Descartes for [Arnauld], 29 July 1648, AT V 222–23; and the *Letter of Mr. Descartes to Mr. C. L. R.* [i.e., Clerselier], AT IXA 213.

14. *Sixth Replies*, AT VII 442.

15. Descartes for [Arnauld], 29 July 1648, AT V 222–23.

16. We don't know Arnauld's reaction, but the tactic *wasn't* particularly successful with Elisabeth. See Elisabeth to Descartes, 10/20 June 1643, AT III 684.

17. This is exactly parallel to the account Descartes often gives of the common belief that material things are really red, or hot, or sweet. See, e.g., Pr I 66–71.

18. Descartes to Elisabeth, 21 May 1643, AT III 665.

19. One might even suggest that when Descartes says that mind and body are united, this claim simply *means* that they are capable of appropriate causal interaction. See, e.g., Henri Gouhier, op. cit., p. 335. For a contrary view, that the mind-body union results in a third substance, a substance over and above the mental and material substances that make it up, see, e.g., G. Rodis-Lewis, op. cit., vol, I, p. 353 and the references cited in vol. II, p. 543, note 29; or Janet Broughton and Ruth Matterri, "Reinterpreting Descartes on the Notion of the Union of Mind and Body," *Journal of the History of Philosophy* 16 (1978), pp. 23–32.

20. See, e.g., Pr I 53, 61.

21. Pr II 45. See also Pr II 27.

22. Descartes to More, August 1649, AT V 403.

23. Despite what Descartes says, this cannot be quite right, since motion, unlike shape, involves time or, at very least, change.

24. Though the question is hotly debated, this is at least *one* reading of what Galileo thought he was up to. For this reading, see, e.g., Stillman Drake, *Galileo Studies* (Ann Arbor, 1970), especially Drake's polemical introduction. For Descartes' nutshell assessment of Galileo's physics, see Descartes to Mersenne, 11 October 1638, AT II 380.

25. This seems to be the strategy Thomas Hobbes adopts, e.g., in *De Corpore*, chapter 15. This is also the strategy that Leibniz sometimes attributed to his own youthful works in physics, the *Theoria Motus Abstructi* and the *Hypothesis Physica Nova*. See, e.g., Leibniz's remarks at the time these works were being written, in Leibniz to Oldenburg, 13/23 July 1670, in Leibniz, *Sämtliche Schriften und Briefe* (ed. Preussischen Akademie der Wissenschaften), series II, vol. I (Darmstadt, 1926), p. 59; or Leibniz's later remarks on this early program in Part I of his *Specimen Dynamicum* (1695), in G. W. Leibniz (ed. C. I. Gerhardt), *Mathematische Schriften*, vol. VI (Halle, 1860), p. 240, translated in P. P. Weiner (ed.), *Leibniz Selections* (New Vork, 1951), p. 128. In some of his polemical writings against the Cartesians, Leibniz gives the misleading impression that for Descartes, too, the laws of motion are to be derived from me nature of body. See, e.g., the essay that Weiner has entitled, "Whether the Essence of a Body Consists in Extension," in Leibniz (ed., C. I. Gerhardt), *Die Philosophischen Schriften*, vol. IV (Berlin,. 1880), pp. 464–66, translated in Weiner, op. cit., pp. 100–2.

26. Descartes to More, August 1649, AT V 403–4.
27. P. H. J. Hoenen has suggested that the "other things" to which God gave the ability to cause motion in bodies are just other bodies. See the excerpt from his *Cosmologia*, translated as "Descartes's Mechanicism" in Willis Doney, ed., *Descartes* (Garden City, 1967), pp. 353–68, esp. p. 359. But it is interesting that in the sections of *Principia* II that deal with the *causes* of motion, properly speaking, sections 36 and following, bodies are *never* mentioned as genuine causes. However, in Pr II 40 Descartes does mention, in addition to human minds, *angelic* minds as possible causes of motion. Angelic minds as causes of motion also come up in the letter Descartes wrote to More that immediately precedes the one from which I quoted. See Descartes to More, 15 April 1649, AT V 347. This suggests that the "other things" in question in the August 1649 letter are not bodies, but angels.
28. Pr II 36. See also Descartes 10 [the Marquis of Newcastle], October 1645, AT IV 328.
29. See *Meditation III*, AT VII 48–49; *Second Replies*, AT VII 165; Pr I 21.
30. The continual re-creation account of God's activity creates a curious difficulty for the mental causation of events in the material world. When God is re-creating the material world from moment to moment, He must put each material thing *somewhere* when He recreates it. But if it is God who determines the position of bodies from moment to moment, how is it possible for *minds* to affect the momentary position of a body? There seems to be no room for minds to act on Descartes' continual re-creation picture. Nicolas Malebranche develops this difficulty into an argument for occasionalism in the seventh of his *Entretiens sur la métaphysique*.
31. Pr II 36.
32. Pr II 37.
33. Pr II 39.
34. Pr II 5–19.
35. Pr II 36. Pr III 46–47.
36. Pr II 42.
37. Descartes to More, August 1649, AT V 403–4.
38. See, e.g., More to Descartes, 11 December 1648, AT V 238–24; More to Descartes, 5 March 1649, AT V 301; More to Descartes, 23 July 1649, AT V 379.
39. More to Descartes, 11 December 1648, AT V 238–39. This seems similar to a point Spinoza makes in defense of his claim that God must have the attribute of extension. See *Ethics* I, prop. 15, scholium, in Spinoza (ed. Carl Gebhardt), *Opera* (Heidelberg, 1925), vol. II, p. 57.
40. Compare, e.g., the discussion of the sense in which God is extended in *potentia* in the letters to More (Descartes to More, 15 April 1649, AT V 342; Descartes to More, August 1649, AT V 403) with Descartes' remarks to Elisabeth about the sense in which it is proper to say that mind is extended (Descartes to Elisabeth, 28 June 1643, AT III 694).
41. Descartes to More, 15 April 1649, AT V 347.

## CHAPTER 4

# Understanding Interaction Revisited

### DEBORAH BROWN

Although Descartes has important things to say about the union of mind and body prior to his correspondence with Princess Elisabeth, it is in his replies to her penetrating questions that we learn most about his thinking on the subject. In his first reply, Descartes makes it clear that he has not been overly concerned with the union because in the *Meditations*, his "principal aim was to prove the distinction between the soul and the body." To that end, conceiving of the mind just as a thinking thing was useful, whereas thinking of it as something that "can act and be acted upon" through its union with the body would only have detracted from the argument. But now, he tells Elisabeth, he will endeavor to explain how he conceives of the union of the soul and the body and how the soul has the power to move the body (AT 3.665, CSM 3.218). Elisabeth's letter is thus a turning point in Descartes' philosophical development.

Elisabeth seeks clarification about the intelligibility of mind-body interaction. She cannot grasp how a thinking substance could cause bodily motion and voluntary actions. For according to Descartes' own physics, all movement is caused by impulse, which requires both physical contact and extension. Extension is excluded from the notion of the soul Descartes develops in the *Meditations*, and Elisabeth takes physical contact to be impossible for an immaterial thing (AT 3: 661). In his replies, Descartes attempts to reassure her that she already possesses the conceptual resources sufficient for understanding the union. These conceptual resources are given by her "everyday experience" of the way in which her mind moves her body and how her mind, through its sensations and passions, is affected by her body.

Narrowly construed, the debate between Elisabeth and Descartes concerns the possibility of interaction between mind and body. More broadly, as Daniel Garber has shown, a host of deeper issues related to causation and God's activity are raised in the process. Against Garber, I argue that the primacy of our knowledge of how minds move bodies does not establish that our idea of the union is the primitive notion on which all understanding of causation depends. I also argue that bodies are real causes just as much as minds are and that Descartes' main goal in replying to Elisabeth is to demonstrate that nothing in Cartesian philosophy demands that all changes of motion occur through collisions.

## Understanding Interaction

Descartes' thinking about the problem of mind-body interaction begins in his reply to the Fourth Objections. There, Arnauld warns him that the separation of mind and body is in danger of reintroducing a form of Platonism that conceives of the human being as a rational soul that simply uses the body like a tool (AT 7.203, CSM 2.143). Descartes rejects this consequence, insisting that the union is "substantial," although what exactly this means for him is obscure.

Later in his reply to Gassendi, moreover, he appears to endorse the very interpretation Arnauld warns him about. In the Fifth Objections (AT 7.339–346, CSM 2.235–240), Gassendi objects that no thing lacking parts could be intermingled or compounded with a body so as to be mutually bound to it. Wouldn't such compounding require physical contact? If Descartes claims that an unextended thing can communicate its feelings or instructions to the body, how can this be achieved without exertion—and how can there be exertion without mutual contact between the mover and the moved? If change of motion is conceived in terms of push and impact, how is mind-body interaction consistent with physics (AT 7.339–340, CSM 2.235–236)? Descartes responds by claiming that although the mind *uses* a body, it doesn't follow that it *is* one, an odd reply given his response to Arnauld, and one decidedly off point (AT 7.389–390, CSM 2.266). Gassendi is assuming that if A *pushes* B, then A and B must be capable of contact, and that is a reasonable assumption given Descartes' physics.

Presumably Elisabeth was aware of this exchange. She would thus have read Descartes' bald assertion that it is not necessary for the mind to be a body in order to move the body (AT 7.390, CSM 2.266). That she raises much the same objection as Gassendi shows that she is not persuaded. In his more gracious response to her, Descartes begins by adding the notion of the union to his collection of "primitive notions," which hitherto included only mind and body (and their essences, thought and extension) and certain "common notions" which connect simple natures together and form the basis for all rational inferences (AT 10.418–419, CSM 1.44). These primitive notions are "patterns on the basis of which we form all our other conceptions." It is from the notion of the union, Descartes writes, that we form the idea of the power the soul has to move the body and the power of the body to act on the soul (AT 3.665, CSM 3.218).

Garber is right to observe that this constitutes real progress. Admitting that the union is a "primitive notion" is intended to serve two purposes. First, it is intended to block attempts to understand mind-body interaction in terms of the concepts of body and extension. Mind-body interaction has to be intelligible on its own terms. Second, it serves as an explanation for certain mistakes in philosophy. Just as we err in using the notions of body and extension to understand mind-body interaction, so too do we err in thinking that there are real qualities of body, such as the Scholastic notion of heaviness, that act like little souls in directing the motion of bodies. Heaviness, on Descartes' (possibly inaccurate) reading of Scholastic physics, is a property of bodies that causes them to move towards the center of the earth. Descartes had already explained in the *Sixth Replies* that this notion of heaviness was simply the result of our taking the idea of how the mind moves the body and using it inappropriately in the explanation of free fall. The Scholastic view is absurd because no quality of bodies could propel them to the center of the earth without possessing knowledge of the center, and that is impossible for non-rational substances. Instead, free fall can be explained entirely in terms of motion and rest and the configuration and situation of the parts of bodies (AT 7.441–443, CSM 2.297–8).[1]

However, the absurd Scholastic theory does serve to illustrate mind-body interaction. If we have no difficulty conceiving of how heaviness, *were it intelligent*, could move bodies, then we should have no difficulty understanding how the mind can be joined to a body so as to move it (AT 3.667–8, CSM 3.219).

What exactly is Descartes hoping to achieve by relying on this analogy? Principally, he is trying to convince Elisabeth that

1. there can be causes of motion other than impact, and
2. she possesses the knowledge of this already, because she is embodied.

Elisabeth professes to have within her no such knowledge. When she thinks of the immaterial, she thinks of something which can have no "communication" with matter. For there could only be communication between an immaterial mind and the material body if the body carries *information*—which it cannot do given that on Descartes' view it lacks intelligence. Nor can she conceive why, if the soul is really distinct from the body, it should be ruled by it. She concludes: "I admit it would be easier for me to concede matter and extension to the soul than to concede the capacity to move a body and to be moved by it to an immaterial thing" (AT 3.685; Shapiro 2007, 68).

This move seems bizarre. Rather than addressing Elisabeth's objection head on, Descartes offers her an account of the origins of the idea of the union. The union is known only obscurely by the understanding but clearly with the senses. The exercise of the notion of the union is hampered by metaphysical thoughts, which focus our attention on the distinctness of mind and body rather than their union. Descartes invites Elisabeth to give more time to the senses so that she may better know the union, an odd recommendation from someone who previously denied that anything can be known clearly and distinctly through the senses (AT 3.691–4, CSM 3.226–228). He further invites her to attribute matter and extension to the soul "for to do so is to conceive it as united with the body."

It is important to understand that he is using 'matter' and 'extension' here equivocally. The soul is not extended in the sense bodies are (AT 3.694–5, CSM 3.228).[2] But if all it means to say that the soul is extended and material is to say that it acts through the body, nothing much has been achieved.

Elisabeth responds with the assertion that while her senses teach her *that* the soul moves the body, they do not teach her *how* it does so. Thus, following Descartes' own rule of not judging what she does not clearly and distinctly perceive, she will continue to think of the soul as extended: "Though extension is not necessary to thought, neither is it at all repugnant to it, and so it could be suited to some other function of the soul which is no less essential to it" (AT 4.2; Shapiro 2007, 72).

## What Should Descartes Have Told Elisabeth?

So far Elisabeth has the upper hand. Through Descartes' physics, she has gained a clear understanding of how bodies produce changes in motion. Now she uses that understanding to begin drawing her own conclusions about mind-body interaction and the nature of the soul.

Garber makes the intriguing suggestion that Elisabeth is not really entitled to assume that she has a clear grasp of how bodies produce motion, simply on the basis of her idea of extension. In fact, he claims, Elisabeth is wrong to think that the idea of body-body interaction is primitive. Rather, for Descartes the idea of body-body interaction really derives from the idea of how the mind moves matter. Had Descartes made that point, it would have effectively stopped Elisabeth in her tracks.

What grounds Garber's suggestion that the whole edifice of Cartesian physics rests on the primitive notion of mind-body interaction? His reasoning is straightforward. First, he notes that although motion can be understood through the notion of extension, *changes in motion* cannot be, and it is the explanation of such changes that Elisabeth is interested in (see pp. 46–47 above). Second, Garber argues that changes in the speed or direction of a body through impact are not explained through the concept of extension *per se.* Rather, they are governed by the laws of motion and impact. Third, Garber argues that the principal cause of motion from which the laws are derived is nothing but God himself (see pp. 46–47 above).

In support of the first point, he notes that Descartes' definition of local motion as the "transfer of one part of matter, or of one body, from the vicinity of those bodies which immediately touch it . . . into the vicinity of others" (*Principles* II, 25; AT 8a.53, CSM 1.233) does nothing to illuminate how *changes* of motion are produced (see pp. 44–45 above). Hence, we must look elsewhere. On the second point, Garber notes that when Descartes discusses the causes of motion, it's in the course of introducing the laws of nature: "the secondary and particular causes of the various motions we see in bodies" (AT 8a.62, CSM 1.240). In relation to the third point, Garber explains how the laws are derived from our idea of God, particularly, his immutability. *Principles* II, 36 prefaces a discussion of the laws with the following remark:

> After having considered the nature of motion, we must consider its cause, and that is twofold: first, indeed the universal and primary cause, which is the general cause of all motions in the world; and then the particular cause, by which it happens that individual parts of matter acquire motions which they did not have before. And it seems obvious to me that the general cause in question is nothing else but God himself.
>
> (AT 8a.61)

This passage suggests that God and bodies constitute two kinds of causes of motion. But Garber denies this.

Descartes' occasionalist followers argued that his doctrine of divine conservation entails that only God is a cause of motion. God's conserving bodies in motion is, they argued, no different from his recreating them in different places at different times, and hence no different from motion. Garber does not endorse all of this occasionalist reading of Descartes, but he does think that Descartes' three laws of motion are "not causes of motion over and above God" but simply how God conserves matter in motion (see p. 44 above). The first and second laws, the so-called "law of inertia" and the law of rectilinear motion, follow directly from God's immutability. The third law, which is about collisions, is also connected with God's immutability: "if God is to preserve motion in the world, as His immutability requires, He *must change* the motion of at least some bodies as they encounter one another" (see p. 47 above).

The final piece of the puzzle comes from establishing that our understanding of how God produces motion derives from our idea of how our own minds move our bodies. The crucial passage comes from a letter Descartes wrote to Henry More, who thought that God must be extended because he can move matter:

It is no disgrace to a philosopher to believe that God can move a body, even though he does not regard God as corporeal; so it is no more of a disgrace for him to think much the same of other incorporeal substances. Of course I do not think that any mode of action belongs univocally to both God and his creatures, but I must confess that the only idea I can find in my mind to represent the way in which God or an angel can move matter is the one which shows me the way in which I am conscious I can move my own body by my own thought.

(AT 5.347, CSM 3.375)

Garber (see pp. 49–50 above) reads this as implying that the way in which God conserves motion derives from the idea of mind-body interaction and hence from our idea of the unity of mind and body. Since the latter is known *a posteriori* through everyday sensory experience, this would make the entire edifice of Descartes' physics not just dependent on the primitive notion of mind-body unity but also upon the *a posteriori* foundation of that notion, sensory experience, a curious outcome indeed for our arch rationalist.

Seventeenth century occasionalists argued that there could be no cause other than God. Garber's weaker view is that it is consistent with Descartes' doctrine that minds are a source of motion, and indeed that we must be able to understand this in order to understand God's efficient causality. But he does not think we need to grant that *bodies* are a source of motion. In the one passage where Descartes appears to list the causes of motion, bodies are curiously absent:

The power causing motion may be the power of God himself conserving the same amount of transfer in matter as he put in it in the first moment of creation; or it may be the power of a created substance, like our mind; or of any other such thing [like an angel] to which he gave the power to move a body.

(AT 5.403–4, CSM 3.381)

Garber thinks that a quasi-occasionalist picture is implied by Descartes' exchange with More, one in which only God and minds are causes of motion. Mind-body interaction is, therefore, a one-way street.

## What Should Descartes Say to Garber?

Implicit in Garber's analysis are assumptions that Descartes may very well not share. First, there is the assumption that our idea of how our minds move our bodies is the same as our idea of how God moves bodies. Second, there is the assumption that because Descartes does not explicitly mention bodies as causes of motion in the letter to More, his account is at least "quasi-occasionalist." Third, Garber assumes that because bodies are inertial, they cannot be causes of change. Let us examine these assumptions.

In regard to the first assumption, Roger Ariew (1983, 36) argues that in the very same letter of April 1649 to More, Descartes states that no mode of action belongs univocally to God and creatures. We might say that God creates the universe and that a human creates a painting, but we do not mean the same thing by 'create' in the two cases. Thus, the idea of how our minds move bodies is at best an analogy for understanding how God moves bodies. If Ariew is correct, body-body interaction does not rest ultimately on the primitive notion of the union and Descartes is not mixing up primitive notions. More likely, he is failing either to show how changes of motion follow from the notion of extension or failing to show how it involves another primitive notion, namely, the primitive notion of how God moves bodies.

Against the second assumption are Descartes' numerous references to bodies as causes of changes, both in the mind and other bodies. The argument for the existence of bodies in the Sixth Meditation seems to depend crucially upon ruling out God and the mind as active causes of our ideas of bodies, leaving bodies as the natural default. In support of the second assumption, Garber notes that in his account of how we know bodies exist in the *Principles*, Descartes' language undergoes a subtle shift and becomes "studiously noncausal." Rather than referring to the "active faculty" of things outside me which produce sensations (AT 7.79, CSM 2.55), the *Principles* passage refers to ideas "coming to us from things outside us" (AT 8a.40–41, CSM 1.223; also AT 9b.63). Garber (1992, p. 74) argues that this shift in terminology is consistent with a weaker position than the one pursued in the *Meditations*, namely, that sensations "come from bodies" with the help of God as an agent. The role bodies play would thus be consistent with their being occasional causes.

If there is indeed a subtle shift in terminology between the *Meditations* and the *Principles* regarding the role bodies play in confirming our knowledge of them, it is isolated (cf. AT 6.141, CSM 1.172). Descartes continues to speak of bodies as the causes of changes in the mind and in other bodies up to 1649 (e.g. AT 11.349, CSM 1.339). The language employed in the *Description of the Human Body*, which dates from 1647–8 is, we might say, "studiously causal." The "body-machine" or, more precisely, the disposition of the organs, is sufficient to "produce in us all the movements which are in no way determined by thought" (AT 11.227, CSM 1.316). Moreover, it is part of Descartes' solution to the problem of evil that there are causes other than minds. Elsewhere, he responds to those who find it problematic that he would explain human procreation by reference to such "light causes" as the laws thus:

But, in truth, who would want heavier [causes] than the eternal laws of nature? Perhaps that they come from some mind? But from which mind?

Immediately from God? Why, therefore, do they sometimes make mon-
sters? Or from a most wise Nature, which would not have originated
except for the dispensation of human thought?

(AT 11.524)

However, none of this explains how bodies can be causes of motion when they
are inert. This brings us to the third assumption. The problem with Descartes'
referring to bodies as having the power to move other bodies, as later thinkers such as Huygens, Leibniz, and Newton were famous for observing, is that
Cartesian bodies do not seem to possess within themselves any *force* which
could explain how motion is initiated or sustained. Occasionalists seized upon
this to argue that force must, therefore, come from God. "It is clear that no
body, large or small, has the power to move itself," wrote Malebranche (SAT
448). To some extent this is correct—a Cartesian body at rest will not begin
to move unless impelled by another body in motion—but it does not follow
that a body does not have a power to act. For Descartes recognizes the need
for a notion that explains why a body would move in a certain direction were
it not impeded. The notion of a tendency or 'striving' appears in his physics in
connection with the first law, which states that "each and every thing, in so far
as it can, always continues in the same state; and thus what is once in motion
always continues to move" (*Principles* II, 37; AT 8a.62, CSM 1.240). In expli-
cating how this law operates, Descartes is often drawn to treat bodies as centers
of activity. This is particularly clear from his dispute with Hobbes.

Hobbes is concerned with the traditional problem in physics of explaining
the first moment of change and ends up believing that even a body at rest must
be in a state of infinitesimal motion. Thus it is active and has what Hobbes calls
'endeavour' (Hobbes 1839, 206). Interestingly, Descartes agrees in this context
that bodies are active, writing to 'Hyperaspistes' (August 1641) that it is absurd
to suppose that there could be a passion without an action for a single moment,
as if, for example, a spinning of a top could persist even though its cause had
ceased to act or was destroyed. Hyperaspistes should not, therefore, reject the
idea that the top acts on itself to sustain its motion (AT 3.428, CSM 3.192–3; cf.
*Optics*, AT 6.93–94). The contrary view is absurd for it amounts to supposing
that the world has no activity within it (AT 3.428, CSM 3.192–193).

Where Descartes disagrees with Hobbes is that he does not conflate a
body's 'action,' 'force,' or 'striving' with motion. In several examples Descartes describes a body as having a tendency to move in a certain direction
without being in motion, or as acting in a way that alters its directional tendencies without its motion being affected. (*Principles* III, 56ff.) In some cases,
these 'causes' are more like dispositional properties or potentialities—they
are understood *counterfactually*, although like any other causal property, they
comply with the laws (AT 1.450–1, CSM 3.74). A striving may "pass through"
a body in a certain direction along the same path that it would travel along

were its motion not being prevented by a greater force. For example, wine in the bottom of a vat has a tendency to move downwards (AT 1.451, CSM 3.74) and a stone in a sling has tendencies to move to points distinct from those it is constrained by the sling to move towards (*Principles* III, 57; AT 8a.108–109, CSM 1.259–260).

This brief sketch of the way in which terms like 'action,' 'force,' 'striving' have broader ranges of signification than 'motion' or indeed other qualities of extension is relevant to our understanding of Descartes' reply to Elisabeth. Bodies 'act' in ways other than through impact or a transfer of motion. At *Principles* II, 43, the terms 'force,' 'action,' 'power' and 'striving,' are brought together: the force of each body to act against another or to resist the action of another consists "in the single fact that each thing strives, as far as is in its power [*quantum in se est*], to remain in the same state" (AT 8a.66, CSM 1.243). What is true of bodies is even more true of minds. As Descartes writes to More (Feb 5, 1649): "we clearly conclude that no incorporeal substances are in any strict sense extended. I conceive them as sorts of powers or forces, which although they can act upon extended things, are not themselves extended . . ." (AT 5.270, CSM 3.361).

Granting that Elisabeth and other critics of Descartes might have been wrong in assuming that all causal interaction between bodies presupposes physical contact, it is less clear why they would be wrong in supposing that all causal interaction presupposes extension. If 'action' and 'force' in Cartesian physics are not reducible to motion, Descartes still owes us an explanation of how the powers of Cartesian bodies are related to extension and its principal modes: size, shape, and motion. How, moreover, using only the primitive notion of extension can we explain all the diversity of effects bodies are capable of producing? And if the power to act applies univocally to incorporeal and corporeal substances, in what sense is this notion derivable from the concept of extension? The worry is that 'force' must really be itself a primitive notion. This is exactly the path Leibniz and Newton would later tread. But, for Descartes, that would perhaps come too close to the view he opposes, namely, one which treats forces as real accidents, which like little intelligences guide bodies to their destinations, sustain them in motion and enable them to resist other bodies. Descartes, however, is quick to dispel any suggestion that his notion of 'striving' bears any resemblance to the forms of Scholastic metaphysics:[3]

> When I say that the globules of the second element 'strive' to move away from the centres around which they revolve, it should not be thought that I am implying that they have some thought from which this striving proceeds. I mean merely that they are positioned and pushed into motion in such a way that they will in fact travel in that direction, unless they are prevented by some other cause.
>
> (AT 8a.108, CSM 1.259)

If I am right, Descartes recognizes that the actions bodies perform on themselves to persist in a state of motion requires that bodies be agents. This is perhaps bad news for the coherence of Cartesian physics, but it should be good news for those worried about how mind-body interaction fits into Cartesian metaphysics. Not all of the actions performed on bodies are to be explained just in terms of motion and impact, and included in this class are our volitions to move our bodies. This is not to say that Descartes does not owe Elisabeth further explication of the nature of mind-body interaction but simply to suggest that the space in which he could have maneuvered was already being shaped by a notion of agency which, to all appearances, supervenes on the essential attributes of thought and extension, but seems reducible to neither of them.

## Acknowledgement

I am grateful to the Australian Research Council Discovery Grant scheme for supporting this research and to the editors of this volume for their excellent suggestions.

## Notes

1. See *Principles* IV, 20–24 for a physical account of gravity (AT 8a.212–214, CSM 1.268–270). See also AT 3.434; AT 5.222–223, CSM 3.358; and AT 11a.213.
2. In a letter to More (15 April, 1649) Descartes refers to the extension incorporeal substances can have as an "extension of power," the power to act on bodies, in contrast with the "extension of substance" of bodies (AT 5.342, CSM 3.372–373). Not surprisingly, More failed to see how something could have a power of extension without being extended (AT 5.379).
3. On Descartes' opposition to forms see AT 3.506, CSM 3.208–209; AT 3.648–649; AT 5.222–223, CSM 3.358; AT 7.441–442, CSM 2.297–298.

# PART III

# Making Sense of Spinoza's *Ethics*

# Editors' Introduction

Spinoza's *Ethics* can seem to be the strangest of canonical philosophical works. This is in part because of the way it is presented as a series of definitions, axioms, propositions, proofs, and scholia. This apparatus can be intimidating and make it hard to see what motivates Spinoza. But the difficulty and strangeness of Spinoza's work are also connected to his views. For instance, there seem to be many things in the world, as I can see just by looking around the room and noticing myself, the table I'm sitting at, and my cat sitting looking sleepily at me. Spinoza argues, however, that there is only one substance, which somehow encompasses all these seemingly independent things. What, one might well ask, could a claim such as that possibly mean? How could there be just one substance, when there appear to be so many? And how could anyone come to believe that?

Michael Della Rocca argues, in his book *Spinoza*, that the central notions in Spinoza's work are things like explicability and intelligibility. Their centrality has two aspects. First, Spinoza believes that every fact has an explanation. There are for Spinoza no brute facts, no things that just are what they are, but for no reason at all. Second, and more controversially, Della Rocca argues that Spinoza thinks that other important notions (e.g. causation, consciousness, representation, goodness, rightness, power) are to be explained in terms of intelligibility. Thus, for instance, "for *a* to cause *b* is nothing more than for *a* to make *b* intelligible, for *a* to explain *b*" (Della Rocca 2008a, 8). On this picture, the world is intelligible, and the world is to be understood in terms of intelligibility.

Yitzhak Melamed, in his response to Della Rocca, agrees that Spinoza has a strong commitment to there being reasons for what happens. But he disagrees with Della Rocca about the second claim, that Spinoza explains many important notions in terms of intelligibility. Della Rocca argues that Spinoza rejects certain views because they involve something being inexplicable. Melamed, considering this, asks how we can know when something is inexplicable. It is one thing to notice that a suggested explanation is inadequate, but another thing to conclude that the phenomenon in question is absolutely inexplicable. Melamed also considers the way Della Rocca's interpretation collapses various distinctions. It appears, for instance, that causation and inherence are different relations. Della Rocca's Spinoza thinks they cannot be, because there would be no reason for the difference between them. Melamed argues that that argument has seriously problematic consequences, and should not be attributed to Spinoza.

## A Note on References

Passages in the *Ethics* are referred to using abbreviations: 'a' for axiom, 'app' for appendix, 'c' for corollary, 'p' for proposition, 'pref' for preface, and 's' for scholium (which means 'note' in Latin). 'd' stands for either 'definition' (when it appears immediately to the right of the part of the book), or 'demonstration' (in all other cases). Thus 1d3 is the third definition of part 1 and 1p16d is the demonstration of proposition 16 of part 1. Some references to longer passages, such as prefaces and appendices, also include references to Gebhardt's edition of Spinoza's works (Spinoza 1925). These give volume numbers, page numbers, and sometimes also line numbers.

## Further Reading

- Don Garrett (1979). "Spinoza's 'Ontological' Argument."
- Yitzhak Melamed (2012). "Inherence, Causation, and Conceivability in Spinoza."
- Yitzhak Melamed and Martin Lin (2010). "The Principle of Sufficient Reason."

## CHAPTER 5

# Excerpts from *Spinoza*

## MICHAEL DELLA ROCCA

**From Chapter 1, "Spinoza's Understanding and Understanding Spinoza"**

All philosophers seek explanation. All philosophers seek to make the world and our place in it intelligible. To grasp such explanations is the perennial hope and promise of philosophy. However, almost all philosophers expect explanations to run out at some point, whether because of the limitations of our cognitive faculties or because of the recalcitrance of the world itself which admits of certain brute facts, facts without any explanation. "My spade is turned," as Wittgenstein famously says when explanations reach a limit (Wittgenstein 1958, §217). This admission is, of course, nothing more than a sober and, perhaps, healthy acknowledgment of our finitude and of the bruteness of reality. And, as I said, almost all philosophers reach this point. Almost all philosophers. But not Spinoza. His spade is never turned. Spinoza's philosophy is characterized by perhaps the boldest and most thoroughgoing commitment ever to appear in the history of philosophy to the intelligibility of everything. For Spinoza, no why-question is off limits, each why-question—in principle—admits of a satisfactory answer.

Spinoza's relentless rational scrutiny extends far and deep. *Far*: his gaze reaches almost all the traditional and important questions of philosophy. Spinoza offers powerful rationalist accounts of causation, of necessity and possibility, of the way in which our minds and our actions take their place in a world governed by strict causal laws. He offers wonderfully rich theories of the human mind, of morality, of political and religious life, of freedom, and of reason itself. *Deep*: Spinoza penetrates to the bottom of each of these issues. He single-mindedly digs and digs until we find that the phenomenon in question is nothing but some form of intelligibility itself, of explicability itself. Thus the causation of one thing by another is nothing but one thing making the other intelligible. Our place in the world simply is the way in which we are explained by certain things and can serve to make intelligible—i.e. explain—certain other things. Our emotions are just different manifestations of our power over, and of our subjection to, other things; they are manifestations of the way in which we explain and are explained by other things. For Spinoza, all philosophical problems bottom out in intelligibility itself.

Spinoza's commitment to intelligibility is extremely ambitious in at least two respects. First, he insists that each thing is intelligible, there are no facts impervious to explanation. Second, he holds that these explanations are—in principle—graspable by us. Our minds are, of course, limited in some ways; there are limits to how many things we can fully grasp. As Spinoza says,

> it would be impossible for human weakness to grasp the series of singu-
> lar, changeable things, not only because there are innumerably many of
> them, but also because of the infinite circumstances in one and the same
> thing.[1]

But this limitation is purely quantitative, not qualitative. While particular things may elude our grasp because of our finite ability to keep many things clearly in mind, no thing is by its nature inaccessible to the human mind. Indeed, as we will see, for Spinoza, our knowledge of the world is of precisely the same kind as the best or highest form of knowledge, the kind of knowledge enjoyed by God (whoever or whatever that is—as we will see, Spinoza has a very non-traditional conception of God).

His ambitions are, of course, not always fully realized, as we will see soon enough, but the boldness of his vision for philosophy, the high-wire act that he performs on each page, makes him a philosopher supremely worth study-ing. This is so especially because Spinoza's ambitious drive for explanation stands in sharp contrast to so much of previous and subsequent philosophy. Sometimes subsequent philosophy in particular seems to be a concerted effort to deny the pretensions of reason. I'm thinking here of, among others, Locke, Hume, and Kant, each of whom wrote a big book that could easily have been, entitled—and in one case actually was entitled—*Critique of Pure Reason*. Per-haps even worse than such clipping of reason's wings is that so much of phi-losophy in the last century seems simply to take the limitations of reason for granted and complacently operates with diminished aims. All too often we find philosophers resorting to primitives, unanalyzable notions, not subject to further explanation but nonetheless extremely important. Thus we encounter philosophers willingly embracing primitive modality (i.e. primitive necessity and possibility), primitive causation, primitive identity, primitive accounts of reference (i.e. accounts of the way words or thoughts succeed in being about things in the world), unanalyzable notions of the good and the right, inexplicable kinds of agency and freedom—the catalogue of philosophy's self-defeats. And we find these philosophers unashamed to do so. Spinoza was and would be appalled—for him, reliance on philosophical primitives is of a piece with the irrational faith or superstition that he devoted his life to fighting. Spinoza, as we shall see, has no objection to belief in God insofar as it is rational, but a less than rational belief in God is objectionable precisely because it is a refusal to dig deeper for an explanation of our place in the world and of the nature of the divinity. In the same way, reliance on philosophical primitives is an irrational refusal, to dig deeper for an explanation. Spinoza's worries about Descartes and other insufficiently rationalist predecessors was—and his worry about so much of philosophy down to the present day would be—that, by appealing to philosophical primitives or inexplicable notions, philosophy has not advanced much beyond irrational faith.

Spinoza thus sees his philosophy as a stronghold against irrationalism in philosophy and as a challenge to other more complacent ways of doing philosophy. For these reasons—in other words, because of the purity of his philosophy—Spinoza enjoys a permanent and essential place in the canon of great philosophers and provides a refreshing and needed contrast to other, less ambitious philosophical approaches.

The purity of Spinoza's commitment to explanation can best be articulated in terms of his commitments to the Principle of Sufficient Reason (hereafter, the "PSR") and to his naturalism. Consider first the PSR, the principle according to which each fact, each thing that exists, has an explanation. The explanation of a fact is enough—sufficient—to enable one to see why the fact holds. The explanation of a fact enables us to see the explained fact coming, as it were. If the explanation of a thing were not sufficient in this way, then some aspect of the thing would remain unexplained, unintelligible. The PSR is thus the embodiment of Spinoza's commitment to intelligibility. Versions of this principle go way back in philosophy and can be found in philosophers such as Parmenides, the Stoics, Aquinas, and others, but the philosopher most often associated with the principle is Leibniz. He built his system—as far as he could—around his commitment to the PSR. But—as we will see in due course—Leibniz's commitment to the PSR is not absolute. In Spinoza, unlike Leibniz, the PSR takes on an outsized importance—it's rationalism on steroids, but for the fact that, in Spinoza's eyes, this total commitment to the PSR is completely natural.

Spinoza's commitment to the PSR emerges most clearly in lp11d2: "For each thing there must be assigned a cause or reason, both for its existence and for its nonexistence." This principle is strong because it requires an explanation not only for existence, but also for non-existence. Consider also 1a2: "What cannot be conceived through another must be conceived through itself." Here Spinoza says, in effect, that each thing must be conceived through something (either itself or another thing). For Spinoza, to conceive of a thing is to explain it.[2] Thus, in presupposing in 1a2 that everything can be conceived through something, Spinoza presupposes that everything is able to be explained, he builds the notion of intelligibility into the heart of his metaphysical system.

Spinoza's commitment to the PSR quickly leads to his commitment to his naturalism. Of course, "naturalism" can mean many different things, but by "Spinoza's naturalism" I mean his thesis that everything in the world plays by the same rules; there are no things that are somehow connected with each other but that are not governed by the same principles. To understand Spinoza's naturalism, it will be helpful to focus on a famous contrast Spinoza draws between his account of the emotions—or affects—and those of his predecessors such as Descartes.

> Most of those who have written about the affects, and men's way of living, seem to treat not of natural things, which follow the common laws of Nature, but of things which are outside Nature. Indeed they seem to conceive man in Nature as a dominion within a dominion. For they believe that man disturbs, rather than follows [*magis perturbare, quam sequi*], the order of Nature.
>
> (3pref; Spinoza 1925, II.137)

He goes on, later in the preface [to part 3 of the *Ethics*], to articulate his own view of the place of man in nature, and in so doing he also gives his clearest statement of what I take to be his naturalism:

> nothing happens in Nature which can be attributed to any defect in it, for Nature is always the same, and its virtue and power of acting are everywhere the same, that is, the laws and rules of Nature, according to which all things happen, and change from one form to another, are always and everywhere the same, namely through the universal laws and rules of Nature.
>
> (3pref; Spinoza 1925, II.138)

Spinoza's problem with Cartesian and other accounts of the affects is that such views introduce an objectionable bifurcation between human beings and the rest of reality. Here we have non-human nature which operates according to one set of laws and here we have another part of reality—human beings—which operates according to a different set of laws or, perhaps, no laws at all.

By contrast, Spinoza's own view is one according to which human beings and the rest of reality are not explained in such different ways, according to which human beings and all else operate according to the same laws. Such a unification of explanatory principles is the heart of Spinoza's naturalism about psychology: human psychology is governed by the same fundamental principles that govern rocks and tables and dogs. Thus no new principles are needed to explain human psychology beyond those principles needed to explain the rest of nature anyway. More generally, Spinoza's naturalism, as I understand it, is the view that there are no illegitimate bifurcations in reality.

What exactly, in Spinoza's eyes, is so bad about such bifurcation? That is, why does Spinoza think that it is illegitimate to have two different kinds of things susceptible to radically different kinds of explanation? A crucial clue comes when Spinoza says that, on the view he rejects, man disturbs rather than follows the order of nature. The fact that, on this view, human beings disturb the order in the rest of reality suggests that human beings and their behavior are related in some way to the rest of reality and that these relations between human beings and the rest of reality cannot be understood in terms of the laws at work generally.

How then are these relations to be explained? First of all, it is important to note that, for Spinoza, the relations must be able to be explained. This is simply a requirement imposed by the PSR. But, again, how to explain the relations? If they cannot be explained in terms of laws at work generally, then perhaps they are explained in terms of special, local laws of nature-human interaction, as it were. These local laws could not be derived from general laws at work throughout nature, for then the behavior of human beings would, after all, be susceptible to, explicable in terms of, general laws. So the behavior, insofar as it is explained in terms of local laws, would be explained in terms of irreducibly local laws. But then a version of our question arises again: why do these local laws hold, if they are not derived from more generally applicable laws? Because they would be local, such laws would, in fact, seem anomalous, inexplicable. From the perspective of the general laws, there is no way, as it were, to see these local laws as coming, no way to derive these local laws. And thus the relations explained by the local laws would be, in a way, still brute precisely because brute laws would explain them. For Spinoza, then, disturbances are disturbing because they are ultimately inexplicable, because their occurrence would involve brute, inexplicable facts.

In general, for Spinoza, whenever there is a dominion within a dominion, that is, whenever there are two kinds of things that operate according to different principles and are related to each other in some way, then the ways in which these things are related to each other are disturbances and, ultimately, inexplicable, that is they would violate the PSR. In this way, we can see Spinoza's naturalism as driven by his rationalist denial of brute facts.

In this move from the PSR to the naturalistic rejection of certain bifurcations in reality, we can see that the PSR initiates a drive for unification. The PSR prompts the naturalistic unification of laws by which certain things are governed. The PSR also motivates other strategies of unification, naturalistic rejections of other bifurcations. Thus, to mention just a few examples which we will return to later in more detail: Spinoza's PSR dictates the collapse of any distinction between necessary truths and possible truths (this amounts to Spinoza's necessitarianism, the thesis that all truths are necessary truths). The PSR also dictates that, for Spinoza, causation and explanation and the inherence of a property in a subject all amount to the same phenomenon. The PSR also dictates the reduction of the consciousness of a mental state (that most recalcitrant notion in recent and not-so-recent philosophy of mind) to the simple fact that the mental state is a representation of, is about, something. The PSR dictates, as we will see, that an action's goodness, rightness, and power all come to the same thing. To view any of these phenomena – necessary truths and possible truths, causation and explanation and inherence, consciousness and representation, goodness and rightness and power – as ultimately distinct from one another would, in Spinoza's eyes, be to introduce illegitimate bifurcations into reality in violation of naturalism and the PSR.

Often these unifications that Spinoza introduces manifest a twofold use of the PSR that I see as characteristic of his rationalism. Let me illustrate this twofold use of the PSR by returning to the case of causation. Spinoza demands that we give an account of what causation is; we must be able to explain what it is for one thing to cause another. (Thus he rejects the position of some recent philosophers who claim that no such account of causation is in the offing and that the notion of causation is thus primitive.) This insistence on an explanation of causation, this demand that causation be intelligible, is the first use of the PSR in this case. The account of causation that Spinoza goes on to offer is, as we will see in Chapter 2, roughly this; for $a$ to cause $b$ is nothing more than for $a$ to make $b$ intelligible, for $a$ to explain $b$. If causation were something over and above explanation then in what would causation consist? How would we explain causation? This analysis of causation in terms of explanation or intelligibility is the second use of the PSR in this case. Thus causation is explained in terms of the notion of explanation itself, it is made intelligible in terms of intelligibility itself. Here we see the notion of intelligibility doubling back on itself: a given phenomenon is explained in terms of explanation itself. This double use of the PSR pervades Spinoza's philosophy. Thus he accounts for consciousness and representation in terms of intelligibility itself; he accounts for goodness, rightness, and power in terms of intelligibility; he accounts for the key phenomena at work in his psychology in terms of intelligibility. Indeed, for him, existence, itself is to be explained in terms of intelligibility. For Spinoza, to be is to be intelligible. This is the most fundamental statement of his rationalism, and it is the most fundamental instance of the twofold use of the PSR. Be on the lookout for the twofold use of the PSR throughout this book: it will provide the key to unlocking many of the mysteries of Spinoza's philosophical system.

## From Chapter 2, "The Metaphysics of Substance"

[According to Curley's interpretation of Spinoza] modes are merely causally dependent on God, they do not inhere in God, they are not states of God. And, while Spinoza does say that modes are in God, by this, for Curley, Spinoza means only that they are caused by God. So, for Curley, there are two different kinds of dependence: inherence and what might be called mere causation or dependence that is not inherence. These are both kinds of conceptual dependence. The states of a thing would be conceived through the thing on which they depend, and Curley-esque modes as mere effects would be conceived through substance.

The question I want to press here is this: in virtue of what are inherence and mere causation different kinds of conceptual dependence? What makes them distinct? This is a pertinent question because, after all, they do have something in common: they are both kinds of conceptual dependence. Wherein do they differ? It's hard to see the difference here as anything other than a brute fact. There seems to be no way to elucidate the difference or to explain what it consists in except to say that mere causal dependence is the kind of conceptual dependence that, for example, bodies bear to God and, perhaps, some bodies bear to other bodies, and inherence is that kind of conceptual dependence that, for example, states of bodies bear to those bodies. Such an answer merely states that there is a difference between inherence and mere causation without explaining what the difference consists in. If the account were to end here, I think Spinoza would regard this account as unacceptably trading in primitive or brute facts.

One can see such a distinction as a violation of Spinoza's naturalism which is, as we saw, the thesis that everything in nature plays by the same rules. There is nothing that operates according to principles that are not at work everywhere. If inherence is found only in some dependence relations but not in others, then that is to see a special kind of principle at work in some cases and not in others. One can put this point by paraphrasing Spinoza: dependence relations are everywhere the same.[3]

The worry here is really just the flip side of the worry that leads Spinoza to reject any kind of Cartesian view which allows for two distinct senses of substance. Descartes holds, as we saw, that we, for example, depend on God, but are nonetheless substances in our own right, albeit in a different sense from the sense in which God, who is absolutely independent of everything else, is a substance. This, as I explained, would be an unacceptable violation of naturalism for Spinoza. The Cartesian account allows different things to play by different rules, to be subject to different sets of requirements when it comes to being a substance. And such exceptions to the rules will seem objectionably ad hoc to Spinoza.

To allow for things that depend on God but are nonetheless substances is already implicitly at least to allow for two kinds of dependence relations. The finite Cartesian substances do not inhere in God or depend on him in that way, yet these finite substances have states that depend on or inhere in those finite substances. Thus, precisely because there are two different kinds of substances in Descartes, there are also two kinds of dependence relations. This duality of kinds of dependence relations seems every bit as objectionable from a Spinozistic point of view as the duality in kinds of substance. There is mere causal dependence and, what might be called, dependence of the inherence variety. But what makes them, distinct kinds of dependence? If they are each a kind of dependence and if there is nothing that makes them distinct, then they are the same after all, Spinoza would argue. If there is something that makes them distinct kinds of dependence, then what is it? For Spinoza, the Cartesian has to say that there are these different kinds of dependence relations, but that, just as with the different kinds of substance, such a difference is a brute fact and a violation of the naturalist ideal of a single uniform set of requirements. Thus in arguing for the non-Cartesian interpretation of Spinozistic modes as *not* states, Curley is making what is in the end a very Cartesian move: he is allowing for an unexplained duality in kinds of dependence.

By contrast, the interpretation of Spinoza according to which bodies and minds are modes of God in the sense that they are caused by God *and* inhere in God preserves the PSR and Spinoza's naturalism Yes, both inherence and mere causation are kinds of dependence, but, for Spinoza, by virtue of his rationalism, they are ultimately the same kind of dependence, and that is conceptual dependence *tout court.*

Here we can see that in an important way Curley is right after all. He denies that Spinoza's in-relation (the relation of being in itself or in another) is an inherence relation. In doing so, Curley affirms that the in-relation just is the relation of causation. While I disagree with Curley about inherence, he is, I believe, absolutely right that the in-relation just is causation or, more generally, conception. And here I depart from Carriero's interpretation in a significant way. Although Carriero holds that Spinozistic modes do inhere in substance— and I agree—he also holds that the in-relation is a completely separate relation from the relation of causation. I find such a distinction inimical to Spinoza's rationalism for reasons I have already given. When Carriero says that the relations are different his claim is based partly on the further claim that Spinoza keeps his talk of causation and his talk of inherence on largely separate tracks. But this is not true. Carriero regards 1p16 as a key place in which Spinoza affirms the causal dependence of things on God. (1p16 says in part, "From the necessity of the divine nature, there must follow infinitely many things in infinitely many ways.") But Spinoza argues for 1p16 by invoking the ways in which the properties of a thing depend on that thing. As Spinoza says in 1p16d:

> This proposition must be plain to anyone, provided he attends to the fact that the intellect infers from the given definition of any thing a number of

properties that really do follow necessarily from it (that is, from the very essence of the thing).

So in 1p16, the supposed bastion of causal talk as opposed to talk of inherence, Spinoza seems to mix the two kinds of locution effortlessly. This is evidence against Carriero's claim that the relations are separate and it is hardier positive evidence for taking causal dependence and inherence to be the same for Spinoza.

In effect, we can see Spinoza as offering an account of the nature of inherence that embodies another twofold use of the PSR. Spinoza would insist on the legitimacy of the demand that inherence be explained. "What is inherence?" is a natural question for Spinoza. Some account must be given beyond the unacceptable treatment of inherence as a relation of conceptual dependence that differs brutely from the relation of mere causal dependence. To make this demand that inherence be intelligible is the first use of the PSR in this case.

Spinoza meets this demand by arguing that inherence just is causal and, ultimately, conceptual dependence. Thus, to say that one thing inheres in another is to say simply that it is understood or conceived through or intelligible in terms of this other. This conclusion is the second use of the PSR or of the notion of intelligibility in this case. For Spinoza, inherence must be intelligible and it is intelligible in terms of intelligibility itself. Here again Spinoza is making the characteristic rationalist move, the kind of move he has already made in treating causation as conception.[4]

## Notes

1. *Treatise on the Emendation of the Intellect,* §100: Spinoza 1985, 100.
2. See, in particular, how Spinoza moves naturally from claims about the way in which substance is conceived to claims about the way substance is explained (1p10s, 1p14d, 2p5). See also the way in which conceiving a thing is identical to understanding it or finding it intelligible (1a5). For further discussion, see Della Rocca (1996a, 3–4).
3. Compare 3pref: "nature is always the same, and its virtue and power of acting are everywhere one and the same."
4. For this reason, we can see that, when Spinoza says that substance is in itself, this simply amounts to the claim that substance is dependent only on itself or is conceived only through itself.

## CHAPTER 6

# The Sirens of Elea: Rationalism, Monism and Idealism in Spinoza

## YITZHAK MELAMED

The main thesis of Michael Della Rocca's outstanding Spinoza book (Della Rocca 2008a) is that at the very center of Spinoza's philosophy stands the *Principle of Sufficient Reason* (PSR): the stipulation that everything must be explainable or, in other words, the rejection of *any* brute facts. Della Rocca rightly ascribes to Spinoza a strong version of the PSR. It is not only that the actual existence and features of all things must be explicable, but even nonexistence—as well as the absence of any feature of any thing—demands an explanation. Della Rocca does not stop here, however. He feeds his PSR monster with some more powerful steroids and suggests that Spinoza advocates what he terms "the twofold use of the PSR." It is not only that everything must be explained and made intelligible, but it must ultimately be explained in terms of explicability or intelligibility itself. This *twofold* use of the PSR is the key to the entire book. Della Rocca's strategy throughout the book is to argue that any key feature of Spinoza's system—be it causality, inherence, essence, consciousness, existence, rejection of teleology, goodness or political right—must be explained, and ultimately it must be explained in terms of intelligibility. "Spinoza single-mindedly digs and digs until we find that the phenomenon in question is nothing but some form of intelligibility itself, of explicability itself" (see p. 71 above).

Della Rocca's book came out together with a cluster of articles in which he develops in detail his new reading of Spinoza.[1] In one of these articles, he warns the reader: "Don't let me start" (Della Rocca 2010, 1). The train that is about to embark leads to very bizarre terrain, and thus one should think twice before embarking on the "PSR Express." In this chapter I argue that the train was hijacked. This was a perfect crime: without anyone noticing it, the engine driver diverted the train to a new route, and as with other perfect crimes, it is only the criminal himself who is capable of bringing about his own demise— as indeed he will. As I will later argue, Della Rocca's "PSR-on-steroids" will eventually cripple reason itself. But let us not run too fast—we'll start at the very beginning. I happily—or at least, so I think—board the "PSR Express." I believe Spinoza is strongly committed to the PSR and makes very significant use of this principle, but, unlike Della Rocca, I do not think the PSR is the key to *all* mysteries Spinozist, nor do I believe Spinoza was committed to the reductionist program of explaining all things through intelligibility (i.e. the second use of the PSR).

Della Rocca's exciting interpretation raises several deep, foundational, questions but unfortunately I can only address a few of them here. In the following I will concentrate on three issues related to Della Rocca's reading. I will first point out the non-trivial danger of misuse of the PSR, and then turn to examine the validity of Della Rocca's inference from the unavailability of explanations of facts to the rejection of the same facts. I will conclude with a critical examination of Della Rocca's claim that the PSR does not allow for any bifurcations in nature.

## On the Possible Misuse of the PSR

The PSR is a powerful tool and, like any other powerful tool, it can be misused. Leonhard Euler (1707–1783), the great Swiss mathematician who was essentially sympathetic to the principle, warned against the "wretched abuse" of the PSR by those who "employ it so dexterously that by means of it they are in a condition to demonstrate whatever suits their purpose, and to demolish whatever is raised again them" (Euler 2009, 224). Euler was particularly alarmed by proofs which rely on the PSR to achieve nothing over and above a *petitio principii* (or question-begging argument) (Euler 2009, 226). But Spinoza, himself, pointed out the tight connection between a rushed use of the PSR and religious superstition. Consider the following example presented by Spinoza in the appendix to Part One of the *Ethics*:

> If a stone has fallen from a roof onto someone's head and killed him, they will show, in the following way, that the stone fell in order to kill the man. For if it did not fall to that end, God willing it, how could so many circumstances have concurred by chance (for often many circumstances do concur at once)? Perhaps you will answer that it happened because the wind was blowing hard and the man was walking that way. But they will persist: why was the wind blowing hard at that time? Why was the man walking that way at that same time? If you answer again that the wind arose then because on the preceding day, while the weather was still calm,

the sea began to toss, and that the man had been invited by a friend, they will press on—for there is no end to the questions which can be asked: but why was the sea tossing? Why was the man invited at just that time? *And so they will not stop asking for the causes of causes* until you take refuge in the will of God, i.e. the sanctuary of ignorance.

(1app; Spinoza 1925, II.80–1)

There are three striking features of the superstitious that contrive together to produce the phenomenon Spinoza examines here. First, the superstitious adhere to the PSR in a very strict and systematic manner, or as Spinoza writes "they will not stop asking for the causes" of things. Second, the superstitious are not willing to allow for coincidences, i.e. the concurrence of events whose cause (i.e. the cause of the *concurrence*) is not easy to explain, and perhaps even impossible to explain, by appealing only to the causes of one or the other concurring events. Finally, the superstitious are satisfied by a unifying and global explanation—the will of God—which upon close examination turns out to be nothing but ignorance (insofar as God's will is taken to be arbitrary or self-explanatory).

Similarly, in chapter 9 of the *Theological Political Treatise*, Spinoza mocks those who believe that every slight abnormality in the Hebrew of the biblical text discloses great secrets and mysteries (Spinoza 1925, III.135). Obviously, Spinoza does believe that all features of the biblical text—just like any features of any text, or anything—deserve an explanation. Yet, the explanation *may not be available to us*, not because it involve great secrets, but rather because we know very little about the precise causal history of almost any particular thing. While the superstitious do have the right urge to insist on asking conscientiously about the causes of things, their use of the PSR is both too strong and too weak: too strong because *when no natural explanation is readily available to them*, they conclude that *there is no natural explanation*, and too weak, because they shelter "the Will of God" from the policing authority of the PSR (i.e. it is not subject to their demand for explanation).

What should we learn from all this? Not much, at this point. We should just be aware of the rather obvious possibility that the PSR can be misused.

### "Unexplainable"

Throughout his book Della Rocca frequently makes truly insightful and illuminating use of the PSR to help motivate various positions of Spinoza's, yet, in several crucial places in the book, he uses the PSR in a manner I find to be flawed.[2] In all of these places Della Rocca attempts to rule out a certain putative state of affairs F, by arguing that if F were the case, F would be—or would bring about—a brute fact, and hence must be rejected since the PSR does not allow for brute facts. Della Rocca uses the same strategy in all of these cases: First, he presents F, the putative fact which he intends to rule out using the PSR. Then, he presents two or three explanations that *could* motivate or justify F, and shows that none of the suggested explanations succeeds in motivating F—so far, so good. At this point comes the announcement that "no explanation of F is available." But if F is not explicable, it is a brute fact, and hence must be rejected by force of the PSR.

The problem with this line of argument is that Della Rocca seems to argue from:

(1) *we have no explanation of F*

to

(2) *F is not explainable*

or, in slightly different fashion, from

(3) *we have no explanation of F*

to,

(4) *F seems to be unexplainable*

to,

(5) *F is a brute fact.*

Such arguments fail to appreciate the modality required for the proper use of the PSR. To claim that so far we have not found any explanation for F is one thing. To claim that there is no possible explanation for F is a completely different thing. As an example of a proper use of arguments from inexplicable facts, consider Leibniz's argument—in his correspondence with Clarke—against the possibility of absolute space. Here, too, Leibniz uses the PSR in order to rule out a certain state of affairs: the existence of absolute, empty space. Leibniz's argument is roughly the following: Suppose space could exist without anything in it. Then, God, when he comes to decide where in space to create the world, could have no reason to create the world in any particular location, because all spatial locations in empty space are qualitatively indiscernible. Whatever reason God could have to create the world at place P1, should equally pertain to any other place (in absolute space) P2, since there cannot be any qualitative difference between P1 and P2. Thus, God *cannot* have a reason to create the world in one place rather than another (AG 324). Notice that the argument does *not* rely on the claim that *so far* we have not found a reason that could motivate God to create the world in P1 rather than P2. Leibniz's argument relies on the far stronger claim that there *cannot be* a reason for God to create the world in P1 rather than P2. In other words, Leibniz argues from:

(6) *there cannot be reason for F*

to

(7) *F is a brute fact.*

While the transition from (6) to (7) is valid, the transitions from (1) to (2) and (3) to (5) are not. It is perfectly possible (and in fact quite common), that no explanation for a certain fact F is available to us right now, but F is still perfectly explicable (and the explanation might even become accessible to us in the future). In other words, in order to be valid, the argument must positively show that *it exhausted all possible explanations*, and that none of these explanations is successful. Proving exhaustibility is, in most cases, quite a daunting task, and demands more work than merely ruling out three or four explanations.

In order not to leave these severe allegations (e.g. of a "hijacked train" etc.) up in the air, let us look quickly at two texts where, I believe, Della Rocca makes an unwarranted use of the PSR. In the first text, the author attempts to show that for Spinoza all mental states are representational. Della Rocca presents the view he attempts to rule out—that for Spinoza some mental states are representational while others are not—and asks by virtue of what both representational and non-representational states are mental. He rightly disqualifies one explanation and then restates the question:

> What is it in virtue of which A and B are both thinking? Perhaps they are both mental in virtue of the fact that they causally interact with mental states. But this won't get us very far. For Spinoza, two things interact only because they belong to the same attribute, for example the attribute of thought. *I know of no other plausibly Spinozistic way to answer the question what is in virtue of which A, a representational mental state, and B, a nonrepresentational mental state, are both thinking. Thus the existence of such disparate mental states would involve a brute fact and so be unacceptable.*
> (2008a, 121)

Notice how Della Rocca moves from the claim that "I know no other plausibly Spinozistic" explanation for the disparity of mental states, to the conclusion that such a disparity is a brute fact. This move is, in my mind, illicit.

Della Rocca could defend his view by suggesting that while his argument may fall short of proving his point conclusively, it still shifts the burden of proof to the opponent of the twofold use of the PSR. Perhaps, so Della Rocca's argument would go, we should *tentatively* consider F (the fact for which we have not yet found any explanation), a brute fact, and thus *tentatively* reject it.[3] I doubt this defense strategy could work. There are far too many things whose explanation is not transparent to us. I, for one, do not know the complete explanation for almost anything I encounter. Should I therefore tentatively conclude that these things do not exist (as long as I have no complete explanation for each)? The counter-commonsense nature of such a radical form of skepticism seems to me much less troubling (since Spinoza frequently rejects common sense) than the inconsistency of this view with Spinoza's disparaging rejection of skepticism.[4] Consider, for example, Spinoza's claim in 2p13c and 2p17s) that "the human body exists as we are aware [*sentimus*] of it." In these passages Spinoza does not require that we know the complete explanation of the human body (this could be achieved only rarely through the Third Kind of Knowledge), but rather feels comfortable enough to pronounce that the human body exists relying merely on our awareness of the body.

There is an even stronger consideration against the inference from tentative lack of explanation for F to the tentative rejection of F, but here I can only point out the direction of that argument. In many cases we cannot provide an adequate explanation for either F or its opposite. Thus, if we follow Della Rocca's line of defense, we should conclude that both F (insofar as we have no adequate explanation for not-F) and its opposite (insofar as we have no adequate explanation for F) are the case, which is clearly absurd.

Another instance in which Della Rocca relies on the unavailability of explanation to rule out a certain state of affairs is in his discussion of divine teleology in Spinoza. Here, I think, the temptation of the easy "no explanation is available" argument leads Della Rocca to an imprecise representation of Spinoza's argument against divine teleology.

Della Rocca's aim in the following passage is to motivate Spinoza's rejection of divine teleology, a view which he cashes out *narrowly* as a rejection of any case in which God acts for the sake of any particular *finite* being *x*. Della Rocca points out (rightly) that every finite mode *x* is part of a strictly necessary and deterministic causal chain of finite modes and then argues that God cannot act for the sake of one of these finite things since God cannot arbitrarily privilege one link in the chain over the other:

> *x*, the finite mode in question, is necessarily in the midst of a series of finite causes and effects, but, we are supposing, *x* nonetheless outstrips other modes in importance to God. Why does God privilege *x* in this way instead of privileging some other finite mode, say, certain of *x*'s causes or *x*'s effects? *X* is neither the culmination of the series of finite modes, nor is it the starting point. So these natural reasons for privileging *x* are not present. Nor can it be said that God privileges *x* because *x* is more like

God than other finite modes. For each divine-like quality that *x* has, there will be other, perhaps infinitely many other, finite modes that have those divine-like qualities to a higher degree . . . For this reason, any privileging of *x* in particular would seem to be arbitrary, a brute fact. And, as such, Spinoza would reject it.

(2008a, 85–6)

Here, too, Della Rocca considers two explanations that *could* justify the view he is arguing against. He shows that neither explanation works, and concludes that in the absence of any explanation, the privileging of *x* is a brute fact. But, here too, as far as I can see, the transition from "no explanation for F is available" to "F is unexplainable" is faulty.

Della Rocca's focus on the question of whether God could privilege one finite mode over the other leads him to misformulate Spinoza's critique of divine teleology. Spinoza does not limit his critique of divine teleology to the rejection of divine action for the sake of a *finite* thing; rather, for Spinoza, God acts for the sake of *no one*, not even *for His own sake* (see 1app; Spinoza 1925, II.80.23). Thus, unjustified privileging of one item over another does not seem to provide the motivation for Spinoza's rejection of divine teleology. God is clearly and *justly* privileged in comparison to the finite modes, but Spinoza's God does not act for the sake of himself as well. Since brute privileging does not seem to be the primary motivation behind Spinoza's critique of divine teleology we must seek an explanation elsewhere.

The lesson I suggest we draw from the teleology issue is that not finding an explanation for a certain fact does not warrant rejecting it as a brute fact. In the case of teleology, we find a purported brute privileging which, upon examination, turns out to be not-brute privileging. Yet Spinoza's refusal to make his God act for the sake of a *justly* privileged entity (such as God himself) shows that the rejection of brute facts cannot provide the principled explanation for Spinoza's rejection of divine teleology.

## Bifurcations and Radical Monism

At the opening of his book, Della Rocca briefly explains Spinoza's naturalism as "the view that there are no illegitimate bifurcations in reality" (see p. 74 above). It is not that difficult to agree with the claim that there are no *illegitimate* bifurcations in reality, but the real question is whether there are *legitimate* bifurcations in reality, and Della Rocca seems to me to be tempted by the Sirens of Elea, and defends the far stronger claim that rejects *any* bifurcations in reality, tout court.

One crucial place where this bold view surfaces is in Della Rocca's attempt to show that, for Spinoza, inherence and causation are strictly identical. According to Della Rocca, both inherence and causation are relations of conceptual dependence (I do not agree with this view, but I'll grant it for the sake of the argument).[5] At this point Della Rocca presses the following question:

> What makes [inherence and causation] distinct? This is a pertinent question, because, after all, they do have something in common: they are both kinds of conceptual dependence. Wherein do they differ? It's hard to see the difference here as anything other than a brute fact. There seems to be no way to elucidate the difference or to explain what it consists in except to say that mere causal dependence is the kind of conceptual dependence that, for example, bodies bear to God . . . and inherence is that kind of conceptual dependence that, for example, states of bodies bear to those bodies. Such an answer merely states that there is a difference between inherence and mere causation without explaining what the difference consists in.
>
> (2008a, 76–7)

I have argued elsewhere that the identification of inherence and causation is inconsistent with some of Spinoza's most important metaphysical doctrines.[6] For shortness of space I will avoid repeating these arguments here, but let me present here four other issues related to the internal consistency of Della Rocca's crusade against bifurcations.

First, one possible answer to the question of what makes inherence and causation distinct is that their *concepts* make them what they are and ground the distinction between them. Oddly enough, in spite of Della Rocca's battle against primitive distinctions, he is, on occasion, amenable to analytic explanations that ground the qualities of things in their essences, or natures, or concepts, and *stop there*. Consider the following passage in which Della Rocca attempts to show that to represent a thing *x* is to represent its essence:

> Given that E is the essence of *x*, and given that for Spinoza, as we have seen, the essence of a thing simply amounts to the very intelligibility of the thing, the way in which the thing must be understood, it follows that to ask why *x* has E is as silly as asking why squares have four equal sides. It's part of the essence, and indeed part of the concept, of squares to have four equal sides—this is how squares must be understood. *In the same way, it's just x's concept or essence to have E.*
>
> (2008a, 97; italics added)

It is somewhat unclear to me why it is sillier to ask why a square has four sides, than to ask why an inherence relation is a relation in which one thing is in another. Let's compare the two cases. Inherence and causation are both allegedly relations of conceptual dependence. Squares and triangles are both polygons. We can ask what distinguishes squares from triangles and the answer we are likely to get will appeal to the very essence of each (i.e. "squares have four sides," etc.). Similarly, we may ask what distinguishes inherence from causation and the answer we are likely to get will appeal to the very essence of each relation (i.e. "an inherence relation is one in which $x$ is in $y$," etc.). Where, precisely, is the difference between the two cases? What kind of analytic explanations, which virtually just restate the essence of the thing, is Della Rocca willing to accept and what kind is he not willing to accept? On its face, the distinction between the two cases seems to be just brute and arbitrary.

Second, for all I can tell, Della Rocca's argument against bifurcation seems to commit him to an extremely radical version of monism that rejects any kind of bifurcations and allows for the reality of merely *one indivisible thing*, and merely *one concept*. Here is a brief outline of the argument leading to this conclusion.[7]

Suppose there were any two distinct concepts, C1 and C2. We could legitimately ask by what virtue C1 is what it is and not C2, and why C2 is what it is and not C1. C1 and C2 have something important in common: we assumed that they are both *concepts* (neither giraffes nor elephants!). Why are they different then? Wherein lies the difference? Of course, we can push the question slightly by saying that C1 has quality Q and C2 doesn't, but here we should employ the same strategy Della Rocca uses constantly against "illegitimate" bifurcations, and ask why C1 has Q and C2 doesn't. (They are both concepts! Where does *this* difference come from?) In this manner, we are not likely ever to reach a satisfactory explanation, and hence the difference between C1 and C2 would seem to be a brute fact.

Similarly, since for Spinoza, *natura naturans* (i.e. the substance) is strictly indivisible, we could (and should) ask where the diversity of things comes from. If at the very beginning of things—at the level of substance—there is strict unity and indivisibility, we should detect the first appearance of diversity, and ask by virtue of what we have two things that are distinct. (In this case, I think the question is *very* powerful since we can show that *the only possible explanation* —i.e. *natura naturans*, from which the diversity sprung—is strictly indivisible and thus cannot explain the diversity. Thus, I take the last question to be a genuine and serious problem for Spinoza, not only for Della Rocca.)[8]

If we take the above arguments against bifurcation seriously, the ensuing view is the acosmist interpretation of Spinoza, suggested by the German Idealists (Maimon and Hegel), according to which Spinoza considered any diversity (the diversity of modes as well as the diversity of attributes) a mere illusion. Let me note that Hegel takes a variant of the PSR—the "*ex nihilo nihil fit*" formula—to be the main motivation behind Spinoza's alleged acosmism (Hegel 1969, 84; Hegel 1991, 144). While I find the acosmist reading fascinating, I believe that in the final account it has to be rejected since it conflicts with far too many important doctrines of Spinoza's. Consider, for example, Spinoza's claims in E1p16d that it is *the intellect* that infers the modes from God's nature.

For Spinoza, the intellect never errs, but were the modes unreal or illusory, the inference of the intellect would clearly be faulty—contrary to Spinoza's view.[9]

To the best of my knowledge, Della Rocca does not wish to endorse the original version of the acosmist interpretation, but rather a certain moderate version of it, according to which modes are neither *fully* real, nor are they illusory.[10] This view is correct in a very trivial sense insofar as modes are less real than the substance (the reality of modes depends on the reality of the substance).[11] However, Della Rocca also suggests that the limited reality of modes reflects the fact that *modes are not fully conceived and fully caused* by the substance (for Della Rocca, degrees of reality reflect degrees of conceivability).[12] This, I think, is not consistent with Spinoza's claim in E1p16d that the modes are inferred by the intellect. Were the modes not fully conceived, the inference of the intellect would have to be faulty.

Third, one of the most interesting results of the claim that only the substance is fully real is that it forces us to reevaluate the status of relations in Spinoza, most crucially the relation of conception.[13] If there is only one fully real thing, and plurality pertains only to partly real things, it would make sense that rationality should be exhibited *fully* at the level of the *fully* real entity (and only partly at the level of the partly real plurality of things). Let's have a closer look at the doings of our fully real entity.

On first sight, our one indivisible entity may appear somewhat boring. Just like the Aristotelian Prime Mover, it keeps on conceiving itself, and conceiving itself, and—surprise, surprise—once again conceiving itself. "Well, what's wrong with that?" you might say, "We have long suspected that heaven is pretty boring." One problem is that it is not at all clear that our entity is even entitled to this kind of activity. According to Della Rocca, there is really only one relation: conceivability is causation is inherence. (If there were any other relation, we would ask, "By virtue of what is it distinct from conceivability?" etc.)

But wait, why is conceivability a two-place relation and not, say, a monadic predicate, such as "$x$ is conceived"? Since there is only one entity in our fully real realm, it would make just as much sense to cash out rationality as a monadic predicate, "$x$ is conceived" or "$x$ is conceiving" (which one? and how can we decide between the two?), or as apolyadic two-place reflexive relation "$x$ is conceived through $x$" or as a zillion-place polyadic relation, "$x$ is conceived through $x$, through $x$, . . . through $x$." There seems to be no reason to privilege a two-place reflexive relation of conceivability over monadic predicate of conceivability, or the other way around. Whatever choice we make would be a brute fact.

But let's assume for a minute that we can justify a choice of one of the disjuncts. Let's say the monadic predicate. Our fully real entity has the one monadic predicate of "$x$ is conceiving." Recall that there are no other concepts (on the pain of there being brute facts: "what makes them distinct from conceiving?"). Here, then, is our *paradigm* of pure rationality and explanation: "The substance is conceiving." What precisely does this explain? How poor does this radical, rock-smashing, rationality end up being?

Finally, let me note that if we push the bifurcation argument slightly further ahead, we could ask: in virtue of what do we distinguish between the subject ("substance") and its predicate ("is conceiving")? Were they strictly the same, I cannot see how in such a world there would be any movement or thought at all. Such a world would be far too poor, far too thin, to entertain thought. Recall that for Spinoza the excellence of minds is a function of their complexity, which reflects the complexity of the parallel bodies (2p13s). When we detach the substance from its modes we seem to get an entity with infinitesimal complexity and an extremely dumb thought.[14] We can reach the same conclusion from a slightly different angle. Since for Spinoza the only vehicles of thought are ideas (2a3 and 2p11d), and ideas are modes (2a3), *it would seem that if the PSR leads to the unreality (or limited reality) of modes, it ends up proving the unreality (or limited reality) of ideas and thought itself.*

The last two points seem, to me, cut not only against Della Rocca's view as an interpretation of Spinoza, but even against an attempt to present this view as an independent venture, going beyond Spinoza. These two points show that the radical, strict, rationalism of the twofold use of the PSR ends up undermining and crippling reason itself. As I warned you at the beginning of this chapter, it was none but the capable, yet PSR-intoxicated, engine driver of our hijacked train who brought about his, and reason's, own demise.

## Acknowledgement

An early version of this chapter was read at an author meets critics session on Della Rocca's book in the 2010 meeting of the Eastern division of the American Philosophical Association. I would like to thank John Brandau, Don Garrett, Mike LeBuffe, John Morrison, Alan Nelson, Sam Newlands, Oded Schechter, and especially, Michael Della Rocca, for their most helpful comments on earlier versions of this chapter.

## Notes

1. See Della Rocca (2003, 2008b, 2010, and forthcoming).
2. I address below the two cases of representation and teleology. For another crucial example of this line of argument, Della Rocca's identification of causation and inherence in Spinoza, see Della Rocca (2008a, 65).
3. Della Rocca actually suggested a response in this spirit in a session on his book at the Eastern Division meeting of the American Philosophical Association in December 2010.
4. See Spinoza's *Treatise on the Emendation of the Intellect*, §§47–48; Spinoza 1985, 22.
5. For Della Rocca's reduction of causation to conceivability see p. 74 above.
6. See Melamed (2012b).
7. Della Rocca seems to embrace this conclusion in Della Rocca, forthcoming.
8. I address this problem in Melamed (2012a).

9. On the German Idealists' acosmist interpretation of Spinoza, see Melamed(2010). For a detailed critique of the acosmist reading, see Melamed (2012a).
10. See DellaRocca (forthcoming, Section III).
11. Consider, for example, an axiom Spinoza adopts from Descartes: "A substance has more reality than an accident or mode" (DPP Part I, Axiom 4; Spinoza 1925, I.154.27).
12. See Della Rocca (forthcoming), Section III, and Della Rocca (2008a, 263).
13. Della Rocca develops and embraces some of the implications I discuss below in Della Rocca (forthcoming).
14. While the human mind can conceive many things (2p14), the substance detached from its modes conceives nothing but one thing: itself.

# The Appeal of Occasionalism

# Editors' Introduction

Christian, Islamic, and Jewish philosophers have typically agreed that God created the world and continues to keep it going after the moment of creation. God isn't just a 'divine watchmaker' who creates the world and then walks away, leaving it going on its own. (It has often been thought that the divine watchmaker view diminishes God in a way that's not acceptable.) But philosophers who have agreed about that have *disagreed* about two related issues. What exactly is involved in God keeping the world going? And what does this imply for 'finite causation' (causal relations between two created things)? Three main schools of thought emerged from such discussions in the seventeenth century.

1. *Mere conservation.* God created things and their powers, but also keeps these created things and their powers in existence. But this is all God does. When the creature causes something, the creature is the sole direct and immediate cause of that effect. God is causally involved only indirectly, in keeping the creature and its power in existence.
2. *Divine concurrence.* God keeps created things in existence but also is directly involved in their activity in some way. Typically, both the creature's activity and God's concurrence are said to be full causes of the effect; it's not like God does half the work and you do the other half. (If this position strikes you as extremely mysterious and difficult, you're right.)
3. *Occasionalism.* God not only keeps created things in existence but also acts in their stead. That is, God is the unique genuine cause and creatures aren't really causes at all.

The best known of the occasionalists is Nicolas Malebranche. One of his main arguments for occasionalism is that creatures cannot be causes because nothing they do is necessarily connected with its effect. Your volition to scratch your head, for instance, isn't necessarily connected with any motion of your hand because you could be momentarily paralyzed. Malebranche's argument assumes that genuine causes *are* necessarily connected with their effects. (This is what Hume later challenged.) But why would anyone think this?

In the first chapter in this part, Walter Ott offers one explanation. In the second, Sukjae Lee argues that Ott's explanation cannot be right and suggests a second explanation. Do you find either one satisfying?

## Note on References

References of the form 'SAT a.b.c, d' are to Malebranche's *Search After Truth*, cited by book, part, and chapter, as well as by page number in the standard English translation.

## Further Reading

- Charles McCracken (1983). *Malebranche and British Philosophy.*
- Sukjae Lee (2008), "Necessary Connections and Continuous Creation: Malebranche's Two Arguments for Occasionalism."
- Steven Nadler (2000), "Malebranche on Causation."

## CHAPTER 7

# Causation, Intentionality, and the Case for Occasionalism

## WALTER OTT

In *The Search After Truth*, Malebranche produces his most famous argument for occasionalism . . .

> A true cause as I understand it is one such that the mind perceives a necessary connection between it and its effect. Now the mind perceives a necessary connection only between the will of an infinitely perfect being and its effects. Therefore, it is only God who is the true cause and who truly has the power to move bodies.
>
> (SAT VI.ii.3, 450)

For any two finite objects or events *a* and *b*, a causal connection between them could obtain only if those events were necessarily connected. But if there were such a necessary connection, it would be impossible to conceive of *a*'s occurring without *b*. God's will and its effects aside, we can always conceive of this happening; thus there is no necessary connection, and hence no genuine causal connection, between *a* and *b*. I'll call this the 'no necessary connection' argument, or NNC for short.

The real puzzle about this kind of argument has never been its form or structure but rather who is supposed to be bothered by it. Even if we accept that the connection between two events is not logically necessary, why should anyone believe that it is not a *bona fide* instance of causation? It is similarly hard to see why anyone would accept that conceivability, even if it is a guide to logical necessity, could tell us anything at all about the natural world and its causal structure.

Jolley (1990, 230) notes that "it is natural to object that while genuine causal connections are indeed necessary, the necessity in question is not logical." In the same vein, (Nadler 2000, 114) argues that Malebranche's identification of logical with causal necessity "does seem strange today, and, I suggest, *should* have seemed strange to a seventeenth century Cartesian." For between the eleventh and seventeenth centuries, "there was a clear and dominant philosophical tendency to distinguish causal or natural necessity—grounded in the operations of real efficient causes—from logical necessity." Thus NNC seems directed at a straw man.

But this should lead us to question, not Malebranche's understanding of his philosophical adversaries, but our own. I shall argue that Malebranche in fact gets it right: his philosophical opponents, and a key strand of scholasticism in particular, do indeed hold that causation requires logical, not nomological, necessitation. This is the burden of §1 below.

Solving this problem leads us straight into another. Even if the conflation of logical and causal necessity is intelligible in its context, why is Malebranche so quick to deny that finite *relata*, and bodies in particular, can be causes? In the passage just quoted, for example, there is no explicit argument for ruling out finite causal *relata*: it is just supposed to be obvious that nothing but God's will can live up to the necessity criterion. But it would have been anything but obvious to Suárez or Aquinas. Thus in §2, I argue that Malebranche's dismissal of bodies as causes makes sense only if the requisite tie between cause and effect involves intentionality.[1] Only by means of this kind of intrinsic directedness can an object or event pick out or be directed toward its cause.

Having taken over key elements of the scholastic conception of causation, Malebranche finds that in the context of mechanism nothing but God's will can fit this conception. Several of Malebranche's arguments bear the stamp of this line of thought. To see this, we shall have to explore the scholastic notion of power, which underwrites the necessary connection between causes and effects. A power is characterized by its '*esse-ad*' or 'being-toward', its intrinsic directedness toward non-actual states of affairs. Malebranche (following Descartes) rejects the attribution of powers to bodies on the grounds that *esse-ad* amounts to intentionality, a feature only minds possess. The flip side of this, however, is that Malebranche accepts the need for precisely the kind of connection intentionality alone can provide. What makes a divine volition a suitable causal *relatum* is the intentional nature that ties it to its effects, since the propositional content of a divine volition *just is* that volition's effect.

These insights can help us understand another of Malebranche's puzzling arguments. Finite minds, he claims, cannot cause physical events. Although it is clear that any finite mind, lacking omnipotence, cannot live up to the demands Malebranche places on causes, he does not rely solely on this consideration to challenge the causal power of minds. Instead, Malebranche offers what I shall call the 'epistemic argument': if a mind were to cause the motion of, say, one's arm, it would have to will the temporal antecedents of that event, which include brain events . . . In §3, I show how this argument comes into focus if we assume, with Malebranche, that a cause must include its effect as its intentional object. This alone lets us see why Malebranche thinks finite minds cannot be causes.

## 1. Logical and Causal Necessity

. . . . If Nadler *et al.* are correct, Malebranche's argument is comically wide of the mark, since none, or very few, of his interlocutors holds that causation is logical necessitation . . . The natural and most common position on causation involves a distinction between logical and non-logical necessities, and the scholastics, particularly Aquinas, were not so foolish as to run the two together.

For my part, I think the claim that Aristotelianism has at its core a commitment to nomological necessity is deeply wrong-headed. I shall argue that the typical Aristotelian position holds that sublunary events are linked by what we would call logical necessity: it is a contradiction, and hence inconceivable, that a cause not produce its effect. I shall also argue that this view is not nearly as odd or indefensible as first appears.

The core position, traceable back to Aristotle, is based on the connection between a form and an object's powers. A substance does what it does in virtue of its form. That fire burns is an analytic truth, although one that can only be discovered through experience. Fire that failed to burn would, for that reason, simply not be fire . . . This rough and ready characterization would need to be refined considerably to stand as an interpretation of Aristotle. But let us look instead to the scholastics and the dominant view, found in both Aquinas and Suárez: concurrentism.

Briefly, concurrentism holds that one and the same effect can be ascribed both to God and to natural agents. God, as the primary cause, is responsible for the *esse* or being of individual beings; creatures, as the secondary cause, are responsible for the properties of those beings . . .

The typical metaphor by which Aquinas explains this curious dual contribution of God and secondary cause is that of craftsman and tool. The tool or instrument by itself does not produce, and is not a sufficient cause, of, say, the wood being carved thus-and-so. Its power depends on the power of the craftsman using it. Nevertheless, that the wood is carved thus-and-so depends partly on the craftsman and partly on the instrument, for which instrument he uses, no less than how he moves his hands, will determine how the wood is shaped. "The whole effect proceeds from [both God and the natural agent], yet in different ways, just as the whole of one and the same effect is ascribed to the instrument, and again the whole is ascribed to the principal agent" (*Summa Contra Gentiles* ch. 70, Aquinas 1945 2.130) . . .

Unlike conservationism, which holds that God merely conserves bodies while their powers operate autonomously, concurrentism requires that God also, as it were, work through the powers of the objects he creates and conserves. And unlike occasionalism, which takes God to be the only real cause, concurrentism assigns genuine causal powers to objects, though these powers are exercised only when God works through his creatures to bring about an effect. But how is it possible for a substance to serve as a secondary efficient cause, if God is nevertheless the ultimate source of all power? Isn't this a case of overdetermination?

Suárez deals with this objection in the course of defending concurrentism from occasionalism. Suárez grants that overdetermination is impossible; that is, it is contradictory "for the same action to proceed simultaneously from more than one total cause," where 'total cause' refers to the sufficient condition for a given event. Unlike two total causes, however, the primary and secondary cause "belong to different orders and are essentially ordered to one another" (Suárez 1994, 41). Just as an ordinary object exists in the fullest sense while depending on God for its existence, so an object's power can depend on that of God without being demoted to a power in name only . . .

The natural world thus appears, much as it did to Aristotle, as a network of causal powers, the combination of which decides the outcome of any event. The scholastics, of course, accord God primacy of place in the causal structure; but, as we have seen, they deny that God acts alone in bringing about natural effects. Once God concurs with a created being's powers, as he does in the majority of cases, it is those powers that 'particularize and determine' the *esse* God provides . . .

I must now defend this reading against two objections, one philosophical, one historical. The philosophical objection is simply that in reading the scholastics as taking causal necessity to be a species of logical necessity, I have done them a disservice. For this then turns their view into a bare tautology. If one packs everything needed to generate a given event into the putative cause, of course that effect will be generated. By appealing to the total cause, cashed out in terms of the instantiation of the relevant active and passive powers plus God's concurrence, I have drained any significance from what seemed like a bold causal hypothesis. And philosophical objections like this one are often transformed into interpretive or historical objections: shouldn't we apply the principle of charity, and look for some other interpretation? This objection is revealing, since it stems from a conception of analyticity that we owe to modern empiricism. It is only by assuming that all analytic truths are true by virtue of convention, and so can in principle tell us nothing about the way the world is, that the objection threatens the Aristotelian view as I have construed it. And to use this view in evaluating the Aristotelians is to ignore their quite different view of concept acquisition and application.

There are two ways to put the objection. First, one might say that on my reading of the scholastics, a claim like 'fire burns paper' amounts to something like 'if everything necessary for fire to burn paper is present, then it will burn.' This of course is tautological. But it is not the scholastic view. Nowhere in a true causal statement would one find such a blanket conditional whose antecedent ranges over the total cause described as such. This is not to say that a true causal statement is not logically necessary (because analytic). There is no possible world in which God concurs with a given power, the empowered object is in the presence of others with the requisite passive powers, and that power does not bring about its defining effect. For this is precisely what makes a power the power it is. The negation of a true causal claim is a contradiction.

There is another way to put this objection. Analytic propositions are knowable *a priori* because the (concept of) the predicate is contained in the (concept of) the subject. But it is hard to believe that the truths of natural science can be discovered by reflecting on our concepts. If causal claims were necessary in this way, natural science would be trivial . . .

This point seems compelling only if we neglect the Aristotelian account of concept formation. True causal claims are, on this view, *a priori* in the justificatory, not genetic, sense. Although the mind must undergo a complex set of experiences and operations to grasp the relevant concepts, causal claims are ultimately justified by virtue of the connections between essences, as captured in the abstracted concepts. We get into a position to know causal claims not by stipulating definitions but by recognizing the true natures of the objects involved, a goal that can only be attained through repeated experience, under different conditions, of those objects. Such experience allows the intellect to distinguish the complex of attributes essential to a thing's being what it is—its substantial form or organizing principle—from its accidental or nonessential characteristics. The scientific concept of a natural kind is nothing but a more thorough and perspicuous working out of what was already present in the mind when it had initial perceptual contact with instances of that kind. Only the modern empiricist assumption that all analytic truths are true by convention stands in the way of grasping these simple points. . . . although true causal claims are *a priori* in the justificatory sense, this does not mean that one can simply define them into existence, or learn them from one's armchair.

At this point a historical objection to my account of the scholastics might be raised. Doesn't the logical necessity of causal claims conflict with God's omnipotence? Surely most, if not all, scholastics are committed to the literal truth of Biblical miracles, as in the case of Daniel iii, where God prevents the furnace from incinerating three young men, while the soldiers pursuing them burn?

This is an important question, and not only from a textual point of view. For it can be tempting to see NNC's conflation of distinct forms of necessity as arising from the medievals' insistence on divine omnipotence rather than from the Aristotelian worldview I have just sketched. Stephen Boulter has recently argued for precisely this position with regard to Hume's use of NNC. On Boulter's view, as on Nadler's, the dominant scholastic tradition as expressed particularly in Aquinas held that causality was governed by natural necessity. But, Boulter argues, this nomological necessity was deemed a threat to God's omnipotence:

> The theologically grounded rationale for what appears to be a confla-
> tion of logical and natural necessity was the claim that if some state of
> affairs is logically possible (or conceivable) it is *ipso facto* physically pos-
> sible because God's omnipotence allows Him to bring about *any* state of
> affairs save those that violate the principle of non-contradiction.
>
> (Boulter 2002, 77)

Now, I have already argued that there simply was no golden age of Aristotelian nomological necessity. And I shall go on to show that the dominant view, running from Aquinas in the mid thirteenth century to Suárez in the late sixteenth, maintains the logical necessity of causal claims even given God's omnipotence. But there's an effective *reductio* in the offing as well. Suppose Boulter were right, and some Aristotelians went in for nomological necessity. Suppose they were then challenged by those who insisted that anything was possible for God. Why would they be bothered by this? Wouldn't they simply appeal to their distinction between kinds of necessity, and happily grant that God can do anything that is logically possible, even violate their laws of nature? After all, Boulter's mythical Aristotelians do not hold that these laws are logically necessary . . .

This still leaves us with the problem of reconciling omnipotence with the necessity generated by the powers of objects. Concurrentism provides a handy way to do just this.

Suárez [counts all created beings except humans and perhaps angels as] "causes that operate necessarily" (Suárez 1994, 280). Now, once the requisite active and passive powers are in place, "natural causes cannot prevent the action of a necessary agent, since they do not have the power to change the nature of things or to remove wholly intrinsic properties" (Suárez 1994, 281). Note what it would take for a natural cause to prevent the action of such an agent, i.e., to change the course of events: one would have to alter its intrinsic properties. In other words, one would have to bring it about that fire was not fire.

Nor is there any exception for God here. God is able "only to remove one of the required things." When the requisite elements obtain, even God himself cannot bring it about that a natural cause fails to act. When Shadrach, Meshach, and Abednego were lifted into Nebuchadnezzar's furnace, God did not remove the fire's power to burn, or flesh's passive power to be burned;

all he did was withhold his ordinary concurrence from the fire (Suárez 1994, 281). Just as Malebranche and Hume suppose, Suárez holds that is logically contradictory, and hence inconceivable, that the presupposition of an action be present and yet that action fail to take place. God can remove his concurrence, but this is no different in kind from a situation in which the intended patient fails to possess the requisite passive power: part of the total cause is not present, and so the action cannot take place.

## 2. 'Little Souls'

We have removed one barrier to understanding NNC: the myth that mainstream scholasticism distinguishes between logical and causal necessity. Malebranche cannot be accused of conflating two types of necessity when there was only one to begin with.

But this raises another problem: why is Malebranche so certain that no physical objects or events, with or without God's concurrence, will be logically necessarily connected with their effects? This question might seem a bit of unnecessary mystery making, since Malebranche's statement of NNC suggests that any true cause will have to be omnipotent. If this is Malebranche's point, then it is trivially true that no physical being is a cause (since it lacks a will), and close to trivially true that no finite mind is a cause. I think this suggestion makes Malebranche's argument implausibly weak . . . More than this, however, it gets the structure of the argument wrong: it is *because* a true cause is one that is necessarily connected to its effects that only an omnipotent being can count as such . . .

Malebranche's typically curt dismissal of the intelligibility of a necessary connection between bodies suggests he takes belief in such a connection to involve a category mistake (see e.g. Elucidation XV: SAT 658). I think we can reconstruct his reasoning if we consider another of his arguments, which itself derives from Descartes.

To make room for their own versions of mechanism, both figures take aim at the scholastic notion of power. And both explicitly argue that power attributions amount to attributions of intentionality; the Aristotelian projects features possessed only by minds on to the inert world of extension. Des Chene (1996) has dubbed this line of thought 'the little souls' argument, as Descartes writes that he does "not suppose there are in nature any real qualities, which are attached to substances, like so many little souls to their bodies, and which are separable from them by divine power" (Letter to Mersenne, CSM 3.216) . . .

This 'little souls' argument is picked up and exploited by Malebranche. In arguing that bodies cannot have the power to move themselves, Malebranche writes,

Well, then, let us suppose that this chair can move itself: which way will it go? With what velocity? At what time will it take it into its head to move? You would have to give the chair an intellect and a will capable of determining itself. You would have, in short, to make a man out of your armchair.

(Dialogue VII in Malebranche 1992, 227)

. . . Like a mind, a body endowed with power would have to be intrinsically directed at states of affairs. Moreover, these states of affairs need never be actual: fire would have the power to burn paper even if it never actually did. Although inhering in a single object, the power is directed toward a range of non-actual states of affairs. This *esse-ad* is the target of Descartes' claim that a body endowed with heaviness, conceived as a power or quality, would have to know where the center of the earth was if indeed it genuinely tended, of its own volition as it were, toward that location. And Malebranche rejects this feature by saying that power attributions require attributions of both intellect and will. In both figures, it is the property of intentionality that is crucial, and this is a property both agree can be possessed only by minds.

We are now in a position to apply these results to NNC. By making explicit what is to count as a genuine cause, NNC lets us take up the issue of intentionality from the other end: once we see what a true cause requires, we shall see that there is no way in principle for bodies to serve as causes.

There is a connection between God's will and its effects that physical events simply cannot have. For a divine volition includes its effect in the sense that that effect is specified as the content of that volition . . . The logically necessary connection between cause and effect requires that they be linked in the right way. But how can a physical event, described in a non-question begging way, point to or be linked with an effect in any way at all? Events described in mechanical terms are not internally connected to their putative effects. For example, 'the ball is dropped from the tower' and 'the ball hits the ground' do not in any sense include or make reference to each other; still less will they do so when analyzed in the appropriate geometrical fashion as mechanism demands. Only intentionality has this feature of directedness. Thus the will is perfectly and uniquely suited to play the role of cause. Unlike a bare event, a volition can be directed at a distinct state of affairs, simply by including that state of affairs as its propositional content. This, I think, is why Malebranche finds the notion that finite *relata* could be causal *relata* so obviously muddle-headed.

As we have seen, the dominant view held by Malebranche's opponents is not the thoroughly 'pagan' one that takes finite objects to be autonomous agents but the concurrentist view that includes God in the total cause of any effect. NNC applies equally well to secondary efficient causes, of course, since even on the scholastic view, there is no necessary connection between these and any states of affairs. God's concurrence is required. But it also applies to the scholastics' total cause. For the necessary connection here is grounded both in God's activity and in the power of the created being. But God's activity is not directed simply at a future state of affairs as such, as it is on Malebranche's view; instead, God works through a created power. The directedness of the total cause, then, must come in part from that created power itself. And this is what Malebranche challenges.

To sum up: Malebranche accepts the scholastic requirement of *esse-ad*; a cause must somehow be intrinsically directed at its effect. But like Descartes, he finds it impossible to conceive how finite objects could have this feature. This, of course, is intimately connected to the abandonment of the Aristotelian ontology. Once a broadly mechanical view is in place, it becomes hard to see how bodies could be causes. Malebranche instead meets the intentionality requirement by ascribing causal power only to the one kind of thing he thinks *can* be directed at non-actual states of affairs: the mind . . .

## 3. The Epistemic Argument

This reading helps illuminate Malebranche's otherwise mysterious argument against the claim that finite minds can be causes. We know that minds, according [to] Malebranche, are at least of the right ontological type; still, lacking omnipotence, they also lack a necessary connection with their effects. For any instance of a finite volition and its putative effect, we can always conceive of the former without the latter [. . . and so] meeting the intentionality requirement is a necessary, but not a sufficient, condition for causal power.

But there is a deeper issue here. For Malebranche does not rely solely on NNC to show the inefficacy of finite minds; he also thinks that our ignorance of the neurophysiological facts prevents our will from being a cause. As we shall see, this argument is another manifestation of the requirement that cause and effect be linked by intentionality.

In what we might call 'the epistemic argument', Malebranche . . . argues that, in order for a finite mind's will to cause its body to move, that mind would have to "know exactly the size and agitation of an infinite number of particles that collide with each other when the spirits are in the muscles" (Eluc. XV: SAT 671). Thus no such mind could, in principle, be a cause of bodily movements.

Let us first distinguish between volitions whose contents are identical with their immediate effects and those that are not. Call the latter 'chain volitions', i.e., volitions whose propositional contents the subject can only bring about by setting a chain of further events into motion. Thus willing that my car start is a chain volition, since I can only bring it about by turning the key, which in turns sends an electrical impulse down the steering column, and so on. In a chain volition, one wills the outcome of a chain of events . . .

We can now reconstruct Malebranche's argument:

1. An effective volition is either a chain volition or not.
2. Willing to move our bodies is a chain volition.
3. In an efficacious chain volition, at least the first member of the chain must be included in the content of the volition.
4. We do not know what this member is in the present case. Thus
5. None of our bodily volitions is efficacious.

The trick is turned by premise (3). For the most natural story here is that the volition sets in motion a series of events that issues in the motion of the arm; why should we assume that the crucial first element must be included in the content of the volition? . . .

To understand the epistemic argument we need to invoke the point I have been pushing toward concerning NNC: Malebranche requires that causes and effects be linked by the content of a volition. Now, in the case of chain volitions, the requisite link obviously does not obtain. For what the physiology shows us is that the connection is not *volition—arm moving* but *volition—brain event x—etc.—arm moving*. And without including the brain event in the content of the volition, that volition cannot be efficacious simply because the p-volition and the alleged effect are not identical.

We saw above in the context of the 'little souls' argument that Malebranche takes this requirement of intentional connection to hold across the board. Entertaining the notion that Malebranche might have imposed an epistemic criterion on causes in general, and not merely on minds, Nadler (2000, 125) observes that "it seems to be a category mistake to extend the epistemic condition to causation by corporeal agents, such as fire and stones". But once we see the need for a tie between cause and effect that only intentionality can supply, we also see that this extension is no category mistake; the category mistake, in fact, is committed by those who claim that physical beings can be causes.

## 4. Conclusion

Occasionalism is a highly counter-intuitive doctrine, and Malebranche surely thinks that he has powerful considerations to advance on its behalf. If these considerations are left opaque, his view cannot but seem a mere historical curiosity. But if I am right, the key element of Malebranche's dialectical strategy falls into place, and the appeal of his arguments, at least in their proper intellectual context, becomes clear.

Why would someone think that causes must logically necessitate their effects? The answer is clear once one has a firm grasp of the Aristotelian tradition, in which powers are defined by their contributions to events. Why would someone think that attributing powers to bodies requires treating them as possessed of little minds, with little wills of their own? Well, powers are supposed to be the sorts of things that of their own nature tie an event to its effect. But the only plausible candidate in Malebranche's intellectual context for such a tie is the relation of intentionality . . . . Finally, why should we think that the first step in a chain volition must be included in the content of that volition? Again, only because a cause must be connected by this relation to its effect.

Where this tie of intentionality is absent, all events are indeed 'entirely loose and separate', as Hume was to write. Malebranche inspired Hume's claim that "[s]olidity, extension, motion; these qualities are all compleat in themselves, and never point out any other event which may result from them" (E 4). For unlike Aristotelian powers (or Malebranchian volitions), these mechanical qualities are not of the right ontological type to be necessarily connected to their effects.

## Note

1. Editors' note: 'intentionality' is a philosophers' term that has little to do with the ordinary English use of the term 'intention'. To say that something has 'intentionality' is to say that it refers to or is about or is directed towards something. Mental states like the idea of a puppy or the desire for a puppy are paradigmatically intentional: they are both, in different ways, about or directed towards puppies.

## CHAPTER 8

# Malebranche on Necessary Connections, Omniscience, and Omnipotence

## SUKJAE LEE

When we think of causation, the idea that effects are necessarily connected to their causes easily comes to mind. If, however, we look back at the 2500-year history of western philosophy, we will find this identification of causation as necessary connection to be a relatively recent development, emerging prominently only in the latter half of the seventeenth century. The Aristotelian worldview, for instance, allowed for types of causation where the *explanation* of an effect rather than its *necessitation* was the primary role of the cause in question. If there were a single philosopher who played the most important role in pushing necessary connections to the fore of our understanding of causation, it was the great French metaphysician, Nicolas Malebranche. (While for some Hume might come to mind, Malebranche preceded him—and, as McCracken (1983) shows, Hume was heavily influenced by Malebranche.) We see this idea in the now famous passage from the *Search After Truth*:

> A true cause as I understand it is one such that the mind perceives a necessary connection between it and its effect. Now the mind perceives a necessary connection only between the will of an infinitely perfect being and its effects. Therefore, it is only God who is the true cause and who truly has the power to move bodies.
>
> (SAT VI.ii.3, 450)

The 'no necessary connection' (NNC) argument, following Nadler's (1996) original coinage, is simple enough. The central positive thesis of occasionalism—that God is the only true cause—is inferred from two premises:

1. a cause is necessarily connected to its effect
2. such necessary connections are uniquely exemplified between divine volitions and their effects.

But, as Walter Ott well points out in the previous chapter these premises are far from being obvious. Ott ingeniously attempts to remedy our puzzlement about these two premises.

The first puzzle concerns premise (1): why would anyone take necessitation to be the criterion of causation? As Ott states,

> The real puzzle about this kind of argument has never been its form or structure but rather who is supposed to be bothered by it. Even if we accept that the connection between two events is not logically necessary, why should anyone believe that it is not a *bona fide* instance of causation?
>
> (see p. 95 above)

This indeed seems to be the right question to ask, especially given the historical background mentioned earlier. If the mature state of an oak tree is the end towards which an acorn strives and hence is its final cause, necessary connection hardly seems to be the right way to describe the causal relation that obtains between the acorn and the oak tree. After raising this insightful question, Ott goes on to present his account as to why Malebranche took necessary connection to be the criterion of causation. This chapter, accordingly, reviews Ott's account, and raises a worry about how Ott is reading other interpretations about Malebranche's motivations.

The second puzzle revolves around premise (2). Why is it the case that necessary connections only obtain between divine volitions and their effects? As Ott puts it, "why is Malebranche so quick to deny that finite *relata*, and bodies in particular, can be causes?" (see p. 96 above) Ott provides us with an interesting account of why Malebranche claimed that "nothing but God's will can live up to the necessity criterion" (see p. 96 above). Central to this account is Ott's emphasis on the role of intentionality in securing necessary connections. In reviewing Ott's account here, we will discuss some reasons to be critical of this account as well.

## The Criterion of Necessary Connection

Complicating the inquiry about the necessity criterion is the question of what type of necessary connection is at issue here. For instance, we typically think of distinguishing *logically* necessary connections from *causally* necessary connections. If so, what type of connection did Malebranche have in mind in presenting the 'no necessary connection' argument? Adding to the confusion is the fact that the recent participants in the debate appear to have distinct notions of what logical and causal necessity are and how they differ. Let us begin by taking a closer look at how Ott carves up the interpretive terrain.

According to Ott, commentators such as Nadler and Jolley have erred in thinking that Malebranche is conflating the two types of necessity in the NNC argument. Ott reads Nadler and Jolley to be arguing that while the necessity in question should be causal, Malebranche is wrongfully requiring that the necessity in question be logical, due to conflating the two types of necessity. Against this reading, Ott argues that rather than inadvertently conflating the two necessities, Malebranche knowingly takes the necessity in question to be logical, and rightfully so, given the historical precedents of Aquinas and Suárez. As his central claim in the first section of Chapter 7 [pp. 97–101 above], "Logical and Causal Necessity," Ott claims that Malebranche continues the tradition of his scholastic predecessors in regarding causal necessity as a species of logical necessity. In a nutshell, when the relevant active and passive powers are instantiated and God concurs with them, it would be a contradiction if the proper event did not result.

Now on to some worries about Ott's view here. Ott, in criticizing Nadler and Jolley, suggests that his opponents hold causal (or nomological) necessity to be distinct from logical necessity in the following sense: while the denial of logical necessity generates a contradiction, the denial of causal (or nomological) necessity does not. But I find this assumption on the part of Ott problematic. For it is not clear that this is the way Nadler understands causal (or nomological) necessity. Here is Nadler on the notion of causal or nomological necessity:

> What is necessary on account of the natural order . . . is not absolutely or logically necessary, because God, in his absolute power, could have established a different natural order. In other words, there is a distinction between nomological necessity (that is, necessity relative to some non-necessary set of laws—for example, the laws of nature) and logical necessity.
>
> (Nadler 2000, 114)

As we can see, Nadler takes the relevant distinction to be grounded in whether the necessity is "relative to some non-necessary set of laws." I take this distinction to mean something like the following: that an apple falls to the ground when dropped, for instance, is nomologically necessary but not logically necessary, since that the apple not falling is contradictory only when we assume the current laws of gravitation. That is, it is not a contradiction in itself that the apple does not fall, since God could have established a different natural order (for instance, where apples float up in the air).

If this reading of Nadler's view is correct, then Ott's assumption that Nadler does not take the denial of causal or nomological necessity to involve contradictions is problematic. For Nadler too thinks that the denial of nomo-logical necessities generate contradictions, only that it takes more, as it were, to generate the contradictions. While the denial of absolute necessities are in themselves inconsistent, in the case of nomological necessities, contradic-tions arise only because additional laws of nature are assumed. It is on the assumption that current gravitational laws obtain that it is contradictory for the apple be dropped and not fall. So, in fact, Ott and Nadler appear to be in agreement in taking the denial of causal or nomological necessity to generate contradictions.

With this point in mind, let us return to the larger question we were hoping to address. Recall that Ott had asked, "even if we accept that the connection between two events is not logically necessary, why should anyone believe that it is not a *bona fide* instance of causation?" Earlier, we had understood this ques-tion as asking why other Aristotelian causes, such as material or final causes, were being banned from the roster of genuine causes. As we can see, Ott's dis-cussion is not aimed at addressing this particular version of the question. But assume that we are on board with the general tendency within early modern philosophy to reject material, formal, and final causation as somehow anti-quated and inadequate. This still leaves us with a question for Malebranche.

Suppose with Ott (and Nadler, if I am right) that causal necessity, tradi-tionally understood, is a type of logical necessity, where if the causal power of the cause is instantiated and all other requisites are posited, it is con-tradictory for the effect not to occur. Now here is a test case for whether Malebranche's identification of causation with necessary connection in the NNC argument would be acceptable to his opponents. Consider a case where the cause in question is a creaturely cause. Given the theological con-sensus of the time, even if the creature's power is instantiated, it was widely accepted that God's concurring activity is necessary as well for the effect to occur. Now Malebranche, given his occasionalism, obviously would deny that the created substances possess any real causal powers. But suppose he were asked the following: hypothetically speaking, if he were somehow convinced that fire possessed the power to burn cotton, would he in this case accept that the fire's power is necessarily connected to its effect? That is, even if the instantiation of the fire's power is not sufficient in itself to bring about the effect, and divine concurrence is an additional requisite, would Malebranche agree that the fire's power is nonetheless necessarily connected to its effect? If Malebranche answered affirmatively, then I take it that his opponents would be hard pressed to complain against Malebranche's claim that causation is necessary connection. If, however, Malebranche denied that fire is a true cause in this case precisely because its power is not sufficient in itself to bring about the burning of cotton, then his opponents would most likely object that his conception of causation is too restrictive. For no one in the debate, including the proponents of genuine creaturely causation, held that creaturely powers were sufficient in themselves to bring about their effects. The crucial issue here is whether Malebranche's conception of necessary connection requires a cause to be sufficient in itself to bring about an effect.

I read Ott as suggesting that Malebranche would indeed deny that a cause must be sufficient in itself to bring about its effects. That is, Ott is arguing that we should not be puzzled about premise (1) in NNC, since, properly understood, premise (1) would be accepted by the Scholastic proponents of genuine creaturely causation as well. In this case, the critical move in NNC would be premise (2), i.e. the claim that there are such necessary connections "only between the will of an infinitely perfect being and its effects." For if a cause need not be sufficient in itself to bring about its effect, then it is not clear why necessary connections should uniquely originate from an agent that is omnipotent.

## Divine Volition and Necessary Connections

On what grounds might we be convinced that necessary connections of the relevant type only obtain between divine volitions and their effects? The question is particularly pointed for Ott, since, on his reading of premise (1), causal powers traditionally thought to be inherent in creatures are not ruled out from having necessary connections to their effects. Malebranche, as the arch occasionalist, naturally would want to resist such powers in creatures, but remember that occasionalism is the conclusion he needs to establish, and this is why he is presenting NNC in the first place. That is, were Malebranche to assume occasionalism in order to support premise (2), this would be a blatant case of circular reasoning.

Fortunately, in his second section, "Little Souls," Ott presents us with an intriguing account of why Malebranche thinks that necessary connections only hold for divine volitions and their effects. The key is that intentionality is what secures the requisite necessary connection between a cause and its effect:

> The logically necessary connection between cause and effect requires that they be linked in the right way. But how can a physical object or event, described in a non-question begging way, point to or be linked with an effect in any way at all? Events (or objects) described in mechanical terms are not internally connected to their putative effects. For example, 'the ball is dropped from the tower' and 'the ball hits the ground' do not in any sense include or make reference to each other; still less will they do so when analyzed in the appropriate geometrical fashion as mechanism demands. Only intentionality has this feature of directedness. Thus the will is perfectly and uniquely suited to play the role of cause.

(see p. 102 above)

The central idea is that necessary connection requires a kind of directedness, an *esse-ad* or being-toward, and only intentionality has this feature of directedness. Ott traces this view back to the Scholastic conception of causal powers, where causal powers were thought to be characterized by their directedness, allowing them to underwrite necessary connections. According to Ott, Malebranche takes over this remnant of Scholastic metaphysics from Descartes.

This interesting account raises a number of questions. On this view, sequences of events count as genuinely causal only if the latter event is somehow included or contained in the prior event as its propositional content. This implies that the prior events must be mental acts that involve propositional attitudes. Our first question is whether this then means that any type of intentionality can underwrite causation. For instance, if I *believe* that there is a cat outside my door, and a cat indeed came over at that very moment and sat outside, then can this belief of mine be thought to be necessarily connected to, and, hence, the cause of this event? For beliefs are just as intentional as volitions, and if intentionality is what underwrites necessary connections, does it matter what type of intentionality is involved? But as the case shows, it seems rather odd that my belief caused the cat to be there. Perhaps not all propositional attitudes can count, and volitions are the only type that provide the right kind of intentionality. But if so, we need to know more about why only volitions are the right kind. If the story is that only volitions are appropriately causal because only volitions brings things about, then Ott's account faces concerns about circularity. For while intentionality was introduced to account for causality, further probing suggests that an account of the right type of intentionality actually relies on a notion of causality.

Here is a different question about how much of a role intentionality plays in securing necessary connections. If intentionality is what underwrites the logical necessities, should not finite intentional agents count as genuine causes as well? In summarizing Ott states that "[w]hat makes a divine volition a suitable causal *relatum* is the intentional nature that ties it to its effects, since the propositional content of a divine volition *just is* that volition's effect" (see p. 96 above). But such conditions are satisfied when I successfully raise my arm intentionally. So why is it that only divine volitions count as genuine causes, when my arm going up *just is* the propositional content of *my* volition as well? Note that at the beginning of this section, the central question we faced was as follows: if we adopt Ott's reading of NNC, the key issue comes down to why it is the case that necessary connections are exclusive to divine volitions and their effects. Given Ott's focus on intentionality as that which plays the critical role in securing this type of connection, the question is all the more pressing, since finite minds fit the bill as well. Ott is aware of this issue and addresses it in the following:

This reading [that emphasizes the role of intentionality in NNC] helps illuminate Malebranche's otherwise mysterious argument against the claim that finite minds can be causes. We know that minds, according to Malebranche, are at least the right kind of ontological type; still, lacking omnipotence, they also lack a necessary connection with their effects. For any instance of a finite volition and its putative effect, we can always conceive of the former without the latter. This shows that the requirement of logical necessity is not fulfilled. Given Malebranche's adoption of the scholastics' analysis of causation as logical necessitation, NNC alone is enough to show that no finite mind, on its own, is a cause. Thus meeting the intentionality requirement is a necessary, but not a sufficient condition for causal power.

(see p. 103 above)

I confess I find this passage rather puzzling. Here Ott states that the reason why finite minds are not causes is that they lack omnipotence. That is, it is conceivable for a finite mind to will some event and for it not occur. But if so, then is it not omnipotence, rather than intentionality, that which underwrites the necessary connections between divine volition and their effects?

Earlier in the chapter, in motivating the 'Little Souls' argument, Ott insisted that NNC cannot rely on assumption that any true cause will have to be omnipotent, for that would make the argument 'implausibly weak' (see p. 101 above). It is against this backdrop that Ott had suggested his alternative, i.e. intentionality. But if it turns out that the intentionality requirement is merely a necessary condition for causal power, and omnipotence is the other requisite, then it seems as though Ott's critique applies to his own account as well.

Perhaps more worrisome is the fact that the intentionality requirement seems to be doing no real work here. For the reason why there is a logically necessary connection between God willing event $p$ and $p$ occurring presumably is that it is contradictory that $p$ not occur, given *divine omnipotence*. That is, without the assumption of omnipotence, there does not seem to be a way to secure the logical necessity relation between the propositional content of a volition and the occurrence of this content. For in the case of a finite mind, despite the fact that the intentionality requirement is met in the finite mind's willing some event $q$ and $q$ does occur, it is not the case that it is contradictory that $q$ not occur. If so, then the intentionality requirement or *ad-esse* component does not seem to be the critical feature underwriting logical necessity. What seemed to be the central motivation behind Ott's move to introduce intentionality seems at this point considerably weakened, since it is not clear at all what role intentionality is doing in securing logical necessity. Insofar as omnipotence is acknowledged to play such a critical role in securing the relevant necessary connection, I remain skeptical of Ott's suggestion that intentionality is the critical feature grounding necessary connections.

## Omniscience Rather Than Omnipotence?

In the last section of Chapter 7 Ott presents us with what is likely the last piece of his puzzle on how to read NNC. In the section entitled "The Epistemic Argument," Ottre marks that "Malebranche does not rely solely on NNC to show the inefficacy of finite minds." Rather

> the chief difficulty with finite minds as causes is their lack, not of omnipotence, but of omniscience . . . Malebranche argues that, in order for a finite mind's will to cause its body to move, that mind would have to "know exactly the size and agitation of an infinite number of particles that collide with each other when the spirits are in the muscles" (Eluc. XV: SAT 671).
>
> (see p. 103 above)

Here we get a distinct, different account as to why finite minds fail to be genuine causes. Despite the fact that they satisfy the intentionality requirement, finite minds fail to cause because they lack the requisite knowledge of the relevant effects. Thus Malebranche seems to be committed to the principle that it is impossible to bring something about unless one knows how to bring it about. Bracketing the question of how plausible this principle itself is, the key issue for us is how this 'epistemic argument' (EP) relates to NNC.

On Ott's reading, EP is critical to the success of NNC, since on its own NNC is not capable of ruling out finite minds from the roster of genuine causes. But I am not convinced this is the right way to view the relation between the two arguments. In fact, that NNC has to be dependent on EP in this manner seems worrisome for a number of reasons. Let us see why. First of all, if EP were being employed for such a purpose, then it would only have limited force. For while we might easily grant that we do not have the requisite knowledge of the nerves and animal spirits involved in moving our body, we might think that we do have the relevant knowledge when the effects in question are things we know much more about, say, mathematical truths.

Suppose a geometer wills to conjure up the Pythagorean theorem, and succeeds in bringing up the theorem in his mind. The geometer in this case would seem to be satisfying both the intentionality requirement and the knowledge principle. On Ott's account then the geometer would be the real cause of this idea of the theorem. But would Malebranche be ready to accept this conclusion? Most likely not. As we know, Malebranche's occasionalism is a broad, sweeping doctrine, which applies with equal force to both cases of minds moving bodies and minds producing ideas. Minds lack the power to bring about changes not only in bodies but also in their own minds. That is, even the ideas we possess are not caused by us. So if we accept Ott's reading and Malebranche is indeed relying on EP to fill a gap within NNC, then EP would seem to have only limited applicability in ruling out the movement of bodies. Moreover, such a strategy would actually open the door to the prospect that finite minds are genuine causes of some effects, namely, their clear and distinct ideas. This is one reason why I am inclined to think, *pace* Ott, that the NNC and EP are in fact independent arguments, with distinct objectives.

But perhaps the geometer case just mentioned assumes something that Ott would not grant. Perhaps the geometer does not satisfy the EP because she does not have perfect knowledge of the Pythagorean theorem (perhaps perfect knowledge requires knowing how it relates to every other geometrical theorem). But if this were Ott's response—that is, if the bar for the requisite knowledge were so high—then a different worry arises for Ott's reading. Remember that a key motivation for Ott's interpretation was that taking necessary connections to be grounded in divine omnipotence made the argument implausibly weak. For if necessary connections are held from the outset to be only exemplified by omnipotent agents, then occasionalism seems to follow from a stipulative conception of causation. But if omniscience is necessary for genuine causation, which seems to be the case on Ott's account here, is the situation any better? Since only one unique agent satisfies the criterion of omniscience, is not this argument implausibly weak as well, since occasionalism once again seems to be had by simply stipulating that genuine causes must be omniscient?

There is one last worry about linking NNC and EP in this way. Imagine there is an intentional agent that is omniscient but not omnipotent. Suppose that this agent wills with perfect knowledge all the relevant physical events that are involved in my arm going up. Would it be a contradiction if my arm did not go up in this instance? I would think not, since intentionality and omniscience do not seem to imply that the intended event occur necessarily. That is, that an intentional agent wills some event with perfect knowledge does not seem to entail that the event itself must occur. In fact, it seems as though any contradiction involving the nonoccurrence of the intended event requires that the agent be omnipotent, since only omnipotence seems to imply that the intended event occur with necessity.

## Concluding Remarks

This observation brings us to the last point I want to make in this chapter. Let us take a look at the following passage, where Malebranche first brings up the term 'necessary connection' in the *Search*:

> But when we examine our idea of all finite minds, we do not see any necessary connection between their will and the motion of any body whatsoever ... But when one thinks about the idea of God, i.e. of an infinitely perfect and consequently all-powerful being, one knows there is such a

connection between His will and the motion of all bodies, that it is impossible to conceive that He wills a body to be moved and that this body not be moved. We must therefore say that only His will can move bodies if we wish to state things as we conceive them and not as we sense them.

(SAT VI.ii.3, 448)

Here the feature that underwrites the necessary connection between God's will and its effect is divine omnipotence. For of the infinite perfections that the divine being possesses, Malebranche calls our attention to God being the 'all-powerful being.' Moreover, this emphasis on omnipotence makes sense, since one obvious way to read omnipotence is that it is impossible for agent $x$ to will event $p$ and $p$ not occur. So the textual evidence and its natural reading, in my view, strongly suggests that Malebranche had omnipotence, rather than intentionality or omniscience, in mind when contemplating necessary connections. This suggestion is not to neglect Ott's charitable intentions in drawing our focus away from omnipotence. As noted earlier, this emphasis on omnipotence does seem to raise the concern of rendering NNC 'implausibly weak.' So some concluding remarks to mitigate this worry seem apt.

What does omnipotence have to do with the causal powers in creatures or lack thereof? Ott himself actually raises this issue in discussing Boulter's reading of NNC (see p. 100 above). Ott's response, briefly put, is that while one might think that "the necessity generated by the powers of objects" might be thought to be a threat to divine omnipotence, the two can be reconciled by divine concurrentism (see p. 100 above). Let us take a closer look at Ott's reasoning here. If one endorsed creaturely causal powers as a concurrentist, which the majority of those who affirmed the genuine causal powers of created substances in fact were, this meant that divine concurring activity was regarded as necessary for the effect to occur. In this respect, divine concurrentists would not affirm claims like the following:

(N) Necessarily, if fire comes into contact with cotton, the cotton burns.

The claim is false for concurrentists, since insofar as God withholds his concurring activity, even if fire comes into contact with cotton, it would not burn. God's power to stop the effectiveness of fire is secured. So the consistency between divine omnipotence and the necessity generated by the causal powers of creatures is in effect maintainable due to the concurrentist's denial of (N). That is, according to Ott, claims like (N) are what threaten divine omnipotence. And by denying (N), concurrentists can affirm divine omnipotence.

Now consider the following claim, which concurrentists would affirm:

(N*) Necessarily, if fire comes into contact with cotton and God concurs, the cotton burns.

Ott is arguing that while (N) is inconsistent with omnipotence, (N*) is not. Perhaps from the concurrentists' perspective. But what about Malebranche? Would Malebranche have thought that (N*) is innocuous as well? If one hangs the causal powers of fire on the fact that we can endorse claims such as (N*), such endorsements have the implication that created substances have certain causal powers essentially. That is, even God cannot remove from fire its power to burn. The Aristotelian causal realist would find such essentialism completely natural. But what of occasionalists of the Malebranchean stripe? What if one is gripped by the intuition that divine omnipotence entails that God could have made fire without its power to burn? This, obviously, would be a juncture at which Aristotelian causal realists and Malebranchean occasionalists would part ways. But this parting of ways tells us that the occasionalist's intuition is as strong as that of the Aristotelian essentialist, and it is in this sense that I think Malebranche takes real causal powers to be a threat to divine omnipotence.

An intuition, of course, does not make an argument, and I do not think that any Aristotelian causal essentialist would have been moved to give up their causal realism in light of this conception of divine omnipotence. But this way of thinking of Malebranche on divine omnipotence, I think, might help us better understand why the notion of omnipotence seems to have such a prominent place in the 'no necessary connection' argument. Furthermore, if so, the argument itself might be thought to be more of an expression of Malebranche's intuition about divine omnipotence than an argument for it.

## Acknowledgement

I would like to thank the graduate students in my Spring 2011 seminar on Early Modern Theories of Causation at Seoul National University for helpful discussion on this material. This work was supported by the College of Humanities Research Fund (CHRF) of Seoul National University.

# PART V

# Did Leibniz Believe in Corporeal Substances?

# Editors' Introduction

This part of the book concerns what looks like a very simple question. Was Leibniz an idealist who thought that the only things that really exist are minds? Or did he also believe that 'corporeal substances' like animals—compounds of mind and body—exist?

This question seems like it should be easy to answer. The question itself is clear, and it's about a fundamental part of Leibniz's system. But many of Leibniz's readers (perhaps including you) have found that it's actually very difficult. In a number of books, articles, and letters written at different points in his career, Leibniz says that only minds exist. But there are *also* many texts, written at many different times, where Leibniz talks about the existence of animals and other corporeal substances.

In Chapter 9 Glenn Hartz argues for two main claims:

1. Leibniz is genuinely committed both to idealism and to the existence of corporeal substance.
2. Leibniz holds these two inconsistent commitments as a result of deep tensions in his system.

Almost everyone agrees that some passages seem like evidence for (1). But many readers have argued that (1) is false: Leibniz may talk about corporeal substances for convenience, but he isn't really committed to their existence. These readers have offered various explanations of why Leibniz's commitment to corporeal substance is merely apparent. Hartz chooses four prominent explanations and explains why all four fail. He thus concludes that (1) is true and explores the tensions that he thinks produced Leibniz's inconsistent commitments.

In Chapter 10 Brandon Look argues, against Hartz, that Leibniz really *is* an idealist. He analyzes some key pieces of textual evidence and shows that their commitment to corporeal substance is merely apparent. And he provides objections to each of Hartz's main arguments. Do you think his objections are compelling? Can you figure out a good response to them on Hartz's behalf? Or is there some third way of making sense of the various pieces of textual evidence that Hartz and Look provide?

## A Note on References

Leibniz wrote *a lot*, in many different venues, and even now his work is scattered in a number of places instead of collected in one standard edition like Descartes'. A lot of Leibniz's work has been translated: in the two chapters that follow, 'AG' refers to the translations by Ariew and Garber in *Philosophical Essays*, 'Leibniz-Des Bosses' refers to Brandon Look and Donald Rutherford's translation in *The Leibniz–Des Bosses Correspondence*; 'Loemker' refers to the translation by Leroy Loemker in *Philosophical Papers and Letters*; 'NE' refers to Peter Remnant and Jonathan Bennett's translation of the *New Essays*; and 'MP' refers to the translation by M. Morris and G. H. R. Parkinson in *Leibniz: Philosophical Writings*. But sometimes there is no translation and the reference is to a French or Latin original. 'Couturat' refers to *Opuscules et fragments inédits*, edited by Louis Couturat; 'Dutens' refers to the *Opera Omnia*, edited by Louis Dutens; and 'Gerhardt' refers to the 7-volume *Die philosophichen Schriften*, edited by C.I. Gerhardt.

## Further Reading

- Robert Merrihew Adams (1983). "Phenomenalism and Corporeal Substance in Leibniz."
- Daniel Garber (2011). *Leibniz: Body, Substance, Monad.*

## CHAPTER 9

# Why Corporeal Substances Keep Popping Up in Leibniz's Later Philosophy

## GLENN A. HARTZ

A problem for Leibniz scholarship today is (in Martha Bolton's words) that 'corporeal substances keep popping up all over the place'. It's a *problem* because many commentators say that while Leibniz is committed to corporeal substances in his 'middle years' (about 1686–1700), he ends up (at least after 1703) rejecting them. In the 'later years', he endorses 'Exclusive Idealism'—where the only substances are purely spiritual monads. Such commentators are embarrassed by any later texts committed to corporeal substances. I argue that corporeal substances pop up later on because Leibniz remained committed to them. Post-1703 Exclusive Idealism cannot be Leibniz's considered view. Any interpretation that says it is faces a formidable list of textual casualties, and undermines several mainstream Leibnizian doctrines. It also flattens out the late-mature system—what it gains in consistency is more than lost in explanatory richness. I present four bad arguments (along with replies) against the claim that post-1703 corporeal substances are genuine substances. I then expound two good arguments to the effect that there is at least a deep tension between the Idealist strain of Leibniz's thought and the realist thread attaching to corporeal substances. My conclusion: no commentator intent on representing the historical Leibniz will ever succeed in eliminating the discord between the idealist and corporeal substance doctrines in the later metaphysic.

## 1. Four Bad Arguments against Post-1703 Commitment to Corporeal Substances

I call these arguments 'bad' because they all force on us a misconception of Leibniz's system.

## A. The Phenomena Argument

C. D. Broad claims that during the De Volder correspondence, "Leibniz definitely comes to the conclusion that corporeal substance is only a *phenomenon bene fundatum*" [well-founded phenomenon]" (Broad 1975, 90). Broad bases this claim on the assumption that corporeal substances are, like aggregates, extended and that thus Leibniz's arguments against the unity of extended bodies apply equally well to 'organic' bodies. He says, "Let [the objects] be as animated and as organic as they will, if their organisms are held to be extended, they are open to this objection" (Broad 1975, 91–92). Stuart Brown writes, "A 'corporeal substance' is a phenomenon produced by monads . . .", adding that "Leibniz himself had tried to defend the hypothesis of 'corporeal substances' and found the task beyond him". Still, "he was just as happy to talk of bodies as 'substances' in a theoretically uncommitted way as he was to talk of bodies causing things to happen in other bodies" (Brown 1984, 148–49).

Catherine Wilson holds that the predominant position in Leibniz's mature work is against corporeal substances: "Under pressure from Des Bosses, Leibniz finally realized, in the last years of his life, that for the sake of logical coherence he would have to choose definitely between monads and corporeal substance" (Wilson 1989, 192–94). He chose monads. Yet when not under "severe pressure", Leibniz often lapsed back into the "exoteric" doctrine of corporeal substance, abandoning for the moment his considered view—namely, a monads-only ontology accompanied by "pure phenomenalism" about bodies. Wilson writes, "around 1703 he stopped actively trying to reconcile monads and corporeal substances."

## Reply to Phenomena Argument

As Robert Adams notes (Adams 1994, 267), Leibniz deliberately denigrates aggregates as 'phenomena' (G III 657; G IV 473; G VII 314), whereas corporeal substances are explicitly contrasted with aggregates and never called phenomena. Moreover, Leibniz clearly distinguished the aggregate-part of a corporeal substance (the 'organic body') from the larger corporeal substance (the organic body + dominant monad). He tells Remond as late as 1715 that the organic body is just a fancy aggregate, and continues,

> secondary matter (for example, the organic body) is not a substance, but . . . a mass of many substances . . . and as a result is called *unum per accidens*, in a word, a phenomenon. A true substance (such as an animal) is composed of an immaterial soul and an organic body, and it is the composite of these two that is called *unum per se* (G III 657).

Corporeal substances must be viewed as genuine . . . Given Leibniz's deep commitment to a substance/accident ontology, his calling *x* a substance (and *unum per se*!) can leave no doubt about his ontological commitment to *x*.

## B. The Aggregate Argument

Benson Mates writes,

> [I]t is clear enough that for Leibniz the only substances are the monads . . . When he is attending to the distinction between individuals and aggregates of individuals, he uses the term "composite substance" to apply to such collections, reserving "simple substance" for the monads themselves'.
>
> (Mates 1986, 194–95)

On Mates's interpretation, when a dominant monad is present, 'the structured aggregate is an animal or a plant' (Mates 1986, 197) . . . And Donald Rutherford holds that, given Leibniz's failure to give an account of the union of soul and body that makes it more than pre-established harmony (that is, the "accidental unit of a being through aggregation"), "we have little choice but to conclude that a dominant monad does not endow its body with the *per se* unity of a substance" (Rutherford 1995, 271–72). Indeed, "Leibniz's deep metaphysics . . . is the metaphysics of monads, in which all other beings, including living creatures, are no more than 'phenomena' and 'results'" (Rutherford 1995, 282). So Rutherford joins Wilson in relegating the corporeal substance doctrine to [exoteric discourse].

## Reply to Aggregate Argument

As is evident from the reply to the last argument, aggregates—the quintessential non-substances—are unities *per accidens*, whereas in [Gerhardt's edition of Leibniz's philosophical works] alone there are at least sixteen texts spanning the period 1686–1715 in which corporeal substances are said to have principles of unity (circa 1694: G VII 444; 1699: G III 260/AG 289: 1703: G II 250/L 529; circa 1705: G VI 550; 1714: G VI 599/AG 207), or a 'strictly genuine identity' (1703–5: NE 232), or 'perfect unity' (1703–5: NE 328) or are called 'true unities' (1687: G II 126; 1695: G IV 473; 1703: G III 457; 1703–5) or *per se* unities (1686: *Discourse on Metaphysics* 34 [G IV 459/AG 65]; 1702: G IV 395/AG 252 & G IV 572; 1703–5: NE 318; 1715: G III 657). Most significant are those texts in which the corporeal substances are explicitly distinguished from aggregates as they are here (1690): "each animal and each plant is also a corporeal substance, having in itself a principle of unity which makes it truly a substance and not an aggregate" (AG 289; cf. AG 252; G VII 501–2; G V1550; G IV 572).

## C. The Reductio ad Vinculum Argument

In 1877 J. E. Erdmann wrote,

> It is chiefly in his correspondence with Arnauld and . . . Des Bosses that such expressions occur as that living things are more than mere phenomena; that there is here an additional element that transforms them into something real . . . which, in the letters to Des Bosses, is called a *vinculum substantiale* [substantial bond or chain]; that on this account, while every mere body is *substantiale* [substantial] . . . a living body is also a *substantia composita* [composite substance].
>
> (Erdmann 1891, 2.188–189)

Erdmann says that maintaining this commitment invites the view that "monads are corporeal", since it involves speaking as if "not merely *materia prima* [prime matter] but also a corporeal nature belonged to the individual monad". His verdict: Leibniz's theory "certainly appears more comprehensive and more consistent if we leave out of account all the statements that affirm the substantial nature of a composite body or the possibility of a *substantia corporea* [corporeal substance]." The *reductio* is roughly this: corporeal substances lead Leibniz down the garden path to bonds, which are inconsistent with his mature philosophy. So we should, as charitable commentators desiring optimal 'comprehensiveness' and 'consistency', leave out of account all references to corporeal substances.

Now the subtle trick in Erdmann's analysis is to liken canonical corporeal substances to the strange 'substantially bonded' substances Leibniz wrote about only to Des Bosses—to see these as of a piece, to be accepted or rejected together. (By 'canonical' here I mean a corporeal substance as described by Leibniz, beginning with the *Discourse on Metaphysics* and continuing through the mature period, as having at least the following traits: (1) has a true unity, or is *unum per se*; (2) is either a form/matter composite or a composite of subordinate monads with a dominant monad unifying them into one organism; (3) is indestructible and immortal (barring divine annihilation); (4) is indivisible (so that the form can't naturally be found without matter, and the dominant monad can't naturally be broken apart completely from some subordinate monads); (5) is a source of force and activity; and (6) has a complete concept.)

Erdmann's '*reductio*' is important because, through Russell,[1] it determined the agenda for nearly all twentieth-century English-language interpretation of Leibniz. The formula is: discuss corporeal substances, show that they lack a principle of unity, show that the best Leibniz could produce for this role was the disastrous substantial bond doctrine, and then suggest that we scrap the entire corporeal substance doctrine.

## Reply to Reductio Argument

There is no necessary connection between canonical corporeal substances and substantial bonds. Of course, the two topics are related conceptually. But I claim that Leibniz should have avoided altogether the substantial bond experiment with Des Bosses. He should have stuck (as he did everywhere but in the Des Bosses correspondence) to his standard line about canonical corporeal substances: there is no knowledge of how their perfect unity comes about—no way humans (at least yet) can explain the basis of their *per se* unity (Loemker 539; cf. Loemker 598; G VI 81). His mistake was to try to supply a "real unifier" for those collections of monads that count as corporeal substances. Most commentators (including many who denigrate corporeal substances) agree with my claim that the substantial bond doctrine is a mistake. They take this as a reason to deny canonical corporeal substances; I take it merely as a reason to deny substantial bonds. It certainly doesn't follow from 'A leads historically to B' and 'B is false' that 'A is false'. Only a logical connection of implication between A and B could give us an instance of *modus tollens* here.[2] But of course the canonical corporeal substance doctrine doesn't entail the *recherché* substantial bond doctrine.

## D. The Philosophical Argument

It seems that many commentators . . . think that Leibniz's theory of monads is his deepest, most profound and interesting philosophical idea. They are led by their metaphysical—perhaps even aesthetic—tastes to emphasize it over the complications that real commitment to bodies would involve. How pristine, neat, clean, simple, powerful—yes, beautiful—is this monadology, which in a single stroke transforms the vulgar empiricist's ragbag world of space, matter, and phenomena into pure intelligibility! If you start with things that can't have parts, the problem of unity is instantly solved—no need to search for 'principles of unity' or worry about borderline cases. It is hard to find commentators explicitly invoking this rationale: thus the 'argument' is a nearly invisible bit of folklore. But I have heard it eloquently defended . . . in the midst of a heated debate over corporeal substances.

## Reply to the Philosophical Argument

One's attitude towards this argument depends on how one views a much larger issue: the commentator's role.[3] Do we merely find ideas that seem to have appeal, and mine those veins until they're empty? Or do we speak as 'impartial spectators', not picking and choosing themes according to their currently perceived interest? Probably there is merit in combining these techniques. But those who favor the former, selective method will more likely be sympathetic to the Philosophical Argument. I myself am sympathetic to it. But I insist on commentator honesty: if the philosophy is what's driving one's interpretation, just say that plainly . . .

So: the Phenomena Argument misapplies the term 'phenomenon' to corporeal substances, while the Aggregate Argument misapplies 'aggregate' to them. The *Reductio ad Vinculum* Argument wrongly squashes corporeal substances and substantially bonded substances down into the same category. And the Philosophical Argument, representing commentator taste rather than historical fact, is not a guide to Leibniz's own thought.

In addition, consider how singularly flat, sterile, and boring Leibniz's late-mature system would be if simple Idealism reigned in it. Leibniz would be expected, if he were clear-headed and speaking esoterically, to wander onto the stage and say, without elaboration, "windowless, purely mental monads are the true atoms of nature, and everything else (except God) exists solely in their representational content." The fact that he *does* elaborate, taking us way beyond this Berkeleyesque picture, indicates that he descended to the most abstract Idealist level *but came back to make connection with bodies and a common world.* Inviting us to ignore the full force of his efforts to come back bankrupts Leibniz's system under the guise of a more charitable, consistent interpretation.

I conclude that commentators who stand upon one or more of these four arguments can't speak for the historical late-mature Leibniz. If they want to expound instead an 'idealized' mature Leibniz who goes the way of pure phenomenalism on bodies, they will find a few texts to support them. Probably many philosophers enamored with desert landscapes of a decidedly spiritual nature will cheer them on. But the corporeal substances that keep popping up will prove a continual distraction . . .

## 2. Two good arguments for a tension between idealism and commitment to corporeal substances in the late-mature system

We must now turn to arguments that aren't based on mistakes, and that raise genuine worries about the coherence of Leibniz's late-mature system once monads and corporeal substances are granted the status of genuine individuals—that is, unities of the strictest metaphysical order.

### A. The No Principle of Unity Argument

[One reason sometimes given] for likening the unity of corporeal substances to that of aggregates [is] Leibniz's failure to provide a decent account ('beyond pre-established harmony') of the union of soul and body. That is a good reason. Most importantly, it is a good Leibnizian reason. For it is Leibniz more than anyone else in the history of philosophy that insisted on principles of unity for individuals. The entire anti-extension campaign is waged with this powerful weapon: any thing that is actually an entity must have a principle of unity—else it isn't.

So if Leibniz has some purported 'thing' lodged in the ground floor of his metaphysic that has no principle of unity, he could fairly be challenged for failing to follow his own precepts at the juncture that he taught us most to insist on in such matters. Indeed, here Rutherford is right. Leibniz does no better than pre-established harmony, and so gives us no principle that can transform all the separate monads in a collection into a true unity.

When Leibniz was pushed on this issue by his later correspondents, he usually says that, while we know there must be such a principle (since we know we have a composite body and are not mere isolated monads), there is no knowledge of what it is (e.g. Loemker 539; Loemker 598). The problem is, of course, that a Cartesian could easily mimic this: she could say that we know a meter-rod has a principle of unity because, well, there it is in all its meter-long splendor. We just don't know what that principle is. If unknown principles of unity will do just fine for corporeal substances, why not for extended aggregates?

What do we, as commentators, do in light of this? [Some commentators march] off to pure Idealism. Since, as I have argued, that is not an option, I think we're stuck with candidly admitting that there is a gaping hole at the center of Leibniz's late-mature corporeal substance doctrine—and that this is a serious shortcoming. He bought, but could not pay for (in his own coin), *per se* unity for corporeal substances.

Now, prospects for meeting the demand for a principle of unity were better back in the good old days of the early and middle mature periods. Here the items to be unified were not collocations of monads, but what Dan Garber calls 'quasi-Aristotelian substances' (Garber 1985) . . . Such substances were indeed nearly dead-on Aristotelian—made from the metaphysical fusion of a substantial form and some primary matter. Here the matter, as in Aristotle, has no separate existence, and form is the principle of being as well as of unity. Thus unity could not emerge as a separate problem because the answer to 'Why is this one?' was the same as the answer to 'Why is this?'

But with the advent of monads in the late 1690s, being was sundered from unity. Leibniz took the Aristotelian prime matter of the 1680s and placed it into the monad as the principle of passivity. The Aristotelian substantial form became the 'primitive entelechy' (Loemker 530) that combined with primary matter to form a monad. Monads then were classified as either subordinate or dominant. But the dominant monads, unlike Aristotelian substantial forms, did not constitute corporeal substances or animals. They functioned, instead, as a metaphysical lasso, surrounding perfectly independent, 'world-apart', solipsistic subordinate monads and 'pulling them together' (in some non-spatial sense). Unlike the mere potentiality of the Aristotelian prime matter—which needed form's actuality to enter existence—the subordinate monads were already fully actual and quite capable of separate existence. So dominant monads were given a crushing burden—unify things that are necessarily independent. All Leibniz could hope for, to be consistent with his mind-body parallelism, was a harmony between subordinate and dominant monads. And that's all he got.

## B. Argument from Inconsistent Ontological Commitments

This argument raises the specter of a logical inconsistency in Leibniz's system. It concerns inconsistent ontological commitments in the following sense. (1) and (2) can't both be true:

1. Exclusive Idealism: In metaphysical rigor, there are only monads.
2. Idealism Plus Corporeal Substances: In metaphysical rigor, there are monads and corporeal substances.

Of the several passages that endorse (1), none is more widely cited than what I call the 'Idealist manifesto' (written in 1704 to De Volder—just one year after Leibniz sent him the five-part anatomy endorsing the reality and unity of corporeal substance): "considering the matter carefully, it may be said that there is nothing in the world except simple substances, and, in them, perception and appetite" (Loemker 537). Ample support for (2) has already been cited.

Most interesting (and frustrating) are the passages that mix (1) and (2). These make it clear that Leibniz wanted both of them. He seems almost unaware of their logical incompatibility—probably because, as Catherine Wilson has argued persuasively (Wilson 1989, 190–196), he was in love with two radically divergent pictures of the ultimate ground-floor metaphysic. A case in point is "Metaphysical Consequences of the Principle of Reason" (c. 1712) . . . where Exclusive Idealism is simply trotted out in the midst of one of later Leibniz's most explicit and adamant endorsements of corporeal ('composite') substance:

A substance is either simple, such as a soul, which has no parts, or it is composite, such as an animal, which consists of a soul and an organic body. But an organic body, like every other body, is merely an aggregate of animals or other things which are living and therefore organic, or finally of small objects or masses; but these also are finally resolved into living things, from which it is evident that what, in the analysis of substances, exist ultimately are simple substances—namely, souls, or, if you prefer a more general term, *monads*, which are without parts. For even though every simple substance has an organic body which corresponds to it—otherwise it would not have any kind of orderly relation to other things in the universe, nor would it act or be acted upon in an orderly way—yet by itself it is without parts. And because an organic body, or any other body whatsoever, can again be resolved into substances endowed with organic bodies, it is evident that *in the end there are simple substances alone,* and that in them are the sources of all things and of the modifications that come to things.

(MP 174–5; last italics mine)

The entire matter turns on what 'in the end' comes to. Does this mean that in the end there aren't corporeal substances because all there are are simple ones? Or does it mean that there still are corporeal substances—that they remain something over and above the separate simple substances? These are deep waters—we must determine whether Leibniz maintains the very same level of ontological commitment to wholes composed of individuals as he does to the individuals . . . Unfortunately, I have been unable to find anything in the corpus that helps sort this out.

(If he, like Scotus . . . recognized different kinds of *per se* unity, he might be able to establish a gradation of kinds of *per se* unity, with simple substances at the highest level, and corporeal substances a bit below. But all indications are that he used this phrase to mark out an absolute feature—one that was 'all or nothing'. Another approach would invoke the occasional reference Leibniz makes to something's having 'more reality' than another thing—as when an aggregate 'borrows' its reality from its genuinely real constituent substances (G II 261; cf. G I 196). This idea of degrees of reality would indeed give Leibniz a way of making a distinction between the kind of reality enjoyed by monads as against that possessed by corporeal substances. The fact that he never uses it for that purpose is instructive in itself.)

Perhaps contemporary commentators have tended towards Exclusive Idealism because there can be, in a broadly Quinean context, no indecision at this point. If someone says 'there are only monads', it's over. There simply can't be anything else, at that level. And this justifies turning a blind eye towards *unum per se* raised like a banner over corporeal substances! Forcing Leibniz to choose between (1) and (2) helps him clarify his Quinean ontological commitments. But the fact that Leibniz refused to choose—like the fact that he recognized degrees of reality—shows he wasn't as concerned about them as we tend to be.

[However, not all commentators who accept Exclusive Idealism can be] charged with inflicting Quinean strictures on Leibniz. [For instance, Don Rutherford] relies on the No Principle of Unity Argument to establish his charge of inconsistency:

in the strictest sense, there is no unitary organism, if this is understood as the composite of a soul-like monad and its associated corporeal mass. If

Leibniz accepts the theory of monads, he is committed to the rejection of organic creatures as animated bodies that possess the property of being an *unum per se*. At the deepest level, the unity of the organism resides in the soul alone.

(Rutherford 1995, 273)

On the other hand, Leibniz's 'panorganicist thesis' is not in the least antithetic to Exclusive Idealism:

for every monad representing itself as an embodied creature . . . there is a ground in reality for that appearance: monads whose perceptions represent them as the organic components of those bodies. In this account, there is clearly no inconsistency between Leibniz's monadic and panorganic models. They represent complementary ways of understanding the universe: one from the point of view of reality as it is in itself, a system of harmoniously related monads; the other from the point of view of the order determined by those monads' expression of themselves as embodied creatures naturally subordinated to one another. There is thus no problem with Leibniz's asserting . . . that reality consists solely of monads and their harmonious perceptions.

(Rutherford 1995, 230)

Panorganicism is compatible with Exclusive Idealism because, on this reading, the embodiment of a monad is simply its mentally representing itself as having a body.

## 3. Conclusion

I conclude that there is no viable way for commentators of later Leibniz to rescue him from the difficulties that corporeal substances create.

All conceivable alternatives have been tried and failed. (1) Leibniz himself insures that corporeal substances can't be likened to extended phenomena or aggregates or substantially bonded substances. (2) He keeps talking about them in important places way past 1703, and so ruins the dream of confining them to an earlier time period. (3) Denigrating all the post-1703 passages as light and fluffy metaphysics leads to textual absurdity. Finally (an alternative I did not discuss because it's very uncommon) . . . ignoring the Exclusive Idealist element and endorsing an 'Exclusive Corporeal Substance' metaphysic also leads to textual absurdity and a dramatic flattening out of the later system.

That leaves us in an uncomfortable spot. One commentator who has faced the discomfort head-on is Catherine Wilson. Despite the fact that she airs certain anti-corporeal-substance arguments, Wilson's later Leibniz is not forced into the mold of Exclusive Idealism by the artifice of explaining away corporeal-substance texts (Wilson 1989, 193–4). Instead, he is committed to two incompatible models: (1) world-apart monads, with purely phenomenal states caused by God, exist in isolation, and there is no common world of bodies; and (2) perception takes place in a common world inhabited by corporeal substances that are composed of dominant and subordinate monads.

She addresses the consistency point in a refreshingly candid way:

> The unspoken assumption [of many commentators] is something like this: the probability of a famous logician and mathematician having been guilty of serious, fundamental inconsistencies is low, while the probability of one of a teeming mass of commentators lacking some crucial bit of textual evidence, or the logical and linguistic skills to decode it, or the insight to realize its significance is high. I think this assumption is incorrect.
>
> (Wilson 1994, 6–7)

So do I. What draws us back to Leibniz is that he isn't easily held to anything, that he experiments with wild abandon, playing at the edge of inconsistency as he grasps for more explanatory richness. As Wilson says,

> What convinces a metaphysician that his system must somehow all fit together, that it is not a poor tattered patchwork of conflicting intuitions is . . . that he discovers motifs, images, patterns, analogies so overwhelming that he is convinced he has the key.
>
> (Wilson 1994, 7)

One of those motifs was Exclusive Idealism, another Idealism Plus Corporeal Substances. Leibniz never managed to choose between them, and neither will any successful interpretation . . .

## Notes

1. One fateful day in 1898–9, Bertrand Russell consulted Erdmann while preparing his Cambridge lectures on Leibniz. Saying that his theory "is substantially that of Erdmann" (Russell 1937, 145). Russell declared that there are "two inconsistent theories, both contained in Leibniz" (Russell 1937, 147) . . .
2. Editors' note: modus tollens is the argument form if p then q; but not q; therefore, not p.
3. Editors' note: this is the subject of Part XIII of this book.

## CHAPTER 10

# Idealism and Corporeal Substance in Leibniz's Metaphysics

BRANDON LOOK

## Introduction

Was Leibniz an idealist? That is, did he believe that the world is composed solely of minds and their ideas? Or did he also admit into his ontology 'corporeal substances,' *embodied* minds, animals, or organisms? These are vexed questions in Leibniz scholarship, and there are a number of interpretive options. One could maintain that Leibniz endorsed some version of idealism from his mid-twenties: his eclectic background of Aristotelian Scholasticism and Renaissance Platonism led to the main tenets of his mature, idealist system—pre-established harmony and simple, mind-like substances—in the mid-1670s (see e.g. Mercer 2001). One could find a change in Leibniz's metaphysics later in the 1670s as a result of his exposure to the philosophy of Descartes, Hobbes, and Spinoza and his rediscovery of substantial forms.[1] One could hold that in the 1670s and early 1690s Leibniz believes that the basic building blocks of the world are 'corporeal substances'—Aristotelian compounds of matter and form—and that only later, by the early 1700s, does he embrace idealism (see e.g. Garber 1985 and 2009). One could maintain that Leibniz is committed to animals, organisms, or corporeal substances as fundamental items in his ontology until the end of his life (see e.g. Loptson 1999, Loptson and Arthur 2006, Phemister 2005, and Smith 2011). Or one could argue that Leibniz endorses inconsistent metaphysical theses and that there is a fundamental tension in his philosophy (Wilson 1989).

In "Why Corporeal Substances Keep Popping Up in Leibniz's Later Philosophy," Glenn Hartz places himself in the last camp. He identifies a number of arguments against corporeal substances in Leibniz's metaphysics and finds problems with all of them. On his view, no serious interpretation of Leibniz can deny that corporeal substances should be admitted into Leibniz's fundamental ontology. Therefore, 'exclusive idealism' must be rejected. At the same time, Hartz believes that the commitment to corporeal substances in Leibniz's late metaphysics creates difficulties for Leibniz that he could not avoid.

I argue that Leibniz should be considered an idealist from his 'middle years' on and that talk of corporeal substances can be explained in terms of the true elements of Leibniz's ontology: monads or simple substances. Moreover, while Hartz may very well be correct about the tensions in Leibniz's metaphysics, I argue that these tensions might actually be reasons to adopt an idealist reading of Leibniz.

## Between Rhetoric and Reality

Leibniz is a very difficult philosopher to study not just because he is a subtle, learned and sophisticated thinker but also because he expresses himself differently depending on his audience. Leibniz speaks one way when talking to Cartesians, another way when speaking to Scholastics; he communicates differently when writing for popular or semi-popular journals, than he does when making notes to himself.[2] In fact, in a letter to Nicolas Remond that accompanied a copy of his *Principles of Nature and Grace*, Leibniz says as much:

> I hoped that this little paper would contribute to better making my meditations understood, by combining it with what I put in the journals of Leipzig, Paris, and Holland. In the journal of Leipzig, I adapted myself to the language of the School; in the others I adapted myself rather to the style of the Cartesians; and in this latest piece I try to express myself in a manner that can be understood by those who are not yet too well accustomed to the style of either.
>
> (G III 624)

Moreover, in a passage much quoted in the scholarly literature, Leibniz says, "he who knows me only from my published writings does not know me" (Dutens VI, 1, 65).

Bertrand Russell, however, saw something more than a mere tendency to alter the *expression* of his system; he saw a wholesale difference in philosophies expressed. And, on Russell's view, this amounts to a character flaw in Leibniz.[3] But we need not consider the matter so strictly. After all, isn't one of the first lessons in rhetoric 'know your audience'? Yet, Leibniz's flexibility in expression raises important questions for any student or interpreter of his thought: When do we take a particular text as an expression of his genuine philosophy? How do we reconcile seemingly inconsistent statements?

There is no doubt that some of Leibniz's best statements of his philosophy are to be found in his major correspondences—especially those with Arnauld, De Volder, Des Bosses, and Clarke. At times, however, even these writings contain apparent contradictions or show Leibniz wrestling with deep problems in his philosophy and working through various options. Given that Leibniz says things that appear contradictory, one can opt for Hartz's position and say that Leibniz is committed to inconsistent claims. Or one can try to determine Leibniz's position by using a number of fixed points in the constellation of his views. If one does this, then one should come to the conclusion that, strictly speaking, Leibniz is an idealist. In the end, however, there is no substitute for philosophical judgment.

## Unity and Being

Much of Leibniz's system can be seen to follow from a number of simple ideas.[4] For example, Leibniz famously said that there are two great principles of all our reasoning: the principle of contradiction and the principle of sufficient reason (*Monadology* 31–32: AG 217). Moreover, Leibniz adopted what for him was a completely uncontroversial account of truth, the '*in-esse* account,' according to which "the predicate or consequent is always in the subject or antecedent, and the nature of truth in general or the connection between the terms of a statement consists in this very thing, as Aristotle also observed" (AG 31). And this account of truth led Leibniz to the strong conclusion that substances have complete concepts that contain all that was, is, and will be true of that substance.[5] Further, it allowed Leibniz to hold that the grounds of the activity of substances are contained within them and that, therefore, substances are causally isolated. (In other words, while each substance acts as the cause of its future states, no substance ever causes the states of *another* substance.) Finally, and most important for the purposes of this chapter, a fundamental axiom of his metaphysics—again inspired by Aristotle and accepted throughout his career—is the reciprocity of unity and being. As Leibniz says in his correspondence with Arnauld, "I hold this identical proposition, differentiated only by the emphasis, to be an axiom, namely, *that what is not truly* one *being is not truly one* being *either*" (AG 86). The logical consequence of this axiom is this: $x$ is a substance if and only if $x$ possesses true unity.

Leibniz uses this conception of unity and being to argue against the then-modern, Cartesian account of matter or body. He claims that, if the essence of body is extension alone, then any body is infinitely divisible. If it is infinitely divisible, then it lacks a principle of unity. And if it lacks a principle of unity, then it cannot be an individual substance. On the other hand, if a body does have a principle of unity, then it can be a substance.

What can that principle of unity be, Leibniz asks, if it's not something material? His answer: it's formal. And, thus, in the correspondence with Arnauld, Leibniz claims that we should accept souls or substantial forms.

> A substantial unity requires a thoroughly indivisible and naturally indestructible being, since its notion includes everything that will happen to it, something which can be found neither in shape nor in motion . . . but which can be found in a soul or substantial form, on the model of what is called *me*. These are the only thoroughly real beings, as was recognized by the ancients, and above all, by Plato, who clearly showed that matter alone is not sufficient to form a substance.
>
> (AG 79)

Only Leibniz would take two Aristotelian principles and draw a Platonic conclusion! And what is that Platonic conclusion? That only a soul or substantial form is thoroughly real. Leibniz puts this more strongly in a later letter to Arnauld:

> I hold that philosophy cannot be better reestablished and reduced to something precise, than by recognizing only substances or complete beings endowed with a true unity, together with the different states that succeed one another; everything else is only phenomena, abstractions, or relations.
>
> (AG 89)

Thus, for Leibniz, a few logical and metaphysical commitments get him to a sharp ontological distinction: there are true unities or substances on the one hand, and phenomena, abstractions, or relations, on the other. While Leibniz is not always as clear as one might like in these 'middle years,' he does seem to think that a *man* or an *animal* counts as a paradigmatic individual substance. Such beings do possess true unity or are 'unities *per se.*' Thus, such beings are real. But 'inanimate' objects, such as tables, chairs, and the like, can at best be said to possess 'unity by aggregation.' They are, as Leibniz will put it, 'mere aggregates'; and, thus, they are relegated to the realm of the phenomenal. This opposition between the real and the phenomenal, a true unity and an aggregate, will prove central to much of Hartz's discussion of Leibniz's later metaphysics.

Two other metaphysical tenets and their corollaries are important for this discussion. First, according to Leibniz, just as there is a reciprocal relation between unity and being, so is there a reciprocal relation between what is active and what is a substance. To be active is to be a substance, and vice versa.[6] Second, substances express the universe from their own perspective. Indeed, "there are as many true substances as there are expressions of the whole universe" (AG 87). From these two positions, Leibniz further concludes that substances, as active, can be said to have *forces* (both active and passive) and that the activity and expressive capacity of substances are *representational.*[7] Through their expressive capacity, substances represent what is going on in the rest of the universe even though they have no causal contact with it.

In the 1680s and early 1690s Leibniz speaks to Cartesians about the union of soul and body through pre-established harmony, and to Scholastics about the unity granted to matter by the presence of a substantial form. The most fundamental elements of his metaphysics—the most real things—seem to be those individual substances that are embodied souls, composites of matter and form, or in short 'corporeal substances.' But by the mid-1690s there is, argu-ably, a change afoot. Consider this from *A New System of Nature*, Leibniz's first major philosophical publication:

> There are only *atoms of substance*, that is, real unities absolutely destitute of parts, which are the source of actions, the first absolute principles of the composition of things, and, as it were, the final elements in the anal-ysis of substantial things. We could call them *metaphysical points*: they have *something vital*, a kind of *perception*. . . Only metaphysical points or points of substance (constituted by forms or souls) are exact and real, and without them there would be nothing real, since without true unities there would be no multitude.
>
> (AG 142)

Here it should be clear that the fundamental beings of Leibniz's metaphysics are souls or forms, rather than composites of form and matter. And by the time of his correspondence with De Volder, the point is made even more clearly:

> [C]onsidering the matter carefully, we must say that there is nothing in things but simple substances, and in them, perception and appetition. Moreover, matter and motion are not substances or things as much as they are the phenomena of perceivers, the reality of which is situated in the harmony of the perceivers with themselves (at different times) and with other perceivers.
>
> (AG 181)

And similarly:

> I don't really eliminate body, but reduce it to what it is. For I show that corporeal mass, which is thought to have something over and above sim-ple substances, is not a substance, but a phenomenon resulting from sim-ple substances, which alone have unity and absolute reality.
>
> (AG 181)

It seems clear what Leibniz intends here: simple substances, monads or minds, are the ultimately real things; everything else is ontologically dependent upon them.

But what about 'corporeal substances'? This is Hartz's question. Even in Leibniz's later works, he seems to claim that they exist. Consider this famous passage from another letter to De Volder:

> I distinguish: (1) the primitive entelechy [i.e. roughly, substantial form] or soul; (2) the matter, namely, the primary matter or primitive passive power; (3) the monad made up of these two things; (4) the mass or secondary matter, or the organic machine in which innumerable subordinate monads come together; and (5) the animal, that is, the corporeal substance, which the dominating monad makes into one machine.
>
> (AG 177)

Now what exactly is a 'corporeal substance' in this new language of monads? It clearly cannot be simply an Aristotelian composite of matter and form because matter has now been reconceived as the result of innumerable monads that are subordinate to one dominant monad. Now, a corporeal substance is a composite of monads unified by a dominant monad.

We now have two questions to address. Do corporeal substances exist? Do corporeal substances possess genuine unity? The first question can be answered in two ways, by saying that corporeal substances are fundamental beings in Leibniz's ontology *or* by saying that whatever reality or being they possess is derivative of the simple substances. The second question is more difficult, and it is the cause of the tension that Hartz correctly sees in Leibniz's late metaphysics.

Ultimately, a strong case can be made that corporeal substances are *not* fundamental and that simple substances alone are the fundamental constituents in Leibniz's ontology. It can also be argued that Leibniz does not truly have the conceptual resources to explain how a dominant monad can unify its subordinate monads, unless that 'unity' is merely a matter of the pre-established harmony that *all* substances experience.

That simple substances alone are fundamental can be seen in the passages from the De Volder correspondence quoted above. Similarly, at the end of his career, Leibniz writes to Remond that "absolute reality rests only in the monads and their perceptions" (Loemker 659) and, in a text written for Remond but never sent, "I believe that the entire universe of creatures consists only in simple substances or monads and their collections" (G III 622). Of course, as Hartz points out, Leibniz also writes this to Remond: "a true substance (such as an animal) is composed of an immaterial soul and an organic body, and it is the composite of these two things that one calls *unum per se*" (G III 657). But Leibniz addresses the complications posed by corporeal substances most clearly in the following passage from an unpublished text probably composed in 1712 and now known as the "Metaphysical Consequences of the Principle of Reason":

> A substance is either simple, such as a soul, which has no parts, or it is composite, such as an animal, which consists of a soul and an organic body. But *an organic body, like every other body, is merely an aggregate* of animals or other things which are living and therefore organic, or finally of small objects or masses; but these also are finally resolved into living things, from which it is evident that all bodies are finally resolved into living things, and that what, in the analysis of substances, exist ultimately are simple substances—namely, souls, or, if you prefer a more general term, *monads,* which are without parts . . .And because *an organic body, or any other body whatsoever,* can again be resolved into substances endowed with organic bodies, it is evident that in the end there are simple substances alone, and that in them are the sources of all things and of the modifications that come to things.
>
> (Couturat 13–14; emphasis added)

Since the organic body of an animal is, in a certain sense, like any other body, it is 'resolvable' into or reducible to simple substances. Thus, it is not a genuine unity. And if it is not a genuine unity, then it cannot be counted among the fundamental existents of Leibniz's ontology.

Now, the claim that the bodies of organisms are *just like* 'inanimate' bodies might seem to beg the question. Surely this cannot be taken as a premise in an argument demonstrating that organisms have the same ontological status as aggregates. Rather, what Hartz and others are trying to show is that corporeal substances can have a unity that is qualitatively different from the merely phenomenal unity or unity by aggregation of tables and chairs. But the unity of corporeal substances would have to be grounded in the relations among monads in that composite, corporeal substance. And it is very difficult to understand what the relations of domination and subordination are and how they can guarantee that organisms are indeed true unities. After all, one of the central tenets of Leibniz's metaphysics is that all substances are causally isolated and exist in pre-established harmony with each other; and it becomes difficult to reconcile the causal isolation of substances on the one hand with the dominant monad's act of *unifying* the monads that make up its body.

Leibniz was very much aware of this problem. In a passage deleted from a draft of a 1706 letter to Bartholomew Des Bosses, Leibniz writes, "The union I find some difficulty explaining is that which joins the different simple substances or monads existing in our body with us, such that it makes one thing from them" (Leibniz-Des Bosses 22–23). Yet Leibniz does not resolve this difficulty in his correspondence with Des Bosses. Indeed, the most natural reading of the correspondence leads to the conclusion that, although Leibniz considered accepting corporeal substances, he ultimately rejects them in favor of idealism.[8]

## Reconsidering the 'Bad Arguments' Against Corporeal Substances

Hartz points to three 'bad arguments' against Leibniz's commitment to corporeal substances in his mature metaphysics. But these 'bad arguments' can be reformulated to have much more bite.

The first two are closely related, as are the supposed deficiencies in them. According to Hartz, advocates of an idealistic interpretation of Leibniz falsely apply the term 'phenomenon' or 'aggregate' to corporeal substances, whereas Leibniz never calls a corporeal substance either a 'phenomenon' or an 'aggregate.' Strictly speaking this is correct; but the point of the idealistic interpretation has not been blunted. If a *corporeal* substance is anything, it is composite of form and *matter*, soul and *body*, or dominant monad and *corporeal mass*. And to the extent that a corporeal substance, an animal, has a body one can speak of it as 'phenomenal'; and to the extent that it is a collection of monads it is an 'aggregate.' If we consider again the passage from the "Metaphysical Consequences of the Principle of Reason" quoted above, we see that Leibniz is explicit: "A substance is either simple, such as a soul, which has no parts, or it is composite, such as an animal, which consists of a soul and an organic body. But *an organic body, like every other body, is merely an aggregate*" (Couturat 13; emphasis added). Likewise, an organic body is a phenomenon. The crucial question is whether a corporeal substance is a *mere* phenomenon or a *mere* aggregate or whether a corporeal substance has more than merely phenomenal unity or is more than a mere being by aggregation. Again, this question can only be resolved by considering whether or not a dominant monad can truly be said to unify the subordinate monads in the animal. But, as we saw above, this is a point that Leibniz confesses that he has difficulty explaining.

Finally, Hartz claims that there is a 'Philosophical Argument' in favor of idealism and against corporeal substance. On his view, some commentators are moved by '*metaphysical*—perhaps even *aesthetic*—*tastes*' to deny a real commitment to bodies. Hartz has a point here. But it is more a methodological point than a metaphysical point. And, indeed, what is the difference between 'metaphysical taste' and philosophical judgment? The methodological point is this: should a commentator engaged in rational reconstruction not seek to attribute the best view to a philosopher—so long as it is consistent with all the textual evidence? The answer is clearly *yes*—which is why what is truly important is whether or not there are plausible 'idealistic' interpretations of Leibniz's references to corporeal substances. It should be clear that there are.

## Being and Being Fundamental

Consider the following questions: Do atoms exist? Do chairs exist? A pre-philosophical answer is certainly that, yes, atoms exist *and* chairs exist. But we would also not hesitate to assent to the claim that, strictly speaking, the building blocks of the universe are atoms and that chairs are ontologically dependent upon the atoms.[9] In fact, there is a compelling case to be made that, strictly speaking, there are only simples or atoms of substance.

This is not only Leibniz's point but also, in contemporary metaphysics, Peter van Inwagen's.[10] It should come as no surprise then to say that, *in some sense*, there are corporeal substances in Leibniz's metaphysics. Indeed, corporeal substances pop up in Leibniz's late metaphysics because Leibniz wishes to describe and explain the world that we experience, and that phenomenal world includes animals, corporeal substances, things that seem to be paradigmatic substances. But *in no sense* should corporeal substances be considered to be fundamental to his ontology unless Leibniz can give an adequate account of their true unity. It is for this reason that Hartz's distinction between 'exclusive idealism' on the one hand and 'idealism plus corporeal substances' is a distinction without a difference. Put differently, one could say that Hartz commits a category mistake in suggesting that *there are, in the same sense*, monads, *and* corporeal substances.[11]

The question of metaphysical fundamentality has returned to the attention of contemporary philosophers.[12] It is also, however, an important theme throughout Leibniz's writings, early, middle and late. In the late metaphysics, there can be no doubt that souls or minds—that is, monads—are metaphysically fundamental: they are the building blocks of the world; they alone are fully real; and all other things—even corporeal substances—depend for their being on the monads. This is what constitutes Leibnizian idealism.

## Notes

1. By 1679 or the early- to mid-1680s, Leibniz is committed to forms or minds as fundamental in his ontology. Although there are a number of differences between the authors on matters of detail, this general view can be seen in Adams 1994, Cover and Hawthorne 1999, Rutherford 1995 and 2008, and Sleigh 1990. Some version of this interpretation is what one might call the 'standard view' of Leibniz, and it is what will be defended here, as it is in Look 2010.

2. This is what led Russell to distinguish the 'exoteric' and the 'esoteric' views of Leibniz: the former "was optimistic, orthodox, fantastic, and shallow; the other, which has been slowly unearthed from his manuscripts by fairly recent editors, was profound, coherent, largely Spinozistic, and amazingly logical" (Russell 1945, 581).

3. So Russell: "Leibniz . . . was one of the supreme intellects of all time, but as a human being he was not admirable" (Russell 1945: 581). The reader may wish to consult the excellent biographies of Monk 1996 and 2000 and Antognazza 2008 and determine for herself which of the two was the more admirable human being.

4. This is what Russell argued in his classic study (1900/1937). While many have argued against this view, there is something right about it; or, at least, it is good way to *begin* to orient oneself with respect to Leibniz.

5. See, for example, how Leibniz continues in *First Truths* (AG 32) or states this explicitly in *Discourse on Metaphysics* 8 (AG 41).

6 .See, for example, *Discourse on Metaphysics* §8 (AG 40) or *On Nature Itself* (AG 160).

7. The other way to arrive at the essential representational character of simple substance is this: since substances must differ among themselves (by the principle of the identity of indiscernibles, which follows from Leibniz's notion of truth and his principle of sufficient reason), simple substances must differ in terms of their representations. This is the way that Kant reconstructs Leibniz's system in the *Critique of Pure Reason*. See the Appendix to the Transcendental Analytic, "On the amphiboly of the concepts of reflection," especially A 283–284/B 339–340.

8. See Look 1999 and the editors' introduction to Leibniz-Des Bosses.

9. Accept this way of speaking for the sake of argument. One could, of course, break the atoms down further to their constituent sub-atomic particles. Or one could conceive of the sub-atomic particles as packets of energy or centers of force—something that is more than a little Leibnizian.

10. See van Inwagen 1990—though Leibniz and Van Inwagen differ in many fundamental ways.

11. Compare this with Ryle's famous critique of Cartesian dualism. What do you say to the campus visitor who sees dormitories, classroom buildings, libraries and asks, "Yes, but where is the university?" Ryle's point is that a mistake to think that there are (a) dormitories, classroom buildings, libraries, *and* (b) a university, existing all on the same ontological level. See Ryle 1949.

12. See, for example, Schaffer 2009.

# PART VI

# The Role of Mechanism in Locke's *Essay*

# Editors' Introduction

In recent years Locke has often been described as a mechanist or mechanical philosopher. The mechanist ideal was of a certain way of explaining the workings of the material world. These explanations were to invoke only a small set of qualities of material things, such as shape, size, solidity, and motion. Thus the workings of much of the natural world would be explained in the same way as the workings of artificial things, such as clocks. A clock is a material thing with the ability to tell the time, but that ability is not a fundamental or irreducible quality of the clock. Rather it is explicable in terms of the internal mechanism of the clock, its parts, and their shapes, sizes, and motions. The mechanists' hope was that features of natural bodies, such as their colors and tastes, could also be explained in terms of the mechanical behavior of their small parts.

Locke was clearly attracted to this sort of view of the world, but there are puzzles about just what he believed in this realm. As Lisa Downing expresses the problem, Locke appears to be committed to three inconsistent views. He apparently believed that:

1. bodies fundamentally have only the mechanical qualities: shape, size, motion, and solidity;
2. bodies' qualities are all explained by their real essences, their fundamental features; and
3. not all of the features of bodies are explained by their shape, size, motion, and solidity.

145

Perhaps Locke was simply inconsistent in his beliefs. But perhaps he did not actually believe all three claims. In different ways, Downing and Edwin McCann both argue for this. McCann denies that Locke believes that all the qualities of bodies flow from their real essences. Instead, he argues, Locke thought that qualities are explained by real essences, plus certain laws that God has instituted, which explain the connection between various essences and the qualities they are associated with. Downing, in contrast, argues that Locke was not fully committed to the view that bodies fundamentally just have the mechanical qualities: shape, size, motion, and solidity. He thought this was an attractive account of the material world but not, ultimately, the correct one.

## A Note on References

References to Locke's *Essay concerning Human Understanding* are given using the abbreviation *Essay*, followed by the book, chapter, and section numbers. So '*Essay* III.vi.17' refers to Book III, chapter vi, section 17.

## Further Reading

- M.R. Ayers (1981). "Mechanism, Superaddition, and the Proof of God's Existence in Locke's *Essay*."
- Lisa Downing (1998). "The Status of Mechanism in Locke's *Essay*."
- Michael Jacovides (2002). "The Epistemology Under Locke's Corpuscularianism."
- Matthew Stuart (1998). "Locke on Superaddition and Mechanism."
- Margaret Dauler Wilson (1979). "Superadded Properties: The Limits of Mechanism in Locke."
- Margaret Dauler Wilson (1982). "Superadded Properties: A Reply to M. R. Ayers." These papers of Wilson's are reprinted in Wilson (1999, 196–214).

## CHAPTER 11

# Lockean Mechanism

### EDWIN McCANN

Locke subscribed to the Mechanical Philosophy, in Gassendi's and Boyle's version of it. On this view, all of the powers and qualities of bodies, and all the changes in these powers and qualities which result from the actions of these bodies one upon the other, issue entirely from the "two grand principles of bodies, matter and motion".[1] The main points of the view, more particularly, were these: (a) all bodies are made up of matter, and only of matter; (b) the essence of matter consists in the qualities of extension and solidity; (c) bodies large enough to be perceived are compounded out of physically indivisible bits of matter too small to be perceived (the so-called *minima naturalia*) and have no other constituents (in particular, no immaterial constituents); (d) in consequence of being extended and finite, each body has a determinate bulk or size and figure; and finally, (e) any change in the qualities of a body is the result of the alteration of the bulk, figure, relative situation and/or motion of the solid parts of the body, the latter alteration being due to the action upon that body, perhaps through a material medium, of the mechanical affections of the solid parts of some other body or bodies. A very strong case can be made for the ascription of these doctrines to Locke; I will not go into this here as Locke's commitment to mechanism is so widely acknowledged . . .

Margaret Wilson has recently argued that Locke is not a consistent mechanist; she maintains that other doctrines of his conflict with his Boylean 'official position', on which the qualities and powers of a body 'flow from' the real essence of that body (Wilson 1979). She instances his view that matter might have the power of thought superadded directly to it by God; his insistence that we cannot conceive there to be any connection between the primary qualities of (the constituent solid parts of) bodies and the sensations they cause in us, and hence between those primary qualities and the sensible secondary qualities of bodies; his pessimism about the prospects for an adequate account of the cohesion of bodies; and his concession that gravity cannot be understood as a mechanical phenomenon, that is, that gravitational attraction does not seem to involve the transfer of motion through impulse.

In this paper I will argue that Locke is in fact a consistent mechanist. He does hold all of the doctrines Wilson mentions, but these doctrines are not inconsistent with mechanism . . . when this is properly understood.

## 1.

I want first of all to identify more precisely the obstacle to a straightforward reading of Locke as a mechanist. This is important, as there are a number of issues here that can get tangled up together.

We should note first that the lacunae in the mechanist account of the world to which Wilson draws our attention are of quite different sorts. Locke's worry about cohesion, for example, is simply that there are objections to all the extant proposals for a mechanical resolution of the phenomenon; he does not suggest that cohesion is inherently non-mechanical, or that it cannot be explained mechanistically, but only that we do not now know how to do so. In this case, as well as in the more problematic case of gravity, Locke does not cite any particular reasons for thinking the phenomenon to be insusceptible of mechanical explanation.[2] In the case of the possibility that certain systems of matter may have the power of thought, the situation is different. Thought and matter as we conceive them are of such different natures that we cannot see how they could possibly be connected; we might put this by saying that thought, sensation, the power of moving the parts of one's body by willing, etc., seem to us to be inherently non-mechanical phenomena. This deep explanatory gap extends to the connections between the primary qualities of bodies and their secondary ones, in view of the fact that these connections depend on the connections between the primary qualities of bodies and the sensations these bodies cause in us. This last problem is especially troubling since, as Locke notes in the chapter on our ideas of substances, most of the powers and qualities we recognize in bodies are secondary qualities, or else powers defined in relation to the sensations they produce in us.

Although the recalcitrant phenomena resist mechanistic explanations for different reasons, Locke puts them in one basket in the following passage from *Essay* IV.iii.29:

> But the coherence and continuity of the parts of Matter; the production of Sensation in us of Colours and Sounds, *etc.* by impulse and motion; nay, the original Rules and Communication of Motion being such wherein

we can discover no natural connexion with any Ideas we have, we cannot but ascribe them to the arbitrary Will and good Pleasure of the Wise Architect.

The problem, at bottom, for those who wish to read Locke as a consistent mechanist lies in the ascription of the recalcitrant phenomena to God's arbitrary will and good pleasure. Bodies would have the powers and qualities in question not simply in virtue of their mechanical constitutions (what Locke calls their real essences), but instead they would have these powers and qualities in virtue of God's arbitrary action. Thus, Margaret Wilson, discussing the problem of primary/secondary quality connections, writes:

> . . . at first thought it might seem that Locke could consistently hold that a body's powers to produce ideas flow naturally from its real essence, while also maintaining that the ideas themselves are arbitrarily annexed to whatever motions of matter habitually cause them. But of course this is not really the case. For it follows from Locke's account that a body has its powers to produce ideas only *because of* the divine acts of annexation. Therefore, . . . we find conflict with the official position that there is in reality an *a priori* conceptual connection between a body's real essence and its secondary qualities.
>
> (Wilson 1979, 147)

We have to be careful how we take Wilson's claim. She might seem to be attributing a sort of occasionalism to Locke, in light of the emphasis on God's action and the consequent arbitrariness of the annexation. Wilson does not suggest, however, that Locke thinks that bodies or their powers and qualities have no causal efficacy; indeed, she suggests that Locke's view is that these powers and qualities do produce the effects in question, but are able to do so only by virtue of God's having ordained the requisite general laws connecting the primary qualities of bodies with these effects. But this means that there are no suitable explanatory connections between the mechanical affections of a body and its secondary qualities.

The connections that are lacking, on this reading, are connections in *rerum natura*, and not merely connections perceived or apprehended by us. It would be a short way with the problem to read the passages we have been discussing as having only an epistemological import. Then, Locke is saying only that we do not know the explanatory connections that are in fact there, connections apprehended by God and the angels. Ayers takes this approach, drawing attention for example to the fact that in the passage I have quoted from *Essay* IV.iii.29 Locke talks of the ideas *we* have, wherein *we can discover* no natural connexions, so that *we cannot but ascribe* them to the arbitrary determination of God's will. There are two reasons why we should resist the suggestion that Locke's point is merely an epistemological one. In the first place, on the face of it the appeal to God's will is more than an epistemological place-holder. If it were only this, it would have been much more appropriate for us to simply admit that while we suspect there are connections here, we do not know what they are or even what they are like; why appeal to God's will, if all we mean to mark is our ignorance of the connections? To ascribe the connections to God's arbitrary will and good pleasure must be to issue an hypothesis, however tentative and unsupported it may be, concerning the causal ancestry of the connections. Ayers himself notes that in some cases Locke's appeal to God's will is meant to carry ontological weight (Ayers 1981, 225–226); I do not see any clear basis for reading *Essay* IV.iii.29 and kindred passages in a different way. Second, and most important, Locke would seem to have no good reason to suppose that there are mechanistically intelligible connections here, of which we are simply ignorant. He does go on to say, in *Essay* IV.iii.29, that

> The Things that, as far as our Observation reaches, we constantly find to proceed regularly, we may conclude, do act by a Law set them; but yet by a Law, that, we know not: whereby, though Causes work steadily, and Effects constantly flow from them, yet their *Connexions* and *Dependencies* being not discoverable in our *Ideas,* we can have but an experimental Knowledge of them.

We conclude that there are law-like connections of some sort because of the regularities we observe in the powers and qualities of bodies. There is no license given here to suppose that these connections must be mechanistically explicable, however, and Locke's talk of a law *set them* certainly has in it the suggestion of divine action. It would sort better with Locke's general agnosticism about the ultimate explanation of the qualities and operations of bodies to see him as issuing the least specific hypothesis available as to the source of the connections, rather than dogmatically insisting that they derive from matter and motion in some as yet unknown manner.[3]

The problem for a mechanistic reading of Locke is therefore this: because of our inability to conceive a mechanistic explanation of such phenomena as the cohesion of bodies, their mutual gravitational attraction, their power to cause sensations in perceivers in a regular manner and thus their possession of secondary qualities and other powers defined in reference to sensation, we are forced to ascribe these phenomena to God's action as determined by his arbitrary will. Since this ascription is not merely an epistemological place-holder but is instead an hypothesis about the causal ancestry of the phenomena, it is inconsistent with the mechanist's claim that all the phenomena of bodies can be explained in terms of the bulk, figure, texture, and motion of their solid parts.

## 2.

At this point I want to consider what might be involved in God's superadding powers or qualities to bodies, for by doing so we shall see how we can square Locke's commitment to mechanism with his concession that God's action is required if bodies are to have the powers and qualities in question. When he first comes to speak, in *Essay* IV.iii.6, of the possibility that God might superadd the power of thought directly to matter, thus making matter capable of thinking, he puts this possibility in the following way:

> We have the *Ideas* of *Matter* and *Thinking*, but possibly shall never be able to know, whether any mere material Being thinks, or no; it being impossible for us, by the contemplation of our own *Ideas*, without revelation, to discover, whether Omnipotency has not given to some Systems of Matter fitly disposed, a power to perceive and think, or else joined and fixed to Matter so disposed, a thinking immaterial Substance . . .

His reason for thinking this is given as follows:

> For I see no contradiction in it, that the first eternal thinking Being should, if he pleased, give to certain Systems of created senseless matter, put together as he thinks fit, some degrees of sense, perception, and thought.

Looked at in the context of our present problem, certain phrases in these passages which might easily be overlooked or treated as throwaways take on importance. It is not simply matter, but certain systems of matter fitly disposed, or put together as God thinks fit, to which God is supposed to have superadded the power of thought. These phrases recur often in Locke's extended defense of his claim that God may endow matter with the power of thought against the objections of Stillingfleet, talking there of God's superaddition of thought to matter "ordered as he sees fit", or "so disposed as he thinks fit", and the like. Perhaps the most interesting passage along these lines is this one, in which Locke is answering Stillingfleet's charge that he will be unable to explain why we are capable of abstract thought, whereas brutes are not, if we and the brutes are, equally, merely material things:

> . . . if Omnipotency can give Thought to any solid Substance, it is not hard to conceive, that God may give that Faculty in an higher or lower Degree, as it pleases him, who knows what Disposition of the Subject is suited to such a particular way or degree of Thinking.
>
> (Locke 1823, 4.465)

These passages suggest a picture of superaddition on which God superadds a power or quality to body by somehow connecting that power or quality with a certain type or types of material constitution, i.e. with a certain disposition of parts.

There is an alternative interpretation of these passages, on which the connections between the primary-quality constitutions of bodies and the powers or qualities that are to be superadded are somehow already there, laid out in the nature of things.[4] God would then be seen as superadding powers or qualities to particular bodies by contriving them so that they satisfy the structural descriptions implicit in the antecedently existing connections. This interpretation, it seems to me, involves the attribution to Locke of an unreasonable commitment to the correctness and adequacy of the corpuscularian hypothesis; it sorts ill with those passages in which Locke agnostically stresses the tentativeness of his espousal of the hypothesis (see e.g. *Essay* IV.iii.11, IV.iii.16 and IV.xii.9–13). It also fails to fit with those central passages in which Locke insists that even if we knew the real essences of bodies we would be unable to tell what their consequent powers and qualities might be; for this we need to know the connections between primary and secondary qualities as well (see e.g. *Essay* IV.iii.12–13 and IV.vi.7). It is hard to see what this "other and more incurable part of our ignorance", over and above our ignorance of the real essences, would consist in, if the relevant connections were a matter of mechanical necessity laid out in the nature of things. For given access to the real essences of the bodies involved, what would stand in the way of our simply working out the powers and qualities that flow from the real essence, given that the connections themselves are a matter of mechanical necessity?

We do better to interpret these passages as implying that God actually forges the connections between types of material constitution and the superadded powers and qualities. Taking this route enables us to avoid the difficulties of the alternative interpretation, and further it chimes in well with those passages in which Locke stresses the arbitrariness of the connections and their dependence on God's will. We have already looked at *Essay* IV.iii.29, in which Locke talks of bodies acting according to a law set them; in the section just preceding that one, Locke has set up this claim by arguing that ordinary experience convinces us that thoughts (acts of will) can produce motion in bodies and that bodies can produce thoughts (sensations) in the mind, although we cannot conceive how this should be so:

> These, and the like, though they have a constant and regular connexion, in the ordinary course of Things: yet that connexion being not discoverable in the *Ideas* themselves, which appearing to have no necessary dependance one on another, we can attribute their connexion to nothing else, but the arbitrary Determination of that All-wise Agent, who has

made them to be, and to operate as they do, in a way wholly above our weak Understandings to conceive.

In *Essay* IV.iii.6, the passage on superaddition, Locke says something similar, and he also suggests that God superadds the power to produce sensations of a certain sort by annexing the sensations to motion of a certain kind:

. . . Body as far as we can conceive being able only to strike and affect body: and Motion, according to the utmost reach of our *Ideas*, being able to produce nothing but Motion, so that when we allow it to produce pleasure and pain, or the *Idea* of a Colour, or Sound, we are fain to quit our Reason, go beyond our *Ideas*, and attribute it wholly to the good Pleasure of our Maker. For since we must allow he has annexed Effects to Motion, which we can no way conceive Motion able to produce, what reason have we to conclude, that he could not order them as well to be produced in a Subject we cannot conceive capable of them [i.e. "in some Bodies themselves, after a certain manner modified and moved"], as well as in a Subject we cannot conceive the Motion of Matter can any way operate upon?

And finally, in *Essay* IV.vi.14 he says that to establish truths about substances that are universal and certain (and non-trifling), we would have to know

. . . what Changes the *primary Qualities* of one Body, do regularly produce in the *primary Qualities* of another, and how. Secondly, we must know what *primary Qualities* of any Body, produce certain Sensations or *Ideas* in us. This is in truth, no less than to know all the Effects of Matter, under its divers modifications of Bulk, Figure, Cohesion of Parts, Motion, and Rest.

And this, he goes on to say, we can know only by revelation.

All this points to the following as Locke's position: God superadds a power or quality to body by ordaining that a law holds connecting a certain type or types of material constitution (i.e. a certain arrangement of the mechanical affections or primary qualities of the constituent parts of bodies) with the power or quality. The law is arbitrary in that it is only one of a number of possible but mutually exclusive connections that might hold between types of constitution and resultant qualities, and that it is the one that does obtain is due only to the undetermined action of God. Nevertheless, the connection thus forged between the primary qualities of the body and the secondary qualities and other of its powers is a necessary connection, in Locke's sense, since God is thought of here as decreeing a *law* connecting the qualities. This will guarantee that every time a body has the appropriate inner constitution it will

have the associated powers and qualities, and it will make true many coun-
terfactuals of the form, 'if a body were to have such-and-such a constitution
it would have such-and-such a quality, and would do so-and-so in such-and-
such circumstances'.

In keeping with Locke's injunction not to limit God's omnipotence by our
narrow conceptions, and his insistence on our ignorance with regard to these
matters, we should take this picture of superaddition to be nothing more than
our best conjecture (or rather, the only even provisionally satisfying one we
can construct) as to how bodies might have powers and qualities which we
cannot see how to connect with their mechanical affections. Even so, the position we have arrived at for Locke is, I will argue in the next section of the paper,
compatible with mechanism and can even serve to bolster it . . .

## 3.

We have arrived at a consistent view for Locke, but is it mechanism? The outstanding reason for doubting that it is stems from the fact that God's action is
required for the appropriate connections to hold, and thus cannot be elimi-
nated from any complete explanation of 'all the phenomena of bodies'. . .

First of all, we should note that God's actions are required only to set the
general background for any particular causal interactions among bodies, and
thus for a particular body's having a certain set of causal powers; he does not
directly work any of the effects which proceed from the superadded powers or qualities, nor need he superadd the qualities to particular bodies on
a case-by-case basis. If we have to appeal to the actions of God only in such
a general way, we needn't see these actions as interventions in the natural
order; far from interfering with or supplementing the natural workings of
matter-in-motion, these actions establish (in part) what are these natural
workings.[5]

At this point we need to remind ourselves of the going alternatives to the
mechanical philosophy, as these presented themselves to Locke (and Boyle).[6]
First and foremost, and most familiar to us, there was the Aristotelian or
Scholastic view (in a number of variants). Roughly speaking, on this view
natural phenomena are explained by appealing to substantial forms and real
qualities as the causal agents in natural change; these causal agents, if not
explicitly immaterial, always operate in the light of final causality, hence non-
mechanically. Less well known to us, but of great concern to Boyle, was what
he called spagyritic chemistry and what we know as iatrochemistry, the 'philosophers by fire', among whom the most prominent were Paracelsus and,
closer to Locke's and Boyle's time, J. B. van Helmont. Their three basic principles (salt, sulfur, and mercury) were held to be essentially active forces, and
hence living or vital forces. Finally, and perhaps of more concern to Locke
than to Boyle, were the Cambridge Platonists. Henry More and Ralph Cud-

worth both argued for the need to recognize immaterial, animate causal agents
– 'plastic natures' or 'plastic principles' – which determine all natural change,
matter being essentially passive, Cudworth even argued for an *anima mundi* to
accomplish the aims with which God created the world.[7]

Although I have given only very sketchy descriptions of these competing
views, it can be seen that they are quite different. They have one thing in common, however, which sets them off from the mechanical philosophy: they all
assert the existence in bodies of non-mechanical (and usually immaterial)
causal agents which are ultimately responsible for some if not all of a body's
natural operations. Seen in this light, it is clear that the distinctive feature of
mechanism is its refusal to postulate any causal agents in bodies except for
the bulk, figure, texture, and motion of their solid parts. Locke's position, as
we have come to understand it, is thoroughly mechanistic. God ordains certain general laws and gives matter its initial disposition and motion; against
this general background or 'frame' of the world the mechanical affections of
bodies come to have certain causal powers which they otherwise would not
have had. But it is the mechanical affections which have these powers; it is the
mechanical affections of body which are the only causally efficacious agents in
any natural change.

Even if Locke is a mechanist in this sense, it might still be thought that his
views on scientific explanation are not consistent with the views we bave been
discussing. In the characterization of the problem given by Wilson (1979, 147),
she gives as Locke's (and presumably Boyle's) 'official position' that there is
an *a priori* conceptual connection between the real essence of a body and its
secondary qualities. She apparently bases this attribution on the strict analogy
she finds in Locke between explanation in natural philosophy and geometrical
demonstration. She says in her original paper that "Many passages show that
Locke conceives the relation of real essence to derivative properties as analogous to that between the definition of a geometrical figure and the properties deducible from the definition" (Wilson 1979, 143), and in her later paper
she glosses the problem she raises for a consistent mechanism in Locke in
this way:

> My claim, however, was just that Locke thought these qualities [second-
> ary qualities, and superadded qualities generally] cannot 'arise naturally'
> from Boylean primary qualities, in the sense that the former cannot be
> 'explained' (through something like geometrical demonstration) in terms
> of the latter.
>
> (Wilson 1982, 249)

Although there is no doubt that Locke did compare explanations in natural philosophy with geometrical demonstrations, it is important to see that
the similarity between them to which Locke points is limited to this, that in

each we have (or would have, if we could achieve the relevant explanations) non-experimental knowledge of the properties of the object in question. The knowledge we would have from explanations in natural philosophy, if we were in a position to give them, would thus be *a priori*; but this does not mean that the connections figuring in such explanations would be conceptual, or just like the ones involved in geometrical demonstrations.

Let us consider the passages which are supposed to show that Locke thinks of the relation between the real essence of a body and its derivative powers and qualities as analogous to that between the definition of a triangle (which, triangles being modes, is both its real and its nominal essence) and its derivative properties. Wilson cites four such passages, of which two are the ones most commonly cited as support for the attribution to Locke of a 'rationalist' or 'deductivist' conception of natural science. These are from *Essay* II.xxxi.6 and IV.iii.25 respectively:

> The complex *Ideas* we have of Substances, are, as it has been shown, certain Collections of simple *Ideas*, that have been observed or supposed constantly to exist together. But such a complex *Idea* cannot be the real Essence of any Substance; for then the Properties we discover in that Body, would depend on that complex *Idea*, and be deducible from it, and their necessary connexion with it be known; as all Properties of a Triangle depend on, and as far as they are discoverable, are deducible from the complex *Idea* of three Lines, including a Space.

> I doubt not but if we could discover the Figure, Size, Texture, and Motion of the minute Constituent parts of any two Bodies, we should know without Trial several of their Operations one upon the other, as we do now the Properties of a Square, or a Triangle.

The first of these passages is concerned not with the relation between the corpuscularian real essence of the body and its qualities, however, but instead with the relation of the nominal essence to those qualities. Locke is giving a *reductio* argument against the Scholastic doctrine of substantial forms, which he interprets as holding, in effect, that the real essence of a body is its nominal essence. If this were so, Locke is arguing, then we would have demonstrative knowledge of the properties of substances, just as we have of those of modes; but in fact we have no such knowledge. The reason for this, Locke goes on to say, is precisely that the real essence of a substance is not its nominal essence: "... it being nothing but Body, its real Essence, or internal Constitution, on which these Qualities depend, can be nothing but the Figure, Size, and Connexion of its solid Parts" (II.xxxi.6).

The other passage, from IV.iii.25, does not say that if we knew the real essences of bodies we could give demonstrations in natural philosophy strictly analogous to those we give in geometry; it only says that we could know "without trial" not all, but "several", of the operations of bodies, just as we know without trial or experiment the properties of triangles, in their case on the basis of geometrical demonstration . . .

Even given the high standards Locke set for explanation in natural philosophy, then, there is no inconsistency between his commitment to mechanism and his treatment of secondary qualities, or of superadded qualities in general. I think we have arrived at a picture of Locke as not only a consistent mechanist, but a sophisticated one as well. Or rather, a relatively sophisticated one. For this picture of Locke does not leave him looking so very modern. In this respect I am quite in agreement with Wilson (1979, 143–144 and 147, n.15) who remarks with disapproval the tendency among recent commentators to see Locke as basing his arguments on a scientific theory that is in essentials the correct one. This underestimates both the very large differences between Boylean corpuscularianism and modern day physics and physical chemistry and the nature and extent of the gaps in arguments for Locke's and Boyle's views based on the scientific adequacy or superiority of corpuscularianism. (I think that Locke rarely, if ever, argues from the scientific adequacy of corpuscularianism, even in the case of the distinction between primary and secondary qualities. But that is another story, to be reserved for another occasion.)

On the other hand, if this picture of Locke does not make him look very much at home in modern science, it does situate him squarely in the tradition of late seventeenth-century English natural philosophy, and particularly in the tradition of natural religion. Starting with the work of Walter Charleton, and particularly prominent in Boyle, and later, in Newton and his acolytes Samuel Clarke and Richard Bentley (both of whom were Boyle lecturers), there was a concerted effort to rid the mechanical philosophy of its taint of atheism, and even to show that the being and attributes of God could be established by rational arguments drawn from natural philosophy.[8] Central to these arguments was the need to call upon the providence and omnipotence of God in order to understand natural phenomena, and this of course is a feature of Locke's mechanism . . .

## Notes

1  Robert Boyle, *The Origin of Forms and Qualities* (1666) in Boyle (1772, III.16), Boyle (1979, 20).

2  On cohesion, see *Essay* II.xxiii.23–27 . . . Locke does not mention the problem of gravity in the *Essay*; the passages cited by Wilson and Ayers are . . . from *Some Thoughts concerning Education* (1693) and from the third of his replies to Stillingfleet (1699) . . .

3  I have in mind the agnosticism expressed in passages such as *Essay* IV.iii.11 and 16 and *Essay* IV.xii.10, as well as the more specific difficulties concerning cohesion, and so on, that are discussed in the chapter on ideas of substances (*Essay* II.xxiii).

4  I take Ayers' view to be something like this. See Ayers 1981, 213–215, 222–231, 244–246.
5  See Boyle's interesting discussion of the universal and particular notions of nature, in *A Free Inquiry into the Vulgarly Received Notion of Nature* (published probably in 1685 or 1686, but started in 1666 (Boyle 1772, V.177; Boyle 1979, 187–188).
6  For discussion of this background see Dijksterhuis (1961, 433ff), Boas (1952), Kuhn (1952), Heilbron (1979, 19–46); and for the best short introduction see Westfall (1971, esp. Chapters 2 and 4).
7  For plastic natures in Cudworth, see the selections from *The True Intellectual System of the Universe* in Patrides (1970, 288–325).
8  See Charleton (1654), a work based very much on Gassendi's *Syntagma*. For general discussions of these issues see Kargon (1966, esp. Chapters 8–9), Redwood (1976, Chapters 2 and 4), and Westfall (1966, Chapter 5, and esp. pp. 108–110).

CHAPTER 12

# Mechanism and Essentialism in Locke's Thought

## LISA DOWNING

In this chapter, I engage with Edwin McCann's interpretation of Locke, which in turn arbitrates an earlier critical dispute between Margaret Wilson and Michael Ayers. Thus, the map of interpretive positions could get complicated quickly. Let's begin with some points that I think all of us agree on: Locke was a participant in the science (better: natural philosophy) of his time.[1] This is in part just a matter of biographical fact: Locke's training as a physician and his interactions with Robert Boyle's circle are well known (see e.g. Woolhouse 2007). More important for our purposes, though, his epistemological and ontological views in the *Essay* show the influence of mechanist/corpuscularian natural philosophy.[2]

As McCann explains, Margaret Wilson's "Superadded Properties: The Limits of Mechanism in Locke" pointed out a tension that appears as one tries to articulate Locke's mechanism and its philosophical implications. On the one hand, Locke seems to accept Boylean corpuscularianism and to enshrine it in his account of what the primary qualities (the qualities they have in and of themselves) of bodies are and what the real essences (the physical constitutions which ground the observable qualities on the basis of which we classify them into kinds) of bodies are like. On the other hand, as Wilson stresses, Locke also seems to hold that some qualities (e.g. thought, gravity, cohesion) cannot be the natural consequences of the operations of Boylean corpuscles. This apparent acknowledgement of the explanatory gaps in corpuscularianism is often accompanied by the suggestion that we must chalk such qualities up to God, or, more specifically, regard them as having been 'superadded' by God. Wilson's interpretation has both negative and positive implications, as she sees it.

It does, of course, attribute to Locke an unresolved tension. However, it clears Locke of a naïve faith in the explanatory power of Boylean mechanism and, instead, attributes to him insight into its limitations (though this insight is not fully realized in his system).

McCann seeks to resolve this tension and to vindicate Locke as a consistent mechanist. He holds that once the nature of Locke's mechanism is properly understood, the apparent conflict between that mechanism and the admission of explanatory gaps can be dissolved.

I too think that Locke holds a consistent position, but not the one that McCann offers him. The best way to zero in on the difference between our two interpretations is to spell out the tension in Locke this way—Locke appears to be committed to an inconsistent triad:

1. Boylean corpuscularianism: Bodies possess only size, shape, solidity, motion/rest as intrinsic and irreducible qualities; they operate only by contact at impact.
2. Essentialism: All of bodies' qualities, powers, and behavior follow from their real essences (that is, their real and ultimate physical constitutions) plus spatial relations among bodies.[3]
3. Gappiness: Not all of bodies' qualities, powers, and behavior follow deductively from corpuscular real essences plus spatial relations.[4]

A quick way to characterize the difference between our interpretations is this: McCann denies that Locke holds (2), while I deny that he holds (1) and thus offer a different account of the role of corpuscularianism in Boyle's thought. We both affirm (3), though we understand its import quite differently, and have correspondingly different accounts of Locke's talk of superaddition. But this is a dry, if accurate, way of putting our differences. I proceed next to lay out the two interpretations, their motivations, and their challenges in more detail. Unsurprisingly, I will argue that the essentialist interpretation of Locke is more attractive than McCann's committed corpuscularian interpretation.[5]

## McCann: Committed Corpuscularianism and Bare Laws

McCann urges that we take Gappiness seriously:

The problem for a mechanistic reading of Locke is therefore this: because of our inability to conceive a mechanistic explanation of such phenomena as the cohesion of bodies, their mutual gravitational attraction, their power to cause sensation in perceivers in a regular manner and thus their possession of secondary qualities and other powers defined in reference to sensation, we are forced to ascribe these phenomena to God's action as determined by his arbitrary will. Since this ascription is not merely an epistemological place-holder but is instead an hypothesis about the causal ancestry of the phenomena, it is inconsistent with the mechanist's claim that all the phenomena of bodies can be explained in terms of the bulk, figure, texture and motion of their solid parts.

(see p. 150 above)

His solution is as follows: The phenomena of bodies are explicable, but not in terms of corpuscularian real essences alone. Rather, important and pervasive reference must be made to God's action. Specifically, "God actually forges the connections between types of material constitution and the superadded powers and qualities" (see p. 152 above). He "forges" these connections by ordaining laws:

> God superadds a power or quality to body by ordaining that a law holds connecting a certain type or types of material [corpuscularian] constitution . . . with the power or quality. The law is arbitrary in that it is only one of a number of possible but mutually exclusive connections . . . and that is the one that does obtain is due only to the undetermined action of God.
>
> (see p. 153 above)[6]

So, bodies have corpuscularian real essences, and their behavior flows from those real essences, but only *given* the laws arbitrarily decreed by God. This is to deny essentialism and to endorse gappiness, as I have defined them. McCann resists Wilson's suggestion, however, that some qualities are not a "natural consequence" of mechanist constitutions, since God's "actions establish (in part) what are these natural workings" of matter (see p. 154 above).

McCann's account has many virtues. It clears Locke of charges of inconsistency. It takes his use of corpuscularianism at face value as indicating commitment to the truth of that scientific theory, which seems a nicely straightforward reading. Its invocation of laws of nature sounds plausible and attractive to our ears. And it fits naturally with some places where Locke speaks of God's superadding qualities or abilities such as thought to bodies (e.g. *Essay* IV.iii.6).

However, the interpretation has vices (or challenges) as well. The most obvious motivation to look for an alternative is provided by the fact that there is solid textual evidence in favor of what I have labeled Locke's essentialism (as both Wilson and Ayers point out). That is, Locke indicates in many places that if we had knowledge of the real essences of bodies, we would be able to deduce their further qualities in a geometrical fashion. Perhaps the most striking passage is this one:

> The whole extent of our Knowledge, or Imagination, reaches not beyond our own *Ideas*, limited to our ways of Perception. Though yet it be not

to be doubted, that Spirits of a higher rank than those immersed in Flesh, may have as clear *Ideas* of the radical Constitution of Substances, as we have of a Triangle, and so perceive how all their Properties and Operations flow from thence: but the manner of how they come by that Knowledge, exceeds our Conceptions.

(*Essay* III.xi.23)

On McCann's interpretation, this just comes out false. For triangles, we know the real essence, according to Locke, as it coincides with the nominal essence (that is, the collection of qualities necessary and sufficient to count as a thing of that kind, namely, a triangle). When we do geometry, we deduce further properties from that real essence. Locke says that angels or the like could do this with corporeal things. But if McCann is right, they could not do these deductions just by consulting the real essences and drawing deductive conclusions; they would also have to know (through experience or some sort of testimony) God's contingent volitions.[7]

A second difficulty, with broad implications, is the importance that McCann's interpretation assigns to God's decreeing laws of nature. The textual evidence for this part of the interpretation is very weak. Locke almost never theorizes in terms of laws of nature in the *Essay*. McCann quotes what is really the only significant passage in which he does refer to such physical laws:

The Things that, as far as our Observation reaches, we constantly find to proceed regularly, we may conclude, do act by a Law set them; but yet by a Law, that we know not: whereby, though Causes work steadily, and Effects constantly flow from them, yet their *Connexions* and *Dependencies* being not discoverable in our *Ideas*, we can have but an experimental Knowledge of them.

(*Essay* IV.iii.29)

While the talk of a law being set to things seems to fit well with McCann's interpretation, the rest of the passage suggests that the law is just a way of summarizing what results from the flowing or following of effects from causes. There is no trace here of McCann's picture of God's "forging" a connection by arbitrarily decreeing a law. Another way to put this point is this: If God merely arbitrarily decreed a law, then our experimental acquaintance with the regularity would be all there is to know, at least as far as the created world goes. Locke, however, clearly holds that there are "connexions and dependencies" out there in the physical world that elude our grasp.

This, in turn, leads to one of the strongest points against McCann's interpretation: If McCann's bare laws account of superaddition were correct, then Locke ought to hold that there is no special problem of how matter could think, nor ought we to be perplexed by gravity. For the only difficulty in either case would be the usual one of comprehending the workings of an all-perfect being. But this is clearly not Locke's view:

> If it be asked, why they limit the omnipotency of God, in reference to the one rather than the other of these substances; all that can be said to it is, that they cannot conceive how the solid substance should ever be able to move itself. And as little, say I, are they able to conceive how a created unsolid substance should move itself; but there may be something in an immaterial substance, that you do not know. I grant it; and in a material one too: for example, gravitation of matter towards matter, and in the several proportions observable, inevitably shows, that there is something in matter that we do not understand . . . it must therefore be confessed, that there is something in solid, as well as unsolid substances, that we do not understand.
>
> (Locke 1823, IV.464)

Again, what Locke concludes here is not simply that God has done something, and we don't fully understand how he could do that, but rather that there is something about bodies themselves, material substances, that we do not understand.

Further, I would like to suggest that the role McCann assigns to laws of nature, while it fits with contemporary theorizing about laws, is in fact not truly in harmony with Locke's seventeenth century context.[8] McCann writes:

> . . . we should note that God's actions are required only to set the general background for any particular causal interactions among bodies, and thus for a particular body's having a certain set of causal powers; he does not directly work any of the effects which proceed from the superadded powers or qualities, nor need he superadd the qualities to particular bodies on a case-by-case basis.
>
> (see p. 154 above)

Suppose, then, that the sun now manages to exert a gravitational attraction on the earth, retaining it in its elliptical orbit, preventing it from leaving on the tangent. What caused that? Not the sun itself, on this account, whose mechanical nature is incapable of action at a distance. Not God, who does not directly work such effects. The law?[9]

Boyle himself raises concerns about breezily invoking laws of nature:

> . . . to speak properly, a law being but a notional rule of acting according to the declared will of a superior, it is plain that nothing but an intellectual being can be properly capable of receiving and acting by a law.
>
> (Boyle 1996, 24)

It is Leibniz's concerns that are most to the point here, however. In the preface to his *New Essays*, provoked by Locke's remarks about thinking matter in the correspondence with Stillingfleet, Leibniz indignantly defends essentialism as something understood by anyone competent in philosophy:

> . . . it must be borne in mind above all that the modifications which can occur to a single subject naturally and without miracles must arise from limitations and variations of a real genus, i.e. of a constant and absolute inherent nature. For that is how philosophers distinguish the modes of an absolute being from that being itself; just as we know that size, shape and motion are obviously limitations and variations of corporeal nature (for it is plain how a limited extension yields shapes, and that changes occurring in it are nothing but motion). Whenever we find some quality in a subject, we ought to believe that if we understood the nature of both the subject and the quality we would conceive how the quality could arise from it. So within the order of nature (miracles apart) it is not at God's arbitrary discretion to attach this or that quality haphazardly to substances. He will never give them any which are not natural to them, that is, which cannot arise from their nature as explicable modifications. So we may take it that matter will not naturally possess the attractive power referred to above, and that it will not of itself move in a curved path, because it is impossible to conceive how this could happen—that is, to explain it mechanically . . .
>
> (NE 65)

Leibniz holds that God could not effect attraction without either giving bodies natures that would ground such powers or bringing about the effect himself, directly. He thinks that Locke has confusedly denied this with his talk of super-added powers. If McCann's interpretation is correct, then Leibniz is right; that is, McCann's interpretation renders Locke vulnerable to Leibniz's criticism. I contend, by contrast, that Locke in fact disagrees with little in Leibniz's indignant lecture. Locke is an essentialist: He agrees that God could not effect attraction, or make matter think, without giving bodies natures that would ground such powers (or bringing about the particular results himself, directly). Now Leibniz holds further that God would not bring about such effects directly, for that is beneath his dignity; it would make him a bad watchmaker. Locke, I think, is agnostic about this issue—while he is not at all attracted to occasionalist accounts, he has no basis for ruling them out in principle. Leibniz holds, further, that because mechanism must be correct (this on the basis of its unique intelligibility, it seems), bodies could not have natures that would ground attraction or thought, so they do not attract or think. Leibniz thinks Locke also holds that mechanism must be correct; on my view this is where both he and McCann go wrong in their Locke interpretation.

And this leads to my last point against McCann's interpretation: Whereas Wilson's interpretation portrays Locke as forward-thinking and astute in being alive to the limitations of corpuscularian mechanism, McCann takes (1) as a fixed point and regards Locke as a committed mechanist. Chapter 11 contains some internal tension on this issue, however, as McCann explicitly cites the passages wherein "Locke agnostically stresses the tentativeness of his espousal of the hypothesis" (see p. 152 above). Despite this, McCann's interpretation makes Locke so sure of corpuscularianism that he is willing to bring in God to shore up its deficiencies! I suggest below that these agnostic passages in fact motivate a different interpretation.

### Downing: Corpuscularianism as Illustration, and Essentialist Superaddition

What motivates my alternative interpretation is, on the one hand, the view that some version of essentialism is central to Locke's metaphysical picture and, on the other, a desire to take seriously Locke's expressed agnosticism about the truth of corpuscularian mechanism. Let me start with the first motivation: If Locke endorses essentialism, but he sees that corpuscularianism is irremediably gappy, then he ought not to be a corpuscularian.[10] I think that in fact this is the right conclusion, and that it can be independently motivated, but we need to work up a subtle story here. The obvious difficulty for this interpretation is that Locke often sounds like Boyle when he discusses the primary qualities and real essences of corporeal things; that is, he sounds like a committed corpuscularian. I think that Locke, around the time of Draft C of the *Essay* (1685–6) and the first edition (1689), is tempted to suppose (with Leibniz) that intelligibility considerations allow us to conclude (albeit tentatively) that the corpuscularians have correctly characterized the nature of bodies. However, by the time of the correspondence with Stillingfleet and the fourth edition of the *Essay* (1700), he has repudiated this temptation. This fits with his official position in the *Essay*, which is that "which ever Hypothesis be clearest and truest" is not his "business to determine" (IV.iii.16). The evolution in Locke's thought looks like this: Locke always holds (as Boyle himself did) that corpuscularianism *might* not be the right account of the nature of bodies, although it is peculiarly natural and intelligible to us (McCann 1994, Downing 1998), and, further, that the core doctrines of the *Essay* are not supposed to depend on the truth of this physical theory. He holds, further, that the explanatory gaps in mechanism (namely, that it can't explain impulse, cohesion, or body-mind interaction) give us reason to back away from our natural commitment to it. Locke concludes from Newton's *Mathematical Principles of Natural Philosophy*, by the time of the correspondence with Stillingfleet, that corpuscularian mechanism *could not* be a correct and complete account of the nature of body:

The gravitation of matter towards matter, by ways inconceivable to me, is not only a demonstration that God can, if he pleases, put into bodies powers and ways of operation above what can be derived from our idea of body, or can be explained by what we know of matter, but also an unquestionable and every where visible instance, that he has done so.

(Locke 1823, IV.467–8)

This represents a correct moral to draw from Newton's success: that the workings of the natural world cannot be explained by attributing only size, shape, solidity, motion, and interaction at contact by impact to bodies.

But what then should we make of the prominent role that corpuscularian theory retains in the *Essay*? The answer is clear if we take our cue from Locke's discussion of real essences (*Essay* III.iii.15, III.iii.17). Locke's central notion of real essence is an abstract one: what makes a thing the thing that it is. Corpuscularianism represents one account, albeit our most intelligible account, of what the real essences of bodies might be like.[11] Now, the notions of primary quality and real essence are logically linked, for Locke (Downing 1998, 394). I suggest that Locke's core notion of primary quality is the correspondingly abstract, metaphysical one, that of intrinsic and irreducible quality (Downing 1998, Downing 2009). And the real role of corpuscularianism in the *Essay* is that of illustrating these metaphysical notions.[12]

This interpretation of Locke's view of primary qualities and real essences is thus not motivated merely as a way of explaining a denial of (1) in order to resolve the conflict among (1), (2), and (3). It is independently motivated as a way of responding to this challenge to a committed corpuscularian interpretation: Why should Locke simply assume that the intrinsic and irreducible qualities of bodies just are size, shape, solidity, and motion? What lies behind the challenge is the point that the core notions of real essence and primary quality are metaphysical, and we should take Locke at his word when he tells us that he regards corpuscularianism as one hypothesis about what fills these metaphysical roles.[13]

I take it that I have answered the most obvious objection to my proposed interpretation and, I hope, answered it in a way that reveals independent virtues of the interpretation—it in fact gets right Locke's subtle and evolving attitude towards corpuscularianism. But there are further questions/challenges to address.

As noted above, an obvious motivation for McCann's account is that it fits naturally with some of Locke's discussions of superaddition. On McCann's view, when Locke speaks of God's superadding powers to bodies, he simply means that God attaches powers to them by fiat. If Locke is an essentialist, however, he could not mean this, so what does he mean? One point to keep in mind is that Locke often brings in superaddition simply as a way of discussing our ignorance—when we cannot conceive how some effect obtains, we can do no better than refer it to God's action. That is to say that the epistemic reading of superaddition is sometimes the right reading: the only thing that all Locke's references to superaddition have in common is our incomprehension. However, Locke does sometimes seem to be sketching a metaphysical proposal about what God has done or could do (as McCann, Wilson, and Stuart rightly observe). In keeping with essentialism, I think Locke's idea is this: God gave (or could have given, in the case of thought) body a nature that goes beyond our (corpuscularian) conceptions of body/matter; that is, he gave body a real essence that is not captured in our nominal essence of body. (Here, the "super" in "superaddition" is relative to our conceptions, but not relative to the actual nature of body.)[14] Further, he may have configured the real essences of particular bodies in a way that allows them to manifest particular qualities that they wouldn't be capable of absent these particular configurations (Locke 1823, IV.460).[15] I call my reading of superaddition "essentialist superaddition," as opposed to McCann's "bare laws" view (Downing 2007).

One further concern follows upon this one: One might worry that there is a puzzle about Locke's treatment of thinking matter that McCann's "bare laws" view can answer, while essentialist superaddition cannot.[16] On the one hand, Locke famously (and notoriously, to his contemporaries) holds that for all we know, matter might think, that is, materialism might be true. He suggests that both materialism and dualism raise inconceivability problems for us, and we aren't in a position to definitively arbitrate between them. On the other hand, in the course of proving God's existence and immateriality, Locke seems to give arguments that purport to show that matter could not think (*Essay* IV.x.14–17). A bare laws reading of superaddition offers an easy resolution to this apparent contradiction: matter on its own, exercising its natural powers, is incapable of thought, but matter after the addition of divinely instituted laws *is* capable of thought.[17] Problem solved. Now, Locke's *Essay* IV.x proof of God's existence is a peculiar context, and there are interpretive questions about it that go beyond what can be addressed here. Nevertheless, I will present the core of an essentialist response to this problem: What Locke takes himself to have proved in *Essay* IV.10 is that Boylean corpuscles cannot think. That is, stuff whose nature is exhausted by size, shape, solidity, motion/rest (mere matter) cannot think. (And here, again, he agrees with Leibniz.) However, what that does not rule out is that stuff which *manifests* size, shape, solidity, and motion/rest can think. That is, stuff which satisfies the nominal essence of matter and thus *is* matter might (for all we know) think (Locke 1823, IV.460–1). This, after all, is what Locke undertakes to defend in the correspondence with Stillingfleet—that something solid, material, whose nature we do not fully understand, might think.

One might wonder, lastly, about how charitable it is to place essentialism at the heart of an interpretation of Locke. Wilson (1999, 205) raises the question (in effect) of whether essentialism would remain well motivated absent a commitment to a quasi-geometrical mechanist theory of matter. I think the answer is "yes," but it is a question worth reflecting on. One point is that Locke's real commitment is to a principle that is broader than essentialism, that is, the thesis that for everything that happens, there is a particular cause (or collection of such causes) that brings it about. If that cause is corporeal, then the effect must derive from the real essences (particular instantiations of intrinsic and irreducible qualities) and spatial arrangements of bodies, because such facts exhaust the basic facts about bodies. God could also be the cause, but if so, that would involve God's direct action on the world. One might still worry that this is too much metaphysics to attribute to an empiricist such as Locke. Locke holds that this is the metaphysics we derive from reflection on experience. He ought to hold that it is defeasible, his epistemic modesty demands this much, but he had no reason to regard it (unlike Boylean corpuscularianism) as defeated.

## Notes

1. Though Anstey's verdict that Locke was not a natural philosopher is reasonable (Anstey 2011, 1).
2. A note on terminology: For the purposes of this chapter, I will use "mechanism" and "corpuscularianism" interchangeably. Robert Boyle coined the term "corpuscularian" to cover both Cartesian and atomist versions of the new mechanical philosophy. "Mechanism" is a term that readily admits a variety of construals, both broad and narrow. Noting the influence of mechanism has become commonplace in Locke interpretation, thanks to the work of many other scholars, prominently including Maurice Mandelbaum (1964) and Peter Alexander (1985).
3. As will become apparent below, this needs a qualification: "absent intervention by God or other incorporeal substance." Also, it is crucial that "bodies" is in the plural here. A single body's powers and behavior will not follow simply from its real constitution because of what Ott (2009, 175) rightly highlights as the "multilateral reducibility" of powers. Both Boyle and Locke emphasize that the rest of the universe would have to be taken into account in order to determine all the powers of a body.
4. Wilson presents the conflict as being between (1) and (3), but that is presuming (2) in the background. That presumption is made explicit and is anchored to Locke's text at Wilson (1999, 197). The question of the relation between Locke's mechanism and his essentialism (in my terminology) is raised at Wilson (1999, 205).
5. In putting (2) at the center of my interpretation, I am in strong agreement with Michael Ayers. Confusingly, what I call "essentialism," Ayers calls "pure mechanism." See Ayers (1991, II.135, II.153, II.190) and Ayers (1981, 210). It is also closely related to what Ott (2009, 36) calls "course of nature mechanism."
6. Compare Matthew Stuart's (1998) "extrinsic powers" interpretation of superaddition.
7. McCann discusses this passage (see p. 150 above), but I find his reading unpersuasive. He also discusses *Essay* II.xxxi.6, IV.iii.25, and IV.vi.11. His remarks go some way towards explaining away these passages, but I think their collective weight in favor of essentialism is still substantial. Matthew Stuart (1996), who also denies that Locke endorses essentialism, attempts a reconstrual of the point of Locke's analogy with geometry, according to which it represents, roughly, a mere commitment to deductivism about explanation.
8. Here I agree with Walter Ott, who argues that accounts of law or power in the early modern period are either top-down (derived from God) or bottom-up (derived from bodies' natures), never freestanding (2009, chapter 1). Now, one might think that McCann's view

falls into the top-down category. But on Ott's view (with which I am in sympathy), the top-down view must ultimately be occasionalist, for if God simply creates the laws and does not carry them out, then he has created them as freestanding: "It is not enough simply to will conditional claims; one must also bring it about that their consequents come to pass when their antecedents are fulfilled. To suppose otherwise is to suppose, in Cudworth's mocking phrase, that the laws of nature could 'execute themselves'" (Ott 2009, 105).

9. Perhaps the answer is supposed to be that God rendered the sun (and all bodies) capable of causing such effects. The reply is that he could not do that without grounding the power in the way the bodies themselves are.

10. This is true even if he merely does not rule out the truth of essentialism, that is, if he does not reject Leibniz's view.

11. Although, again, Locke concludes in the end that Newton's results show that it could not be a complete and correct account.

12. See *Essay* IV.iii.16 where Locke writes that he has "instanced" the corpuscularian hypothesis. Of course, as indicated above, corpuscularianism is more than a *mere* illustration, in that it is uniquely intelligible/natural to us. One way of characterizing that naturalness is that corpuscularianism asserts that the real essence of body coincide with the nominal essence we assign to "body." Ayers 1981, 229 notes that "for Locke 'extended solid substance' gives a sort of nominal essence of matter rather than its real essence." See also Atherton (1984, 418.)

13. An alternative would be to suppose that Locke thinks that his grain of wheat example in *Essay* II.viii.9 (or relativity arguments) suffices to definitively establish the intrinsic and irreducible qualities of bodies. I find this uncharitable. What the grain of wheat argument does do is to show that reflection on sensory experience brings us to corpuscularianism; that is, it is a uniquely natural and intelligible hypothesis. Further, I think Locke holds that it would be reasonable to suppose that the hypothesis was correct if there were no problems with it, that is, if it could follow through on its promise of grounding explanations of all the phenomena.

14. This is a kind of epistemic reading, but different from the broad "just chalk this phenomenon up to God as a way of registering our ignorance" epistemic reading. It is to say that God has *made* bodies in a way that isn't captured by our conceptions.

15. McCann seems to prefigure part of this interpretation on p. 152, where he describes an alternative that understands superaddition as God's contriving particular bodies so that their constitutions can work appropriately. He suggests that this "involves the attribution to Locke of an unreasonable commitment to the correctness and adequacy of the corpuscularian hypothesis." On the contrary, it reflects Locke's conclusion that there is something in solid substances that we do not understand (Locke 1823, IV.464). "Contriving" must be understood abstractly, however (see Downing 2007, 373).

16. In fact, this seems to me the best argument for McCann's interpretation, which he makes use of in McCann (1994, 74), though not in the chapter in this volume. See Stuart 1998 for a nice development of the argument.

17. Again, I think this picture makes little sense to Locke: something must be carrying out any laws that there are: either bodies do so by their natures, or God does so directly.

PART **VII**
# Locke on Personal Identity

# Editors' Introduction

Many things change over time. Seeds become shoots and then saplings and finally fully-grown trees, all of which look very different from each other. If I planted a tree today that grew successfully for twenty years, in twenty years it would still be the tree that I planted. What explains it being the same tree? The tree's shape and size and external appearance cannot explain it being the same tree, as all those will have changed over twenty years. So where does the explanation lie?

In Book II, chapter xxvii of his *Essay Concerning Human Understanding*, Locke addresses these issues about identity and change. Two claims that Locke makes while explaining his views about these issues are particularly puzzling to our authors in this part.

One puzzle involves changes to an object. Consider a growing tree. After growing, there is more matter in the tree than there was before. So we appear to have the same tree, but not the same mass of matter. But what exactly does this mean? And, someone might ask, is the same thing there or not? Or can there be no definitive answer to that apparently simple question?

The second, and related, puzzle is about Locke's use of the word 'substance.' Usually in the *Essay* (at least outside II.xxvii) it appears that Locke counts people as substances, as individual things that exist over time and have features, rather than as properties or qualities or events or any of the other sorts of things there seem to be in the world. However, in *Essay* II.xxvii Locke seems to say that the presence of the same substance is neither necessary nor sufficient for the presence of the same person. If a person was a substance, this could not be the case. So what is going on?

William P. Alston and Jonathan Bennett argue that Locke uses 'substance' differently in *Essay* II.xxvii than he does elsewhere in the *Essay*. In that chapter the notion of substance involves a sort of basicness, and other things (trees, for instance, or even people) are thought of as composed of substances. Matthew Stuart argues, against Alston and Bennett, that we should not take Locke to use 'substance' in this ambiguous way. Rather, the puzzles about Locke's text can be resolved by seeing that Locke thought identity was relative. As Stuart himself puts it:

> On the view that identity is relative, (i) '*x* is the same as *y*' is always short-hand for '*x* is the same *F* as *y*,' and (ii) *x* can be the same *F* as *y* without being the same *G* as *y* even if *x* and *y* are both *G*s. Substituting 'person' for '*F*' and 'substance' for '*G*', we see that the relativist about identity can allow that *x* is the same person as *y* while denying that *x* is the same substance as *y*, even if *x* and *y* are both substances.
>
> (see pp. 187–188 below)

### Further Reading

- Vere Chappell (1989). "Locke and Relative Identity."
- Dan Kaufman (2007). "Locke on Individuation and the Corpuscular Basis of Kinds."
- Antonia LoLordo (2011). "Person, Substance, Mode and 'the Moral Man' in Locke's Philosophy."
- Ruth Mattern (1980). "Moral Science and the Concept of Persons in Locke."
- Kenneth Winkler (1991). "Locke on Personal Identity."

## CHAPTER 13

# Locke on People and Substances

## WILLIAM P. ALSTON AND JONATHAN BENNETT

## The Problem

In the famous chapter on identity in the *Essay* (II.xxvii), Locke notoriously denies that sameness of substance is either necessary or sufficient for sameness of person. In thus denying that the identity of a person is determined by "unity of substance," Locke denies that a person is a substance. If people were substances of some kind, then for me to be the same person through a stretch a time would just be for me to continue to be the same substance of that sort. And yet through most of the *Essay* the term 'substance' is used in a comprehensive contrast with 'mode' and 'relation': this is, roughly speaking, the trichotomy of thing, property, and relation. If Locke were thinking of substance in this way in the "Identity" chapter, he ought to find it obvious that people are substances, that people are squarely on the *substance* side of the great divide that has substances (things, beings) on one side of it, and modes and relations on the other. Indeed, he not only ought to find it obvious; he *does*. At the very outset of the treatment of personal identity he writes:

> [T]o find wherein *personal Identity* consists, we must consider what *Person* stands for; which, I think, is a thinking intelligent Being, that has reason and reflection, and can consider it self as it self, the same thinking thing in different times and places.
>
> (*Essay* II.xxvii.9)

Surely a *thinking intelligent being* belongs on the list of those items that have properties and stand in relations to things, rather than on the list of properties and relations. And since a person is the same item in different times and places, it passes another standard requirement for substancehood. Thinking of a person in this way, how can Locke suppose that one and the same person can "involve" different substances, and vice versa?

Here is a further compounding of the puzzle. In the section but one before the passage just quoted Locke is setting up that passage by enunciating the general methodological point that

> to conceive, and judge of it [identity] aright, we must consider what *Idea* the Word it is applied to stands for: It being one thing to be the same *Substance*, another the same *Man*, and a third the same *Person*, if *Person*, *Man*, and *Substance*, are three Names standing for three different *Ideas*; for such as is the *Idea* belonging to that Name, such must be the *Identity*.
> (*Essay* II.xxvii.7)

There can be no doubt, of course, that the general idea of *substance* is different from the general idea of *person*. Nevertheless if, as the above quoted passage from section 9 seems clearly to say, the idea of a person is the idea of a certain kind of substance, Locke is left with no possibility of holding that he is the same person as the one who went to Cleves with Sir Walter Vane in 1665 but not the same substance (of the appropriate kind) as Vane's travelling companion.

Thus the problem of this essay. Locke's handling of 'substance' and of 'person' seems clearly to imply that a person is a substance of a certain kind, and he often says as much, outright; this implies that to continue to be the same person is to continue to be the same substance; yet Locke flatly denies this. What is going on?

The problem arises in connection with other kinds of things also, not just with people. In the "Identity" chapter, Locke firmly declares that to have the same man or the same horse at one time as at an earlier time, one need not have the same substance: "Animal Identity is preserved in Identity of Life, and not of Substance" (*Essay* II.xxvii.12), he says, citing *man* (*Essay* II.xxvii.8) and *horse* (*Essay* II.xxvii.3) as examples. Yet only four chapters earlier *man* and *horse* are two of Locke's prime examples of substances (see *Essay* II.xxiii.3–4).

How can this be? Is Locke flatly contradicting himself, or can he be understood in such a way as to make all this consistent?

*Relative Identity*

This difficulty was first raised against Locke by Reid, and was reiterated by Shoemaker.[1] But in the voluminous secondary literature about the "Identity" chapter the matter seems to have been neglected except by those who take it as evidence that Locke accepted the relative identity thesis, according to which

1. the proper form of an identity statement is not '*x* is (the same as) *y*' but rather '*x* is the same *F* as *y*', and
2. *x* can be the same *F* as *y* without being the same *G* as *y* (even if *x* is a *G* and *y* is a *G*).

This doctrine would let Locke say that we are now listening to the same *person* but not to the same *thinking thing or substance* as we were listening to an hour ago, even though every person is a thinking thing or substance.

We will offer to explain this performance of Locke's quite differently. Our explanation will provide a key to the chapter as a whole, helping to exhibit its real unity and the integral connections that obtain—for better and for worse—among Locke's discussions of people, oaks, masses of matter, and atoms. The relative identity explanation does not have that virtue.

Even if we did not have that alternative explanation, we would hesitate to credit Locke with accepting the relative identity theory when he does not explicitly express it. Nothing in the "Identity" chapter comes close to having the form '*x* is the same *F* as *y* but is not the same *G* as *y*', let alone expressing the theory that would license such a statement.

The relative identity explanation has been most fully deployed by Noonan, who points out something else in the chapter that it could also explain (Noonan 1978). Regarding masses of matter, Locke is a mereological essentialist:[2]

> [While] two or more Atoms be joined together into the same Mass, . . . the Mass, consisting of the same Atoms, must be the same Mass, or the same Body, let the parts be never so differently jumbled; But if one of these Atoms be taken away, or a new one added, it is no longer the same Mass or the same Body.
>
> (*Essay* II.xxvii.3)

He goes on immediately to explain that he does not take the same line about organisms:

> In the state of living Creatures, their Identity depends not on a Mass of the same Particles; but on something else. For in them the variation of great parcels of Matter alters not the Identity.

So we have mereological essentialism for masses of matter—*which Locke also calls "bodies"*– but not for animals. Add to that Locke's subsequent statement that "An Animal is a living organized Body" (*Essay* II.xxvii.8) and there is a problem. If an animal is a body, and the same body cannot lose or gain any parts, it should follow that an animal cannot gain or lose any parts; but an animal can do just that, and this is a central theme in the "Identity" chapter. If Locke held the relative identity thesis, on the other hand, he would think it all right to say that animals are bodies and yet *x* may be the same animal as *y* without being the same body as *y*.

But there is another explanation, which is less drastic and closer to the text. It is that Locke uses 'living body' with a special sense of its own, in which *living bodies* don't conform to the mereological essentialism that Locke attributes to *bodies simpliciter*. This special sense is at work in the closing sentence of the very section we have been considering. Locke says there: "In these two cases of a Mass of Matter, and a living Body, *Identity* is not applied to the same thing" (*Essay* II.xxvii.3; see also II.xxvii.4, II.xxvii.8).

On a few occasions he apparently uses 'body' to mean "living body," for example when he speaks of "our bodies," when he asks "why the same individual Spirit may not be united to different Bodies" (*Essay* II.xxvii.6), and when he speaks of "the Body of an Animal" (*Essay* II.xxvii.5) and of a metabolizing machine as "one continued Body" (*Essay* II.xxvii.5). Even in this last case, he could have allowed himself to say 'living body', for he does speak of the particles that successively comprise the machine as involved in "one Common Life." If we are right about this part of Locke's thought, all these uses of 'body' are imperfect, but mildly and understandably so.

And there are fewer of them than one might expect. Sometimes when Locke explains 'animal' through "collection of matter" or through "body" (not "living body"), the topic seems to be, or is explicitly said to be, an animal at an instant. There is no problem there, for Locke can say that an animal is at each instant constituted by a mass of matter. (See *Essay* II.xxvii.4, II.xxvii.6, II.xxvii.8.)

When Locke says that an animal is a living body, this doesn't tell us much, because our only handle on 'living body' is through his extended account of animals. But how could he—how indeed can we—do better? The whole truth about an animal is a truth about particles or masses of matter, which are somehow more fundamental than animals; so it is natural to think that "An animal is . . ." can be helpfully completed in the language of particles or masses. But how? There seems to be no way, unless we bite the bullet and say with Grandy (1979) that an animal is a function from times to particles or masses of matter. Now consider this, the only remaining relevant occurrence of 'body' in the early sections of the "Identity" chapter:

> 'Tis not the *Idea* of a thinking rational Being alone, that makes the *Idea* of a *Man* in most Peoples sense; but of a Body so and so shaped joined to it; and if that be the *Idea* of a *Man*, the same successive Body not shifted all at once, must as well as the same immaterial Spirit go to the making of the same *Man*.
>
> (*Essay* II.xxvii.8)

We suggest that the awkward, ingenious phrase "the same successive body not shifted all at once" shows Locke straining with the difficulty to which we have referred. . . .

## Atoms and Masses

Locke's treatment of the diachronic identity of bodies goes in carefully controlled stages.

It starts with *atoms*. Locke can hardly be said to throw any light on atomic identity. He writes:

> Let us suppose an Atom, i.e., a continued body under one immutable Superficies, existing in a determined time and place: 'tis evident, that, considered in any instant of its Existence, it is, in that instant, the same with it self. For being, at that instant, what it is, and nothing else, it is the same, and so must continue, as long as its Existence is continued: for so long it will be the same, and no other.
>
> (*Essay* II.xxvii.3)

This tells us that an atom continues to be the same atom so long as *its* existence is continued. Undeniable, but hardly illuminating. For any $x$ whatever, $x$ continues to be the same $x$ so long as $x$ continues to exist. Apart from this truism (and the still idler truth that an atom is identical with itself at an instant), all the passage offers is the suggestion that atoms are marked out by their fixity of size and shape ("a continued body under one immutable Superficies"). As it stands, this is no use at all. Atom $x$ has a certain size and shape at $t_1$, and atom $y$ has that very same size and shape at $t_2$; but whether this is a case of one immutable superficies depends on whether $x$ is $y$, and thus cannot help us to determine whether $x$ is $y$.

If Locke means fixity of size and shape only to be necessary and not sufficient for atomic identity, that puts him in the clear; for then the "immutable superficies"-phrase is only part of his account—the part that says that if $x$ ever has a shape or size that $y$ at some time doesn't have, then $x$ is not the same atom as $y$. This, however, is a modest triumph unless Locke completes the story, presenting other necessary conditions for atomic identity that jointly constitute a sufficient condition. Well, perhaps he is trying to do that too. His phrase "a continued body," rather than meaning merely "a body that continues to exist," might mean something about *spatiotemporal continuity*. That, together with fixity of size and shape, could put Locke on the path towards a true theory of atomic identity. It would, however, be only a tiny first step, and we are not sure that Locke took even that step.

Rather than continue to squeeze this turnip, let's simply assume atomic identity, and see what Locke has to tell us about the identity of more complex entities.

Next he turns to *masses of matter*, which he takes to be aggregates of atoms. Locke deals with them simply: if $x$ is a mass of matter and $y$ is a mass of matter, then $x$ is $y$ just in case $x$ contains all and only the atoms that $y$ contains. A mass of matter can stand any amount of internal rearrangement, but not the slight-est turnover of material:

> Whilst they exist united together, the Mass, consisting of the same Atoms, must be the same Mass, or the same Body, let the parts be never so dif-ferently jumbled: But if one of these Atoms be taken away, or a new one added, it is no longer the same Mass, or the same Body.
>
> (*Essay* II.xxvii.3)

In passing, it may be noted that Locke stays away from two hard problems about sameness through time. By rooting his "Identity" chapter in atomism, Locke escapes having to wrestle with "same mass of matter" when atomism is not assumed, that is, when it is allowed that matter may be infinitely divisible. And he simply omits to discuss "same pebble" and "same island," for which exact sameness of constituent atoms is neither necessary nor sufficient.

## Oaks and Horses

The next topic is *organisms*. Locke notes that throughout the history of an oak tree (or any other organism) there is a continuous turnover of constitu-ent matter, which implies that we can have "the same tree" out in the garden although we do not have "the same matter." Locke says that this is because a tree is different from the mass of matter that makes it up at a given time, as follows:

> [I]n these two cases of a Mass of Matter, and a living Body, *Identity* is not applied to the same thing.
>
> We must therefore consider wherein an Oak differs from a Mass of Matter, and that seems to me to be in this; that the one is only the Cohe-sion of Particles of Matter any how united, the other such a disposition of them as constitutes the parts of an Oak; and such an Organization of those parts, as is fit to receive, and distribute nourishment, so as to continue, and frame the Wood, Bark, and Leaves *etc.* of an Oak, in which consists the vegetable Life.
>
> (*Essay* II.xxvii.3)

This is offered as a snapshot of an oak, an account of what makes a material system count, at a particular moment, as an oak. Locke evidently thinks that it entails the diachronic story that he wants to establish, that is, the truth about what distinguishes an alteration in an ongoing oak from the death of one oak and the birth of a new one. He is wrong about that, however. His snapshot account, however charitably interpreted, is consistent with a diachronic story that is absurdly wrong, being in one way too strong and in another too weak, namely: the oak that is $F$ at $t_1$ is the oak that is $G$ at $t_2$ just in case a single aggregate of atoms constitutes at $t_1$ the oak that is then $F$ and constitutes at $t_2$ the oak that is then $G$. Still, Locke's snapshot *suggests* the diachronic story that he does tell, which is excellent:

> That then being one Plant, which has such an Organization of Parts in one coherent Body, partaking of one Common Life, it continues to be the same Plant, as long as it partakes of the same Life, though that Life be communicated to new Particles of Matter vitally united to the living Plant, in a like continued Organization, conformable to that sort of Plants. For this Organization being at any one instant in any one Collection of *Matter*, is in that particular concrete distinguished from all other, and is that individual Life, which existing constantly from that moment both forwards and backwards in the same continuity of insensible succeeding Parts united to the living Body of the Plant, it has that Identity, which makes the same Plant, and all the parts of it, parts of the same Plant, during all the time that they exist united in that continued Organization, which is fit to convey that Common Life to all the Parts so united.
>
> (*Essay* II.xxvii.4)

This is extraordinarily good. It brings in the notion of continuity, and of turnover of constituent matter (that is, of constituent atoms), and unifies it all with help from the notion of an "individual life." Even though we can think of improvements on points of detail, the core of the truth is here.

Locke adds a little about animals, but the differences between oaks and horses don't matter for our purposes in this paper, or for his in the "Identity" chapter.[3] Later on in the chapter, he mentions the possibility that some people will reject his account of animal identity on the grounds that although it is right to focus on "Identity of Life" and not of constituent matter, what "makes the same Life in Brutes" is "one immaterial Spirit," one immaterial substance (*Essay* II.xxvii.12); so that a strictly physicalist account such as Locke's must be wrong or at least incomplete. He remarks that "the *Cartesians* at least will not admit [this], for fear of making Brutes thinking things too." Although Locke does not have that reason for denying that equine identity involves the identity of an immaterial substance, and although he offers no other reason, he proceeds as though he could safely ignore this possibility, and after this one mention no more is heard about it.

## Organisms and Material Substances

In Sections 4 and 5 of the chapter, where organisms are treated, the term 'substance' does not occur. However, when Locke says later that "animal Identity is preserved in Identity of Life, *and not of Substance*" (*Essay* II.xxvii.12, emphasis added), he clearly means to be referring back to these sections, and is equating identity of substance with identity of constituent matter or atoms. This is implied by the whole tenor of the discussion, and especially by a clause in which the phrase "material Substances" is closely allied with the phrase "particular Bodies" (*Essay* II.xxvii.12). Locke's thought is just that if we leave immaterial substances out of the picture, the question "Same person, same substance?" can only be interpreted as asking "Same person, same mass of matter (that is, same aggregate of atoms)?" to which the answer is obviously "No."

A full deployment of this negative answer would take us through the twists and turns of Locke's relatings of 'same person' to 'same man', but our purposes don't require us to enter that labyrinth. It is enough to grasp that the first part of Locke's answer to "Same person, same substance?" relies on earlier discussions, and can coherently do so only if he is here equating "substance" with "atom" or "aggregate of atoms."

## People and Immaterial Substances

The second half of Locke's answer to "Same person, same substance?" is based on the assumption that the substances that are in question are immaterial substances, and thus are not atoms or aggregates of them. Locke no longer has his treatment of oaks and horses as a basis for answering "No," but he warns the reader not to assume too hastily that the right answer is "Yes." The mere hypothesis that people involve immaterial substances doesn't imply that each person involves just one substance, Locke says, for it is consistent with a person's relating to his constituent immaterial substances as a horse or an oak does to its atoms, constantly ingesting and excreting them.

Locke says that nothing we know rules out the possibility that each person involves a succession of substances, as each animal involves a succession of masses of matter:

> As to the . . . Question, whether if the same thinking Substance . . . be changed, it can be the same Person. . . . I answer, that cannot be resolv'd, but by those, who know what kind of Substances they are, that do think; and whether the consciousness of past Actions can be transferr'd from one thinking Substance to another.
>
> (*Essay* II.xxvii.13)

He is depending here on his positive view about the diachronic identity of people, according to which: *If* x *and* y *are differently dated total temporary personal states, then they are states of a single person if and only if one of them includes states of "consciousness of" items belonging to the other.*[4] Locke offers two kinds of argument for this. One is the inference of a conclusion about the diachronic identity of people from a snapshot account of a person at a moment (*Essay* II.xxvii.9). This is not rigorously valid, any more than the corresponding inference for the oak is valid, and Locke probably knows that it is not—in sec. 26 he seems to connect the two more loosely.

The other is an appeal to thought experiments. We are invited to contemplate a range of actual and possible cases and to agree with Locke that our intuitive judgments on them seem to be guided by the principle "One person, one consciousness." The spirit of these thought experiments is well expressed in this passage from the first chapter of Book II: "If we take wholly away all Consciousness of our Actions and Sensations, especially Pleasure and Pain, and the concernment that accompanies it, it will be hard to know wherein to place personal Identity" (*Essay* II.i.11). There is an enormous amount to be said about the positive theory, none of it relevant to this paper.

Locke has his thesis (1) "Same person, same consciousness" firmly in hand, though not soundly argued for, when he addresses the question (2) "Same person, same substance?" which he therefore equates with (3) "Same consciousness, same substance?" He sees the truth of (1) as a matter of conceptual analysis, as discoverable by attending properly to our ideas. (He does not imply that our general idea of identity needs scrutiny: the problem about personal identity, he rightly thinks, is chiefly a problem about *person*. "To find wherein *personal Identity* consists, we must consider what *Person* stands for" (*Essay* II.xxvii.9; see also II.xxvii.15).) But just because that analysis palpably does not bring in the concept "same substance," he holds that what the right answer is to (2) or (3) is a sheer matter of fact.

What kind of matter of fact? What is at issue here, and how might the issue be resolved? That depends on what Locke's notion of immaterial substance is. We shall describe it first in general terms and then in application to his treatment of (3) "Same consciousness, same substance?"

## How "Substance" is used in the "Identity" Chapter

If Locke's "Identity" chapter is to have a decent degree of unity, we need a uniform understanding of 'substance' all through it. For a start, then, how does Locke come to equate *material substance* with *atom*? We need to know that, if we are to have an understanding of the unqualified 'substance' that will carry over into 'thinking substance'.

In fact, Locke does not explicitly say that all and only atoms are material substances. His discussion of oaks and horses implies, at most, that material substances are *at least as basic* as atoms; nothing in the argument rules out the possibility that each atom relates to a sequence of material substances as each oak relates to a sequence of atoms. Locke's main point is that oaks themselves are not substances, because there are items of a *more* basic kind—items that are *nearer* to being substances—many of which flow through a single oak; and from this it follows also that many material substances flow through a single oak, whether those substances are atoms or something more fundamental out of which atoms are, so to speak, constructed. But Locke's discussion of atoms themselves strongly suggests that he thinks of them as basic; what he says about the integrity of their boundaries may be intended to imply that they don't have any turnover of constituent matter; so we have little hesitation in speaking of his equation of atoms with material substances.

Our thesis is not that Locke uses 'material substance' to mean *atom*. We hold rather that he uses it in this chapter to mean *thing-like[5] item that is quantified over at a basic level in one's ontology of the material world*. Using the term 'substance' in that way, he argues that oaks are not substances, and that their relationship to atoms suffices to show this.

From that account of what Locke means by 'material substance' in the "Identity" chapter, it is easy to extract a meaning for 'substance', namely: *thing-like item that is quantified over at a basic level of one's ontology*. And then 'thinking substance' means *thing-like item that is quantified over at a basic level in one's ontology of the mental world*, so that a thinking substance is a *basic* subject of thoughts, sensations, and the rest. And 'immaterial substance' will mean, of course, *thing-like non-material item that is quantified over at a basic level of one's ontology* (presumably, one's ontology of the mental world).

The term 'basic' needs to be explained, especially since it is our term for a notion we find Locke employing in this chapter. Locke may not have worked out in hard detail the notion of basicness that (according to us) is at work here. His actual use of the notion in this chapter—that is, his operative constraint on his application of 'substance' in this chapter—requires only that a basic thing does not have parts that it loses or gains, as masses of matter and oaks do, or even parts that it could conceivably lose or gain. And since the notion of having a part that one could not conceivably lose or gain is incoherent, that means that a basic substance has no parts at all. But he probably derived this from a deeper and more abstract constraint on 'substance', requiring substances to be self-sufficient, independent in their existence, or the like. For if a thing has parts it is, in a sense, dependent on them; since it *could* lose the ones it now has, it is, so to say, at their mercy so far as retaining its integrity is concerned. Thus no composite being is totally self-sufficient. If this is what is behind Locke's criteria for basicness in this chapter, it places him in a long intellectual tradition. Think for example of Aquinas's view that God, being absolutely self-sufficient, must be absolutely simple, and Leibniz's view that no substance could have parts.

If you prefer not to think of 'substance' as bearing different meanings in Locke, all the above explications can just as well be put in terms of how Locke was thinking about substance in these passages, or of what kinds of substances he was focusing on. Thus what we have expressed as an account of what 'substance' means in these passages could be reformulated as a statement about what substances Locke is addressing himself to: "In these passages when Locke speaks of substance he is restricting himself to thing-like items that are quantified over at a basic level in his ontology."

So far as we know, it is only in this one chapter that the term 'substance' carries this special emphasis on basicness, non-compositeness, or the like. Throughout the rest of the *Essay*, substances are just *things*, and include oaks and horses and people.

Because of the way he uses the term in the "Identity" chapter, Locke there understands the question "Same person, same substance?" to be the question "When you have one enduring person, do you have one enduring thing of a basic kind?" His discussion offers a coherent answer to this question, but not to either "When you have one enduring person, do you have one enduring substratum?" or "When you have one enduring person, do you have one enduring thing?"

That completes our resolution of the puzzle with which we began. In the widest understanding of substance—that which has properties and stands in relations, in contrast to the properties that are had and the relations that bind—Locke does take people to be substances. But where 'substance' is restricted to the most basic thing-like entities out of which all others are in some sense composed or constructed, neither people nor oaks are substances, but are rather composed of, or derived from, substances, in such a way that one and the same oak (person) may be composed of, or otherwise derived from, many different substances. A person is a substance, where that term is taken in its widest usage; but it is a substance in such wise that one and the same person may "involve" any number of fundamental substances, whether the latter be material or immaterial. Hence the identity of a person does not necessarily carry with it the identity of a single basic substance of the sort of which people are composed . . .

## Notes

1. Reid (1969, 356); Shoemaker (1963, 45ff).
2. Editors' note: mereological essentialism is the view that objects (or objects of a certain type) have all their parts essentially, so that an object cannot survive the loss of even the smallest part.
3. Locke adds that "machines" are like organisms in how they are re-identified across time; that is why we charged him with neglecting "same pebble" and "same island," but not "same clock." Incidentally, if shoes and ships are "machines" in Locke's sense, his discussion covers shoes and ships and sealing wax, cabbages and kings; otherwise it doesn't.
4. We borrow "total temporal state" from Grice (1941).
5. The qualification is needed because Locke might well have been prepared to allow non-substances to figure in his basic ontology, for example, ideas. The point is that material substances are the items in the category of substance over which he is prepared to quantify in his basic ontology of the material world.

## CHAPTER 14

# Revisiting People and Substances

MATTHEW STUART

## I

William Alston and Jonathan Bennett's chapter "Locke on People and Sub-stances," is a gem. They raise a puzzle that takes us right to the heart of Locke's metaphysics, offer an ingenious and original solution to it, and they do it all in sparklingly clear philosophical prose. The puzzle is that on Locke's ontology people seem to count as substances, and yet in the chapter on identity (*Essay* II.xxvii) he denies that the persistence of a person is the same thing as the per-sistence of a substance. If a person *is* a substance of a certain kind, then how can the persistence of a person be anything but the persistence of a certain kind of substance? One might dismiss this as yet another example of Locke's sup-posed failure to engage seriously with metaphysical issues, but Alston and Ben-nett do better. They offer a solution that accommodates the Lockean claims that seem to give rise to it, and that locates his theory of substance in a vener-able philosophical tradition.

Though I find much to admire in Alston and Bennett's chapter, I am not in the end convinced by their reading. They claim that in one chapter Locke uses a key term ('substance') differently than he uses it everywhere else, though he makes no mention of doing so. We should be reluctant to say such a thing about any philosopher unless the other interpretive options are even more unpalatable. In this chapter, I try to develop a line of interpretation that seems to me more attractive, and to defend it against some of Alston and Bennett's criticisms. I begin, in section II, by explaining their solution. In section III, I argue that they are too hasty in dismissing the reading of Locke as a relativist about identity. However, as I show in section IV, we do not solve the puzzle about people and substances merely by saying that Locke takes identity to be relative. We must also show how to make sense of his claims that something is or is not the same substance as an earlier one. In section V, I explore two ways this might go. On one, he uses 'substance' as what I call a quasi-sortal; on the other, he uses it as a dummy sortal.

## II

As Alston and Bennett are quick to point out, the puzzle they raise is not just a difficulty about the metaphysical status of people (see p. 176 above). The same difficulty can be raised about the status of other complex things, including plants, animals, and machines. Each tree or horse would seem to count as a substance for Locke, and yet he says that the persistence of an organism is a matter of "Identity of Life, and not of Substance" (*Essay* II.xxvii.12).

The key to Alston and Bennett's solution is their claim that Locke uses 'substance' differently inside II.xxvii than he does outside that chapter. Outside II.xxvii, a substance is any thing-like item, which is to say anything that is not a property or a relation. Inside the identity chapter, according to Alston and Bennett, Locke operates with a narrower conception of substance, one on which a substance is any "*thing-like item that is quantified over at a basic level of one's ontology*" (see p. 184 above). They say that the items that Locke counts as basic are only those that cannot gain and lose parts (see p. 184 above). They suggest that he may count these as basic because he sees them as enjoying a self-sufficiency not possessed by items whose persistence depends on the union of, or the orderly exchange of, their parts. Alston and Bennett claim that only atoms—or things more basic than atoms—will be basic in this sense, but in fact Lockean masses will qualify as well. Locke takes any change in the material constitution of a coherent group of atoms to be the end of one mass and the beginning of another, so no mass can possibly gain or lose parts.

Alston and Bennett solve the puzzle about people and substances by saying that Locke takes people, organisms, and machines to be substances in the broad sense, but not in the narrower sense (see p. 185 above). As they read him, he holds that the persistence of a person does not entail the persistence of a substance because he holds that a single persisting person, organism, or machine may 'involve' more than one basic substance at a time, or over time.

## III

Before offering their solution to the puzzle about people and substances, Alston and Bennett consider and reject the possibility that Locke is a relativist about identity. On the view that identity is relative, (i) '$x$ is the same as $y$' is always shorthand for '$x$ is the same $F$ as $y$,' and (ii) $x$ can be the same $F$ as $y$ without being the same $G$ as $y$ even if $x$ and $y$ are both $G$s. Substituting 'person' for '$F$' and 'substance' for '$G$,' we see that the relativist about identity can allow that $x$ is the same person as $y$ while denying that $x$ is the same substance as $y$, even if $x$ and $y$ are both substances. Alston and Bennett offer two reasons for resisting this interpretation of Locke (see p. 177 above). First, they say that it does a poorer job than theirs of explaining the unity of *Essay* II.xxvii and the connections among Locke's discussions of people, organisms, masses, and atoms. Second, they contend that there is inadequate textual support for taking Locke to be a relativist about identity. They say that nothing in the identity chapter comes close to having the form '$x$ is the same $F$ as $y$ but not the same $G$ as $y$,' and that he does not articulate a theory licensing claims of that form. These arguments strike me as indecisive.

It is true that if we look for explicit pronouncements that identity is relative, or that some $x$ is the same $F$ as some $y$ without being the same $G$ as that $y$, we are largely disappointed. On the other hand, there *is* the very passage they cite as giving rise to the puzzle. Locke says:

> 'Tis not therefore Unity of Substance that comprehends all sorts of *Identity*, or will determine it in every Case: But to conceive, and judge of it aright, we must consider what *Idea* the Word it is applied to stands for: It being one thing to be the same *Substance*, and another the same *Man*, and a third the same *Person*, if *Person, Man*, and *Substance*, are three Names standing for three different *Ideas*; for such as is the *Idea* belonging to that Name, such must be the *Identity*. . .
>
> (*Essay* II.xxvii.7)

One might, like Alston and Bennett, read this as implying that a man is not a substance. Or one might take Locke to be suggesting that something that is both a man and a substance can be the same man as some $y$ without being the same substance as that $y$. His observation at the end of this passage (". . . such as is the *Idea*. . . such must be the *Identity*") might be understood as telling us that judgments of identity are relative to sortal ideas.

One reason for thinking that Locke is a relativist about identity is that otherwise it looks as though he must countenance the co-location of distinct material bodies, something that he seems to explicitly reject. As we have noted, Lockean masses cannot survive changes in material composition. So if identity is absolute and organisms are persisting things that outlast the masses that compose them, then organisms must be distinct from those masses. Although some philosophers countenance distinct, co-located bodies, Locke seems not to. He says that we

> have the *Ideas* but of three sorts of Substances; 1. God. 2. Finite Intelligences. 3. *Bodies* . . . though these three sorts of Substances, as we term

them, do not exclude one another out of the same place; yet we cannot conceive but that they must necessarily each of them exclude any of the same kind out of the same place.

(*Essay* II.xvii.2)

A possible reply here would be to say that in the passage just quoted Locke is introducing three types of *basic* substances, and that he should not be understood to be ruling out the co-location of basic with non-basic material substances. Yet just after the passage last quoted, Locke offers an argument against the co-location of bodies, and it is one that seems to apply to non-basic bodies as well as to basic ones. He says:

[C]ould two Bodies be in the same place at the same time; then those two parcels of Matter must be one and the same, take them great or little; nay, all Bodies must be one and the same. For by the same reason that two particles of Matter may be in one place, all Bodies may be in one place: Which, when it can be supposed, takes away the distinction of Identity and Diversity, of one and more, and renders it ridiculous.

(*Essay* II.xxvii.2)

Locke contends that if we were to allow that two bodies could be at the same place at the same time, then we would entirely lose our grip on the individuation of bodies. He does not explain why, but we can plausibly reconstruct his reasoning. If the possibility of co-location threatens our grip on the individuation of bodies, it must be because it is possible for there to be bodies distinguished only by their locations. Locke might think this because he thinks that all of the other features that could distinguish one body from another supervene on its structure. Two bodies with the same structure will have everything but location (and the extrinsic features determined by location) in common, so nothing would distinguish them if they were at the same place at the same time. The worry would apply not just to a pair of basic substances with the same structure, but also to a basic and a non-basic substance composed out of the same atoms.

Another reason for reading Locke as a relativist about identity is that relativism about identity fits comfortably with his rejection of essentialism, whereas the view that organisms and masses are distinct, co-incident entities does not. Locke holds that the distinction between essence and accident is nominal-essence relative (*Essay* III.vi.4–5). He holds that each thing conforms to many abstract ideas, and that each abstract idea to which a thing answers yields a different division between its essential features and its accidental ones. According to Locke, we have no conception of anything that could privilege one such division above the others, making it right and the others wrong. To say that a feature is essential is to say that its possessor cannot survive the loss of it, so Locke's view about the distinction between essence and accident already entails that the persistence conditions of things are to some degree nominal-essence relative. If he is a relativist about identity, then he goes further in that direction, holding that nominal essences supply more of the criteria that we rely on when we make judgments about identity. By contrast, suppose that he holds that an organism and the mass that composes it are distinct but co-located things. In that case, he must say that part of what distinguishes them is that the organism has certain features (its shape, the arrangement of its internal parts) necessarily that the mass has only contingently. It is very difficult to see how to reconcile this with his rejection of essentialism.

These arguments seem to me to answer both of the concerns that Alston and Bennett raise about the relative identity reading: the concern that there is too little textual evidence in its favor, and the concern that it does a poor job of exhibiting the unity of Locke's thought. There are, it is true, few if any passages in which Locke says unambiguously that something is the same $F$ as an earlier thing but not the same $G$ as that thing. However, indirect textual evidence can have considerable force, especially if we approach a text in a spirit of charity, favoring those readings on which it offers us a consistent and coherent set of answers to the questions that it addresses. Thus does the question of textual support become tied up with that of theoretical unity. If we are to reconcile Locke's remarks about organisms and masses with his repudiation of co-located bodies, we do best to read him as a relativist about identity. If we are to reconcile his account of identity with the anti-essentialist program in Book III, we do best to read him as a relativist about identity. The relative identity reading also does a better job of exhibiting the unity of Locke's account—both in *Essay* II.xxvii and in the *Essay* as a whole—because it allows us to see his remarks about people, masses and organisms as fitting into a single, broader account of identity and individuation.

## IV

To say that Locke is a relativist about identity does not, all by itself, solve the puzzle generated by his claims about people and substances. At most, it points us in the direction of a solution. If we are to solve the puzzle that Alston and Bennett raise, we must be able to explain how Locke can meaningfully and consistently say both (i) that people are substances, and (ii) that being the same person does not entail being the same substance.

Claim (i) can be parsed in more than one way. The absolutist about identity may want to understand it as the claim that for every $x$ that is a person, there is a $y$ that is a substance and $x = y$. The relativist should say that the 'is' in 'Each person is a substance' is that of predication rather than that of (absolute) identity. In Lockean terms, to say that each person is a substance is to say that anything answering to the abstract idea 'person' also answers to the abstract idea 'substance.' To make sense of this, we need to understand what it means for something to answer to the idea 'substance.'

Locke says that ideas of substances are "such combinations of simple *Ideas*, as are taken to represent distinct particular things subsisting by themselves; in which the supposed, or confused *Idea* of Substance, such as it is, is always the first and chief" (*Essay* II.xii.6). His examples include ideas of individuals, such as those of a man (*Essay* II.xii.6) and a sheep (*Essay* II.xii.6); ideas of collections, such as those of a flock (*Essay* II.xii.6) and a fleet (*Essay* II.xxiv.2); and such ideas as those of lead (II.xii.6) and gold (II.xxiii.3), which he may be thinking of either as ideas of kinds or as ideas of stuffs. Locke may count collections, kinds, and stuffs as substances. Or, more likely, he calls the ideas of these things 'ideas of substances' just because they are ideas of collections of substances, ideas of kinds of substances, and ideas of stuffs that are composed of substances.

Locke seems to hold that something is a substance if it does not depend on something else for its existence in the way that modes are supposed to do. One might challenge this characterization of substance for various reasons, but I will let it pass, turning instead to a worry about claim (ii). The relativist about identity holds that $x$ can be the same $F$ as $y$ without being the same $G$ as $y$, even if $x$ and $y$ are both $G$s. This formula presumes that we possess some criteria of identity for $F$s and for $G$s, and that these are different criteria. So to understand claim (ii), on the relative identity reading of it, we must see Locke as holding that there are criteria of identity for people and for substances, and as holding that these are different criteria. There is no doubt that Locke offers an account of the criteria of identity for people in terms of psychological relations (though of course there is controversy about the details). Less clear is whether he has any account of the criteria of identity for substances.

Nowadays, discussions of criteria of identity often make reference to 'sortals.' It was Locke who first coined the word, deriving it from 'sort' as we do 'general' from 'genus' (*Essay* III.iii.15). As he uses the word, a sortal term (or '*Sortal* Name') is any general term, any term that stands for an abstract idea. Today 'sortal' is often used in a more restrictive sense, as standing for a term that supplies criteria of identity sufficient for counting $S$s (Strawson 1959, 168; Griffin 1977, 34; Lowe 2009, 13). In order to supply criteria for counting $S$s, a term must not only supply criteria for distinguishing $S$s from non-$S$s, but also criteria for individuating $S$s over time, so that we do not count the same $S$ twice. Henceforth, I will use 'sortal' in this more restrictive sense.

The term 'book' is a sortal, because we can easily make sense of the request to count the books in a room, and of the question whether the book in one's hand is the same book as one held earlier. To say that 'book' is a sortal is not to say that there can be no difficulties about how to count books. It is easy enough to count them in most cases, but it may be less clear what to do when one literary work occupies several volumes, when novels by several authors are bound together, or when a collection of writings are first bound together and later broken up and bound separately. A term can supply some criteria of identity without providing criteria so thorough as to settle every question that might arise. Still, there does seem to be an important difference between a sortal term such as 'book' and a non-sortal such as 'thing.'

If we are instructed to count the things in a room, we might begin by counting the table, the chairs, the lamps, and the pictures on the wall. Yet soon we run into trouble. Do we count the table legs? The left halves of the pictures? Do we count momentary table stages as well as tables? Is there a thing composed of the back of one chair and the left half of a picture? Many of us find ourselves at a loss about how to answer such questions. There are philosophers who do defend answers to them, but even their success would not necessarily show that 'thing' is a sortal. For 'thing' to be a sortal, it would have to be the case that the answers to the above questions are delivered by criteria that are grasped implicitly by understanding the meaning of, or mastering the use of, the ordinary word 'thing.' If that were the case, then we would expect to be able to answer those questions as easily, and with as much consensus, as we do questions about which items are books. The unsettled state of the debate about the metaphysics of physical objects suggests that this is not the case.

Some point out that we sometimes use 'thing' and 'object' to mean something like "bounded, coherent material object" (Geach 1968, 145; Xu, 1997), and that we sometimes do count such things. If a child's six wooden blocks sit alone on a table, it does seem very natural to say that there are just six things on the table. If a car drives across a plain, it seems likely that even an observer who had never before encountered a transporting vehicle would conceptualize it as a single moving thing (Hirsch 1976, 361). Yet problems arise about how to cash out the notions of boundedness and coherence. Is a desk lamp that is plugged into an outlet a bounded thing? What about a light fixture on the ceiling? A steam radiator that is connected to other radiators by pipes? To be sure, problems also arise about how to count books, but the counting and tracking of bounded, coherent material objects seems to involve more vagueness, and less easily remedied vagueness, than does the counting of books. So if we do sometimes use the concept of a bounded, coherent material object to count and to track 'things' or 'objects,' it may be best to say that in such cases 'thing' and 'object' function as quasi-sortals rather than as genuine sortals.

Terms that take the grammatical form of count nouns, but that do not supply criteria for counting, are sometimes called 'dummy sortals.' A dummy sortal can stand in proxy for one or more genuine sortals. Even if we cannot track 'things' or 'objects' *per se*, we can understand someone who says: "Those things on the table were there yesterday." We can understand this remark because we see, or presume that we could come to see, that there are sortals that do apply to the things on the table and that might be used to ground diachronic identity judgments about them. Dummy sortals can function as labor-saving devices.

It would have been more cumbersome to say that the six books, three pencils, one fountain pen, one stapler, and seventeen loose sheets of paper that are on the table were there yesterday.

## V

Is 'substance,' in Locke's hands, a sortal, a quasi-sortal, or a dummy sortal? If his conception of a substance is just that of an ontologically independent thing, then it is not a sortal. We may be able to sort the ontologically independent things from the ontologically dependent ones, but how are we to track and count the ontologically independent things? If every ontologically independent thing is a substance, then 'substance' has much the same status as 'red thing.' We can sort red things from the non-red things, but counting red things presents us with much the same challenge as counting things.

Perhaps Locke uses 'substance' as a quasi-sortal? It cannot be that he reserves 'substance' for bounded, coherent material objects, since he countenances immaterial substances as well as material ones. However, it may be that he reserves the term for bounded, continuous, ontologically independent things whose persistence involves some degree of spatio-temporal continuity. Locke holds that immaterial substances, like material ones, have spatial locations (*Essay* II.xxvii.2) and move about (*Essay* II.xxiii.19). His claim that "*Continued Existence makes Identity*" (*Essay* II.xxvii.29, section heading) might be understood as requiring continuous existence for persistence. If all substances occupy places, and if continuous existence is required for persistence, it is but a short step to the view that spatio-temporal continuity of some sort is required for the diachronic identity of substances.[1] If Locke thinks that continued existence makes for identity across time, he may also think that it is required for identity across space. That is, he may deny that substances can have scattered parts.[2] All of this might be enough to make 'substance' a quasi-sortal in his hands. This would give Locke some account of the criteria of identity associated with 'substance,' and of how these differ from the criteria associated with 'person.' It would not commit him to any very specific principles of individuation for substances, but it would explain why sameness of person does not entail sameness of substance. For on this reading, sameness of substance requires some degree of spatio-temporal continuity, and sameness of person does not.

Another possibility is that Locke uses 'substance' as a dummy sortal. In that case, 'substance' functions for him much as 'red thing' does. Any ontologically independent thing will qualify as a substance, and diachronic identity judgments about substances rely upon criteria of identity supplied by other, unvoiced sortals. If we are to make sense of such judgments, we need to be able to say something about the truth conditions that govern them. Consider this affirmation:

(A)  $x$ is the same substance as $y$

If 'substance' is a dummy sortal, then we may say that (A) is true just in case there is some sortal, 'S,' such that each S is ontologically independent and $x$ is the same S as $y$. If we read Locke as a relativist about identity, we will need to make sense of (A) as it appears in the following relativistic claim:

(R1)  $x$ is the same substance as $y$, but $x$ is not the same person as $y$

If one supposes that the substance in question is a material one, one might take (A) as it appears in (R1) to be true because one thinks that $x$ is the same mass as $y$, or because one thinks that $x$ is the same organism as $y$. If we suppose that the substance is immaterial, it is less clear what might be the sortal for which 'substance' stands in proxy. Since Locke takes immaterial substances to occupy places and to move about, one possibility would be a sortal concept modeled on his notions of atom and mass. This would be the idea of a kind of immaterial substance whose diachronic identity is a matter of perfect spatio-temporal continuity. We might call such a substance an 'immaterial mass.'

If we say that 'substance' is a dummy sortal in Locke's hands, then we must also be able to offer some account of the truth conditions for the following denial:

(D)  $x$ is not the same substance as $y$

There would seem to be two possibilities. The first is to say:

(i)  (D) is true just in case there is no sortal, 'S,' such that each S is ontologically independent and $x$ is the same S as $y$

The second is to say:

(ii)  (D) is true just in case there is some sortal, 'S,' such that each S is ontologically independent and $x$ is not the same S as $y$

On the relative identity reading of Locke, we need to consider (D) as it appears in the following relativistic claim:

(R2)  $x$ is the same person as $y$, but $x$ is not the same substance as $y$

If everything that is a person is a substance, then reading (i) is a non-starter. For if we plug reading (i) into (R2), we turn (R2) into a contradiction. So we must go with reading (ii). On this reading, (R2) is equivalent to:

(R3)  $x$ is the same person as $y$, but that there is at least one sortal 'S' such that an $S$ is ontologically independent and $x$ is not the same $S$ as $y$

Locke will hold that (R3) is true if $x$ and $y$ stand in certain psychological relations and $x$ is not the same mass as $y$ (or not the same organism as $y$, or not the same immaterial mass as $y$, etc.).

A possible worry is that (R2) seems an awkward way to express (R3). This may lead one to doubt whether Locke could mean anything like (R3) when he says something like (R2). Consider a parallel case. Suppose that a relativist about identity wants to solve the Ship of Theseus problem by endorsing the following:

(R4)  $x$ is the same ship as $y$, but $x$ is not the same collection of planks as $y$

We would not expect the relativist to express himself by saying:

(R5)  x is the same ship as $y$, but $x$ is not the same thing as $y$

We would not expect him to do this because there is a natural reading of (R5) on which it is a contradiction. By the same token, one might not expect the relativist who holds (R3) to assert (R2), because there is a natural reading of (R2) on which it is a contradiction.

Is this a decisive knock against reading Locke as a relativist about identity who uses 'substance' as a dummy sortal? I do not think so. One thing to notice is that (R2) and (R5) are not simply awkward *as* expressions of (R3) and (R4), respectively. They are simply awkward. In the Ship of Theseus case, the relativist has no reason to employ the potentially misleading dummy sortal formulation (R5), and will instead opt for the clearer formulation with a proper sortal (R4). Locke, however, may well have reason to employ the dummy sortal, even at the cost of some awkwardness. He wants to remain agnostic about thinking matter, and this means adopting a non-committal stance about what is the sortal for which 'substance' stands in proxy in (R2). He does not know whether that which thinks within us is material or immaterial, and he does not go so far as to explicitly formulate sortal concepts for immaterial things. We should thus not be surprised if he resorts to using a dummy sortal in (R1) and (R2). This makes him rather like the person who is unsure about what specific sorts of things are on the table (machines? works of art?), and yet who can say that they are, or are not, the same things as were there yesterday.

On Alston and Bennett's solution, 'substance' is a dummy sortal outside of II.xxvii, but a proper sortal inside it. It is an advantage of the relative identity reading that it does not portray Locke as guilty of this particular inconsistency. However, it is not much of an advantage if we cannot explain what diachronic identity judgments about substances come to on the relative identity reading.

I have suggested two possibilities: that Locke consistently uses 'substance' as a quasi-sortal, and that he consistently uses it as a dummy sortal. I have not tried to decide between them. Either way, we are talking about the presumptions that lie behind certain of Locke's identity statements, and not about positions that he self-consciously forwards.

## Notes

1. There is the possibility of a continuously existing substance that hops instantaneously from one place to another, but we can forgive Locke for silently passing over that.
2. On the other hand, he may not. Locke seems to count water as a substance (*Essay* II.xxiii.3), and Michael Jacovides has argued that he takes fluids to be scattered objects (Jacovides 2008).

# PART VIII

# Idealism Without God

# Editors' Introduction

Berkeley's most famous philosophical works are his *Treatise Concerning the Principles of Human Knowledge* (1710) and *Three Dialogues between Hylas and Philonous* (1713). In them Berkeley argued against skepticism and atheism, and for his remarkable-sounding view that there is no such thing as matter and that God causes all the things we think matter causes. Both authors in this part also refer to Berkeley's *Essay Towards a New Theory of Vision* (1709)—a book about how vision works, and *Alciphron* (1732)—a series of dialogues in which Berkeley defends Christianity against 'free-thinkers' or atheists.

Religion was a central theme for Berkeley. For instance, an argument for God's existence is the main topic of the second of his *Three Dialogues*. Indeed, God is so entwined in Berkeley's system that it can be hard to see how to make sense of that system without God. That perception drives Margaret Atherton's central question in "Berkeley Without God." What would Berkeleianism without God look like? Would it just be "the unlikely view that things exist only when they are actually being perceived" (see p. 201 below)? Or did Berkeley have other philosophical views that can stand independently of his commitment to God's existence?

Atherton approaches this question by beginning with Berkeley's *New Theory of Vision*. The *New Theory* does not talk about God, but it does contain substantive philosophical views about sensory representation. And although the *New Theory* is an early work of Berkeley's, Berkeley reissued it when *Alciphron* was published, so we know he continued to endorse the views of the *New Theory* throughout his career. Indeed, in *Alciphron* he uses its theory of sensory representation as the basis of a proof for God's existence. Atherton argues that we can see the same theory of sensory representation that is independent of Berkeley's arguments for God's existence in the *Principles* and the *Three Dialogues*. This theory is Berkeleianism without God.

Tom Stoneham argues against several of Atherton's main claims. He disagrees with her reading of *Alciphron*, and also argues that the arguments for God's existence in the *Principles* and *Three Dialogues* are significantly different from the arguments in *Alciphron*. Finally he considers whether the theory of sensory representation could be a viable Berkelianism without God. He argues that it could not, for reasons connected to Berkeley's anti-skeptical aims.

## A Note on References

Both authors refer to the text of Berkeley's works in the edition edited by Luce and Jessop (Berkeley 1948–57). References to individual works generally use abbreviations of their titles: 'PHK' for Berkeley's *Principles*, ' *Dialogues*' for his *Three Dialogues between Hylas and Philonous*, 'NTV' for the *New Theory of Vision*, and 'TVV' for the *Theory of Vision Vindicated*. References to PHK, NTV, and TVV are to the numbered sections within those works. The *Three Dialogues* have no sections, so these are referred to by page number in volume two of the Jessop and Luce edition. The *Alciphron*'s seven dialogues are divided into sections which are also used for referencing, so ' *Alciphron* IV.7' refers to section 7 of the fourth dialogue.

## Further Reading

- Margaret Atherton (1990). *Berkeley's Revolution in Vision*.
- Tom Stoneham (2002). *Berkeley's World*. Chapters 5, 7, and 8 explore in more detail the interpretation presented in the final section of Stoneham's chapter here.
- Arthur Collier, who supplied the epigraph to Stoneham's paper, defended a position similar to Berkeley's in *Clavis Universalis* (1713).
- Robert J. Fogelin. (2001). *Routledge Philosophy Guidebook to Berkeley and the Principles of Human Knowledge*.

## CHAPTER 15

# Berkeley Without God

## MARGARET ATHERTON

In much of his work, Berkeley set himself the twin goals of combating atheism and skepticism. Nowadays, it is the second enterprise that interests philosophers more than the first, especially since Berkeley's proofs for the existence of God are not thought to be any more successful than anyone else's. There has been, then, some interest in the question, What does Berkeley's theory amount to if he is not allowed his proofs for the existence of God? Can there be a viable position that is Berkeleianism without God? To many, the answer to this question must be no, God plays far too important a role in Berkeley's thinking to be eliminable. For Berkeley maintains that for ideas to be perceivable, they must actually be perceived. Thus, things not currently perceived by any finite mind can only be perceivable if God is actually perceiving them. Berkeley's theory, it is said, is unavoidably theocentric. Without God, it collapses into the unlikely view that things exist only when they are actually being perceived.

There is, however, one consideration that suggests a different way of looking at Berkeleianism without God. Berkeley's first book, *An Essay Towards a New Theory of Vision*, in its first and second editions, made absolutely no reference to God whatsoever. (In the third edition, in two places, the phrase "language of nature" is changed to "language of the Author of Nature" [NTV 147 and 152].) The *New Theory* criticizes a theory of perception based on realist or materialist assumptions and, in its place, puts forward a theory of sensory representation, in which ideas represent only other ideas. This theory of sensory representation might be said, in effect, to constitute a Berkeleianism without God. This suggestion is plausible, however, only if the Berkeleianism of the *New Theory* is compatible with the Berkeleianism of the later works. If the proofs for the existence of God Berkeley subsequently introduces require adjustments to his theory that render it incompatible with the God-free *New Theory*, then perhaps those who say that Berkelelanism is unavoidably theocentric are in the right. If this is the case, then it will also mean that in suppressing all mention of God from the *New Theory*, Berkeley was doing something with more far-reaching consequences than his notorious suppression of the facts about *tangibilia*. He was putting the *New Theory* at odds with his final doctrine.[1]

# I

When we consider the relation between the *New Theory* and Berkeley's proofs for the existence of God, it is highly significant that when Berkeley published *Alciphron*, he chose to reissue the *New Theory* along with it. *Alciphron's* most important goal is theological. It is a defense of traditional religion against free-thinkers, and it contains very elaborate proofs for the existence of God. In the *Theory of Vision Vindicated*, Berkeley tells us that he published the *New Theory* along with *Alciphron* because he was "persuaded that the *Theory of Vision*, annexed to the *Minute Philosopher*, affords to thinking men a new and unanswerable proof for the existence and immediate operation of God, and the constant condescending care of his providence" (TVV 1). Thus, in 1732, when Berkeley published *Alciphron*, he indubitably considered the *New Theory* not only to be compatible with but also to provide significant support for the proofs for the existence of God to be found there. What remains at issue, how-ever, is the extent to which the position Berkeley lays forth in *Alciphron* is com-patible with what is found in *Principles* and *Three Dialogues*, with the position that is generally identified as Berkeleianism.

Berkeley's ultimate proof for the existence of God in *Alciphron* depends heavily on the results he had achieved in the *New Theory*. He builds to this proof by way of a subproof, which is not found satisfactory by Alciphron, one of Berkeley's representative freethinkers. This subproof sets the stage for the final proof and helps establish its nature. In this first proof, Alciphron concedes that while we can be sure of the existence of whatever we sense, we may also infer the existence of imperceptible things from their sensible effects. What is involved in these sorts of causal inferences is further refined: we can make inferences about the nature of the cause from the nature of the effects, and so, in particular, from rational acts we infer a rational cause. The proof there-fore is going to be a matter of showing that there are a number of events that would be otherwise inexplicable unless we assume the existence of a particular rational cause. Euphranor, Berkeley's spokesman, cites a number of examples of such rational events, or motions, as he calls them: "A man with his hand can make no machine so admirable as the hand itself; nor can any of these motions by which we trace out human reason approach the skill and contrivance of those wonderful motions of the heart, and brain, and other vital parts, which do not depend on the will of man" (A IV, 5, 146). These are, then, examples of motions that are rational but in need of an explanation because they are independent of any human reason. Therefore, we can infer the existence of some rational or, indeed, suprarational cause.

Berkeley does not, however, take this proof as it stands to be sufficient to establish the existence of a single God. He therefore adduces some further evidence: these rational motions exhibit a unity in that they are governed by single set of immutable laws. It is concluded that they must be the product of a single agent or mind, which can be identified with God. This first proof is, as I read it, causal. It attempts to establish the existence of God as the best explanation for certain natural events.[2] It depends upon our willingness to admit as evidence that there are events or motions in nature that are both rational and independent of a human will and that are law-governed. For the proofs to go through, we have to be in a position to accept these as facts.

Alciphron recognizes that the proof for the existence of God just given, depending as it does on the premise that from rational effects we can infer a rational cause, is a version of an argument to the existence of other minds. It requires that we have just as good evidence for the existence of God as we do for other rational human beings. This Alciphron refuses to admit. He is then casting doubt on the strength of the evidence Euphranor has cited, claiming it is not as powerful as the evidence Euphranor has that Alciphron exists, whom he sees and talks to. Euphranor responds by asserting he has better evidence for the existence of God than for the existence of Alciphron (A IV, 5, 147).[3] What is at stake here is the nature of the evidence Euphranor claims to have. Alciphron is maintaining that truly to be evidence of a rational cause, it would have to be of the same sort as the evidence that convinces him of the existence of a human mind, and that is the presence of language. Alciphron is introducing a condition on what it is for natural events or motions to be rational: they must be languagelike.

Berkeley's demonstration that the rational natural motions are languagelike amounts to a lightning tour through the *New Theory of Vision*. What he is seeking to establish is that vision is a language, that our ability to see the world around us, to see people, trees, and houses, is a matter of having learned to understand visual signs. Berkeley's demonstration consists, first, in a discussion of what he regards as a clear case of his account of how we learn to see, that of distance perception. We are undeniably able to see how far away objects are from us, even though this is not information available to us in the visual stimulus. Our success at seeing distance is the result of connecting visual cues, such as faintness, which in its own nature has nothing to do with distance, with distance information. Faintness can come to stand for distance because it is reliably correlated with distance in our experience. Seeing distance is therefore something we learned how to do; we learned to read visual distance cues such as faintness as signifying distance information. Berkeley generalizes from the distance case very rapidly. Just as we have to learn to see distance because distance information is not immediately present in visual stimulation, so most of what we see, trees, people, and houses, must be suggested by the lights and colors we are built to register visually. Thus, Berkeley claims that upon the whole, "it seems the proper objects of sight are light and colours, with their several shades and degrees; all which, being infinitely diversified and combined, form a language wonderfully adapted to suggest and exhibit to us the distances, figures, situations, dimensions, and various qualities of tangible objects: not by similitude, nor yet by inference of necessary connexion, but by the arbitrary imposition of Providence, just as words suggest the things signified by them" (A IV, 10, 154). This is the conclusion, of course, that Berkeley took most of the *New Theory* to demonstrate, that the natural motions of Alciphron are rational because they can be fit into the rational structure of a language. On the basis of what we see, we can learn what to expect so as to govern our conduct rationally.

Berkeley's proof for the existence of God follows quite straightforwardly from the claim that vision is the language of nature. If there is a language of nature, there must be a speaker of the language, there must be a divine mind to which we owe the language of nature. The only plausible explanation for the highly rational phenomenon that is the language of nature is that it is due to God. The last proof in *Alciphron* is intended by Berkeley to be understood as a convincing version of the first, and exemplifies the same causal principle, that from rational effects we can infer rational causes. For this proof to go through, we have to accept Berkeley's account of the evidence, his characterization of rational causes. We have to accept the demonstration of the *New Theory*, that sensory ideas constitute a language in which visual ideas represent other ideas. For the proofs in *Alciphron* to hold, we have to, at least, accept that what Berkeley says in the *New Theory* is true. Berkeley must first establish his theory of sensory representation as the correct way to understand our knowledge of the natural world; then he can use it as evidence for the existence of God. So Berkeley's theory, as developed in the *New Theory*, must be independent of the theological use to which he puts it, and cannot require the existence or the cooperation of God in order to be true. The *New Theory*, then, from the perspective of *Alciphron*, constitutes Berkeleianism without God.

There is, however, a problem with drawing conclusions about the nature of Berkeleianism based on *Alciphron*. This is because *Alciphron* makes no mention of the issue of the mind-dependent status of the natural world. Indeed, the effects that in *Alciphron* are explained by appealing to God are referred to as "motions." There is no indication of the fact that, for Berkeley, these motions have the status of ideas. There is a sense, then, in which Berkeley's attitude in *Alciphron* is a throwback to the one he expressed in the *New Theory*, where he failed to point out that the tangible objects that visual ideas signify are themselves mind-dependent. Since the need to make use of God, which

Berkeley's theory faces in its canonical form, is generally supposed to arise from the absence of a mind-independent material world to provide stability, it might be supposed that it is not appropriate, based on *Alciphron* to make generalizations about the nature of Berkeleianism. It might be the case that there are two versions of Berkeleianism. In the one laid out in the *New Theory* and *Alciphron*, Berkeley's account of the natural world is not theocentric and can be used as evidence in a proof for the existence of God. In the other, found in *Principles* and *Three Dialogues*, Berkeley's account of nature is unavoidably theocentric, and God's existence is proved by other means. It is not, on the face of it, likely that in the course of his life Berkeley leapt back and forth between two incompatible positions, but since the way in which *Principles* and *Three Dialogues* are often read has this result, it is necessary to show that the complete statement of his position that Berkeley gives in *Principles* and *Three Dialogues* is nonetheless compatible with the somewhat more cautiously expressed claims of the *New Theory* and *Alciphron*.

## II

Berkeley proves the existence of God twice in *The Principles of Human Knowledge*, once in sections 25–33, at the end of the introductory section summarizing his doctrine, and once in sections 145–55, at the very end of the book. The placement of these proofs not only indicates the importance of this issue within Berkeley's overall plan, but also supports the view that Berkeley took his proof for the existence of God to be the culmination of his theory, for which the rest provided support. While the occurrences of the proof differ in detail, they do not differ significantly from each other, in the sense that each relies on roughly the same body of evidence. The second occasion on which Berkeley proves God's existence, a proof that makes reference to other minds, ought appropriately to be regarded as an enrichment of the first. While in both cases the primary evidence Berkeley relies on are ideas rather than, as in *Alciphron*, "rational motions," the arguments do not otherwise differ significantly from that of *Alciphron*.

Berkeley begins his proof in PR 26 by claiming ideas need causes, and proceeds to establish by a process of elimination that they must be caused by spiritual substance or mind. (Ideas, being inert, cannot cause other ideas, and so must be caused by a substance. Since there is no such thing as corporeal substance, they must be caused by spiritual substance.) Although I experience some of my ideas as having been caused by myself ("It is no more than willing, and straightway this or that idea arises in my fancy" PR 28), many other ideas, in particular, sensory ideas, are not like this but are experienced as involuntary. These ideas, the ones that are independent of my will, are caused by some other will or spirit (PR 29). Thus, this proof, like the *Alciphron* proof, is causal. Since the "rational motions" of *Alciphron* have been identified in the *Principles* as ideas, Berkeley is able to argue more straightforwardly that their cause must be something mental, or rational, and argues that God is the best explanation for our ideas.

As in *Alciphron*, the nature of the evidence must be further refined before Berkeley can plausibly argue that the cause of our ideas is God.[4] Berkeley gives a description of the ways in which the ideas he is going to ascribe to God differ from human productions.

> The ideas of sense are more strong, lively, and distinct than those of the imagination; they have likewise a steadiness, order and coherence, and are not excited at random, as those which are the effects of human wills often are, but in a regular train or series, the admirable connexion whereof suf-ficiently testifies the wisdom and benevolence of its Author. Now the set rules or established methods, wherein the mind we depend on excites in us the ideas of sense, are called the *Laws of Nature:* and these we learn by experience, which teaches us that such and such ideas are attended with such and such other ideas, in the ordinary course of things.
>
> (PR 30)

This passage, in a highly condensed form, refers to the same sorts of reasons that led Berkeley in *Alciphron* to describe our ideas as language-like: they have the order and coherence that allows us to learn what to expect, that is, to learn to understand them. As in *Alciphron*, Berkeley argues the specific character of our ideas of nature indicates they must be the effects of a suprarational mind, or God. While the reference to language is lacking, otherwise this proof paral-lels the proof in *Alciphron*. Like that one, this depends upon the claim that our ideas are law-governed and independent of our will.[5]

The proof for the existence of God Berkeley gives at the end of the *Principles*, like the proof in *Alciphron*, is enriched by a comparison with the way in which we know other persons, or other minds. Berkeley's point is that the inference that leads us to God is as good as and in fact better than the inference we make to the existence of other minds. Just as we do not see a person directly, but rather infer the person's existence from "such a certain collection of ideas, as directs us to think there is a distinct principle of thought and motion like to our selves" (PR 148), so we infer the existence of God. Presumably (this is not spelled out with respect to other finite minds) it is not just any ideas that lead us to suppose we are in the presence of another person, but only those to be explained as deriving from a rational agent. Similarly, in the proof for the existence of God, the emphasis is on the complexity of the evidence that leads us to attribute some of what we experience to God.

> But, though there be some things which convince us human agents are concerned in producing them; yet it is evident to every one that those things which are called the words of Nature, that is, the far greater part of

the ideas or sensations perceived by us, are not produced by, or dependent on the wills of men. There is therefore some other spirit that causes them; since it is repugnant that they should subsist by themselves. See *Sect* 29. But if we attentively consider the constant regularity, order, and concatenation of natural things, the surprising magnificence, beauty, and perfection of the larger, and the exquisite contrivance of the smaller parts of the creation, together with the never enough admired laws of pain and pleasure, and the instincts or natural inclinations, appetites, and passions of animals; I say if we consider all these things, and at the same time attend to the meaning and import of the attributes, one, eternal, infinitely wise, good, and perfect, we shall clearly perceive that they belong to the aforesaid spirit, *who works all in all*, and *by whom all things consist.*

(PR 146)

Berkeley's proof here, as in *Alciphron*, requires us to see the effects that we attribute to God not just as independent of our will but as exhibiting a certain kind of rational structure.

While the language analogy, the explicit comparison between our ideas of the natural world and a language, is absent from Berkeley's proof for the existence of God in the *Principles*, it is not entirely missing from the *Principles* itself. Berkeley refers to the language analogy explicitly in PR 44, in which he goes over the results of the *New Theory*,[6] and makes use of it in PR 65, in his answer to the eleventh objection. This objection asks why there appears to be a clockwork of nature, if all the various inner parts have no causal efficacy. Berkeley's answer, in part, is that the connections observed are not causal but those of sign to thing signified. Further, he writes:

[T]he reason why ideas are formed into machines, that is, artificial and regular combinations, is the same with that for combining letters into words. That a few original ideas may be made to signify a great number of effects and actions, it is necessary they be variously combined together: and to the end their use be permanent and universal, these combinations must be made by *rule*, and with *wise contrivance*. By this means abundance of information is conveyed unto us, concerning what we are to expect from such and such actions, and what methods are proper to be taken, for the exciting such and such ideas: which in effect is all that I conceive to be distinctly meant, when it is said that by discerning the figure, texture, and mechanism of the inward parts of bodies, whether natural or artificial, we may attain to know the several uses and properties depending thereon, or the nature of the thing.

Finally, in PR 108, he compares natural scientists to grammarians, who are able to go beyond the ability of ordinary people in understanding the signs of nature and to write the grammar or rules for their use.[7] It seems reasonable to suppose that the rational structure that, in the *Principles*, Berkeley argues must be the effect of God is the same as the language of nature, whose existence he demonstrated in the *New Theory* and referred to in *Alciphron*. Berkeley's proof for the existence of God in the *Principles* does not require the traditional argument from design, as Grayling has it, but rather the enriched version of this argument, as found in *Alciphron*, which presupposes the results of the *New Theory*. As in *Alciphron*, the proofs for the existence of God in the *Principles* assume the truth of the theory of sensory representation developed in the *New Theory*.

## III

But even if the proof of the *Principles* is entirely compatible with the proof given in *Alciphron*, it might be supposed that the same cannot be said of the way in which Berkeley sets about proving the existence of God in *Three Dialogues Between Hylas and Philonous*. For it is generally supposed that in *Three Dialogues* Berkeley introduces a new proof for the existence of God, a proof Jonathan Bennett has called the continuity argument.[8] And it is, after all, the continuity argument that has led people to claim Berkeley's theory is intrinsically theocentric, because it purports to show God must exist to perceive the tree when there is no one about in the quad. The crucial passage runs as follows:

> When I deny sensible things an existence out of the mind, I do not mean my mind in particular, but all minds. Now it is plain they have an existence exterior to my mind, since I find them by experience to be independent of it. There is therefore some other mind wherein they exist, during the intervals between the times of my perceiving them: as likewise they did before my birth, and would do after my supposed annihilation. And as the same is true, with regard to all other finite created spirits; it necessarily follows, there is an *omnipresent eternal Mind*, which knows, and comprehends all thing, and exhibits them to our view in such a manner, and according to such rules as he himself hath ordained, and are by us termed the *Laws of Nature*.
>
> (D 230)

This argument is supposed to differ from the one given in the *Principles* because it argues God must exist, not to be the cause of the ideas we do have, but to perceive the ideas we do not have. The *Principles* God functions as a cause—He is to be seen primarily as an agent, a will—whereas the *Three Dialogues* God preserves the continuing existence of things and is primarily (or, rather, additionally) a perceiver, an understanding. Such an assessment, however, not only requires a particular way of reading *Three Dialogues*, which can be questioned, but also requires taking the *Principles* to be about God only as a cause. According to this assessment, the *Principles* argument is what has been called a "pure passivity" argument. The account I have given so far of the *Principles* suggests this is not the case. When the *Principles* argument is properly understood, it is clear that the arguments of the *Principles* and *Three Dialogues* are very similar.[9]

Since the proof in the *Principles* does not stop with the conclusion that some other spirit causes our involuntary ideas, it does not simply establish the existence of God as a will or agent. The ideas whose existence depend upon God do not occur randomly or incoherently, but instead display the sort of order that leads Berkeley to describe them as languagelike. God is not a random cause or blind agent, but causes our ideas according to a plan, the laws of nature, by virtue of which our ideas are meaningful. It cannot be correct, therefore, to see Berkeley as offering at any stage an argument that just trades on God's volitions, an argument to be otherwise supplemented by another about his role as an understanding. The argument that establishes that the cause of our ideas is *God* rests on the claim that these ideas are rational in structure, requiring a rational cause.[10]

In arguing that our involuntary ideas are also orderly or meaningful, Berkeley is presenting a picture of our ideas as having an existence that is distinct from any particular (finite) perceiver. Consider the case of distance perception, discussed extensively in the *New Theory of Vision*. When I stand on my front steps and look to the corner, I may be said to see how far away the corner is from me. But, of course, all that I register visually, all that I immediately perceive, is light and colors. These lights and colors, therefore, suggest to me distance, which, according to Berkeley, I experience tangibly or kinesthetically. There is a way or ways it feels to go from where I am standing to the corner. Because visual experiences are reliably correlated with tangible experiences, I come to learn what distance looks like, or I come to read my visual experiences as having a distance meaning. Just as the immediate visual experiences are independent of my will, so the distance meanings with which my visual experiences are invested are also involuntary. They are a habit I fall into when my visual and tangible experiences are regularly correlated. The existence of the distance meaning is dependent on these regular correlations and is therefore distinct from my own existence. The standards I learn and employ, while cashed out in terms of my tangible and kinesthetic experiences, are nevertheless independent of my mind.

Exactly the same can be said about any of my experiences of sensible things. If I am seeing a cherry, then my immediate visual experiences stand for a range of perceptual experiences with which these immediate visual experiences are reliably correlated and which they have come to mean. The cherry, although mind-dependent, has an existence that is distinct from and independent of *my* mind. Berkeley's claim that our sensory ideas are governed by law amounts to the claim that the sensible things for which our ideas stand have a distinct existence, independent of any particular finite perceiver. From the fact that we do, and therefore can, make sense of our experience because of its regular and orderly (language-like) nature, we can conclude the items of our experience have a distinct existence. This claim is established entirely through the God-free resources of the *New Theory of Vision*.

It is useful, in getting a handle on the way in which sensible things have an existence that is distinct from any particular (finite) perceiver, to keep Berkeley's distinction between immediate and mediate perception in mind. According to Berkeley, I may be said to immediately perceive whatever my sense organs are equipped to register, whereas I mediately perceive those meanings I have learned to attach to what I immediately perceive, which constitutes the greatest part of what I may be said to perceive. I immediately perceive lights and colors, but mediately perceive distance or cherries. Things that are sensible, like cherries or coaches or trees, are all mediately perceived.[11] While it seems reasonable to say what I immediately perceive exists in my mind for only so long as I am perceiving it, the same is not true for the sensible things I mediately perceive. Two people do not feel the same twinge of pain or sense the same flash of light, but they do see the same distance or the same cherry. Just as the immediate ideas I hear and see are different but of the same coach (so long as they form part of the same congeries of ideas I have come to expect to mean coach), so the immediate ideas you and I have are of the same coach. On the basis of what I immediately see, I expect to be able to touch the coach, and I expect you to be able to touch it too. We can be confident we attach the same meanings to what we perceive, because our perceptions are governed by the same laws of nature.

The distinction between immediate and mediate perception is also useful in understanding how Berkeley thinks he can argue it is God who causes our ideas. Berkeley himself says God causes ideas in us in the same way in which I cause ideas in myself, but it is, I believe, more helpful to think about the more strictly analogous situation where I cause ideas in someone else by speaking to them, by making noises they hear as meaningful. Berkeley thinks, after all, it is a strength of his position that his argument that God is the cause of our ideas relies on the same evidence as that by which we convince ourselves that other minds exist. But it is not apprehension of immediately perceived sounds that convinces us that we are in the presence of another mind, but rather the mediate perception of meaningful language. Similarly, what convinces us of the existence of God is the meaningful units we mediately perceive. Looking at things in this way not only makes plain why Berkeley is so clear that the cause of our sensible ideas must be a mind, but also shows that Berkeley's proof for the existence of God depends upon his theory of sensory representation.

Not perhaps surprisingly, what I am saying is that, according to Berkeley, the natural world is mind-dependent, but independent of any particular mind, such as my own, in exactly the same way language is a mind-dependent phenomenon, but independent of any particular mind. If all minds were annihilated, clearly language would also be annihilated; but the existence of language is distinct from that of any one mind, in the same way that the law-governed world we learn about via our senses is independent of any one (finite) mind. The annihilation of a single English speaker does not cause English to go out of existence, and similarly, the items of the natural world are not dependent on the ideas of some one perceiver.

This point is consonant with various remarks Berkeley makes in the *Principles* that have been cited as reflecting his interest in the continued existence of objects. Consider his reply, in PR 48, to the objection that so long as the existence of things depends on their being perceived, then everything goes out of existence whenever it is not being perceived:

> For though we hold indeed the objects of sense to be nothing else but ideas which cannot exist unperceived; yet we may not hence conclude they have no existence except only while they are perceived by us, since there may be some other spirit that perceives them, though we do not. Wherever bodies are said to have no existence without the mind, I would not be understood to mean this or that particular mind, but all minds whatsoever. It does not therefore follow from the foregoing principles, that bodies are annihilated and created every moment, or exist not at all during the intervals between our perception of them.

To be a sensible body is reliably to present a certain range of experiences to perceivers. Sensible bodies will continue to exist so long as the conditions exist that enable perceivers to make sense of their experiences, to experience them as bodies.[12] Berkeley, of course, further supposes that God is the cause of those conditions that enable perceivers to understand what they are perceiving. Ultimately, through the laws that preserve the regularities that allow us to make sense of what we perceive, God preserves the continued existence of sensible things. The issue of the distinct and continuous existence of sensible things is not absent from the *Principles*. In the *Principles*, the proof for the existence of God, from the premise that our experiences are orderly and according to the laws of nature, establishes the existence of a God who is responsible through these laws of nature for the distinct and continued existence of sensible things.

It is finally interesting to note there are two entries in the *Philosophical Commentaries* that are relevant to our understanding of Berkeley's proof for the existence of God. PC 838 reads: "Every sensation of mine which happens in consequence of the general, known Laws of nature and is from without i.e. independent of my Will demonstrates the Being of a God. i.e. of an unextended incorporeal Spirit w$^{ch}$ is omniscient, omnipotent etc." This entry indicates Berkeley considered the proof for the existence of God to follow not only from the fact that ideas are independent of my will but also from the fact that my sensations are in accordance with the laws of nature. A further entry also shows Berkeley's conception of the independence of my ideas is not limited to their independence of my will: "I will grant you that extension, Colour etc may be said to be without the Mind in a double respect i.e. as independent of our Will & as distinct from the Mind" (PC 882). These entries make clear Berkeley was thinking about the issues surrounding the distinct existence of ideas before he published the *Principles,* and further suggest it is unlikely they would form part of a new proof, introduced only in *Three Dialogues.*

Once it becomes clear the position in the *Principles* is that God is the cause of ideas that are both independent of my will and distinct from my understanding, then it is hard to find any new element introduced in *Three Dialogues.* Berkeley's proof for the existence of God spreads over several pages of the second dialogue, or more accurately, it is discussed twice, once at D 212–13 and again, after a digression where Berkeley distinguishes his position from that of Malebranche, at D 214–15. The second occurrence is a fairly straightforward causal argument, not different in any way from that of the *Principles*:

> It is evident that the things I perceive are my own ideas, and that no idea can exist unless it be in a mind. Nor is it less plain that these ideas or things by me perceived, either themselves or their archtypes exist independently of my mind, since I know myself not to be their author, it being out of my power to determine at pleasure, what particular ideas I shall be affected with upon opening my eyes or ears. They must therefore exist in some other mind, whose will it is they should be exhibited to me.

Michael Ayers says of this argument that Berkeley has built into it "certain elements of the Passivity Argument,"[13] and if by this he means that it relies, as does the *Principles'* proof, on the claim that sensible ideas are independent of my will, then this is certainly the case. Ayers is also of the opinion, however, that the first occurrence of the proof, at D 212–13, lacks any reference to passivity, but this seems to me less clear. Berkeley says, in D 212: "To me it is evident, for the reasons you allow of, that sensible things cannot exist otherwise than in a mind or spirit. Whence I conclude, not that they have no real existence, but that seeing they depend not on my thought, and have an existence distinct from being perceived by me, *there must be some other mind wherein they exist.* As sure therefore as the sensible world really exists, so sure is there an infinite omnipresent spirit who contains and supports it." The only reason I can see for distinguishing this proof from the one given slightly later in *Three Dialogues,* or from the proof in the *Principles,* is that here Berkeley speaks of his ideas as independent of his *thought* instead of independent of his *will.* But I think this is to place too much weight on an implied sharp distinction between will and understanding. Berkeley is quite prepared to use "thought" as a general term for what goes on in his mind, and he is suspicious of attempts to separate the will from the understanding. I think it is reasonable to see this proof, too, as arguing for the need to provide an explanation for ideas that are both causally independent and ontologically distinct from my mind. There is no serious discrepancy between the proofs of the *Principles* and the proofs of the second dialogue.

Furthermore, once it becomes clear Berkeley was arguing from the start that sensible things, while mind-dependent, are distinct from my mind, then it is also clear, as Ayers and Grayling argue, that the "continuity argument" of D 230 does not present a startling departure from what has gone before. For since what makes it possible for us to perceive the world of sensible things is their dependence on the laws of nature, then it is obvious this world is not only distinct but continuous, preserved by the continuing operations of the laws of nature. Thus the "continuity argument," far from introducing any novelties, is, as Ayers says, an "enrichment," doing no more than spelling out the implications of what has gone before.

## IV

It seems reasonable to say, then, that from the beginning, Berkeley intends our sense experience to be of sensible things having a continued and distinct existence. From entries in his philosophical notebooks to *Alciphron*, Berkeley has based his argument for the existence of God on the claim that the natural world is governed by law, and hence is meaningful to us. We can reject Berkeley's proof for the existence of God and still accept his theory of sensory representation. We can accept that we live in a world in which, thanks to the regular and orderly nature of our experience, we perceive distance or cherries or trees in the quad. Without God, we obviously lack a cause or an explanation for the theory of sensory representation, but the theory itself stands.[14]

In arguing for the existence of a viable Berkeleianism without God, I am not trying to downplay the importance of theological considerations in Berkeley's own motivations. On the contrary, I believe them to be central. I am only claiming that Berkeley's theological purposes required him to have a free-standing theory of sensory representation to which he could then appeal in proving the existence of God. If it is concluded that Berkeley's proof for the existence of God is unconvincing, then we have no account of the cause of sensory representation, but the details of the theory are untouched.[15]

## Notes

1. The issues are not unconnected, of course. It is maintained Berkeley does not need God in the *New Theory* as he does in the later works, because in the *New Theory* tangible objects are

mind-independent. This claim is not entirely compatible with the way in which I prefer to read the *New Theory*. See Margaret Atherton, *Berkeley's Revolution in Vision* (Ithaca: Cornell University Press, 1990).

2. The proof is sometimes taken as an analogical argument. The claim we infer rational causes from rational effects is taken to be licensed by a comparison with explanations for human actions. Even those, however, who take the initial proof to be analogical suppose that the final "successful" proof is a best-explanation argument. See Michael Hooker, "Berkeley's Argument from Design," in *Berkeley: Critical and Interpretive Essays*, ed. Colin M. Turbayne (Minneapolis: University of Minnesota Press, 1982), pp. 261–70, and A. David Kline, "Berkeley's Divine Language Argument," in *Essay on the Philosophy of George Berkeley*, ed. Ernest Sosa (Boston: Reidel, 1987), pp. 129–42; hereafter, Sosa.

3. This passage is sometimes considered a second subproof, analogical in nature, which is not usually regarded as satisfactory. Since, in the passage in question, Euphranor does not in fact give any of the evidence he alleges he has, I think it better to regard this not as a proof at all but rather as an introduction to the proof Euphranor eventually gives.

4. Jonathan Bennett, as A. C. Grayling points out, has unaccountably ignored this part of Berkeley's proof in his influential discussion of Berkeley's proofs for the existence of God, although he does nevertheless criticize Berkeley for having given a proof that falls far short of theism. It is certainly true that at the place where Bennett halts his discussion of Berkeley's proof, Berkeley has done no more than show that my involuntary ideas are caused by some mind or other besides my own. See Jonathan Bennett, *Locke, Berkeley, Hume: Central Themes* (Oxford: Oxford University Press, 1971); idem, "Berkeley and God," reprinted in *Locke and Berkeley: A Collection of Critical Essays*, ed. C. B. Martin and D. M. Armstrong (Notre Dame, Ind.: University of Notre Dune Press, 1968), pp. 380–99; and A, C. Grayling, *Berkeley: The Central Arguments* (LaSalle, Ill: Open Court, 1986).

5. For those who like to see proofs laid out in a series of numbered steps, the one just discussed might go something like this:

    (1) Ideas can only be caused by a mind.
    (2) I am not the cause of ideas of sense.
    (3) Therefore they are caused by some other mind.
    (4) Ideas of sense are more coherent and orderly than any caused by a finite mind.
    (5) Therefore they are caused by God.

6. "It is, I say, evident from what has been said in the foregoing parts of this treatise, and in *Sect* 147, and elsewhere of the essay concerning vision, that visible ideas are the language whereby the governing spirit, on whom we depend, informs us what tangible idea he is about to imprint upon us, in case we excite this or that motion in our own bodies." It is clear from this passage Berkeley regards the language analogy as established by the argument of the *Principles*.

7. Curiously, in the first edition, Berkeley made much more explicit use of the language analogy in PR 108, writing, for example, "It appears from *Sect.* LXVI, etc. that the steady, consistent methods of Nature, may not unfitly be stiled the *language* of its *Author*, whereby he discovers His *attributes* to our view, and directs us how to act for the convenience and felicity of life." I have no theory to account for Berkeley's deletion of this and other sentences from PR 108.

8. Although Jonathan Bennett has focused attention on the problem of the two proofs for the existence of God and given them the names by which they are now commonly known, the idea that *Dialogues* contain a new proof is not new with him. See the editor's introduction, *Works* II, 152; "In the *Principles* (Sect. 29) God was adduced as the *cause* of *our* percepts, and of our perceptual experiences, and only incidentally (Sects. 48 and 91) is He brought in as the *upholder* of sensory things when they are not being perceived by us. The emphasis is now transposed: the argument is that the existence of God must be granted in order to account for the continuous existence of the natural order; the notion of God as cause is slipped in in a quite casual way."

9. This position is also shared by Grayling and Winkler and is compatible with Winkler's claim that Berkeley's Divine Agent is both will and understanding. Michael Ayers has shown the continuity argument of D 230 is an enrichment of and not otherwise distinct from the central proof for the existence of God in D 212–15, but he wants to distinguish what he renames the "distinctness argument" from the "pure passivity argument" he finds in the *Principles*. It is not like Ayers to be taken in by Bennett, but I think he is wrong in agreeing with Bennett that the *Principles* contains a "pure passivity" argument. See Grayling, *Berkeley: The Central Arguments*; Kenneth P. Winkler, *Berkeley: An Interpretation* (Oxford: Oxford University Press, 1889); and M. R. Ayers, "Divine Ideas and Berkeley's Proofs of God's Existence," in Sosa, pp. 115–28.

10. The best evidence, according to Ayers, Berkeley thought he had two arguments for the existence of God comes at D 240, where Berkeley says: "From the effects I see produced, I conclude there are actions; and because actions, volitions; and because there are volitions, there must be a will. Again, the things I perceive must have an existence, they or their archtypes, out of my mind; but being ideas, neither they nor their archetypes can exist otherwise than in an understanding: there is therefore an understanding. But will and understanding constitute to the strictest sense a mind or spirit. The powerful cause of my ideas, is in strict propriety of speech a *spirit*." The conclusion of this passage suggests, however, that a single causal argument requires the operation of a being who has both will and understanding.

11. NTV 9, D 174–75. The account I am giving here is the one I defend in *Berkeley's Revolution in Vision*. It is not entirely in accordance with others that have appeared in the recent literature. See Winkler's *Berkeley*, pp. 149–61, and George Pappas, "Berkeley and Immediate Perception," in Sosa, pp. 195–213.

12. This thought seems to be what is captured by the more phenomenalist passages of the *Principles*, such as PR 3: "The table I write on, I say, exists, that is, I see it and feel it; and if I were out of my study I should say it existed, meaning thereby that if I was in my study I might perceive it, or that some other spirit actually does, perceive it."

13. Ayers, "Divine Ideas," p. 121.

14. In what I am saying here, I am agreeing with Grayling, who argues there is a lot of value left to Berkeley's theory even if God is removed. I am going slightly beyond his claims, however, in seeing the residue as consisting not only in the view of the world, as Grayling has it, as mental, together with a negative thesis about materialism, but also in a positive theory of sensory representation. I have written more about this in *Berkeley's Revolution in Vision*.

15. This essay took its inspiration from a paper Charles McCracken read at an International Berkeley Society session at the 1991 Central Division Meetings of the APA, in which he complained that the doctrine of the *New Theory* cannot be used as a guide to understanding the theologically based doctrines of the *Principles* and *Dialogues*. I do not know that what I have written here satisfies him any more than what I said to him there, but this is my considered response. I am also grateful to Robert Schwartz and Robert McKim for their help, as well as to Lorne Falkenstein, who commented on this essay at the University of Western Ontario's conference on Berkeley's Metaphysics.

## CHAPTER 16

# Response to Atherton: No Atheism Without Skepticism

## TOM STONEHAM

> Nay, I will . . . uphold against him that he himself is the man who is guilty of the scepticism of denying the existence of all visible objects; nay, that he cannot shew another in the world, besides Mr. Berkeley and myself, who hold the testimony of sense to be infallible as to this point.
>
> (Rev. Arthur Collier, 8th March 1713/4)

We should begin by noting that Margaret Atherton does not ask the question "What is left of Berkeley's philosophy if we deny the existence of God?" but the subtly different:

> Can there be a viable position which is Berkeleianism without God?
>
> (see p. 201 above)

This question has two important features. The first is that she asks whether there is a 'viable' position. Thus she is interested in the question of whether Berkeley without God has a philosophical position which is of interest ahistorically, a position which contemporary philosophers might want to discuss and consider. If Berkeley without God is just solipsism of the present moment, then the question doesn't receive an interesting answer, and presumably Atherton would not have bothered writing on the topic.

The second is that what remains for the non-theist must be recognizably 'Berkeleian.' At a minimum, it must be something Berkeley agrees with. More substantially, it should be something which is distinctive or original to Berkeley. But I think there is a further condition being imposed here as well, which will become important later: Atherton's question only gets an affirmative answer if the resulting, non-theistic position is not merely one which we regard as viable but also one which Berkeley himself would regard as viable. Here we have to be careful, because Berkeley was himself a deeply religious man and saw his philosophy as fundamentally directed to theological ends, so any non-theistic position would not be seen by him as viable. After all, his favorite Biblical quotation was "In God we live and move and have our being" and it was a matter of great pride to him that his philosophy showed how it was true. Yet we can still ask, with reference to Berkeley's purely philosophical concerns, whether he would regard the resulting non-theistic position as viable. And here we should pay attention to the subtitles of his two major philosophical works: *A Treatise concerning the Principles of Human Knowledge: Wherein the Chief Causes of Error and Difficulty in the Sciences, with the grounds of Scepticism, Atheism, and Irreligion, are inquired into* (1710); and *Three Dialogues between Hylas and Philonous: The design of which is plainly to demonstrate the reality and perfection of human knowledge, the incorporeal nature of the soul, and the immediate providence of a Deity: in opposition to Sceptics and Atheists. Also to open a method for rendering the Sciences more easy, useful, and compendious* (1713). Here Berkeley shows himself just as concerned with skepticism as he is with atheism. So we can see that answers to Atherton's question, in being constrained to find a position that Berkeley would think viable, should be constrained to find a position which is anti-skeptical.

Atherton claims that what remains of Berkeley's philosophy without God is the theory of sense perception he puts forward in the *New Theory of Vision* (1709): "Without God, we obviously lack a cause or explanation for the theory of sensory representation, but the theory itself stands" (see p. 213 above).

In what follows I shall firstly show that Atherton's argument for this claim is flawed, for it depends upon a mis-reading of *Alciphron* IV. However, even when we read *Alciphron* IV correctly, it remains the case that the theory of sensory representation is independent of the existence of God within Berkeley's system. My second point will be that the theory of sensory representation, when separated from the rest of Berkeley's philosophy, is not a position he would find 'viable' because it would not suffice to refute the skeptic. In the passage just quoted, Atherton acknowledges that on such a position we would lack an explanation of sensation, but seems to think that this does not impugn the viability of the position because such an explanation could be added by the non-theist. This will not do, because the only 'cause or explanation' which Berkeley thinks is adequate to rule out skepticism commits him to theism.

## The Premises in *Alciphron* IV

Atherton's argument starts with an account of Berkeley's proof of the existence of God in Dialogue IV of his 1732 book *Alciphron, or the Minute Philosopher*, which was originally published with a new edition of the *New Theory of Vision*. In this Dialogue, Berkeley's spokesman Euphranor tries to persuade the atheist Alciphron of the existence of God. Atherton shows that the *New Theory* has the status of a premise in the argument and is thus something which Berkeley thought could be accepted by an atheist. She then goes on to argue that essentially the same argument is used to prove the existence of God in both the *Principles* and the *Three Dialogues*, allowing her to conclude that also in those early works, the *New Theory* is Berkeley without God.

Thus the argument turns upon whether the proofs of the existence of God in the early works are essentially the same as that given in the *Alciphron*. In this section and the next, I propose to challenge this by showing that the proof in the *Alciphron* depends upon a premise which is not present, implicitly or explicitly, in the earlier works, and thus the proofs cannot be essentially the same.

What Atherton calls the 'first subproof' given in *Alciphron* IV.4–5 is a form of the argument from design, inferring a rational cause from the complex character of the effects. The inference used here is taken to be analogous to the inference to 'animal spirits' from 'their effects and operations.' Now while it is likely that Berkeley would accept this as a good reason to believe in the existence of God, he is smart enough to realize that it will not convince an atheist, so he has Alciphron object to it by saying that it is only language that really convinces him of the existence of another mind:

> I have found that nothing so much convinces me of the existence of another person as his speaking to me. It is my hearing you talk that, in strict and philosophical truth, is to me the best argument for your being. And this is a peculiar argument, inapplicable to your purpose; for, you will not, I suppose, pretend that God speaks to man in the same clear and sensible manner as one man doth to another?
>
> (*Alciphron* IV.6)

Euphranor accepts the challenge and gives the second argument. Before we consider that argument, we should note the dialectical position. Alciphron is making an epistemological point: arguments from design are weak because there are plenty of alternative possible explanations of the existence of complexity, but there is one really strong and convincing argument for the existence of another mind and that is speech. He is asserting that he has much greater confidence in the existence of fellow humans than he does in the existence of any alleged mental cause of complexity in nature. In response, Euphranor is explicitly aiming to put our knowledge of God and of other human minds on an exactly equal footing. If his argument works, knowledge of God and of other minds will stand or fall together, i.e. an atheist must be a solipsist.

Berkeley uses the literary form of dialogue to great effect, and at the beginning of *Alciphron* IV.7 the exchange between Alciphron and Euphranor establishes exactly what has to be done to meet Alciphron's challenge to show that we know God through his speech, just like we know other minds:

> Alciphron: I am for admitting no inward speech, no holy instincts, or suggestions of light or spirit. All that, you must know, passeth with men of sense for nothing. If you do not make it plain to me that God speaks to men by outward sensible signs, . . . you do nothing.

Alciphron is challenging Euphranor to show that God literally speaks to men in the same way they speak to each other: analogies and language-like phenomena will not suffice. The challenge is accepted and Alciphron's definition of speech agreed upon:

> the arbitrary use of sensible signs, which have no similitude or necessary connexion with the things signified; so as by the apposite management of them to suggest and exhibit to my mind an endless variety of things, differing in nature, time, and place; thereby informing me, entertaining me, and directing me how to act, not only with regard to things near and present, but also with regard to things distant and future.
>
> (*Alciphron* IV.7)

The discussion then proceeds to a quick summary of the arguments of the *New Theory of Vision* which are taken to show that visual experience is a language by these standards. While the details of this argument are fascinating and important, for present purposes we can skip to the objections Alciphron raises before being finally persuaded. One objection is that if vision is a language, so are all the other senses. Euphranor replies:

> That they are signs is certain, as also that language and all other signs agree in the general nature of sign, or so far forth as signs. But it is as certain that all signs are not language: not even all significant sounds, such as the natural cries of animals, or the inarticulate sounds and interjections of men. It is the articulation, combination, variety, copiousness, extensive and general use and easy application of signs (all which are commonly found in vision) that constitute the true nature of language. Other senses may indeed furnish signs; and yet those signs have no more right than inarticulate sounds to be thought a language.
>
> (*Alciphron* IV.12)

It is this passage which undermines Atherton's interpretation. If the argument rests just on a general theory of sensory representation, then whatever linguistic qualities vision has would be possessed by the other senses as well, for they are equally involved in mediate perception (e.g. the famous example of hearing the sound of a coach in the *Three Dialogues*). It only makes sense for Berkeley to insist on this distinction between mere sign systems and genuine languages if his proof requires that vision is *literally* a language and not merely language-like or analogous to a language. We can see why the argument requires such a strong claim when we remember that it is a response to Alciphron's challenge to show that God *literally* speaks to men in just the same way they speak to each other. Merely showing that vision is a sign system would not meet this challenge. This is because inferences from a sign system, such as the honey bee's waggle dance, to the existence of an intelligent cause are just variations on the argument from design, which Alciphron has already rejected as insufficient to give him as much certainty in God's existence as he has in other humans'. Berkeley's divine language argument is entirely original, and avoids all the standard objections to arguments from design, precisely because of the premise that vision is not just a sign system but is literally a language.

## Language in the Early Works

Let's call this claim the 'Literal Language Premise.' It rests upon applying a definition of language to the theory of visual representation in the *New Theory*. It is not our purpose here to evaluate this argument but to consider Atherton's thesis that the arguments for the existence of God in the *Principles* and *Three Dialogues* are essentially the same as the argument in *Alciphron*.

Atherton herself allows that neither the Literal Language Premise nor anything like it appears in the *Principles* argument for God. After quoting the first formulation of the argument at PHK 30, she writes:

> This passage, in a highly condensed form, refers to the same sorts of reasons that led Berkeley in *Alciphron* to describe our ideas as languagelike ... While the reference to language is lacking, otherwise this proof parallels the proof in *Alciphron*.

(see p. 206 above)

But without the reference to language, and in particular, without the Literal Language Premise, it is simply a different proof. The Alciphron who challenged Euphranor to show that God speaks to men just as they speak to each other would not accept that ideas displaying 'steadiness, order, and coherence' and 'in a regular train or series' adds anything to the weak argument from design. What Atherton seems to have missed is that it is essential to the argument of

*Alciphron* that vision is not merely analogous to language but is a language, so when she identifies in the *Principles* the same sort of phenomena as are being used in the *Alciphron*, she takes the argument to be the same, whereas in fact it is very different.

In the third section of her chapter, Atherton addresses the question of whether the so-called 'continuity argument' which Jonathan Bennett claimed to have found exclusively in the *Three Dialogues* (at *Dialogues* 230) constitutes a new proof for the existence of God. Her main line of argument is that Berkeley's way of accounting for continuity—the publicity and persistence of ordinary physical objects such as tables and trees in contrast with the privacy and fleetingness of ideas—depends upon the distinction between immediate and mediate perception, which is the core of the theory of sensory representation given in the *New Theory*. Despite Atherton's attempts to emphasize the language analogy at this point (see p. 209 above), it does not seem that this line of thought needs the Literal Language Premise, not least because continuity and mediate perception occur in all five senses—they are all sign systems—but only vision is literally a language.

The early works, then, involve no use of the Literal Language Premise in their arguments for the existence of God or elsewhere, and thus cannot contain essentially the same argument as *Alciphron*. It is worth noting that this gives us a neat explanation of a textual problem which Atherton notes but cannot solve (n. 7 on p. 214 above). In the first, 1710, edition of the *Principles*, PHK 108 began:

> It appears from sect. 66, etc. that the steady, consistent methods of Nature, may not unfitly be stiled the *language* of its *Author*, whereby he discovers His *attributes* to our view, and directs us how to act for the convenience and felicity of life.

When the book was reissued in 1734, after the publication of *Alciphron*, this sentence and another about ways of learning languages were deleted. It is clearly problematic for Atherton's claim that the *Principles* contains essentially the same divine language argument as *Alciphron* that Berkeley should delete such a comment just two years after making the importance of language in that argument so explicit. It seems as if he wanted to reduce the emphasis on language in the *Principles* in the light of his formulation of the argument in the *Alciphron*, which would make sense if he wanted to clarify the differences between the two. By the time of writing *Alciphron*, he realized the importance of distinguishing languages from mere sign systems, and that not all of the natural world is a language, though all of it may be a sign system. And it is precisely this claim which makes that sentence originally in PHK 108 incorrect and in need of deletion.

## God and Sensation

While Atherton is wrong that the arguments for the existence of God in the *Principles* and *Three Dialogues* are essentially the same as the argument in *Alciphron*, she may yet be right that the theory of sensory representation in the *New Theory* is a viable Berkeleianism without God. I have not challenged her interpretation of the arguments for the existence of God in the early works as depending upon the theory of sensory representation, and instead only denied that they involve the Literal Language Premise. I now want to question whether the theory of sensory representation, considered in a non-theistic philosophical context, is a position Berkeley would consider viable (setting the non-theism aside, of course). In particular, I want to consider what Berkeley the anti-skeptic would say about Atherton's Berkeleianism without God. In order to do that, we must first digress a little on the topic of the role or function of God in Berkeley's theocentric philosophy.

Standard interpretations of Berkeley take the issue of existence unperceived—the famous tree in the quad which no one sees—to force a choice. Either Berkeley holds that when no finite mind is perceiving the tree, its existence is upheld by God's perceiving it, or he holds that 'the tree exists unperceived' means no more than 'were someone to look, they would perceive a tree.' The latter interpretation is implausible, despite a few supporting texts, because "for ideas to be perceivable, they must actually be perceived" (see p. 201 above). But then "Berkeley's theory is intrinsically theocentric, because it purports to show God must exist to perceive the tree when there is no one about in the quad" (see p. 208 above).

As already noted, Atherton thinks that the theory of sensory representation can give the non-theist Berkeleian an account of existence unperceived. For the theory gives us an account of what it is to perceive a tree or a coach rather than merely lights and colours, sounds and textures. What the theory says is that to perceive a tree is to ". . . mediately perceive those meanings I have learned to attach to what I immediately perceive [lights, colours etc.]" (see p. 210 above).

We are each only able to attach those meanings in the first place, and any two of us are only able to attach the same meanings to the different immediately perceived ideas we have when looking at the same tree, because of the Laws of Nature which govern our experiences. This orderly, lawful structure in immediate perception is thus the necessary condition for mediate perception and thus what enables us to perceive 'sensible bodies,' i.e. public, persisting physical objects. Which deals with existence unperceived:

> Sensible bodies will continue to exist so long as the conditions exist that enable perceivers to make sense of their experiences, to experience them as bodies. Berkeley, of course, further supposes that God is the cause of those conditions . . .

(see p. 211 above)

The further supposition is, for Atherton, unjustified. It is not needed to ensure continuity and it is not the best explanation in a causal inference. In fact, we are left with the impression that God is a slightly gratuitous prejudice in Berkeley's system.

It is worth noting that the argument in *Alciphron*, with its use of the Literal Language Premise, offers a distinct and very different route to the existence of God. Hence, it is possible that Berkeley's further supposition, while not required by the theory of sensory representation and the account of continuity, is in fact justified by independent considerations. But even if that argument succeeded, Atherton could claim to have identified a viable Berkeleian philosophy which is not intrinsically theocentric.

However, it is not clear that Atherton has got the 'choreography' of Berkeley's argument right here. She notes that:

> . . . the proof in the *Principles* does not stop with the conclusion that some other spirit causes our involuntary ideas, it does not simply establish the existence of God as will or agent . . . The argument that establishes that the cause of our ideas is *God* rests on the claim that these ideas are rational in structure, requiring a rational cause.
>
> (see p. 209 above)

While this is correct, Atherton appears to pay insufficient attention to the fact that the argument has a two-step structure. First of all Berkeley establishes the existence of 'some other mind' as the cause of his ideas of sense, then he establishes the *attributes* of that mind by considering the character of the effects it causes. And for Berkeley, it is not just the 'rational structure'—presumably the Laws of Nature which support mediate perception—which is important here, but also 'immediate providence' (cf. subtitle to the *Three Dialogues*). Now, even if the second step is Berkeley's 'further supposition' based upon the inference to the best explanation which Atherton finds so dubious, it may be the case that the first step is an unavoidable element of Berkeleianism.

What I shall now argue is that the element of the theory of sensory representation which makes it anti-skeptical also mandates the inference to 'some other mind' as the cause of our ideas of sense. Whether this mind is unique, let alone divine, is a different matter.

## Skepticism and the Causes of Sensation

In the *Three Dialogues*, Berkeley discusses the nature of the skepticism he is rejecting and, in a rhetorical question, asserts a sufficient condition for being a skeptic: "What think you of distrusting the senses, of denying the real existence of sensible things, or pretending to know nothing of them. Is not this sufficient to denominate a man a *skeptic*?" (*Dialogues* 173).

And when asked which are the sensible things, he identifies them with those *immediately* perceived, contrasting immediate objects of perception with those that are represented, using the example of words and their meanings. So it seems that in Berkeley's most explicit discussion of skepticism, it is crucial that sensible objects are immediately perceived. Yet Atherton's account of the theory of sensory representation has sensible things only mediately perceived: "I immediately perceive lights and colours, but mediately perceive distance or cherries. Things that are sensible, like cherries or coaches or trees, are all mediately perceived" (see p. 210 above).

We need to be clear about the difference between two claims which might be attributed to Berkeley. The first is that mediate perception is a necessary condition for the sense perception of things such as cherries and coaches, that hearing a sound couldn't be the perception of a coach for a person who did not have several other ideas suggested by that sound. The second is that sensible things such as coaches are the objects of mediate perception. Atherton seems to attribute the latter to Berkeley, but that makes the perception of coaches always epistemically indirect: though the represented congeries of ideas may spring directly to mind, the process relies upon suggestion which, like inference, is a means of moving from idea to idea. Suggestion not merely makes the perception indirect, it also makes it fallible precisely because those connections upon which mediate perceptions rely are not necessary, a point Berkeley often makes by pointing to illusions of distance in mirrors and paintings. While Atherton may think that such fallibility does not inevitably lead to skepticism, it is clear that Berkeley would not accept it as a *refutation* of skepticism.

Unfortunately, Berkeley never fully spells out how his theory delivers the 'reality and perfection of human knowledge' and thus refutes skepticism. However, his account of knowledge must rely heavily upon the thesis that the immediate objects of sense are ideas and thus that they are perfectly known:

> Colour, figure, motion, extension and the like, considered only as so many *sensations* in the mind, are perfectly known, there being nothing in them which is not perceived. But if they are looked on as notes or images, referred to *things* or *archetypes* existing without the mind, then are we involved all in *scepticism*.
>
> (PHK 87)

The problem is to explain how this perfect knowledge of our ideas can give us knowledge of persisting, public objects like trees and cherries. Atherton thinks that since cherries and coaches are collections of ideas and thus do not exist "without the mind," though they are "independent of any particular mind" (see p. 210 above), this skepticism is avoided. However, it is only individual ideas which are here claimed to be perfectly known and the defeasibility of the process of suggestion excludes knowledge of collections of ideas from being similarly perfect.

Consider how the passage just quoted continues:

> We see only the appearances, and not the real qualities of things ... Things remaining the same, our ideas vary, and which of them, or even whether any of them at all represent the true quality really existing in the thing, it is out of our reach to determine ... All this scepticism follows, from our supposing a difference between *things* and *ideas,* and that the former have a subsistence without the mind, or unperceived.
>
> (PHK 87)

Here the position which generates skepticism is contrasted with one on which the ideas, the objects of immediate perception are the 'real qualities of things,' such that when our ideas change, so do the qualities of things and vice versa. One interpretive option here is to take Berkeley literally: the idea of orange I am perceiving and the colour property of the fruit I can see are *one and the same thing.* Since fruit, and other sensible things, are not substances but collections of qualities (PHK 1), my orange idea is a property, i.e. part or aspect, of the persisting, public object which sits on my desk.

Interpreting Berkeley literally shows how perfect knowledge of ideas defeats the skeptic: my ideas are components of the real world of trees and cherries and coaches, so in knowing them infallibly I thereby have infallible knowledge of (some parts of) reality. As he puts it: "I am not for turning things into ideas, but rather ideas into things; since those immediate objects of perception, which according to you, are only appearances of things, I take to be the real things themselves" (*Dialogues* 244).

Is the literal interpretation viable? The problem here is that each idea is a private mental event or object in the mind of a particular person, but cherries, trees etc. are public objects which are experienced by different people at different times. Atherton's view that sensible objects are only mediately perceived fails to address the skeptic, so how can Berkeley reconcile the claim that the immediate objects of perception are ideas, that their *esse* is *percipi,* with the claim that they are sufficiently independent of the mind which perceives them to be the real qualities of persisting, public objects? The answer lies in that very feature of our sense experience which leads Berkeley to make the first step in his argument for the existence of God, namely to there being some other mind. Consider this version of the inference, which Atherton quotes:

> The far greater part of the ideas or sensations perceived by us, are not produced by, or dependent on the wills of men. There is therefore some other spirit that causes them; since it is repugnant that they should subsist by themselves.
>
> (PHK 146)

Setting aside the missing premise that only minds can cause ideas or sensations, the final clause should make us think a bit harder about what is going on here. The conclusion is that some other mind causes these ideas, so one would naturally expect a premise to the effect that they cannot be uncaused, but instead we get the claim that they cannot "subsist by themselves." Berkeley is appealing to the thought that some things, and in particular ideas, depend upon their cause in a stronger sense than merely that had the cause not existed, they would not. Rather, the cause explains not only their coming into existence but also their subsistence. The allusion seems to be to the doctrine that there are grades of being, with necessary existents at the top and everything else depending in some way upon a being of a higher grade.

Thus Berkeley is saying that ideas, of their nature, stand in two distinct dependence relations to minds. Because their *esse* is *percipi*, they depend upon being perceived by some mind; and because they are not self-subsistent, they depend upon being willed by some mind. In some cases, such as ideas of imagination, the perceiving and the willing minds are one and the same, but since the dependence relations are distinct, the depended on minds could be distinct. Which sets up the inference that, since most ideas of sense are not willed by any human mind, they must be willed by some other mind.

It is precisely these two different dimensions of dependence which solve our problem. My ideas of sense can be components of a public world precisely because they do not subsist in my mind (that is what distinguishes them from ideas of imagination) but in some other mind. They are necessarily perceived by me, but that is not sufficient for them to subsist in my mind, and not subsisting in my mind gives them the independence from me that is needed to answer the skeptic. What we need to add to the theory of sensory representation to provide an answer to the skeptic is the subsistence-independence of my ideas of sense from my mind, and that gives us the first step in the inference to the existence of God. For Berkeley there can be no atheism without skepticism and Berkeley without God is not Berkeley at all.

# PART IX

# Hume on Causation

# Editors' Introduction

The following two chapters discuss Hume's views about causation. This relation appears to be central to our understanding of the world around us. And Hume's thoughts about causation have been very influential—and very puzzling to interpreters.

Our two authors agree that there is a traditional interpretation of Hume on causation. According to this view, there is nothing to causation over and above regularity, or what Hume calls constant conjunction. Very roughly, this is the view that there is nothing more to A being the cause of B than the fact that As are always followed by Bs. This is sometimes thought of as a way of understanding causation, and sometimes as skepticism about causation (the view that there isn't really causation, just constant conjunction).

Some recent interpreters, including Galen Strawson, have argued for a skeptical realist understanding of Hume on causation. Advocates of this reading argue that Hume believes there really are causal powers in the world that are more than just constant conjunctions. So Hume was a realist about causation. But they also think that Hume thought we couldn't know much at all about these powers. So he was a skeptical sort of realist.

In Chapter 17, Strawson argues for a skeptical realist reading. In doing so, he argues that we should pay particular attention to what Hume says in his *Enquiry concerning Human Understanding*, which Hume described as containing the "same doctrines" as the earlier *Treatise*, but "better illustrated and expressed." He also argues for an analogy between what Hume says about causation and what he says about mind-independent objects that give rise to our impressions.

In Chapter 18, Helen Beebee argues against Strawson's version of skeptical realism. In doing so, she pays a good deal of attention to the analogy between causation and external objects. She argues that Hume thinks talk about secret causal powers does not play an indispensible role in our interactions with the world, in the way that talk about external objects does. Thus she opposes attributing to Hume the belief that we have a natural, important, and irremovable belief in causal powers.

## A Note on References

References to Hume's works use two abbreviations: 'T' for his *Treatise of Human Nature*, and 'E' for his *Enquiry concerning Human Understanding*. References to these texts are to the book, part, section, and paragraph in the *Treatise*, or the section and paragraph in the *Enquiry*. Thus 'T 1.1.1.1' refers to the first paragraph of the *Treatise*, and 'E 9.1' to the first paragraph of section 9 of the *Enquiry*. These paragraph numbers are printed in Hume (1999) and Hume (2001), as well as in the versions at www.davidhume.org.

Both authors also refer to texts of Berkeley's: his *Principles of Human Knowledge*, using the abbreviation PHK and giving section numbers; his *Three Dialogues*, using the abbreviation *Dialogues* and giving page numbers from the edition of Luce and Jessop, and also *De Motu*, again giving section numbers. Both authors quote the text from the edition of Ayers (Berkeley 1975).

## Further Reading

- Galen Strawson (1989). *The Secret Connexion: Causation, Realism, and David Hume.*
- John P. Wright (1983). *The Sceptical Realism of David Hume.*
- Rupert Read and Kenneth A. Richman (2000). *The New Hume Debate.*

## CHAPTER 17

# David Hume: Objects and Power

GALEN STRAWSON

## 1

Many people think that Hume holds a straightforward 'regularity' theory of causation, according to which causation is nothing more than regular succession or constant conjunction. . . . "Hume's conclusion," according to Roger Woolhouse, is "that so far as the external objects which are causes and effects are concerned there is only constant conjunction"; so far as the "operations of natural bodies" are concerned, "regularity and constant conjunction are all that exist" (Woolhouse 1988, 149-50). I will call this the standard view. I will argue that it is wrong, and that Hume believes in causal power, or 'natural necessity', or 'Causation', as I will sometimes call it.

## 2

If you want to know what Hume thought about causation, you have to give priority to his first *Enquiry*, which begins as follows:

Most of the principles, and reasonings, contained in this volume, were published in a work in three volumes, called *A Treatise of Human Nature*: a work which the author projected before he left college, and which he wrote and published not long after. But not finding it successful, he was sensible of his error in going to the press too early, and he cast the whole anew in the following pieces, where some negligences in his former reasoning and more in the expression, are, he hopes, corrected. Yet several writers, who have honoured the author's philosophy with answers, have taken care to direct all their batteries against the juvenile work, which the author never acknowledged, and have affected to triumph in any advantages, which, they imagined, they had obtained over it: *a practice very contrary to all rules of candour and fair-dealing, and a strong instance of those polemical artifices, which a bigotted zeal thinks itself authorized to employ.* Henceforth, the author desires, that the following pieces *may alone be regarded as containing his philosophical sentiments and principles.*

(E Advertisement; my emphases)

These are strong words for Hume, and they express hurt . . .

Hume's public response was to write the *Enquiry* (1748). He wrote it to counteract the misinterpretation of the Treatise, and to correct certain mistakes: "The philosophical principles are the same in both: but I was carried away by the heat of youth and invention to publish too precipitately . . . I have repented my haste a hundred, and a hundred times" (Hume 1932, 1.158). "I . . . acknowledge . . . a very great mistake in conduct, viz. my publishing at all the *Treatise of Human Nature* . . . Above all, the positive air, which prevails in that book, and which may be imputed to the ardor of youth, so much displeases me, that I have not patience to review it" (Hume 1932, 1.187). He expected a much better reception for the *Enquiry*, in which "the same doctrines [are] better illustrated and expressed": a striking remark when one is trying to establish Hume's views about causation, given that all the main support for the view that Hume was an outright regularity theorist derives from the *Treatise*, and vanishes in the *Enquiry* . . .

In asking that the *Enquiry* alone should "be regarded as containing his philosophical sentiments and principles," Hume lays a clear obligation on us. We can read the *Enquiry* back into the *Treatise*, when trying to understand his considered view; we can't go the other way. Everything in the *Treatise* that is or appears incompatible with the *Enquiry* must be discarded. Nothing in the *Treatise* can legitimately be used to throw light on any passage in the *Enquiry* unless two conditions are fulfilled: the passage in the *Enquiry* must be unclear (this is not often the case), and the passage from the Treatise must not be incompatible with anything in the *Enquiry* that is not in dispute. Even when a passage from the *Treatise* is called in evidence, its claim to make a contribution to interpretation must be weak when compared with competing claims from passages in the *Enquiry* other than the passage under consideration.

If we also respect Hume's insistence that "the philosophical principles are the same in both" the *Treatise* and the *Enquiry*, we have a further obligation. In order to understand the *Treatise*— in order, in particular, to avoid being misled by the dramatic and polemical exaggerations of the "ardor of youth"—we must read the *Enquiry* back into the *Treatise* wherever possible, and give it priority. For it was written to correct the misunderstanding of the *Treatise*.

Nearly all present-day commentators ignore this obligation, and many of them have their exegetical principles exactly the wrong way round. Hume deserves sympathy, for it is bad to be attacked for views one never held, and worse to be praised and famous for holding them. I know of no greater abuse of an author in the history of philosophy. Many love the *Treatise* because they love argument, and this is understandable; many excellent philosophers are condemned to the lower divisions in philosophy because, consciously or not, they are more attached to cleverness and argument than truth. Hume is not among them, however, and no one can avoid the obligations described in the preceding paragraph. It cannot be plausibly argued that there is early Hume and late Hume, that they are importantly different, and that each deserves study in his own right. Hume was at work on the *Treatise*-clarifying *Enquiry* within five years of the publication of the *Treatise* and probably earlier, and (once again) was most insistent that the philosophical principles are the same in both. We have no reason to judge him to be self-deceived on this matter.

## 3

When Hume talks of 'objects' he usually means genuinely external objects, in a sense to be explained further below. Sometimes, however, he only means to refer to mental occurrences, or what he calls 'perceptions', and it may be suggested that this is always so: that he only means to refer to the 'immediate', mental objects of experience, in talking of objects. This suggestion is worth mentioning, because if it were correct it would be easy to understand why Hume might wish to adopt a regularity theory about causation in the 'objects'. But it is not correct—Hume didn't mean to refer only to mental occurrences or perceptions, and when I use the word 'object' I will mean what he usually meant in the contexts with which I will be concerned: objects that are genuinely non-mental things, things that exist independently of our minds.

I will argue for this soon. For the moment I will take it for granted, because it allows me to state the main objection to the standard view of Hume. It is that the standard view fails to distinguish clearly between two fundamentally different notions, one ontological, the other epistemological. It fails to distinguish sufficiently between the ontological notion of causation as it *is* 'in the objects', and the epistemological notion of causation so far as we *know* about it in the objects. But this distinction is crucial. In the end Hume's regularity theory of causation is only a theory about causation so far as we can know about it in the objects, not about causation as it is in the objects. As far as causation as it is in the objects is concerned, Hume believes in Causation.

In other words: the 'standard' view confuses Hume's epistemological claim

(E) All we can ever know of causation is regular succession

with the positive ontological claim

(O) All that causation actually is, in the objects, is regular succession.

It moves, catastrophically, from the former to the latter. The former is arguably true. The latter is fantastically implausible. It is 'absurd', as Hume would have put it.

Although (E) and (O) are clearly distinct, Hume sometimes abbreviates his main claims, in the *Treatise*, in such a way that he seems to slide from (E) to (O), propelled by his theory of ideas or meaning. In these cases, the passage from the merely epistemological claim (E) to the ontological claim (O) appears to be made via the semantic claim

(S) All we can legitimately *manage to mean* by expressions like 'causation in the objects' is regular succession.

The transition is made as follows. (1) (E) is true. (2) If (E) is true, (S) is true (that's strict empiricism for you). (3) If (S) is true, (O) is true. Hence (4) (O) is true. Why does (O) follow from (S)? Because, given (S), when the phrase 'causation in the objects' comes out of our mouths or pens, or occurs in our thought, it inevitably just means regular succession. So (O) causation in the objects—here is the phrase, meaning 'regular succession'—just is regular succession. After all, regular succession is regular succession.

I am going to reject this view of the consequences of Hume's theory of ideas (or theory of meaningfulness). Let me raise an initial doubt. Suppose there were good grounds for thinking that Hume's theory of ideas did license the (very strange) move from (E) to (O) via (S), and hence licensed the claim that all we can suppose a thing to be is what we can detect or experience or know of it, simply because we cannot manage to mean anything more than what we can detect or experience or know of it, when we think or talk about it. Even if this were so, the following decisive objection to attributing (O) to Hume would remain: (O), the claim that causation is definitely nothing but regular succession, and that there is definitely no such thing as Causation, makes a positive ontological assertion about the ultimate nature of reality. It is therefore violently at odds with Hume's skepticism—his skepticism with respect to knowledge claims about what we can know to exist, *or know not to exist*, in reality. As a strict skeptic with respect to knowledge claims about the nature of reality Hume does not make positive claims about what definitely does exist (apart from mental occurrences or 'perceptions', whose existence he rightly takes as certain). But, equally clearly, he does not make positive claims about what definitely (or knowably) does not exist. For such claims are equally unwarranted, from the skeptical point of view. Ignorance, as he says, is never a "good reason for rejecting any thing" (E73). This point about Hume's skepticism is enough to refute any attribution of (O) to him.

## 4

The following objection may be put. As a strict skeptic with respect to knowledge claims, Hume will not claim that we can know that there is definitely nothing like Causation in reality. Equally, though, he will not claim that there definitely is something like Causation in reality.

This is true. It requires us to take note of the distinction between knowledge and belief. Those who think that Hume is a straightforward regularity theorist with respect to causation standardly suppose that he makes a *knowledge* claim on the question, claiming that causation is definitely just regular succession, and that therefore there is definitely nothing like Causation. Such a knowledge claim is ruled out by his skepticism. The *belief* that there is some such thing as Causation is not ruled out, however. Skepticism can acknowledge the naturalness of this belief, and grant that it may well be something like the truth; it will merely insist that although we believe it, we cannot prove it to be true.

Some think that Hume cannot even admit to *believing* in the existence of anything like Causation, given his skepticism. I will discuss the motivation for this view in §§5 and 6. For the moment it suffices to say that Hume is not a Pyrrhonist. This objection fails to take account of his doctrine of 'natural belief', according to which we have certain natural beliefs (for example in the existence of external objects) which we find it practically impossible to give up. Skepticism of the Humean kind does not say that these beliefs are definitely not true, or unintelligible, or utterly contentless (see §6). Genuine belief in the existence of *X* is fully compatible with strict skepticism with regard to knowledge claims about the existence of *X*.

In fact Hume never really questions the idea that there is Causation—something in virtue of which reality is regular in the way that it is. Following Newton, he repeatedly insists on the epistemological claim that we know nothing of the ultimate nature of Causation. "The power or force, which actuates the whole machine . . . of the universe . . . is entirely concealed from us" (E 7.8), and "experience only teaches us, how one event constantly follows another; without instructing us in the secret connexion, which binds them together, and renders them inseparable" (E 7.13). We cannot know the nature of Causation. But to say that is not to doubt that Causation exists.

## 5

These quotations seem very clear. But it may now be objected that Hume cannot mean what he says. He cannot mean what he says because he holds that the idea of causation as something more than regular succession—the idea of Causation—is completely *unintelligible*. What's more, he says the same about the notion of 'external objects'.

The fact that he said the same about the notion of external objects may, however, be part of the solution, not part of the problem. I will now approach the general issue of Hume's attitude to questions of meaning and intelligibility by defending the view that he was committed to the intelligibility of the realist conception of objects. This commitment is obvious in the *Enquiry*, and also in the *Treatise*, but some doubt it, believing that Hume is some sort of idealist about objects, and is forced to be so by a theory of meaning which entails that talk of external objects is unintelligible.

The central point is simple. When present-day philosophers say that something is unintelligible they mean that it is incoherent and cannot exist. But Hume—with Locke, Berkeley, and many others—uses the word 'unintelligible' in the literal sense, which survives in the standard non-philosophical use of the word—as when we say that a message is unintelligible, meaning simply that we cannot understand it, although it exists ('Ni chredai Hume nad yw achosiaeth yn ddim ond cydddigwyddiad rheolaidd'). When Hume says that something is unintelligible, then, he means that we cannot understand it. In particular, he means that we cannot form an idea of it, or term for it, that has any positive descriptive content on the terms of the theory of ideas. To say this, however, is not to say that we cannot refer to it, or that the notion of it is incoherent.

Hume's position on this matter is like Locke's position with respect to the 'real essence' of gold. Locke takes it that the real essence of gold is completely unknown to us. This leads him to say that in so far as the word 'gold' carries a "tacit reference to the real essence" of gold, as it does in common use, it has "*no signification at all*, being put for somewhat, whereof we have no idea at all." In other words, the word 'gold' is *completely meaningless*—it lacks any positive descriptive content on the terms of the theory of ideas—in so far as it is taken to refer to the unknown real essence of gold. And yet it does so refer, as Locke concedes. We can perfectly well talk about the real essence of gold and take it to exist.

Berkeley makes a similar move when he proposes that the term 'notion' be used as a "term for things that cannot be understood" (*De Motu* 23). It is, he says, "absurd for any man to argue against the existence of [a] thing, from his having no direct and positive notion of it." It is only where "we have not even a relative notion of it" that we "employ words to no manner of purpose, without any design or signification whatever" (*Dialogues* 223). But "many things, for anything I know, may exist, whereof neither I nor any other man has or can have any idea or notion whatsoever" (*Dialogues* 232). This is Berkeley speaking.

Kant makes a similar move. On the one hand, he says that the categories, which include the concept of cause, "have only an empirical use, and have *no meaning whatever* when not applied to objects of possible experience." On the other hand, he says that "in *thinking*," and *a fortiori* in intelligible—hence contentful, hence meaningful—thinking, "the categories are not limited by the conditions of our sensible intuition, but have an unlimited field. It is only knowledge of what we think . . . that requires intuition."[1]

The point is routine in Hume's time. He continually stresses the fact that there may be aspects of reality of which we can form no positively descriptive conception on the terms of the theory of ideas, and which are in that sense wholly unintelligible by us. This is an integral part of his skepticism. It is, in fact, an integral part of any sound philosophy.

The claim about Hume may still be doubted. So I will consider what happens in the *Treatise* when Hume explicitly considers the thought that talk of realist external objects is 'unintelligible', given his theory of ideas.

## 6

Speaking of the notion of external objects, Hume says that it is "impossible for us so much as to conceive or form an idea of any thing *specifically different* from ideas and impressions" (T 1.2.6.8). By 'specifically different' he means 'of a different species or kind'; so his claim is that we cannot form any idea of anything which is of an entirely different species or kind from ideas and (sensory) impressions. Why not? Because the content of our ideas is entirely derived or copied from our impressions, and such impression-copy content can never amount to a genuine representation of something entirely different from impressions. But this means it can never amount to a genuine representation of an external object. For an external object is by hypothesis an essentially non-mental thing, and is obviously of an entirely different species from an essentially mental thing like an impression and an idea.

Hume, then, seems to be saying that we can never conceive of or form any idea of such a thing as an external object. But he goes straight on to grant that we can after all form some sort of conception of external objects:

> The farthest we can go towards a conception of external objects, when [they are] suppos'd specifically different from our perceptions, is to form a *relative* idea of them, without pretending to *comprehend* the related objects (T 1.2.6.9).

This is the farthest we can go; external objects are 'incomprehensible'; we have only a 'relative' idea of them. But a relative idea of X is not no idea at all. An everyday example of a case in which one has a referentially efficacious, but in a sense contentless and hence merely 'relative' idea of something X is the idea one has of something when one can refer to it only as, say, 'whatever it was that caused this appalling mess'. In this case, one may have no positive conception of the nature of X.

In the case of Causation, our merely relative idea of it is 'that in reality in virtue of which reality is regular in the way that it is'; or, in Hume's terms, it is "the power or force, which actuates the whole machine . . . of the universe" (E 7.8) and on which the "regular course and succession of objects totally depends" (E 5.22). It is "that circumstance in the cause, which gives it a connexion with its effect" (E 7.29), "that very circumstance in the cause, by which it is enabled to produce the effect" (E 7.17). Or—to quote the *Treatise* rather than the *Enquiry*—it is that which is in fact the "reason of the conjunction" of any two objects (T 1.3.6.15). This description suffices to pick Causation out in such a way that we can go on to refer to it while having no descriptively contentful conception of its nature on the terms of the theory of ideas.

. . . Hume writes that "we may *suppose*, but never can *conceive* a specific difference betwixt an object and an impression" (T 1.4.5.20). This contrast is important. It occurs at several other points in the *Treatise* (for example, T 1.2.6.9, already quoted), and the idea behind it, expressed in one way or another, is routine in Hume's time. Anything that is to count as a genuine *conception* of something must be descriptively contentful on the terms of the theory of ideas: it must have directly impression-based, impression-copy content. By contrast, a supposition that something exists or is the case can be a genuine *supposition*, genuinely about something, and hence intelligible in our present-day sense, without being contentful (or meaningful or intelligible) on the terms of the theory of ideas. So the natural supposition that there are external objects "specifically different from perceptions" is an intelligible one in our sense, and may well be true. All that follows from the theory of ideas is that we cannot form any well-founded descriptively contentful conception of external objects.

Here as elsewhere Hume respects the principles of his skepticism, which prohibit the claim that we can know that there *isn't* anything to which the merely 'relative' idea of objects realistically conceived might relate or refer. Hume grants that there may be such external objects, firmly believes that there are, and merely insists that there will always remain a sense in which their nature is "perfectly inexplicable"' by us (T 1.3.5.2). The conclusion of the famous discussion of objects in I.iv.2 of the *Treatise* is not that there are no external objects, or that the notion of such things is incoherent: unintelligible in our strong, modern sense. On the contrary. In the penultimate paragraph Hume remarks that he began his discussion of objects by "premising, that we ought to have an implicit faith" in our natural, sense-and-imagination based belief in external objects (T 1.4.2.56). He concludes that this is indeed what we ought to do, announcing in the final paragraph that he will proceed upon the "supposition . . . [that] there is both an external and an internal world" (T 1.4.2.57).

His conclusion, then, is certainly not that there are no external objects. Nor is it that the idea of external objects is incoherent (unintelligible in our strong modern sense). He has two main points, of which the first is that we can supply no decent rational foundation or justification for the belief that there are external objects: "By what argument can it be proved, that the perceptions of the mind must be caused by external objects, entirely different from them, though resembling them...?" (E 12.11). It cannot be proved, he says. For "it is a question of fact, whether the perceptions of the senses be produced by [such] external objects, resembling them," and if we ask "how shall this question be determined?", the answer is "By experience surely; as all other questions of a like nature. But here experience is, and must be entirely silent" (E 12.12).

In other words: it is either true or false that there are external objects, but we cannot know which. *A fortiori*, the supposition—and natural belief—that there are external objects is intelligible, and hence meaningful. Hume himself takes it that it is true, for the belief that it is true is part of natural belief.

His second point is that there is nonetheless something profoundly problematic, incomplete, misleading—defective, relative, inadequate, inaccurate, imprecise, imperfect, vulgar, loose, uncertain, confused, indistinct, 'fiction'-involving (see for example T 1.4.7.6, T 1.4.2.56, T 1.3.14.10, T 1.2.5.26n, E 7.15n, E 7.28-9, E 7.29n)—about any conception of external objects (or Causation) that purports to be anything more than a merely 'relative' notion of external objects. This view is a consequence of his theory of ideas, and the question he faces is then this: 'What exactly is the content of natural beliefs featuring defective conceptions of this sort?' He does not answer this question in any detail, however. It is a question which tormented many in the twentieth century, but it was not one about which Hume felt he needed to say any more. The point he insists on is that we are deluded if we think we have any sort of complete, adequate, accurate, precise, perfect, philosophical, tight, certain, distinct, legitimately sense-based conception of external objects (or Causation) . . .

## 8

. . . Some have suggested that when Hume talks of secret or concealed powers or forces, all he really means are constant conjunctions, or objects, that are too small to be detected. But even if this interpretation were thought to have some plausibility for the plural uses of terms like 'power' and 'force', it would have none for the more common singular uses. When someone speaks of the "power or force, which actuates the whole machine . . . of the universe", and says that it is "entirely concealed" from us, it is very implausible to suppose that all he really means are all those hundreds of constant conjunctions that are too small to be seen.

[At E 4.21,] after speaking of 'our natural state of ignorance with regard to the power and influence of all objects', Hume goes on to give an argument against the appeal to past experience in justifying induction that makes essential use of the idea that causal power exists. Although particular experiences of objects at particular times may indeed show us "that those particular objects, at that particular time, were endowed with . . . *powers and forces*", still, he says, we can never be sure that the objects in question will continue to have just those same powers in the future. The reason why induction cannot be justified by appeal to past experience, therefore, is precisely that "*the secret nature* [of bodies], and consequently all their effects and influence, may change", between now and the next time we observe them. So the reason why induction is not rationally justifiable by appeal to past experience is certainly not that there isn't really any power governing bodies. It is not that bodies do not really have any secret nature or powers governing their effects and influence, so that anything might happen. On the contrary. Bodies do have a secret nature which determines their effects and influence. The trouble with appeals to past experience is simply that past experience can never provide a guarantee that the secret nature of bodies will not change in the future, bringing change in their effects and influence.

This clarifies something that is obvious on reflection but often misunderstood: *there is no special link between inductive skepticism and the regularity theory of causation.* The argument for inductive skepticism just quoted appeals essentially to Causation . . .

## 12

Hume's principal targets are those philosophers (mechanists or mentalists) who think that they mean or know more than it is possible to mean or know; those who think that the intrinsic nature of causation is 'intelligible' (whether partly or wholly), and that they have some sort of genuine understanding of it. Hume thinks that it is dangerous to use words like 'power', 'force', and 'energy' without continual stress on our ignorance, for the use of these terms is likely to delude us into thinking that we do after all have some positively contentful or 'perfect' grasp of the nature of causation—a grasp that goes beyond what is given in experience of regular succession and the feeling of determination to which regular succession gives rise in human minds. This, just this, is, he insists, a mistake. Our best grasp of causation is very imperfect. We are ignorant of its nature. This ignorance is what has to be shown and argued for from all sides.

That's what Hume believed. At no point in the *Enquiry*, which must "alone be regarded as containing his philosophical sentiments and principles", does he even hint at the thesis for which he is so unjustly famous: the thesis that all there is to causation in the world is regular succession; the thesis that there is (provably) nothing at all in the nature of things in virtue of which reality is regular in the way that it is, so that the regularity of the world is, from moment to moment, and knowably, an 'outrageous run of luck'.

One might summarize the dispute about Hume as follows. Two things in Hume are incompatible: (1) the theory of ideas, strictly and literally interpreted, and (2) the view that a straightforwardly realist view of objects and causation is at least coherent and intelligible ("it is a question of fact . . ." E 12.12). Most people this century have argued that his adherence to (1) proves his rejection of (2). This is the wrong way round. Hume's adherence to (2) proves his rejection of (1). And he not only thinks that a straightforwardly realist view of objects and causation is coherent and intelligible; he standardly takes it for granted that such a view is true.

## Note

1. Kant 1787, B724 (see also B298–9); B166n (see also B309). Kant gives a clear indication of what he means by the word 'meaning' in the phrase "no meaning whatever" on B300: when the categories are not applied to what is given in sensible intuition, he says, "all meaning, that is, all reference to the object, falls away".

## CHAPTER 18

# Reply to Strawson: 'David Hume: Objects and Power'

## HELEN BEEBEE

### Introduction

In Chapter 17 Strawson argues that "Hume believes in causal power, or 'natural necessity', or 'Causation', as I will sometimes call it" (see p. 231 above). He thus aligns himself with the 'skeptical realist' interpretation of Hume, according to which Hume believes in causal powers (hence 'realist') but holds that we cannot know their nature (hence 'skeptical'). This interpretation differs markedly from what I'll call the 'traditional' interpretation, according to which Hume holds a 'regularity' theory of causation—so Hume is neither a realist (there is no such thing as Causation with a capital 'C') nor skeptical, at least in the above sense (there being no more to causation than regularity, we *can* fully grasp its nature).

A central feature of Strawson's argument is an analogy between Hume's attitude to Causation and his attitude to external objects. According to a skeptical realist interpretation of Hume on the latter issue, we 'naturally' believe that external objects exist, and those objects are the intended referents of our ordinary talk about the world: when I say that the table is wooden, I am intending to refer to a real, mind-independent table, and do in fact refer to it, if the table really does exist. And this is so even though we can form only 'relative' ideas of mind-independent objects: "The farthest we can go towards a conception of external objects, when suppos'd specifically different from our perceptions, is to form a *relative* idea of them, without pretending to *comprehend* the related objects" (T 1.2.6.9). When it comes to Causation, Strawson thinks, Hume takes the same basic view: we naturally believe that Causation exists (see p. 235

242

above), and our ordinary causal talk refers to Causation, even though we can only form a 'relative' idea of it (see p. 236 above).

My approach in this chapter will be as follows. In the next section, I shall cast some doubt on Strawson's claim that the second thesis above—that our ordinary causal talk refers to Causation despite its being 'unintelligible' to us—has historical precedents in the work of Locke and Berkeley. I shall argue that while Locke and Berkeley hold that there are, or may be, features of reality that are 'unintelligible', they also hold that such features are what I shall call 'cognitively idle': they do not, or should not, play a role in either our ordinary talk and thought or our philosophical theorizing.

In the third section, I shall argue that Causation—but not belief in external objects—is similarly cognitively idle for Hume. Suppose that Strawson is right that Hume takes our causal talk to refer to Causation. What difference does this make to the issues Hume cares about—in particular, issues concerning the epistemology and psychology of causation? The answer, I shall suggest, is 'none.' All of Hume's central epistemological and psychological claims concerning causation are independent of whether or not he believes in—and takes our causal talk to refer to—Causation.

In other words, there is a striking disanalogy between Hume's view (interpreted in a skeptical realist light) about belief in external objects and his view about belief in Causation, namely that the latter, but not the former, plays no useful role in our cognitive lives. And this gives us *prima facie* reason to reject Strawson's interpretation of the latter: Hume simply has no need for a belief in some regularity-guaranteeing feature of reality. On the other hand, the cognitive idleness of belief in Causation also, I shall argue in the final section, goes some way towards explaining why the interpretative controversy surrounding his views on causation has proved to be so intractable.

## Intelligibility and Reference: Locke and Berkeley

Strawson argues that the traditional, regularity interpretation of Hume attributes to him an inference from the epistemological claim

(E)  All we can ever know of causation is regular succession

to the ontological claim

(O)  All that causation actually is, in the objects, is regular succession

via the semantic claim

(S)  All we can legitimately *manage to mean* by expressions like 'causation in the objects' is regular succession. (see p. 234 above)

In effect, Strawson's contention is that (S) is ambiguous. Disambiguating, we have:

> (S1) The only legitimate *descriptive content* of expressions like 'causation in the objects' is regular succession; and
>
> (S2) The only legitimate *reference* of expressions like 'causation in the objects' is regular succession.

The central issue then becomes whether Hume takes (S1)—a claim he undoubtedly subscribes to—to entail (S2). If he does, then it seems that we have grounds for attributing (O) to him as well; if he doesn't, then we don't.

Hume's theory of ideas, according to which the content of an idea is determined solely by the impression of which it is a copy, makes (S1) true: 'Causation,' that feature of the world upon which regular succession depends, is in this sense 'unintelligible' to us. But does Hume think that (S1) entails (S2)? The traditional interpretation, it would seem, answers 'yes': the reference of terms like 'causation in the objects' is determined solely by their descriptive content, and so they can only succeed in referring to regular succession. Strawson argues, however, that Hume rejects (S2): our idea of causation *refers* to Causation, even though Causation is 'unintelligible' to us. We can, and indeed do, 'suppose' that Causation exists, even though we cannot grasp its nature, and this is because we have a 'relative idea' of it:

> ... our merely relative idea of [Causation] is "that in reality in virtue of which reality is regular in the way that it is"; or, in Hume's terms, it is "the power or force, which actuates the whole machine ... of the universe" (E 7.8) and on which the "regular course and succession of objects totally depends" (E 5.22). This description suffices to pick Causation out in such a way that we can go on to refer to it while having no descriptively contentful conception of its nature on the terms of the theory of ideas.
>
> (p. 238 above)

Thus the inference from (E) to (O) is blocked.

My point of entry into this dispute about the truth (according to Hume) of (S2) will be to reconsider the historical precedents that Strawson claims for Hume's (alleged) view that unintelligibility, or lack of 'meaning' in the sense of (S1), is no impediment to reference. My claim here will be that while both Locke and Berkeley accept that there can be (and in Locke's case, there definitely are) 'relative' ideas that succeed in referring to things that are unintelligible to us, such ideas do *not* include the ideas that we (legitimately) deploy in our ordinary talk and thought about the world: ideas such as *gold*, or *table*, or *cat*. I shall argue that they therefore set no precedent for holding that the idea of *causation* refers to what Strawson calls Causation.

First, then, Strawson likens Hume's position on causation to Locke's position with respect to real essences. Strawson notes, rightly, that "Locke takes it that the real essence of gold is completely unknown to us" (see p. 236 above). He continues:

> This leads [Locke] to say that in so far as the word 'gold' carries a "tacit reference to the real essence" of gold, as it does in common use, it has "*no signification at all*, being put for somewhat, whereof we have no idea at all". In other words, the word 'gold' is *completely meaningless*—it lacks any positive descriptive content on the terms of the theory of ideas—in so far as it is taken to refer to the unknown essence of gold. And yet it does so refer, as Locke concedes.
>
> (see p. 236 above)

On Locke's view, the *nominal* essence of a kind, such as gold, is constituted by those features that we gather together in our 'abstract idea' of gold: "the *nominal essence* of *gold*, is that complex idea the word *gold* stands for, let it be, for instance, a body yellow, of a certain weight, malleable, fusible, and fixed" (*Essay* III.vi.2). The real essence, by contrast, is "the constitution of the insensible parts of that body, on which those qualities, and all the other properties of *gold* depend" (ibid.). In other words, Locke firmly believes that the presence of the observable features of gold (colour, malleability, etc.) *in principle* has a causal explanation in terms of the constitution of its 'insensible parts,' but that inner constitution remains hidden from us.

Locke is standardly taken, however, to hold that the extension of the term 'gold' is determined *solely* by its nominal essence. So it is somewhat surprising to find him apparently saying, in the passage quoted by Strawson, that 'gold' actually refers to the *real*—and not the nominal—essence of gold, and hence, given the unknowability of the real essence, that "the word 'gold' is *completely meaningless*—it lacks any positive descriptive content."

What has happened here? Well, in the section in which the passage occurs, Locke is discussing what he regards as a common *mistake* (indeed, the passage quoted by Strawson appears in a chapter titled 'On the abuse of words'). People "secretly . . . suppose [the name 'gold'] annexed to a real immutable essence of a thing existing, on which those properties depend" (*Essay* III.x.19). In other words, we 'secretly' take it that the name refers not to whatever happens to have the *nominal* essence of gold, but to whatever has a particular, but unspecifiable because unknown, *real* essence. But it is "preposterous and absurd . . . to make our names stand for *ideas* that we have not, or (which is all one) *essences* that we know not" (*Essay* III.x.21).

Strawson is thus right to attribute to Locke the view that we do, in fact, often use general names such as 'gold' with the intention of referring to real essences. But Locke does not endorse that usage; on the contrary, he regards it as an abuse of language. So his charge that the word 'gold', thus abused, has "*no signification at all*" is not by any means an endorsement of the view that it is perfectly legitimate to use words that (in Strawson's words) "lack any positive descriptive content." On the contrary: Locke's point is precisely that to use a word in such a way that it has "no signification" is a very bad idea indeed.

Locke does, admittedly, take the expression 'real essence' itself to be something like a relative idea, in that it genuinely refers but to something whose nature is unknowable; all we can say about the real essence of a kind is that it is "the constitution of the insensible parts of that body"—whatever that might be—"on which [the observable] properties of *gold* depend." So, by Locke's lights, Hume might well be allowed to take expressions such as "that on which the regular course and succession of objects totally depends" to be referring expressions. But what he would *not* be allowed is the further claim that "this description suffices to pick Causation out," if (as Strawson does) we take Causation to be the referent of the term 'causation.' The move from the former to the latter is analogous to the move from the claim that the expression 'the real essence of gold' refers to the real essence of gold to the claim that the expression 'gold' *itself* refers to the real essence of gold—a move that Locke clearly regards as illegitimate.

Let's turn now to Berkeley. As Strawson notes, Berkeley says that it is "absurd for any man to argue against the existence of [a] thing, from his having no direct and positive notion of it" (*Dialogues* 223). It is only where "we have not even a relative notion of it" that we "employ words to no manner of purpose, without any design or signification whatsoever" (*Dialogues* 223) (see p. 236 above).

Berkeley here appears to be endorsing the claim that we *can* employ words with 'design' and 'signification' when they express relative ideas, which of course is just what Strawson needs, given that 'causation' is a relative idea according to his interpretation of Hume. In fact, however, it turns out that Berkeley's only explicit example of a purported 'relative idea' is one that he dismisses as illegitimate; and that example bears a striking resemblance to Strawson's conception of the relative idea of Causation.

Berkeley, an idealist, argues against the existence of "*matter* or *corporeal substance*" (PHK 9). He says:

> The table I write on, I say, exists, that is, I see and feel it; and if I were out of my study I should say it existed, meaning thereby that if I was in my study I might perceive it, or that some other spirit actually does perceive it ... This is all that I can understand by [this] and the like expressions. For as to what is said of the absolute existence of unthinking things without any relation to their being perceived, that seems perfectly unintelligible. Their *esse* is *percipi*, nor is it possible they should have any existence, out of the minds or thinking things which perceive them.
>
> (PHK 3)

So Berkeley's view seems to be that it is *impossible* for unthinking things to exist outside the minds that perceive them; in other words, all that exist are thinking substances and their ideas. Thus tables, for example, are mere ideas; and this must be so *because* it is 'unintelligible' that they should exist outside the mind.

Again, it is hard to square this latter claim with the passages quoted by Strawson, where Berkeley seems to accept that there may well be many things "whereof neither I nor any other man has or can have any idea or notion whatsoever"—including, presumably, things that are neither ideas nor thinkers. So in fact he would appear to hold the more modest view that *when we are talking with 'purpose', 'design', and 'signification'*—as, for example, when we talk about tables or cats or trees—our words can only refer to ideas. In other words, Berkeley concedes that there may be more things in heaven and earth than are dreamt of in his idealist philosophy; but those things are not the things that our everyday and philosophical talk is *about*.

A key point in Berkeley's argument comes in response to the possibility that the notion of material substance is a relative idea. Grant that 'sensible qualities,' such as color, extension, and solidity, cannot exist but as ideas in the mind of a thinking subject. Perhaps we can nonetheless conceive of matter as the mind-independent 'substratum' that 'supports' sensible qualities or 'accidents' (such as extension), so that (for example) our talk about tables is after all talk about mind-independent material objects, *qua* substrata.

Berkeley's response to this objection is this:

> if you have any meaning at all, you must at least have a relative idea of matter; though you know not what it is, yet you must be supposed to know what relation it bears to accidents, and what is meant by its supporting them. It is evident support cannot here be taken in its usual or literal sense, as when we say that pillars support a building: in what sense therefore must it be taken? (PHK 16)

He evidently thinks no sensible answer to this question can be given.

Berkeley thus has no time for the view that we have a relative idea of material objects. And I think it is pretty clear that he would respond in a similar fashion to Strawson's proposed account of the relative idea of causation: "that in reality *in virtue of* which reality is regular in the way that it is," or "the power or force, which *actuates* the whole machine . . . of the universe," or that on which the "regular course and succession of objects totally *depends*" (my italics). As with Berkeley's complaint about the notion of 'support,' the relations supposedly picked out by the italicized phrases cannot be taken in their usual or literal senses, as when we say that the machine was actuated by someone pulling a lever, or that my punctual arrival depends upon the traffic. Such relations are clearly causal relations, and presumably Causation *itself* cannot stand in the causal relation to the regularities that it is supposed to underpin.[1]

My point here is that for Berkeley, lack of intelligibility (as in (S1)) does indeed entail failure of reference (as in (S2)). If a purported entity X lacks intelligibility, *or* if it is supposedly understood merely insofar as it stands in a relation to something intelligible (such as sensory experience) but the relation itself is unintelligible, then we cannot refer to X. By Berkeley's lights, Causation—conceived as something of which we have only a relative idea—falls into this second category.

There are three conclusions that I want to draw from the above discussion of Locke and Berkeley. First, *pace* Strawson, the claim that Causation, conceived as the ground of regularity, is the referent of our ordinary causal talk is one that finds no indirect support in the work of Locke or Berkeley. Second, and relatedly, the claim that there is or may be more to the world than mere ideas (Berkeley) or nominal essences (Locke) or regular succession (Hume) is one that does not, just by itself, undermine the traditional conception of Hume as a regularity theorist about causation, any more than it undermines the standard reading of Berkeley as an idealist. *Pace* Strawson, the fact that Hume "does not make positive claims about what definitely (or knowably) does not exist" is *not* "enough to refute any attribution of (O) [all that causation actually is, in the objects, is regular succession] to him" (see p. 235 above). It is one thing to say that there is, or may be, more in the world than mere regularity (or in Berkeley's case, ideas); it is quite another to assert that the 'more' in question is the referent of the word 'cause' (or, again in Berkeley's case, 'cat' or 'table').

Third, Locke and Berkeley appear to take unintelligibility to be grounds for what I'm calling 'cognitive idleness.' Locke's commitment to real essences plays no role in his account of the legitimate use of substance names, and, as we've seen, this is precisely because real essences are unintelligible. Similarly, Berkeley takes the unintelligibility of 'matter' to show that our talk and thought about the world is talk and thought about ideas, and not about extra-mental reality. So again, while he leaves it open that extra-mental entities may exist, their unintelligibility renders them unfit to play any positive role in our thinking. In the next section, I consider whether Causation, considered as a regularity-guaranteeing feature of reality, might similarly be cognitively idle for Hume.

## Causation, the External World, and Cognitive Idleness

Grant that the skeptical realist interpretation of Hume on external objects, as sketched briefly in the first section above, is broadly correct. Hume's view, thus construed, differs radically from Berkeley's idealism: Hume agrees with Berkeley that we can have no contentful idea of external objects considered as 'specifically different' from impressions but, unlike Berkeley, he holds that we nonetheless refer to them when we talk about chairs and tables.

Belief in external objects is a 'natural belief' for Hume, in the sense that it is "'inevitable', 'indispensable', and . . . thus removed beyond the reach of our sceptical doubts" (Kemp Smith 1941, 87). It arises, Hume thinks, by a 'natural instinct':

> It seems evident, that men are carried, by a natural instinct or preposs-session, to repose faith in their senses; and that, without any reasoning . . . we always suppose an external universe, which depends not on our perception, but would exist, though we and every sensible creature were absent or annihilated.
>
> (E 12.7)

And both its inevitability and its indispensability are demonstrated by Hume's response to the skeptic:

> Thus the sceptic. . . must assent to the principle concerning the existence of body, tho' he cannot pretend by any arguments of philosophy to main-tain its veracity. Nature has not left this to his choice, and has doubtless esteem'd it an affair of too great importance to be trusted to our uncer-tain reasonings and speculations.
>
> (T 1.4.2.1)

The skeptic cannot help but believe in the existence of body—it is simply inev-itable that we believe this, no matter how hard we try to suspend judgment. And that belief is indispensable: it is "of too great an importance to be trusted to our uncertain reasonings and speculations." Indeed, "[e]ven the animal creation are governed by a like opinion, and preserve this belief of external objects, in all their thoughts, designs, and actions" (E 12.7).

It is indispensability, as opposed to mere inevitability, that I want to con-trast with cognitive idleness. Our (and other animals') "thoughts, designs and actions" would not be as they are if we (*per impossibile*) gave up our belief in external objects: our ability to make our way around the world would be severely compromised. For Hume, belief in external objects plays a vital role both in our thinking and in our ability to get around in the world.

What about the case of Causation? On Strawson's view of Hume, belief in Causation, like belief in external objects, is a natural belief (see p. 235 above). I shall argue, however, that we cannot characterize Hume as holding that belief in Causation is *indispensable*—a belief without which we would be unable to function in some crucial respect—in the same way as he holds that belief in external objects is indispensable.

To see why, we need to take a brief detour into Hume's account of causal or 'inductive' reasoning, that is, reasoning from causes to effects. That account is summarized in Hume's discussion of skepticism in section 12 of the first *Enquiry*, where he says that the skeptic:

> justly insists, that all our evidence for any matter of fact, which lies beyond the testimony of sense or memory, is derived entirely from the relation of cause and effect; that we have no other idea of this relation than that of two objects, which have been frequently conjoined together; that we have no argument to convince us, that objects, which have, in our experience, been frequently conjoined, will likewise, in other instances, be conjoined in the same manner; and that nothing leads us to this inference but custom or a certain instinct of our nature.
>
> (E 12.12)

Strawson notes that in his earlier discussion Hume considers, and dismisses, an attempted rational justification for induction that appeals to the 'secret nature' of objects (see p. 240 above). The idea here is that if we could infer *a priori* from past regularity that objects of kind *C* have a secret 'power of production' that necessitates a particular effect *E*, then we could infer *a priori*, on observing a *C*, that an *E* will follow. And Hume points out that we cannot infer *a priori* that *all* *C*s have this power of production, since it is perfectly possible that the secret powers of *C*s have changed, so that they are no longer guaranteed to produce *E*s.[2] Strawson stresses in a footnote that he has "no wish" to "invoke fundamental physical forces 'to soothe away inductive vertigo' (Blackburn 1990, 244)," since "[n]othing could do it, as Hume's argument shows."[3]

Strawson is clearly right about Hume's argument: as far as inductive skepticism is concerned, belief in Causation fares no better than the mere belief that the future will resemble the past, since neither belief admits of rational justification of the kind demanded by the skeptic, and so neither can be used to shore up inductive inference. What is important when it comes to cognitive idleness, however, is whether belief in Causation plays an indispensible role in our *actual* practice of inferring effects from causes—granted that no satisfactory response (by the skeptic's own lights) to the skeptic can be given. And the answer to that question, I think, is 'no.' We infer effects from causes via custom or habit, which takes us from past regularity to expectations about the future. To additionally conceive of the relation between cause and effect as that of Causation adds nothing at all to our ability to do this. Hume thinks that if we gave up the expectations generated by custom, "[a]ll discourse, all action would immediately cease; and men remain in a total lethargy, till the necessities of nature, unsatisfied, put an end to their miserable existence" (E 12.23). So the inference from causes to effects is certainly not cognitively idle: it is central to our very survival. Belief in Causation, however, is not required in order for us to be able to infer effects from causes in just the way that we do. What would happen to us, then, if (perhaps, as with the case of the external world, *per impossibile*) we gave up on Causation? Nothing at all: we would carry on in just the way that we do. In order to get about the place, we only need to believe that the universe is regular; we do not additionally need to believe that there is a reason *why* it is regular.

Let's return to Locke and Berkeley for a moment. I argued above that for both Locke and Berkeley, unintelligibility goes hand-in-hand with cognitive idleness. When it comes to the external world, Hume breaks that connection: he holds that belief in external objects is not cognitively idle, but cannot see a way of rendering external objects intelligible. Hence their existence must be something we automatically 'suppose' despite the fact that we cannot form a contentful idea of what they *are*. But Hume has no need to think that the same is true in the case of Causation, because belief in Causation *is* cognitively idle on his view. Reasoning from causes to effects is what enables us to make our way in the world—to 'act and reason and believe.' The belief that there is an item of ontology that underpins that inference—a reason *why* the universe is regular—is a belief that we can do without, without coming to any harm. So Hume has no motivation for holding that 'cause' refers to Causation. Strawson may be right that Hume himself never seriously doubts that there is some "power or force, which actuates the whole machine." But Hume has no reason to suppose that this is a 'natural belief' shared by all normally-functioning human beings, akin to the belief in external objects, since it is a belief that (unlike belief in external objects) does not play a central role in our cognitive lives. Correspondingly, he has no reason to suppose that this regularity guaranteeing 'power or force' is the referent of 'cause.'

## Why is the Debate about Hume on Causation so Intractable?

Why has the debate about Hume's views on causation proved to be so indecisive? I want to suggest two answers to this question. The first engages with Strawson's prescription (see p. 232 above) that we ignore everything in the *Treatise* that appears to be incompatible with the *Enquiry*, and that we read the *Enquiry* back into the *Treatise* wherever possible. If we follow Strawson's advice, some version of the skeptical realist interpretation seems fairly plausible. (The worries expressed in this paper are directed at Strawson's own particular brand of skeptical realism, and in particular his claim that Hume believes in a 'reason' why the universe is regular. Other brands of skeptical realism do not attribute this particular view to Hume, and correspondingly fare better against the objection I have been pressing.) But it is not at all obvious that we *should* follow Strawson's advice. We are under no *moral* obligation to Hume to do as he asks—that the *Enquiries* "*may alone be regarded as containing his philosophical sentiments and principles*" (E Advertisement). So the issue turns on whether we have good epistemic reasons for taking him at his word. And here there is considerable room for doubt: it is very hard to read the first *Enquiry* as *merely* correcting "*some negligences in his former reasoning and more in the expression*" (Ibid.), and hence as presenting essentially the same view as the *Treatise*. Perhaps (*pace* Strawson) we should simply regard the *Treatise* and the *Enquiry* as expressing views that are different but related in interesting ways.

The second answer connects with the issue of cognitive idleness. Disputes about which passages in Hume should be taken literally, how many times he uses the expression 'secret power' referentially, and so on obviously play a legitimate role in the interpretative dispute. But a broader question is: what purpose does Hume take his discussion of causation to serve? My own view is that he is considerably more interested in psychology and epistemology than in semantics and metaphysics: in the case of causation and causal reasoning, he is primarily interested in how we come to form expectations and think of the world as a world of causes and effects, and in refuting any attempt to claim that we can have *a priori* access to the causal structure of reality.

If that's right, then there is a sense in which Hume simply does not need to resolve the kinds of issues that are the main bones of contention in the interpretative dispute about causation. The precise semantic content of our idea of causation, and hence what we intend to refer to when we use causal language, is largely irrelevant to the issues Hume is interested in, since his account of inference from causes to effects and his claim that the idea of causation arises as a result of that inference do not depend on what, if anything, the intended referent of the idea of causation is. The cognitive idleness of belief in Causation may, as I have argued, be a reason to think that Hume does not take the case of causal belief to be analogous to the case of belief in external objects. But even if I am wrong about that, it may be part of the explanation of why Hume managed to be so unclear on the semantic and metaphysical questions that have so exercised recent interpreters.

## Notes

1. The expression 'in virtue of' appears to have virtually no currency outside philosophy, theology, and law—a fact that only serves to heighten the suspicion that it has no clear meaning, at least by Berkeley's standards.
2. Part of Strawson's point here is that Hume is here (once again) using terms like 'power,' 'force,' and 'secret nature' referentially. I argue elsewhere (Beebee 2006, §7.2) that Hume's use of these expressions in his discussion of induction is not persuasive evidence in favor of the skeptical realist interpretation.
3. Editors' note: that footnote is in a part of Strawson's chapter not included in the above abridged version.

# PART X

# Hume on Miracles

# Editors' Introduction

In section 10 of his *Enquiry concerning Human Understanding*, Hume considers the topic of miracles. He suggests that his argument might "be an everlasting check to all kinds of superstitious delusion." And ultimately he thinks he can show that "no human testimony can have such force as to prove a miracle, and make it a just foundation for" any of the "popular religions" (E 10.35). This argument has attracted a good deal of attention. There was no shortage of people writing responses to Hume's essay in the eighteenth century. And readers continue to puzzle over just what Hume's argument was, and whether we ought to accept it, or anything like it.

John Earman regards Hume's argument as a disaster. He titled his book on the topic *Hume's Abject Failure*, and in the related chapter that appears here, he describes Hume's essay as "a shambles," "tame and derivative," "something of a muddle," and as having "that combination of vagueness, obscurity, and aphorism that philosophers find irresistible." Central to Earman's rejection of Hume's argument is his view that Hume has a seriously defective account of how we should weigh up the evidence we get from the testimony of others.

In his response, Peter Millican argues that Earman misinterprets Hume's arguments. So even if the view Earman discusses is radically mistaken, that does not show that Hume was radically mistaken. Now Millican does grant that there are difficulties with Hume's position, even when it is correctly understood. But he ends by recommending a revised Humean view that could avoid these difficulties.

## A Note on Probabilities and Bayesianism

Earman believes that, rather than following Hume's remarks, we should instead adopt a form of Bayesianism. Thomas Bayes, after whom Bayesianism is named, was indeed a contemporary of Hume, though unknown to him. Bayesianism is a way of thinking about evidence and probabilities. Suppose you already have a view about how likely an event is to happen, and you then get some new relevant evidence. How should you change your view about the likelihood of the event?

Both Earman and Millican think about evidence in terms of numerical probabilities, between 0 and 1. $P(A)$ is the probability of event $A$. In this context, you might think of it as the degree of confidence you have that $A$ will happen. If $P(A) = 1$, you are completely certain that $A$ will happen; if $P(A) = 0$ you are completely convinced that it will not; if $P(A) = 0.6$, you regard $A$ as somewhat more likely than not; and so on.

$P(A|B)$ is the probability of $A$, given $B$.[1] So if, for example, $P(A|B) = 0.8$, your degree of confidence in $A$ happening, given that $B$ happens, is 0.8. If you also think that $P(A|\neg B) = 0.4$, you think $A$ is twice as likely to happen if $B$ happens than if it doesn't.

Your initial assessment of the likelihood of an event is sometimes called the prior probability you assign to the event. However, you should update the probability you assign to the event in the light of subsequent evidence (e.g. testimony of witnesses). Suppose you think that some event $M$ is rather unlikely: $P(M) = 0.1$. Suppose then that a friend tells you that $M$ just happened: call the event of receiving this testimony $t(M)$. This gives you a reason to increase the probability you assign to $M$. But it shouldn't make you *certain* that $M$ happened: your friend might be mistaken, lying, or joking. Rather, the new value of $P(M)$ should be somewhere between 0.1 and 1. But how can you decide where exactly it should be? How do you determine the probability of $M$, given the evidence of your friend's testimony?

Bayes's Theorem answers this question. According to Bayes's Theorem,

$$P(M|t(M)) = P(t(M)|M) \times [P(M)/P(t(M))]$$

This tells us that the probability of $M$, given $t(M)$, depends on three things: the probability of $M$, the probability of $t(M)$, and the probability of receiving that testimony $t(M)$ given that $M$ happened.

Consider our example. You assigned the prior probability of 0.1 to $M$. Suppose that the probability of $t(M)$ is 0.2. But the probability of $t(M)$, *given M*, is 0.9: although neither $M$ nor your friend's testimony are themselves likely, if $M$ did happen, your friend would probably have seen it and told you about it. So, according to Bayes's Theorem, the probability of $M$ given $t(M)$ is 0.45. Thus, when $t(M)$ happens, you should update $P(M)$ to 0.45.[2] This method can be used over and over, as we acquire more evidence, to further revise the probabilities we assign to events.

## A Note on References

References to Hume's works use two abbreviations: 'T' for his *Treatise of Human Nature*, and 'E' for his *Enquiry concerning Human Understanding*. References to these texts are to the book, part, section, and paragraph in the *Treatise*, or the section and paragraph in the *Enquiry*. Thus 'T 1.1.1.1' refers to the first paragraph of the *Treatise*, and 'E 9.1' to the first paragraph of section 9 of the *Enquiry*. These paragraph numbers are printed in Hume (1999), Hume (2001) and Hume (2007), as well as in the versions at www.davidhume.org. The *Enquiry* edition Hume (2007) also includes excerpts of Hume's letters that pertain to miracles.

## Further Reading

- John Earman (2000). *Hume's Abject Failure: The Argument Against Miracles*. This also includes reprints of a variety of relevant discussions, from chapters of Locke's *Essay concerning Human Understanding* to Charles Babbage's 1837 *Ninth Bridgewater Treatise*.
- Robert J. Fogelin (2003). *A Defense of Hume on Miracles*.
- Peter Millican (1993). "'Hume's Theorem' Concerning Miracles."
- Peter Millican (2011). "Twenty Questions about Hume's 'Of Miracles'."
- William Talbott (2011). "Bayesian Epistemology."

## Notes

1. By definition, $P(A|B) = P(A\&B)/P(B)$.
2. This example involves initial probabilities of 79% for $(\neg M\&\neg t(M))$, 11% for $(\neg M\&t(M))$, 9% for $(M\&t(M))$, and 1% for $(M\&\neg t(M))$.

## CHAPTER 19

# Bayes, Hume, Price, and Miracles

JOHN EARMAN

My topic is the Bayesian analysis of miracles. To make the discussion concrete, I will set it in the context of eighteenth-century debate on miracles, and I will focus on the response to David Hume's celebrated argument against miracles that Thomas Bayes would have made and did in part make, albeit from beyond the grave, through his colleague Richard Price.

## 1.  My trinity: Bayes, Price, and Hume

It is irresistible to think that Thomas Bayes had read Hume and that Bayes' "Essay Towards Solving a Problem in the Doctrine of Chances" was at least in part a reaction to Hume's skeptical attack on induction.[1] But while the Appendix of the published paper is surely making reference to Hume, that Appendix was penned not by Bayes but by Richard Price. It is also nice to think that Hume read Bayes' essay and then to speculate about what Hume's reaction would have been. But while there is a reference to Bayes' essay in Price's *Four Dissertations*, a copy of which was sent to Hume who duly acknowledged receiving and reading it (see below), there is no evidence that Hume followed up the reference. And even if he had, it is unlikely that he would have understood Bayes' essay since he was largely innocent of the technical developments that were taking place in the probability calculus.

While there is no evidence of a direct connection between Bayes and Hume, the indirect connection that goes through Price is solid. Although we know little of the relationship between Bayes and Price, it must have been reasonably close since Bayes' will left £200 to be divided between Price and one John Boyl (see Barnard 1958) and since it was Price who arranged for the posthumous publication of Bayes' essay. In the other direction, Price was a persistent critic of Hume—not just on induction but on matters of religion and ethics as well. Despite the sharp differences in opinion the two men remained on remarkably cordial terms, dining together in London and in Price's home in Newington Green (see Thomas, 1924). In the second edition of *Four Dissertations* Hume is lauded by Price as "a writer whose genius and abilities are so distinguished as to be above any of my commendations" (Price 1768, 382). And Hume in turn praised Price for the "civility which you have treated me" (Hume 1954, 233–4). More intriguingly, Hume goes on to say that "I own to you, that the Light in which you have put this Controversy [about miracles] is new and plausible and ingenious, and perhaps solid". Unfortunately, Hume left the matter hanging by adding that "I must have some more time to weigh it, before I can pronounce this Judgment with satisfaction to myself" (Ibid.).

I will finish Hume's unfinished task. I will claim that Price's criticisms of Hume's argument against miracles were largely solid. More generally, I claim that when Hume's "Of miracles" is examined through the lens of Bayesianism, it is seen to be a shambles.[2]

## 2. The context

The debate on miracles which took place in eighteenth-century Britain is rich and endlessly fascinating. One of the key philosophical problems underlying the debate was posed before the beginning of the century in Locke's *Essay Concerning Human Understanding*, namely, how should one apportion belief when the two main sources of credibility, "common observation in like cases" and "particular testimonies", are at odds? The case of eyewitness testimony to miraculous events—the central focus of Hume's "Of miracles"—presents the extreme form of this problem. The miraculous event around which the eighteenth-century debate swirled was, of course, the Resurrection of Jesus of Nazareth, though the more prudent naysayers took care to make oblique reference to this matter—Hume, for example, couches his discussion in terms of the hypothetical case of the resurrection of Queen Elizabeth.

To convey a bit of the flavor of the debate I will trace one of the many threads—the one that starts with Thomas Woolston, one of the incautious naysayers. His *Six Discourses on the Miracles of Our Saviour* (1727–29) was an undisguised and broadsided attack on the New Testament miracles. As attested by Swift, it created a minor sensation:[3]

Here is Woolston's tract, the twelfth edition
'Tis read by every politician:
The country members when in town
To all their boroughs send them down:

You never met a thing so smart;
The courtiers have them all by heart.

What the courtiers learned from reading Woolston was that the New Testament accounts of miracles were filled with "absurdities, improbabilities, and incredibilities". While Woolston's charges and his sarcasm and obvious contempt for the Church authorities won him a large readership—reportedly, 30,000 copies of *Six Discourses* were printed—they also earned him a fine and a stay in prison, where he died.

Six Discourses received a number of replies, the most influential being Thomas Sherlock's *Tryal of the Witnesses* (1728), which itself went through fourteen editions. Sherlock was answered by Peter Annet (I744a, 1744b), and Annet in turn was answered by Chandler (1744), Jackson (1744), and West (1747). And so it went.

Set in this context, Hume's essay on miracles seems both tame and derivative. It is also something of a muddle. What appears on first reading to be a powerful and seamless argument turns on closer examination to be a series of considerations that don't comfortably mesh. And worse, Hume's thesis remains obscure—the possibilities range from the banal to the absurd:

(T1)  One should be cautious in accepting testimony to marvelous and miraculous events, and doubly so when religious themes arise.

(T2)  The testimonies of the Disciples do not establish the credibility of the resurrection of Jesus.

(T3)  In no recorded case does the testimony of eyewitnesses establish the credibility of a miracle deemed to have religious significance.

(T4)  Eyewitness testimony is incapable of establishing the credibility of a miracle deemed to have religious significance.

(T5)  Eyewitness testimony is incapable of establishing the credibility of any miraculous event.

Hume deserves no credit—save for pompous solemnity—for uttering various forms of the banality (T1), since even the pro-miracle proponents in the eighteenth-century debate were at pains to acknowledge the pitfalls of eyewitness testimony and the need to carefully sift the evidence, especially in the case of religious miracles. Hume believed (T2), but refused to join Annet, Sherlock, Woolston, et al. in arguing the specifics. He surely also believed something in the neighbourhood of (T3), but his cursory recitation and rejection in Part II of his essay of a number of sacred and profane miracles hardly counts as much of an argument for this sweeping thesis. What Hume manages beautifully is the creation of an illusion that he was in possession of principles for evaluating evidence that allowed him to remain above the nastiness of the fray. This would have been the case if he had been in possession of principles that entailed (T4) or (T5). But there are no such principles since (T4) and (T5) are absurd. A skilful oscillation among these various theses is what helps to create the illusion of a worthy argument against miracles.

Stripped of the theology, the key issue addressed in Hume's essay is how to evaluate the evidential force of fallible witnesses. The obvious tool to apply was the probability calculus, and one of the first published applications in English was the anonymous (George Hooper?) essay "A Calculation of the Credibility of Human Testimony", which appeared in the 1699 *Transactions of the Royal Society*. Some advances were made in the eighteenth century—for example, by Price—but it was not until the work of Laplace (1812, 1814) and Charles Babbage (1838) that definitive results were obtained. Hume's pronouncements on the key issue have that combination of vagueness, obscurity, and aphorism that philosophers find irresistible, and, consequently, have led to an endless and largely unfruitful debate in the philosophical literature, the contributors to which are willing to go to extraordinary lengths in an attempt to show that Hume had something interesting to say on the matter.

To state what should be obvious, but still manages to elude some commentators, the core issues in Hume's essay are independent of the theological subtleties of that vexed term 'miracle'. For what an eyewitness testifies to in the first instance is the occurrence of an event which can be characterized in purely naturalistic terms, e.g., the return to life of a dead man. How such an event, if its credibility is established by eyewitness testimony, can serve theological purposes is a matter I will take up in due course. But first I have to substantiate my negative evaluation of Hume's treatment of eyewitness testimony. At the same time I hope to show how the issues can be advanced with the help of Bayes' apparatus.

## 3. Hume's 'proof' against miracles

Here is Hume's 'proof', such as it is:

> A miracle is a violation of the laws of nature; and as a firm and unalterable experience has established these laws, the proof against a miracle, from the very nature of the fact, is as entire as any argument from experience can possibly be imagined.
>
> (E 10.12)

For Hume 'proofs' are "such arguments from experience as leave no room for doubt or opposition" (E 6, note to title). He thought his proof against miracles fitted this bill since it is 'full and certain when taken alone, because it implies no doubt, as in the case of all probabilities' (Hume 1932, 1.350). In probability language, Hume seems to be saying that if $L$ is a lawlike generalization, such as 'No dead man returns to life', and $E$ records uniform past experience in favor of $L$, then $P(L \mid E) = 1$; hence, if $M$ asserts a violation of $L$, then it follows from the rules of probability that $P(M \mid E) = O$.

Price opposed Hume's wildly incautious and inaccurate account of inductive practice: "It must be remembered, that the greatest uniformity and frequency of experience will not offer a proper proof, that an event will happen in a future trial" (Price 1768, 393) ... The relevant thing to note for present purposes is that Hume's account of inductive practice is descriptively inaccurate: scientists don't think that uniform experience in favor of a lawlike generalization leaves no room for doubt—if they did it would be hard to explain their continued efforts to search for exceptions.

But the crucial point is that Hume recognized that his 'proof' only applies when the evidence consists of uniform experience (recall the qualifier 'when taken alone'). The real issue is joined when that proof is opposed by a counterproof from eyewitness testimony. Many commentators from Hume's day to the present have read Hume as saying that this contest has a preordained outcome. The idea is that the probative force of eyewitness testimony derives from the observation of the conformity between the testimony and reality; but whereas our experience in favor of the relevant lawlike generalization and, thus, against an exception that constitutes a miracle, is uniform, our experience as to the trustworthiness of witnesses is anything but uniform. Thus, Price took Hume to be arguing that to believe a miracle on the basis of testimony is to "prefer a weaker proof to a stronger" (Price 1768, 385).[4] Such a reading makes Hume's essay into a puzzle: if this was Hume's argument, why did the essay have to be more than one page long? And apart from the puzzle, the position being attributed to Hume implies the absurd thesis (T5).

The anti-miracle forces in the eighteenth-century debate sometimes asserted that uniform experience always trumps testimony. Such assertions were met with variations of Locke's example of the king of Siam who had never seen water and refused to believe the Dutch ambassador's report that, during the winter in Holland, water became so hard as to support the weight of an elephant. Thus, in the *Tryal of the Witnesses* (1728), published almost a decade before Hume got the idea for his miracle essay,[5] Sherlock puts the rhetorical question: "[W]hen the Thing testify'd is contrary to the Order of Nature, and, at first sight at least, impossible, what Evidence can be sufficient to overturn the constant Evidence of Nature, which she gives us in the constant and regular Method of her Operation?" (Sherlock 1728, 58). Sherlock answers his rhetorical question with a version of Locke's example: what do the naysayers against the Resurrection have to say "more than any man who never saw Ice might say against an hundred honest witnesses, who assert that Water turns into Ice in cold Climates?" (Sherlock 1728, 60). That Hume's contemporaries were not impressed by his miracles essay is partly explained by the fact that he seemed to be offering a warmed-up version of the past debate, and a defective version at that, since the 1748 edition of the *Enquiry* is silent on the issues raised by Locke's example.[6]

Let's be charitable to Hume by not subscribing to the reading that takes him to be saying that uniform experience always trumps eyewitness testimony. The issue then becomes how to tell when the balance tips in favor of one or the other. Hume's famous 'maxim' might be thought to provide just such a prescription.

## 4. Hume's maxim

Hume announces the 'general maxim'

> That no testimony is sufficient to establish a miracle, unless the testimony be of such a kind, that its falsehood would be more miraculous, than the fact, which it endeavours to establish.
>
> (E 10.13)

Most commentators have seen profound wisdom here. I see only triviality. Suppose that we are in a situation where witnesses have offered testimony $t$ $(M)$ to the occurrence of the miraculous event $M$. Let $E$ be the record of our past experience in favour of the lawlike generalization to which $M$ is an exception. Then, as good Bayesians, our current degree of belief function should be the conditionalization on $t(M)\&E$ of the function $P(\cdot)$ we had before obtaining this evidence. Thus, the relevant probability of the event which the testimony endeavors to establish is $P(M \mid t(M)\&E)$, while the relevant probability of the falsehood of the testimony is $P(\neg M \mid t(M)\&E)$. To say that the falsehood of the testimony is more miraculous than the event which it endeavors to establish is just to say that the latter probability is smaller than the former, i.e.

$$P(M \mid t(M)\&E) > P(\neg M \mid t(M)\&E) \tag{1}$$

which is equivalent to

$$P(M \mid t(M)\&E) > 0.5. \tag{2}$$

On this reading, Hume's maxim is the correct but unhelpful principle that no testimony is sufficient to establish the credibility of a miracle unless the testimony makes the miracle more likely than not.

A number of other renderings of Hume's maxim have been offered, but either they fail to do justice to the text of Hume's essay or else they turn Hume's maxim into a false principle (see Earman 2000 for details) . . .

## 5. Hume's diminution principle

This principle is enunciated by Hume in the following passage:

> [T]he evidence, resulting from the testimony, admits of a diminution, greater or less, in proportion as the fact is more or less unusual.
>
> (E 10.8)

In citing the proverbial Roman saying, "I should not believe such a story were it told me by Cato", Hume intimates that in the case of a miracle the diminution of the evidential force of testimony is total.

Price responded that "improbabilities as such do not lessen the capacity of testimony to report the truth" (Price 1768, 413). This is surely right, as was Price's further claim that the diminution effect operates through the factors of the intent to deceive and the danger of being deceived, either by others or by oneself. Unfortunately Price overstepped himself in claiming that when the first factor is absent, testimony "communicates its own probability" to the event (Price 1768, 414). It was left to Laplace (1814) to give a correct and thorough Bayesian analysis of when and how the intent to deceive and the danger of being deceived give rise to a diminution effect. Two cases suffice to illustrate the results that can emerge from the analysis.

The first case—one considered by Price—concerns a witness who testifies $t$ ($W_{79}$) that the winning ticket in a fair lottery with $N$ tickets is #79. Assuming that when the witness misreports, she has no tendency to report one wrong number over another, then

$$P(W_{79}|t(W_{79}) \& E) = P(t(W_{79})|(W_{79}) \& E) \qquad (3)$$

where $E$ records the background knowledge of the lottery. And this is so regardless of how large $N$ is and, thus, regardless of how small the prior probability $P(W_{79}|E) = 1/N$. In such a case the testimony does, in Price's words, communicate its own probability to the event. But, as Price was well aware, (3) does not hold if the witness has some ulterior interest in reporting #79 as the winner.

The second case concerns the testimony $t(W)$ that a ball drawn at random from an urn containing one white ball and $N–1$ black balls is white. As long as there is a non-zero probability that the witness misperceives the color of the ball drawn, or else there is a non-zero probability that the witness misreports the correctly perceived color, the posterior probability $P(W|t(W) \& E)$ does diminish as $N$ is increased and, thus, as the prior probability $P(W|E) = 1/N$ is reduced.[7]

The difference between the two cases lies in the fact that in the urn case, as the prior probability is reduced the likelihood factor $P(t(W)|\neg W \& E)/$

$P(t(W)| W \& E)$ remains the same because the visual stimulus presented to the witness when either a black or a white ball is drawn is independent of the numbers of black and white balls in the urn. By contrast, in the lottery case the corresponding likelihood factor changes in such a way as to cancel the change in the prior factor, quenching the diminution effect.

Two comments are in order. First, I see no *a priori* reason to think that cases of reported miracles are always or even mostly like the urn case in that they are subject to the diminution effect. Even when the reported miracle is subject to the diminution effect, Hume gets his intended moral only for one order of quantifiers; namely, for any given fallible witness (who may practise deceit or who is subject to misperception, deceit, or self-deception), there is a story so *a priori* implausible that we should not believe the story if told by that witness. It does not follow that there is a story so *a priori* implausible (unless, of course, the prior probability is flatly zero) that for any fallible witness, we should not believe the story if told by that witness. To get this latter implication one needs the extra postulate that there are in-principle bounds below which the probability of errors of reporting cannot be reduced. Hume's cynicism suggests such a postulate, but cynicism is not an argument.

## 6. Multiple witnesses

Hume makes some nods to the importance of multiple witnessing, but he seems not to have been aware of how powerful a consideration it can be. In fairness, the power was clearly and fully revealed only in the work of Laplace (1812, 1814) and more especially the work of Babbage (1838), whose *Ninth Bridgewater Treatise* devotes a chapter to a refutation of Hume's argument against miracles.

Suppose that there are $N$ fallible witnesses, all of whom testify to the occurrence of an event $M$. For simplicity suppose that the witnesses are all equally fallible in that for all $i = 1, 2, \ldots, N$

$$P(t_i(M)| M \& E) = p, \quad P(t_i(M)|\neg M \& E) = q \tag{4}$$

And suppose that conditional on the occurrence (or non-occurrence) of $M$, the testimonies of the witnesses are independent in the sense that

$$P(t_1(M) \& t_2(M) \& \ldots \& t_N(M) | \pm M \& E)$$
$$= P(t_1(M)|\pm M \& E) \times P(t_2(M)| \pm M \& E) \times \ldots \times P(t_N(M)| \pm M \& E) \tag{5}$$

where $\pm M$ stands for $M$ or $\neg M$, and where the choice is made uniformly on both sides of the equality. Then the concurrent testimony of all $N$ witnesses gives a posterior probability

$$P(M \mid t_1(M) \& t_2(M) \& \dots \& t_N(M) \& E) = \cfrac{1}{1+\left[\dfrac{P(\neg M \mid E)}{P(M \mid E)}\right]\left(\dfrac{q}{p}\right)^N} \tag{6}$$

The witnesses may be very fallible in the sense that $q$ can be as close to 1 as you like. But as long as they are minimally reliable in the sense that $p > q$, it follows from (6) that the posterior probability of $M$ can be pushed as close to 1 as you like by a sufficiently large cloud of such fallible but minimally reliable witnesses—provided, of course, that $P(M \mid E) > 0$. Using this result Babbage was able to give some nice examples where just twelve minimally reliable witnesses can push the posterior probability of an initially very improbable event to a respectably high level.

In sum, if we set aside Hume's wildly optimistic account of induction on which $P(M \mid E) = 0$, then he must agree that fallible multiple witnesses can establish the credibility of a miracle, provided that their testimonies are independent in the sense of (5) and that they are minimally reliable in the sense that $p > q$. Which of these provisos would Hume have rejected? The answer is 'Neither', at least in some cases of secular miracles, such as in his hypothetical example of eight days of total darkness around the world.

> [S]uppose, all authors, in all languages, agree, that, from the first of January 1600, there was total darkness over the whole earth for eight days: Suppose that the tradition of this extraordinary event is still strong and lively among the people: that all travellers, who return from foreign countries, bring us accounts of the same tradition without the least variation or contradiction: It is evident, that our present philosophers, instead of doubting the fact, ought to receive it as certain. . . .
>
> (E 10.36)

But in cases to which religious significance is attached, Hume professed to be unswayed by even the largest cloud of witnesses. In the hypothetical case of the resurrection of Queen Elizabeth, Hume declared that he would 'not have the least inclination to believe so miraculous an event' (E 10.37), even if all the members of the court and Parliament proclaimed it. Here it is less plausible than in the previous case that the independence assumption is satisfied since the witnesses can be influenced by each other and the general hubbub surrounding the events. But there seems to be no in-principle difficulty in arranging the circumstances so as to secure the independence condition. The minimal reliability condition becomes suspect if the alleged resurrection is invested with religious significance because witnesses in the grip of religious fervor tend to be more credulous and because they may give in to the temptation to practise deceit in order to win over the unconverted. But it is an insult to the quality of the eighteenth-century debate to think that the participants needed a sermonette on this topic from Hume. The pro-miracle proponents were acutely aware of the need to scrutinize the contextual factors that might give clues as to the reliability of the witnesses. The conclusions they drew from their scrutiny may have been mistaken, but if so, the mistakes did not flow from a failure to heed the empty solemnities of Hume's essay. Hume's treatment of the hypothetical Queen Elizabeth case drips with cynicism:

> [S]hould this miracle be ascribed to any new system of religion; men, in all ages, have been so much imposed on by ridiculous stories of that kind, that this very circumstance would be a full proof of cheat, and sufficient, with all men of sense, not only to make them reject the fact, but even reject it without farther examination.
>
> (E 10.38)

The cynicism remains just cynicism unless it is backed by an argument showing that, in principle, the witnesses cannot be minimally reliable and independent when the alleged miracle is ascribed to a system of religion. Such an argument is not to be found in Hume's "Of miracles".

## 7. Miracles as a just foundation for religion

Grant that nothing in principle blocks the use of eyewitness testimony to establish the credibility of a miracle—say, a resurrection—of supposed religious significance. It might still seem that Hume has safe ground to which to retreat. On his behalf one can argue that to serve as a 'just foundation for religion', the miracle must not only satisfy Hume's first definition of 'miracle' as a violation of a (putative) law of nature but must also satisfy the second definition, according to which a miracle is "a transgression of a law of nature by a particular volition of the Deity, or by the interposition of some invisible agent" (E 10.12n). But (still continuing on Hume's behalf, now in the voice of John Stuart Mill), nothing can ever prove that the resurrection is miraculous in the sense of Hume's second definition because "there is still another possible hypothesis, that of its being the result of some unknown natural cause; and this possibility cannot be so completely shut out as to leave no alternative but that of admitting the existence and intervention of a being superior to nature" (Mill 1843, 440).

This line is used over and again across the decades by commentators sympathetic to Hume. It is apt to strike the innocent reader as a powerful consideration, but when the context is filled in it is seen as unavailing against the more sophisticated eighteenth-century pro-miracles proponents. For . . . the role these proponents saw for miracles was not that of a direct and full proof of the presence of God by marks of a supernatural intervention in human affairs.

Rather, the miraculous figured in an argument whose goal was to render religious doctrines highly credible and, ideally, to give them the kind of moral assurance needed to render a jury verdict of beyond reasonable doubt. And to fulfill this role, miracles need not be conceived as supernatural interventions; they need only serve as probabilistic indicators of the truth of the religious doctrines.

To illustrate how miracles can serve to confirm religious doctrines, suppose that testimonial evidence $t(M)$ has incrementally confirmed M:

$$P(M \mid t(M) \& E) > P(M \mid E) \tag{7}$$

Suppose also that the testimony bears on the religious doctrine $D$ only through M in that

$$P(D \mid \pm M \& \pm t(M) \& E) = P(D \mid \pm M \& E) \tag{8}$$

And suppose finally that

$$P(M \mid D \& E) > P(M \mid \neg D \& E) \tag{9}$$

Then it follows that

$$P(D \mid t(M) \& E) > P(D \mid E) \tag{10}$$

that is, $t(M)$ incrementally confirms $D$.

Condition (8) is surely unobjectionable. Condition (9) is the sense in which M serves as a probabilistic indicator of the truth of $D$, and to fulfill this role M need not be the result of a supernatural intervention that disrupts the order of nature. And condition (9) is seemingly easy to satisfy. For example, isn't it obvious that the miracle of the loaves is more likely on the assumption that Christian doctrine is true than on the assumption that it is false? In fact, it is not obvious. In general, whether or not (9) is satisfied depends on what alternatives are included in ¬D and what their prior probabilities are.[8] Consider, for example, the case where a high prior is given to the possibility that there is a non-Christian deceiver God who actualizes a world containing events designed to mislead people into falsely believing Christian doctrine. And even when $D$ is incrementally confirmed by $t(M)$, there is no assurance that evidence of other miracles will push the probability of $D$ anywhere near that required for moral certainty—again, it depends on the available alternatives and their prior probabilities.

So the discouraging word is that Bayesianism does not pave an easy road for religion. But by the same token there is no obvious difference here with theoretical physics: whether and how much a physical theory $T$ that postulates unobservable properties of unobservable elementary particles is confirmed by direct or testimonial evidence about streaks in cloud chambers depends on what alternatives to $T$ are entertained and what priors these alternatives are assigned.

## 8. Parting company

Let us agree for present purposes . . . that the subjectivist form of Bayesianism captures the logic of inductive reasoning. . . . By these lights it is rational to give high degrees of belief to miracles; indeed . . . given various kinds of eyewitness testimony that it is in principle possible to obtain, it would be irrational not to give a high credibility to miracles. Further, miracles can be used to support rational credence in theological doctrines.

Thus far I have marched shoulder to shoulder with the pro-miracle forces. But now I drop out of the parade, and this for two reasons. First, my degree of belief function—which I immodestly assume to satisfy the Bayesian strictures—disagrees with, for example, Professor Swinburne's (1970, 1979) function—which I have no doubt satisfies the strictures.[9] Second, and more important, I think that these differences are matters of taste in that there is no objective basis to prefer one over the other. One way to find objectivity in the framework of subjective Bayesianism is through an evidence-driven merger of opinion (aka 'washing out of priors'[10]). Such a consensus, however, is hollow unless it is in principle possible that the accumulating evidence produces the merger of opinion by driving the posterior probability to 1 on the true hypotheses and 0 on the false hypotheses. But for theological hypotheses, whose truth values do not supervene on the totality of empirical evidence—no matter how liberally that evidence is construed—the desired convergence to certainty is impossible . . .[11]

## 9. Conclusion

I trust that I have displeased all parties. I hope to have upset the devotees of Hume's miracles essay by showing that a Bayesian examination reveals Hume's seemingly powerful argument to be a shambles from which little emerges intact, save for posturing and pompous solemnities. At the same time I hope I have given no comfort to the pro-miracle forces. I personally do not give much credibility to religious miracles and religious doctrines. And while I acknowledge that those who do can be just as rational as I am, I suspect that degrees of belief in religious doctrines cannot have an objective status if a necessary condition for such a status is the existence of a reliable procedure for learning, from all possible empirical evidence, the truth values of these doctrines. The proof, or disproof, of this suspicion would, I think, constitute an important contribution to the philosophy of religion.

## Notes

1. Bayes' essay was published posthumously in 1763. It was probably written in the 1740s.
2. A first draft of Hume's essay on miracles was written (probably) in 1737. But the essay did not appear in print until 1748 when it was published as Chapter 10 ('Of miracles') of Hume's Philosophical Essays Concerning Human Understanding, later called Enquiry Concerning Human Understanding. The internal evidence indicates that the published version of Hume's miracles essay was written in the 1740s.
3. Quoted in Burns (1981). Burns's book provides a good overview of the eighteenth-century miracles debate.
4. And C. D. Broad took Hume to be saying that "we have never the right to believe any alleged miracle however strong the testimony for it may be" (Broad 1916–17, 80).
5. Hume tells us that he got the idea during his stay in La Flèche (1736–37); see Hume (1932, 1.361).
6. Hume's 'Indian prince' example makes its appearance in a hastily added endnote to the 1750 edition. In later editions a paragraph and a long footnote on the Indian prince were added to the text.
7. Editors' note: the original printing of this paper stated the second formula as '$P(W|E) = 1/(N–1)$', which appears to be a misprint
8. An exception is the hypothetico-deductive case where D entails M.
9. It is only here that I part company with Professor Swinburne, from whom I learned to apply Bayesianism to religious matters.
10. This phrase is misleading since the likelihoods, which in many cases are just as subjective as the priors, have to wash out too.
11. Editors' note: The remainder of §8 gives technical support to this claim.

## CHAPTER 20

# Earman on Hume on Miracles

## PETER MILLICAN

John Earman, in his book *Hume's Abject Failure: The Argument Against Miracles* (2000) and his chapter in this volume "Bayes, Hume, Price, and Miracles" subjects Hume's essay on miracles (in Section 10 of the *Enquiry concerning Human Understanding*) to an abusive and merciless attack. According to Earman, Hume's argument is "a confection of rhetoric and *schein Geld* [German for *false money*]" (Earman 2000, 73), and "a shambles from which little emerges intact" (see p. 269 above). More specifically, he alleges that it is "tame and derivative [and] something of a muddle," presenting a hopelessly obscure thesis (see p. 260 above), based on a "proof" that amounts to little more than the dogmatic assumption that "uniform experience in favor of a lawlike generalization leaves no room for doubt" (see p. 262 above). According to Earman, Hume's only achievement in the essay is to disguise the crudity of his position through misleading "posturing and pompous solemnities" (see p. 262 above) which have seduced his readers into viewing his key "maxim," in the final paragraph of *Enquiry* 10 Part 1, as an expression of "profound wisdom." Instead, alleges Earman, this maxim is at best merely trivial and tautological, amounting to "the correct but unhelpful principle that no testimony is sufficient to establish the credibility of a miracle unless the testimony makes the miracle more likely than not" (see p. 263 above). He goes on (in §5) to criticize what he calls Hume's "diminution principle"—that the evidential force of testimony for any event diminishes in proportion to the unusualness of that event—and to propose (§6) that multiple witnesses can provide a clear counterexample to Hume's apparent belief that a miracle could never be established by testimony.

Earman then turns to the specific case of religious miracles (§7), arguing—here more against Mill and other Humean sympathisers than against Hume himself—that there is no reason in principle why testimony for a miracle should not support a religious doctrine. Earman is doubtful, however, whether such support could ever amount to an objective proof, though for reasons quite different from Hume's (§8).

All this might seem quite damning for Hume, but let us see what can be pleaded on his behalf. I shall argue that his essay on miracles does indeed have some significant flaws, but it is far better than alleged by Earman, whose interpretation of it can indeed be decisively refuted.

## Hume's "Proof" Against Miracles

Since he is so confidently abusive about Hume's argument and the obscurity of its main thesis, it is especially disappointing that Earman himself is so careless in his exposition of it, for example talking quite inappropriately of "Hume's 'proof' against miracles" as though this referred to his overall philosophical argument. In fact, when Hume talks of a *proof* in *Enquiry* 10 he always means a strong *inductive* argument, extrapolating from uniform experience of a specific phenomenon, and providing full assurance *when taken alone*. As he makes clear in a 1761 letter to Hugh Blair:

> The proof against a miracle, as it is founded on invariable experience, is of that *species* or *kind* of proof, which is full and certain when taken alone, because it implies no doubt, as is the case with all probabilities.
>
> (Hume 1932, 1.350)

Earman (see p. 261 above) suggests—perhaps with a hint of caution—that Hume "seems to be saying" that if *L* is a lawlike generalization backed by such a proof, then *L* should be assigned a probability of 1 (i.e. 100%), thus effectively ruling out from the start any possibility of testimonial evidence counting significantly in favor of any violation of *L*. In his earlier book, Earman was far more forthright in presenting this interpretation:

> So here in a nutshell is Hume's first argument against miracles. A . . . miracle is a violation of a presumptive law of nature. By Hume's [principles], experience confers a probability of 1 on a presumptive law. Hence, the probability of a miracle is flatly zero. Very simple. And very crude.
>
> (Earman 2000, 23)

On this interpretation, once "the proof against a miracle" has been established, there is no way that any further observation or testimony—however good it might be—could make any difference whatever to the miracle's probability, which even if multiplied by an enormous factor (due to that further evidence) must remain fixed at zero. But this is entirely contrary to much that Hume says, not least the final clause of the sentence quoted above from his 1761 letter to Blair: ". . . but there are degrees of this species, and when a weaker proof is opposed to a stronger, it is overcome."

Earman (2000, 23, and see p. 261 above) omits this final clause, but it is crucial to Hume's position, providing the entire basis for the main scenario of his essay on miracles, in which there is "proof against proof" (E 10.11), with new testimonial evidence potentially *overruling* a previous proof from experience. So we have very strong grounds for rejecting the crude interpretation that Earman initially proposes.[1]

## Earman on Hume's Maxim

Earman then moves on to another simplistic reading, but seems curiously unwilling to engage in careful consideration of Hume's text, gliding above it by referring vaguely to other commentators' views, while including not a single quotation from Hume himself:

> Hume recognized that his "proof"[2] only applies when the evidence consists of uniform experience . . . The real issue is joined when that proof is opposed by a counterproof from eyewitness testimony. Many commentators from Hume's day to the present have read Hume as saying that . . . uniform experience always trumps testimony . . . Let's be charitable to Hume by not subscribing to [this] reading . . . The issue then becomes how to tell when the balance tips in favor of one or the other. Hume's famous "maxim" might be thought to provide just such a prescription.
>
> (see p. 262 above)

It seems odd to describe this treatment as "charitable," when no evidence has been presented to suggest that Hume's argument is anything like as crude as "many commentators" have thought. Moreover in other circumstances, Earman himself is quite happy to dismiss the views even of "most commentators," as we find when he gives his own—somewhat uncharitable—account of Hume's maxim. Here is how Hume himself states it:

> The plain consequence is (and it is a general maxim worthy of our attention), "That no testimony is sufficient to establish a miracle, unless the testimony be of such a kind, that its falsehood would be more miraculous, than the fact, which it endeavours to establish . . ."
>
> (E 10.13)

And here are Earman's comments on the quoted "maxim":[3]

> Most commentators have seen profound wisdom here. I see only trivial-
> ity ... the relevant probability of the event which the testimony endeavors
> to establish is $P(M \mid t(M) \& E)$, while the relevant probability of the false-
> hood of the testimony is $P(\neg M \mid t(M) \& E)$. To say that the falsehood of
> the testimony is more miraculous than the event which it endeavors to
> establish is just to say that the latter probability is smaller than the former,
> i.e.
>
> $$P(M \mid t(M) \& E) > P(\neg M \mid t(M) \& E) \qquad (1)$$
>
> which is equivalent to
>
> $$P(M \mid t(M) \& E) > 0.5. \qquad (2)$$
>
> On this reading, Hume's maxim is the correct but unhelpful principle
> that no testimony is sufficient to establish the credibility of a miracle
> unless the testimony makes the miracle more likely than not.
>
> (see p. 263 above)

Earman's argument for this reading—both in this chapter and his earlier
book—makes very little further reference to Hume's text, but consists mainly
of criticism of rival probabilistic interpretations, which are shown to fail in
various ways.[4] But all of the rivals that Earman considers share the same fault,
of completely ignoring the significance, within Hume's maxim, of the words
"testimony ... of such a kind." They are all thus *token* interpretations of the
maxim—focusing on the probability of *individual items* of testimony—rather
than *type* interpretations, which take seriously Hume's apparent concern with
the typical probability of *kinds* of testimony.[5]

   It is fairly easy to show that Earman's interpretation is incorrect, by examining Hume's argument leading up to his maxim, and the evidential weighing operation that generates it. Hume starts by pointing out that all evidence
about the unobserved is derived from experience, with the weight of such evidence determined by the consistency of the relevant experience. "A wise man,
therefore, proportions his belief to the evidence" (E 10.4). He then emphasizes
that this principle of inductive rationality applies not only to inference from
personal observation but also to arguments from testimony, for "our assurance in any argument of this kind is derived from no other principle than our
observation of the veracity of human testimony, and of the usual conformity
of facts to the reports of witnesses" (E 10.5). That being so, it is important to
recognize that not all kinds of testimony are found to be equally reliable:

And as the evidence, derived from witnesses and human testimony, is founded on past experience, so it varies with the experience, ... according as the conjunction between any particular kind of report and any kind of object has been found to be constant or variable ... Where ... experience is not entirely uniform on any side, it is attended with an unavoidable contrariety in our judgments ...

This contrariety of evidence ... may be derived from several different causes; from the opposition of contrary testimony; from the character or number of the witnesses; from the manner of their delivering their testimony; or from the union of all these circumstances. ... There are many other particulars of the same kind, which may diminish or destroy the force of any argument, derived from human testimony.

Suppose, for instance, that the fact, which the testimony endeavours to establish, partakes of the extraordinary and the marvellous; in that case, the evidence, resulting from the testimony, admits of a diminution, greater or less, in proportion as the fact is more less unusual.

(E 10.6–8).

In this last sentence, the unusualness of the reported event is identified—alongside contrary testimony and the character, number, and manner of the witnesses—as one additional factor that bears on the credibility of testimonial reports. But Hume then immediately isolates this particular factor, and views it as balanced *on the other side of the scale* against the characteristics of the testimony that incline us to believe it, resulting in "a counterpoize, and mutual destruction of belief and authority" (E 10.8).

After a couple of short paragraphs illustrating such "destruction of belief" (through the famous examples of Cato and the Indian prince), Hume quickly goes on to present the most extreme possible case of "counterpoize," where the reported fact;

instead of being only marvellous, is really miraculous; and ... *the testimony, considered apart and in itself,* amounts to an entire proof; in that case, there is proof against proof, of which the strongest must prevail, but still with a diminution of its force, in proportion to that of its antagonist.

(E 10.11, my emphasis)

Two very important points should be noted here. First, Hume's argument so far has treated a miracle as just an extreme case of an extraordinary (i.e. inductively improbable) event, and the general principles involved in this treatment are no different from those that he applies to any other extraordinary event.[6] Second, in sketching out how the counterpoise takes place, Hume has understood the strength of the testimony—"considered apart and in itself"—as yielding a single overall measure of *proof* which can then appropriately be weighed against the strength of the counter-proof that arises from the miraculousness (i.e. the extreme lack of conformity to our uniform experience) of the alleged event. The stronger of these two proofs "must prevail, but still with a diminution of its force, in proportion to that of its antagonist." So the confidence we place in the testimony (or—depending on which is weightier—in the inductive evidence against the supposed event) will depend on the extent to which the testimonial proof (or alternatively the proof from experience) over-balances its antagonist. We have "proof against proof," *with the overall credibility given not by either "proof" individually, but by the result of weighing them against each other.* Neither side of the contest *alone* yields the appropriate credibility measure: that comes only from the *comparison* between them.

This point, which is absolutely clear from Hume's text, refutes Earman's interpretation outright. For on his account, Hume's intended criterion of credibility is:

$$P(M \mid t(M) \& E) > P(\neg M \mid t(M) \& E) \tag{1}$$

On this criterion, *both* sides of the inequality represent an overall probability measure, on the left-hand side the probability of the miracle (conditional on the testimony and our past experience), and on the right-hand side the probability of no such miracle (conditional on the testimony and our past experience). Hume's own maxim is nothing like this. On the contrary, as we have seen clearly from his text, his maxim involves a comparison between two quite different "proofs," one concerning the relevant *kind* of testimony "considered apart and in itself" (in terms of the character, number, and manner of the witnesses etc., but *not* the specific event reported), and the other concerning the event reported (in terms of its lack of conformity to our experience). We have yet to see whether this maxim can be given a suitable probabilistic representation, let alone one that is philosophically defensible. But what is quite clear is that Earman's interpretation of Hume's maxim is seriously mistaken.

## A "Type" Interpretation of Hume's Maxim

If the preceding discussion is correct, then Hume's maxim must be understood in such a way that the probability of the testimony "considered apart and in itself" is distinguished from, and weighed against, the improbability of the reported event considered independently of that testimony.[7] Hume's idea seems to be that different "kinds" of testimony (specified in terms of the character and number of the witnesses, the manner of delivery etc.) carry a different typical probability of truth and falsehood *independently of the event reported*.[8] Let us call this his *Independence Assumption*. Suppose, then, that we focus on a particular kind of testimony—whose characteristic probability of falsehood is $f$—which either asserts, or denies, the occurrence of a particular type of event $M$—whose probability of occurrence is $m$. If the reliability of that kind of testimony is probabilistically independent of what is being reported, then we can apparently calculate the probability of a "true positive" and a "false positive" report as follows (as before using "$t(M)$" to mean that $M$ is testified to have occurred):

True positive ($M$ occurs, and is truly reported)

$$P(M\&t(M)) = P(M) \times P(true\ report) = m.(1-f)$$

False positive ($M$ does not occur, but is falsely reported as having occurred)

$$P(\neg M\ \&\ t(M)) = P(\neg M) \times P(false\ report) = (1-m).f$$

If positive testimony has been given, therefore, this testimony will be probably true only if a "false positive" is less likely than a "true positive," and hence in accordance with the formula:

$$P(M/t(M)) > 0.5 \rightarrow (1-m).f < m(1-f)$$

which simplifies to:

$$P(M/t(M)) > 0.5 \rightarrow f < m$$

This result neatly corresponds to Hume's maxim, since its right-hand side is exactly equivalent to saying that *the falsehood of the testimony, considered apart and in itself* is more miraculous (i.e. less probable) than *the event reported, considered independently of the testimony*. Hume's own route to this result was not, of course, so mathematical: he seems to have viewed the situation as involving a relatively simple trial of strength between the inductive evidence for the testimony and the inductive evidence for the relevant "law of nature." But given his apparent Independence Assumption, this yields exactly the formal result calculated above, which can thus stand as a faithful mathematical elucidation of his position, rather than an anachronistic distortion.[9]

## The Non-Triviality of Hume's Maxim

If Hume's Independence Assumption applies to testimony for miracles in this way (for doubts, see the next section), then his maxim can indeed be of real practical value. To illustrate with a non-miraculous example, suppose that

Fred wants to know whether he suffers from some genetic condition G which afflicts one person in a million. He has no other evidence either way, but a test is available which seems very reliable, in that whoever is tested, and *whether they actually have the condition or not*, the chance that the test will give a correct diagnosis is 99·9%, and an incorrect diagnosis only 0·1% (so Hume's Independence Assumption plausibly applies: the test can be assigned a consistent probability of delivering truth rather than falsehood, independently of what the facts happen to be). When Fred later leaves the clinic in distress at having tested positive for G, how convinced should he be that he does indeed have that condition?

Most people would, in my experience, judge Fred's likelihood of having G in this situation to be very high, but in fact the reverse is the case, as Hume would recognize. As Fred stumbles out despondently through the clinic door, Hume might greet him with a consoling comment something like this: Consider whether it be more probable, that this kind of test should be mistaken, or that you should really have condition G(cf. E 10.13).[10]

Given that the test is wrong one time in a thousand, while G afflicts only one person in a million, there is clearly a far greater likelihood of a mistaken test than of Fred's actually suffering from G. And so a positive test report does relatively little to indicate that he actually has the disease: in fact, it changes the probability from a negligible one in a million to the only slightly more worrying 1 in 1,002.[11] Hume's maxim, therefore, is entirely correct in this case, and it also gives the correct answer for other relevantly similar cases. If, for example, we increase the "initial probability" of the disease to over one in a thousand, then the test indeed becomes credible. And this last point demonstrates a kernel of truth in what Earman calls Hume's "diminution principle": whether some alleged fact can be rendered rationally credible by some testimony depends on its prior probability (or in Hume's terms how "miraculous" or "unusual" the alleged fact is) as well as on the characteristics of the testimony.

We have already seen enough to counter Earman's insultingly dismissive view of Hume's treatment of miracles. Certainly there are problems, as will become apparent shortly, but Hume deserves credit for enunciating a principle which clearly anticipates—by two and a half centuries—the identification of the *base rate fallacy* by psychologists Amos Tversky and Daniel Kahneman.[12] This is a very common error in human thinking, whereby we naturally find it all too easy to ignore the background "base rate" of some phenomenon when assessing the significance of evidence for it. So on receiving a disappointing test report for condition G, most people would be far more struck by the specific immediacy of that result—and the test's apparent reliability of 99·9%—than by the memory of the general probability for G of one in a million. They would thus be seriously mistaken, and Hume's maxim is potentially of considerable value as a vivid reminder of the need to take base rates into account.

**Difficulties for Hume's Position**

Let us now take a more critical look at Hume's implicit Independence Assumption: that it is in general possible to consider a *kind* of testimony as conferring a typical evidential probability, independently of what it reports. Admittedly this assumption was not confined to Hume, and some of his opponents—notably Richard Price (1768, §2, pp. 413–6)—themselves took it for granted when arguing *in favor* of miracle stories. Earman (§5) discusses Price on just this theme:

> Price responded that "improbabilities as such do not lessen the capacity of testimony to report the truth" (Price 1768, 413). This is surely right, as was Price's further claim that the diminution effect operates through the factors of the intent to deceive and the danger of being deceived, either by others or by oneself. Unfortunately Price overstepped himself in claiming that when the first factor is absent, testimony "communicates its own probability" to the event.
>
> (Price 1768, 414)

Hume's argument, however—somewhat paradoxically—itself undermines the Independence Assumption from which it apparently starts, since the upshot of the argument is precisely to show that the same *kind* of testimony can yield very different probabilities, depending on the prior probability of what it reports. In the diagnostic example of the section above, a positive test report yields a probability for G of 1 in 1,002; but a negative test report yields virtual certainty for ¬G (with the probability of G now close to one in a billion).[13] Moreover there is no good reason for expecting such a diagnostic test to have the same probability of error in both directions: for example an over-sensitive test for G might have a relatively high chance of erroneously identifying G (a false positive), while having very little chance of failing to detect its presence (a false negative). Likewise, there is no reason why someone, gazing over a foggy Scottish loch at twilight, should mistake a floating log for a sea monster with exactly the same probability as he would mistake a sea monster for a floating log. Indeed Hume himself is clearly aware that such mistakes are likely to be biased in one direction rather than the other, given "the strong propensity of mankind to the extraordinary and the marvellous" (E 10.19). So his own attachment to the Independence Assumption seems to be at most lukewarm, and his argument in "Of Miracles" is perhaps best understood as *starting* from the assumption but then *discarding* it, on the basis of both his maxim and also the psychological considerations presented in his Part 2. Price, by contrast, holds firm to the assumption, and hence has an untenable position.

Price nevertheless raises a serious problem for Hume's position through his examples such as the lottery discussed by Earman (§5). The same problem—

identified previously by Joseph Butler (1736, II ii 3 [§11]) and George Campbell (1762, I §1, p. 31)—also arises in the case of everyday reports, which we very reasonably believe even when the prior probability of the fact reported is far less than the prior probability of a false report. Imagine listening to a BBC radio announcement on 8th April 1967:

> Foinavon, a 100-to-1 outsider ridden by John Buckingham, won the 1967 Grand National after a dramatic pile-up stopped all the leading horses at the 23rd fence.

What is the prior probability that the radio announcer would get something wrong here? To be very ungenerous to the BBC, let us suppose that it is 5% (so 1 in 20 such announcements will involve a mistake). This is clearly *vastly* greater than the prior probability that a 100-to-1 horse with that particular (previously unfamiliar) name, ridden by a jockey with another particular (unfamiliar) name, should win after such a specific and unlikely calamity at that particular fence. So the testimony is *not even close* to being "of such a kind, that its falsehood would be more miraculous, than the fact, which it endeavours to establish";[14] and yet we quite properly believe it. Hence Hume's maxim is mistaken.

The fundamental flaw in Hume's reasoning, as I have interpreted it, derives from the faulty calculation of a "false positive" report:

> False positive (*M* does not occur, but is falsely reported as having occurred)
>
> $$P(\neg M \ \& \ t(M)) = P(\neg M) \times P(\text{false report}) = (1 - m).\, f$$

Imagine if the 1967 Grand National had been an unremarkable race won by one of the favorites, but reported *falsely* on the radio. How likely is it, in those circumstances, that the report would be false *in precisely the way quoted above*—naming Foinavon (wrongly) as the winner, alleging (falsely) a dramatic pile-up, and so forth? Clearly it is vanishingly unlikely; indeed it is so unlikely that the probability of such a "false positive" is far less than the probability of Foinavon actually winning as described. So any listener to the report is quite right to believe it, albeit with some slight reservation in proportion to the general fallibility of BBC reports. And Hume's maxim is indeed refuted, as likewise in Price's lottery example, where again the crucial point is that the probability of ticket number 79's being *falsely* reported as winning is even less than the prior probability of its *actually* winning.[15]

So Hume's maxim fails, except in a limited range of (typically artificial) cases such as the diagnostic test, where it serves as a useful warning against the "base rate fallacy." However, I believe that much more can be salvaged from

Hume's position by dropping his Independence Assumption and taking his arguments as pointing instead towards a revised maxim which encapsulates the point just made:

> No testimony is sufficient to establish a miracle *M*, unless the testimony is of such a kind, that the occurrence of an *M* report of that kind (*given that M does not in fact occur*) would be even less probable than *M* itself.

Such an approach would shift the emphasis from Part 1 of Hume's essay towards Part 2, from abstract probability to the psychological factors that falsely generate miracle reports. But further discussion of all this must wait for another occasion.[16]

## Multiple Witnesses and Religious Miracles

Since Hume does not attempt to rule out the *possibility* of testimony sufficient to establish a miracle,[17] and he never denies that a genuinely established miracle could provide evidence for a religion, Earman's discussions in his sections six and seven do not refute any position that Hume is committing to holding. From a Humean point of view, however, Earman's treatment of independent multiple witnesses seems surprisingly complacent, especially his suggestion that "there seems to be no in-principle difficulty in arranging the circumstances so as to secure the independence condition" (see p. 266 above). Note that his results here *crucially* depend on the assumption that the multiple witnesses are indeed *independent*, so that the probability of some witness $w_2$ reporting that *M* occurs is completely unaffected by what another witness $w_1$ reports: they must not be colluding, or subject to any other common influence except for their perception of *M* itself (or its absence). But Hume's own main concern is *epistemological*, so it is not enough that the multiple witnesses be *actually* independent (as assumed in Earman's calculations); they must also be *known to be* independent. And in any situation involving miracle stories propagated by the adherents of a particular religion, it is almost inevitably going to be more reasonable—our experience of human nature being what it is—to suspect that the witnesses are *not* independent (through either collusion or delusive influences, external or psychological), rather than to believe that some astonishing event favoring their religion has actually happened. That, at any rate, will be the natural Humean suspicion, and Earman has done nothing to refute it.[18] So again, although he makes some interesting points on the Bayesian treatment of miracles, his discussion sheds relatively little light on Hume's philosophy, which is far richer and more defensible than such a narrowly mathematical treatment can reveal.

## Notes

1. There is no space here for further interpretative discussion of Hume's understanding of probabilities and proofs, which can be found in Millican (2011, §2, §6) and Fogelin (2003, 43–53).
2. Note here the point I make in the first paragraph of the firstsection above.
3. In what follows, $M$ is some potential event (typically a would-be miracle), $t(M)$ is the occurrence of testimony for that event, and $E$ is the background evidence (typically the observation of uniformities in accordance with the law of nature of which $M$ would be a violation).
4. Earman's only substantial further quotation of Hume in this discussion is his (correct) point that the final sentence of E 10.13 treats the maxim as providing a *sufficient* as well as *necessary* condition for credibility. The previous two sentences of E 10.13 also suggest this, and the three sentences together strongly corroborate Earman's presumption (which he explains in a part of section 4 omitted from the chapter in this collection) that "sufficient to establish a miracle," for Hume, means to render the miracle *more likely than not*, rather than to render the miracle *certain*.
5. To illustrate the type/token distinction, consider how many letters the word "error" contains. Two different answers are possible, because the word contains five *token* letters ("e," then "r," "r," "o," "r"), but only three letter *types* ("e," "r," "o"). The related distinction between kinds and individual items of testimony is applied to Hume's maxim in Millican (1993), which independently proposes essentially the same formula that Earman favors as a *relatively* plausible *token* interpretation (Millican 1993, 490). But Earman also expresses serious reservations about it, indicating the likely superiority of a *type* interpretation (Millican 1993, 490, 491, 495 n. 8), though without attempting to work out the latter. Earman's book references the paper (Earman 2000, 93), but unfortunately he ignores the reservations expressed there about his favored formula.
6. In a note to the paragraph which mentions the Indian prince's incredulity about ice (E 10.10), Hume sketches a distinction between *extraordinary* and *miraculous* events, but this plays no significant role in his argument. Unlike Earman (see pp. 262–263 above), therefore, I do not see Hume's relative lack of engagement with these sorts of examples and complications as particularly relevant to the assessment of his position.
7. Note that this distinction cannot easily be drawn within a *token* interpretation of Hume's maxim, which can only consider "the probability of the testimony" to refer to *the probability of the particular item of testimony* (in favor of some specific reported event), which is therefore hard to distinguish—given that the testimony has been presented—from *the resulting probability of the reported event itself*. Hence it is not surprising that Earman's attempts to identify a coherent token interpretation lead quickly to triviality.
8. In his maxim, Hume talks of the falsehood of a *kind* of testimony as being "more miraculous" than the event reported, and in the following sentences, he clearly understands miraculousness as the inverse of probability. So he indeed seems committed to viewing *kinds* of testimony as having a typical probability.
9. Nor is there anything un-Humean about attempting to make these things mathematically precise. Hume himself did not have our modern probability theory to hand, but at E 10.4 he explicitly recommends calculation in cases of opposing probabilities, "to know the exact force of the superior evidence."
10. Note that this is quite different from asking: "Which is more probable, in the light of this result: that this specific test is mistaken in saying that you have condition $G$, or that you really have condition $G$?" which would be trivially equivalent to asking whether the test result makes it more probable than not that Fred has the condition. Earman reads Hume's maxim as expressing just this useless equivalence.
11. Consider a population of a billion, of whom one thousand have the disease while 999,999,000 do not. If all were tested, we would expect 999 true positives against 999,999 false positives.
12. Their best-known article is Tversky and Kahneman (1974), with a striking example of the

base rate fallacy at pp. 1124–1125, under the heading "*Insensitivity to prior probability of outcomes.*"

13. Testing a billion people, we could expect just one false negative result, and 998,999,001 true negatives. We might notice here that the test, in either case, impacts on the initial probability of $G$ by a factor of approximately 1,000, which corresponds to the 1 in 1,000 probability of a mistaken test occurring. This might seem to revive the idea that the test can be seen as having a consistent force, and perhaps Hume himself was thinking along these lines, because the same sort of pattern will indeed hold for any similar case in which the relevant initial probability is very small (as with miracles). But unfortunately it breaks down as soon as we move to examples which involve more than two possible outcomes, as in the racing report and lottery cases discussed in the main text.

14 Recall that "more miraculous" here is simply to be understood as "less probable," and that Hume's argument purports to be based on general considerations of probability (n. 8 above). So he would be begging the question against miracles if he attempted to erect some special hurdle against them without providing an argument to justify such discrimination.

15. The difference in Earman's urn example (see pp. 264–265 above) is that the prior probability of reporting a black ball as a white one is taken to be constant, irrespective of the number of balls in the urn, whereas in the lottery case, as the number of available tickets rises, the probability that a mistaken report will happen upon the number 79 reduces. The urn case would become closer to the lottery case if the reporter were under the mistaken impression that the balls are all of different colors; then his reporting "white" when in fact the ball is black will get less probable as the number of balls increases.

16. For a sketch, see Millican (2011, §§19–20).

17. For more discussion of this point, see Millican (2011, §12).

18. Moreover his talk of "arranging the circumstances so as to secure the independence condition" is rather bewildering: are we supposed to organize some rigorous experimental setup, and then just wait for a miracle to present itself?

# Editors' Introduction

Kant's claim that geometry is synthetic *a priori* is very important to him. It's the basis of one of his main arguments for transcendental idealism. (What exactly transcendental idealism amounts to is the subject of Part 12). But many readers find it hard to believe that geometry is synthetic instead of analytic. They suspect that Kant's way of thinking about geometry is out of date or just plain wrong.

James Van Cleve and Emily Carson both defend Kant's claim that geometry is synthetic *a priori*. However, they defend him on very different grounds. And, as you'll see, they use very different methodologies. (Look at Part 13 of this book for a general discussion of methodology.) So as well as making Kant's claim more plausible, this section helps us see some of the different ways you can write papers in the history of philosophy.

Kant's explanation of why geometry is synthetic *a priori* clearly has something to do with pure intuition. But what? On Van Cleve's view, geometry is synthetic *a priori* because we usually arrive at geometrical knowledge by using pure intuition. Consider a geometrical claim like *the shortest path between two points is a straight line*. All you have to do to see that this is true is visualize space with two points and a line. Van Cleve grants that we could also give a proof of this proposition that made it analytic. Nevertheless, he argues, we have synthetic *a priori* knowledge in geometry because we need only the visualization (not the proof) to know that the shortest path between two points is a straight line.

Carson explains how Kant's view of geometry emerged from his disagreement with Leibniz and his followers. Kant worried that Leibniz's philosophy of monads turned mathematics into a set of 'fictions.' (For more on Leibniz and the monads, see Part 5). He found this result completely unacceptable. Kant's theory about the role of intuition in geometry is thus intended to restore the certainty and real-world applicability of math. And this theory about the role of intuition in geometry implies that geometry is synthetic.

## Note on References

The *Critique of Pure Reason* is typically referred to by page number in the original first, or 'A', and second, or 'B' editions. Hence (A84/B116) is a passage that appears on p. 84 in the first edition and p. 116 in the second edition, while (B19) is a passage that appears on p. 19 of the second edition and did not appear at all in the first edition. There are two standard English translations of the *Critique*—by Kemp Smith (1933) and Guyer and Wood (1988). We have not noted which translation an author is using, or whether they are using their own translation.

## Further Reading

- Michael Friedman (1998). *Kant and the Exact Sciences.* (Especially the preface.)
- Charles Parsons (1967). "Kant's Philosophy of Arithmetic."
- Bertrand Russell (1917). *Mysticism and Logic.*
- Lisa Shabel (2006). "Kant's Philosophy of Mathematics."

## CHAPTER 21

# Necessity, Analyticity, and the *A Priori*

## JAMES VAN CLEVE

We are in possession of certain modes of *a priori* knowledge, and even the common understanding is never without them.

Kant, *Critique of Pure Reason* (B3)

Necessity and strict universality are thus sure criteria of *a priori* knowledge.

(B4)

In all theoretical sciences of reason synthetic *a priori* judgments are contained as principles.

(B14)

Now the proper problem of pure reason is contained in the question: How are *a priori* synthetic judgments possible?

(B19)

## A. Three Distinctions

In the introduction to the *Critique of Pure Reason* Kant draws three important distinctions: *a priori* versus empirical, necessary versus contingent, and analytic versus synthetic. Although some philosophers lump them together, we should not assume at the outset that the three distinctions divide things up in the same way. Even if it should turn out that they do, each of the distinctions must be given its own explanation.

*A priori/Empirical.* Kant distinguishes *a priori* from empirical knowledge as follows:

[K]nowledge that is thus independent of experience and even of all impressions of the senses . . . is entitled *a priori,* and distinguished from the *empirical,* which has its sources *a posteriori,* that is, in experience.

(B2)

The term *a priori* is in the first instance an adverb modifying verbs of cognition: person S knows proposition p *a priori* iff S knows p in a way that is independent of experience. We may then go on to define a related sense in which *a priori* is a predicate of judgments or propositions: a proposition p is *a priori* iff it is possible for someone to know p *a priori.* I leave aside the interesting question of whether it is possible for some beings to know *a priori* things that other beings cannot. (E.g., might an infinite intelligence have *a priori* knowledge of propositions about the distribution of primes in the number series that is not available to a finite intelligence?)

The notion of independence that figures in the primary definition of *a priori* must not be misunderstood. In saying that we know a given proposition independently of experience, Kant is not saying that we would still have known it even if we had never had any experience. On the contrary, he allows that experience may be requisite for the knowledge even of an *a priori* proposition in either of two ways. First, it may well be that if we had never had any experience, our cognitive faculties would never have developed to the point that we could entertain any propositions or do any thinking at all. Still, once our faculties are up and running, there are some propositions that we can know to be true without any further need of experience. That is the point of Kant's famous remark that "though all our knowledge begins with experience, it does not follow that it all arises out of experience" (B1). Second, it may be that some of the constituent concepts in a given proposition are concepts that can only be acquired through experience, such as the concept of *red* or the concept of an *event.* In that case, experience would be necessary for us to grasp the proposition or get it before our minds, but once we have framed it in our consciousness, we may be able to ascertain that it is true without any further aid from experience. Kant acknowledges this possibility when he distinguishes (within the class of *a priori* propositions) between the pure and the impure, an impure proposition being one some of whose constituent concepts are derivable only from experience (B3). He gives the example 'every alteration has a cause'; the concept of an alteration (or event) is one that can be got only through experience, but the proposition as a whole Kant takes to be *a priori.* For another example (in which the *a priori* status of the proposition is less controversial), I cite 'nothing is simultaneously red and blue'. In the *Prolegomena,* Kant gives 'gold is a yellow metal' as an example of a proposition that is *a priori* (because analytic) even though it contains empirical concepts (p. 14).

The point of the previous paragraph may be made by invoking the familiar tripartite analysis of knowledge. Someone knows a proposition only if (i) he believes it, (ii) it is true, and (iii) he is adequately justified in believing it. (See Kant's discussion of opining, believing, and knowing at A822/B850 for an account roughly along these lines.) Experience may be necessary in either of the two ways I have mentioned—in many cases or even in all—for the obtaining of condition (i), the belief condition of knowledge, But if experience is not necessary in a given case for the obtaining of condition (iii), the justification condition, the knowledge will still qualify as *a priori.*

The relevant points here were nicely summed up by Frege:

[When we classify a proposition as *a priori,*] this is not a judgment about the conditions, psychological, physiological, and physical, which have made it possible for us to form the content of the proposition in our consciousness; nor is it a judgment about the way in which some other man has come . . . to believe it to be true; rather, it is a judgment about the ultimate ground upon which rests the justification for holding it to be true.[1]

*Necessary/Contingent.* The second distinction relates not to how a proposition is known, but to its manner or mode of being true. Among all the things we recognize as true, there are many that (as far as we can see) need *not* have been true—for example, that stones fall when released near the earth, or that the sun is shining as I write these lines. Such truths are contingent. There are others, however, that *had* to be true. That two and three together make five and that a thing never both has and lacks a given property are truths of this sort. They are necessary truths, the necessity of which may be characterized in any of the following ways:

p could not have been false;
p not only *is* true, but *must* be true;
the opposite of p is impossible;
p holds in every possible world.

I will not try to elucidate these notions further, as they are among the most familiar in philosophy, and I doubt that anything much can be done to explain them to anyone who does not already have a grasp of them anyway. (Such, indeed, is one ground for Quine's misgivings about necessity, discussed later.) Here I simply note that the sense of 'necessary' that is now at issue is what Plantinga calls the "broadly logical" sense.[2] It is logical as opposed to merely physical necessity (i.e., the necessity with which stones fall when released), so laws of nature are not necessary in this sense. And it is broadly logical as opposed to narrowly logical necessity, so laws of formal logic are not the *only* things that are necessary in this sense.

Though the two distinctions drawn so far differ in intension (one relating to the manner of being known and the other to the manner of being true), Kant believes they that they coincide in extension—that they divide up the field of true propositions in the same way. He believes that propositions are necessary iff they are *a priori*, and contingent iff they are empirical *or a posteriori*. As he puts it, "Necessity and strict universality are . . . sure criteria of *a priori* knowledge, and are inseparable from one another" (B4).[3] But Kant famously—and in my opinion correctly—thinks that the next distinction runs at right angles to the first two.

*Analytic/Synthetic.* I come now to the distinction in this trio with which Kant is most associated. Kant's predecessors drew distinctions in the same general area as the analytic/synthetic distinction; for example, Leibniz distinguished between truths of reason and truths of fact, and Hume distinguished between relations of ideas and matters of fact. But Kant is often regarded as the first major thinker to draw the analytic/synthetic distinction in a way that exhibits it as clearly different from the necessary/contingent and *a priori*/empirical distinctions.[4]

My concern in what follows is not so much with elucidating exactly what Kant meant by the analytic/synthetic distinction as with exhibiting connections between his account of it and more recent accounts. I do not think it requires an undue amount of squinting to see Kant's distinction as essentially agreeing with its twentieth-century descendants. When Kant affirms that there are synthetic *a priori* truths and Ayer or Quine denies it, I think they are engaged in the same debate.

*The Containment Characterization.* Kant gives two different accounts of the analytic/synthetic distinction, one in terms of conceptual containment and the other in terms of contradiction. The first and better known runs as follows:

> Either the predicate B belongs to the subject A, as something which is, (covertly) contained in this concept A; or B lies outside the concept A, although it does indeed stand in connection with it. In the one case I entitle the judgment analytic, in the other synthetic.
>
> (A6/B10)

Note that Kant does not merely say that the predicate in an analytic judgment belongs to its *subject,* that is, to that which the judgment is about—that much is presumably the case in *any* true subject predicate judgment. Instead, he says the predicate is contained in the *concept* of the subject. He goes on to explain that in an analytic judgment, the predicate concept is one of the "constituent concepts that have all along been thought in the subject, although confusedly," whereas a synthetic judgment has a predicate "which has not been in any wise thought in [the concept of the subject], and which no analysis could possibly extract from it" (A7/B11).[5] In another place, he equates "what I am actually thinking in my concept of a triangle" with "nothing more than the mere definition" (A718/B746). If we put these two passages together, we arrive at the result that the judgment that S is P is analytic iff the property of being P is included by definition in the concept of S. In fact, Kant would not have said this, owing to special views he held about the nature of definition.[6] But this gloss at least has the virtue of bringing out that whether a judgment is analytic or synthetic depends on what we mean by the terms used to express it.

I now turn to Kant's own examples for illustration. 'All bodies are extended' expresses an analytic judgment, because by 'body' we mean among other things an extended, impenetrable thing. The proposition we express is therefore equivalent to 'all extended and impenetrable things are extended', in which the inclusion of the predicate in the subject concept is visible to the mind's eye. 'All bodies are heavy,' on the other hand, expresses a synthetic judgment, since being heavy is not part of what we mean by 'body'. Our concept of a body allows us to acknowledge the possibility of bodies (e.g., those placed outside all gravitational fields) that do not have any heaviness at all.

*Too Subjective?* It is a perennial objection to the containment account that it yields a distinction that is merely subjective and variable. What one person includes in his or her concept or definition of the metal gold may include more attributes than another does; in consequence, whether a judgment about gold is analytic or synthetic may vary from person to person. This objection was raised against Kant in his own day by J.G. Maass.[7]

It was also answered in Kant's own day. It is quite true that one person's definition of a term may include more than another's, but this turns out to be harmless. Kant's disciple J.G. Schulze, replying to Maass, explained why:

> Now, suppose that I find, in a judgment which two philosophers express in the same words, that one of them connects the subject with a rich concept in which the predicate is already contained, while the other, on the other hand, connects it with a concept in which the predicate in question is not contained. I would then be entirely correct in saying that the judgment of the first one is analytic, and of the second one synthetic. For although their judgments seem to be one and the same, since they are expressed with the same words, they are nevertheless in this case in fact not one but two different judgments.[8]

Schulze's point is that if it is judgments or propositions that we are classifying as analytic or synthetic, then nothing is ever analytic for one person and synthetic for another. The fact that one person uses a more inclusive definition would only show that he or she operates with a different subject concept and therefore frames a different judgment.

On the other hand, if it is *sentences* that we wish to classify as analytic or synthetic, we do indeed get relativity: the same sentence may be analytic for Smith and synthetic for Jones. But such relativity will not undermine Kant's project in the slightest. As I argue below, there are cases in which a sentence that is synthetic for a given person expresses a proposition that is known *a priori* by that person. Such cases still present us with the central question of the *Critique of Pure Reason,* though now it needs to be phrased as follows:

> How are judgments that are known *a priori* by a given person and expressed by sentences that are synthetic for that person possible?

That lacks the fanfare of Kant's "How are *a priori* synthetic judgments possible?" (B19), but it raises the same profound issues.

*Too* Narrow? There is another common objection to Kant's containment definition that has more bite—namely, that it is too narrow. In the first place, it applies only to judgments of subject-predicate form, whereas Kant wishes to classify as analytic or synthetic many judgments not of that form. For example, it does not apply to existential judgments (such as 'there are lions'), which (if we accept the dictum that existence is not a predicate) are not of subject-predicate form. Nor does it apply to compound judgments, such as disjunctive judgments, which need not have a single subject. In the second place, even restricting our attention to judgments of subject-predicate form, the containment definition does not classify as analytic all the judgments that Kant himself would wish to classify as analytic. Consider a judgment of the form 'all ABCD is A'; under the containment definition, this will certainly count as analytic. The equivalent contrapositive judgment, 'all non-A are non-(ABCD)', should therefore also count as analytic, yet clearly one might think of something as non-A without taking any thought of B, C, or D, and therefore not of non-(ABCD).[9] Nor need non-(ABCD) be part of the definition of non-A. So, the contrapositive judgment is not analytic by the containment account. It is not even obvious that the containment account properly classifies as analytic those judgments in which the predicate is extractable from the concept of the subject, but only after a great many steps of definitional replacement.[10]

*The Contradiction Characterization.* Fortunately, Kant has another characterization of analyticity that is less open to the charge of narrowness. There is a first hint of it at B12, where Kant speaks of extracting the predicate of extension from the concept of body "in accordance with the principle of contradiction." The role of contradiction is explicitly recognized later in the section of the *Critique of Pure Reason* entitled "The Highest Principle of All Analytic Judgments," in which Kant says that the truth of any analytic judgment "can always be adequately known in accordance with the principle of contradiction" (A151/B190). Later still, in his critique of the ontological argument for the existence of God, he says that the following feature is "found only in analytic judgments, and is indeed precisely what constitutes their analytic character": their predicates cannot be rejected without contradiction (A598/B626).

What all of this suggests is the following commonly given definition of an analytic judgment:

> A is analytic iff its opposite, −A, is a contradiction.

But what is a contradiction? Many so-called contradictions are not official or formal contradictions in the hard objective sense that they have the logical form 'P & −P'.[11] If we say that a statement is analytic only if its negation is a formal contradiction, nothing will count as analytic except the law of contradiction itself C−(P & −P)') and its instances—and they will count only with the aid of the ruling that the double negation of a contradiction is itself a contradiction. Not even that paradigm of analyticity, 'all bachelors are unmarried', has an opposite that is contradictory in the formal sense. So, what is intended in the definition above is presumably that −A either is or *implies* a formal contradiction.

Now we need to ask another question: "imply" in accordance with which rules and with the help of which auxiliary premises? *Anything* can be shown to imply a contradiction if there is no limit on what rules and premises we may use in the proof. So, which rules and premises may we use? If we look at the transformations to which we must subject the negation of 'all bachelors are unmarried' to arrive at a formal contradiction, the following answer suggests itself: we may appeal to laws of logic, and we may appeal to definitions. This gives us the following revised account:

> A is analytic iff from its negation, −A, a formal contradiction may be derived, using in the derivation only laws of logic and substitutions authorized by definitions.[12]

*Twentieth-Century Accounts.* What we have just arrived at is perhaps the most common twentieth-century conception of analyticity. It is equivalent to each of the following:

| | |
|---|---|
| *Frege:* | "If (in tracing the proof of a proposition) we come only on general logical laws and on definitions, then the truth is an analytic one."[13] |
| *Carnap:* | "The first type of theorem can be deduced from the definitions alone (presupposing the axioms of logic, without |

which no deduction is possible at all). These we call *analytic* theorems."[14]

C.I. Lewis:     "Every analytic statement is such as can be assured, finally, on grounds which include nothing beyond our accepted definitions and the principles of logic."[15]

Quine:          "Statements which are analytic by general philosophical acclaim . . . fall into two classes. Those of the first class are logical truths; those of the second class can be turned into logical truths by putting synonyms for synonyms."[16]

These accounts of analyticity apply in the first instance most readily to sentences—for it is sentences that have meanings, that contain terms that can be interchanged with others having the same meaning, and so on. But we can define a related sense of 'analytic' that applies to propositions: a proposition is analytic iff any sentence expressing it would be analytic.

The resulting conception of analyticity is not open to the charge discussed above of excessive narrowness. It applies to propositions of any logical form, not just those of subject-predicate form. Moreover, it classifies as analytic propositions of the form 'all non-A are non-(ABCD)', whereas the containment definition does not. It also classifies as analytic propositions in which the predicate is extractable from the concept of the subject only after a great many steps of logical or definitional recasting.

I believe also that the resulting notion agrees tolerably well with Kant's own, at least in extension if not in intension. In any case, it is the conception I operate with in this book. If I sometimes use "the opposite implies a contradiction" as my short gloss on analyticity, the reader should remember the unstated provisos that bring the gloss into line with the Fregean conception: from the negation of the statement it must be possible to derive a formal contradiction using only definitions and laws of logic.

## B. Synthetic A Priori

As I said above, Kant believes that his first two distinctions, *a priori*/ empirical and necessary/contingent, make the same divide in the field of judgments, while the third distinction, analytic/synthetic, cuts across the field at right angles to the first two. That makes four compartments in all. Kant believes three of the four to be occupied: analytic *a priori*, synthetic *a posteriori*, and (the famous new possibility) synthetic *a priori*.[17] *A priori* knowledge is perhaps not unduly mysterious when it is of analytic truths, for it is explained in that case by whatever explains our knowledge of logic and our knowledge of our own meanings.[18] But if our *a priori* knowledge extends also to some synthetic truths, what could explain that? Disdain of having to invoke an *oculis rationis* or some other mysterious faculty led the positivists and others to maintain that *a priori* knowledge is to be had only of analytic propositions. But Kant was convinced otherwise, and that set for him the central problem of the *Critique of Pure Reason:* How are synthetic *a priori* judgments possible (B19)?

In the introduction to the *Critique,* Kant asserts that there are three important classes of synthetic *a priori* propositions: the truths of arithmetic, the truths of geometry, and certain framework principles of natural science, such as the principle that every event has a cause. (He also lists as synthetic and putatively *a priori* certain propositions of metaphysics, such as that the world had a beginning, but these turn out for him not to be *a priori* because not knowable at all.) Few agree with Kant nowadays about the synthetic *a priori* status of the propositions in these three classes. Arithmetic is generally thought to be *a priori* but (given the work of Frege, Russell, and Whitehead) not synthetic. Geometry is generally thought to be synthetic but (given the rise of non-Euclidean geometries in the nineteenth century and their subsequent incorporation into physical theory in the twentieth) not *a priori.* Nor are the framework principles of natural science generally thought to be *a priori.*

Although I cannot do justice here to the status of arithmetic and geometry, I offer below a few words in defense of what Kant has to say about a specimen from each subject matter. Then I move on to two more favorable examples of the synthetic *a priori.* Even if Kant is wrong about arithmetic and geometry at large, I believe he is emphatically right in thinking that there are synthetic *a priori* propositions.

$7 + 5 = 12$. '$7 + 5 = 12$' is Kant's well-known example of a synthetic *a priori* proposition in arithmetic. He argues for its synthetic character as follows: "[I]f we look more closely we find that the concept of the sum of 7 and 5 contains nothing save the union of the two numbers into one, and in this no thought is being taken as to what that single number may be which combines both" (B15). Here Kant is invoking the containment characterization of analyticity, and he is clearly right about the results of applying it, at least to some cases if not to this one. There are true arithmetic equalities of the form '$7 + 5 = m - n$', where m and n are numbers so large no human being has ever thought of them; here, of course, one may entertain the subject concept without having any thought of the predicate.[19] Nor need the concepts of m and n enter into the definition of $7 + 5$, or else no concept would have a finite definition, there being infinitely many (m—n) pairs that similarly yield true equations. Thus, by the containment criterion, much of arithmetic is synthetic.

But we know that the containment criterion is too narrow, and that Kant has a better criterion in terms of contradiction. Might it be that arithmetical propositions are analytic by the superior standard? Such, of course, is precisely the contention of the logicism of Frege, Russell, and Whitehead. If they are right, there are definitions of arithmetical concepts in purely logical terms that permit the derivation of any truth of arithmetic from purely logical axioms. That would make arithmetic analytic in Kant's wider sense. But whether the logicists are right is unclear for at least two reasons. First, the status of some of their axioms (e.g., the axiom of infinity, which guarantees the existence of infinitely many objects) as purely logical is controversial. Second, Gödel's incompleteness theorem shows that there cannot be any finite and consistent set of axioms from which every arithmetical truth may be derived, thus apparently dooming the logicist project.[20]

*The Straight Line Between Two Points Is the Shortest.* 'The straight line between two points is the shortest' is Kant's official example of a synthetic *a priori* proposition in geometry.[21] As with the previous example, he thinks its *a priori* status will be generally conceded. He supports its syntheticity with the following observation: "For my concept of *straight* contains nothing of quantity, but only of quality" (B16). In an interesting discussion of the same proposition, Hume observes, "In common life 'tis establish'd as a maxim, that the streightest way is always the shortest; which wou'd be as absurd as to say, the shortest way is always the shortest, if our idea of a right line was not different from that of the shortest way betwixt two points."[22]

Geometers nowadays often define a straight line in just the way Hume and Kant say we should not: as a geodesic, or shortest line (in the space in question) between two points. That makes analytic the sentence Hume and Kant take to express a synthetic proposition.[23] In the bargain, it threatens to undermine the *a priori* status of another of Kant's favored examples: two straight lines cannot enclose a space. In Riemannian geometry, two lines that are geodesics *can* enclose a space.

Of course, if rival geometries undo the apriority of Kantian theses only by redefining terms, they do not really undo it; they make the same sentence express a different proposition, and it need come as no surprise that the new proposition is not *a priori*. Indeed, on first exposure to the non-Euclidean properties of straight lines in Riemannian geometry, many students claim that the meaning of 'straight' has been changed, in which case there is no challenge to Kant. The impression of meaning change may be heightened when the student is told that great circles on a sphere may serve as models of straight lines. "Those lines aren't really straight," the student may be tempted to say, "for it is obvious that there are straighter lines, so you haven't really shown me how *Euclidean* principles might fail." The standard reply to the student is that *in the space in question,* the line really is straight, for there is no straighter. The student is imagining a more inclusive space in which the line would not be straight, but that is not the space that counts.

I think it is significant that to reply to the student we must use a relativized notion of straightness, and I would like to exploit this fact in defending Kant. For a preliminary illustration, let me switch the example from straightness to congruence. Consider the figures a and b in the one-dimensional space of Lineland:

—— ——
a    b

Are a and b congruent or not? Many writers would say no, for there is no motion in the space that will enable one to be superimposed on the other. But Wittgenstein claimed to the contrary that a and b are in fact completely congruent. "It is quite irrelevant," he said, "that they cannot be made to coincide."[24] I agree with Wittgenstein: because there are *possible* spaces (of two or more dimensions) in which a and b could be made to coincide, they are congruent absolutely speaking, even if they cannot be made to coincide in the limited space to which they are actually confined.[25]

In effect, we are now distinguishing two notions of congruence. The relativized notion may be defined thus: two figures are congruent *in S* iff there is a motion in S by which the figures may be brought into coincidence. This notion must be what the writers who deny the congruence of a and b have in mind. But we may also define an absolute notion of congruence as follows: two figures are *absolutely* congruent iff there is a possible space in which they would be congruent in the relative sense. Wittgenstein's remark is defensible in light of the absolute concept.

To return now to the concept of straightness, any geodesic in a space S may be said to be straight in *S*, for no line is shorter or straighter in S. But whether a line is straight *absolutely* is a function not of the space it happens to inhabit, but of what spaces are possible, and if there are possible spaces in which a line would not be the shortest, then it is not straight in the absolute sense.[26]

We are now in a position to defend what our student says on behalf of Euclid and Kant. When she says, "Your so-called straight lines that return on themselves, enclose spaces, and behave in other non-Euclidean ways aren't really straight," she is right—the lines are not absolutely straight. The necessity of Euclid's principles as governing absolutely straight lines is not put in doubt by the fact that non-Euclidean principles govern lines that are straight relative to one or another special space. At the same time, we are not securing the necessity of Euclidean principles simply by making them analytic. That Euclid holds sway over the absolutely straight is a matter not of definition but of intuition.[27]

I pass now to two putative examples of synthetic *a priori* truths that should be less controversial than the two just discussed: 'nothing is red and green all over' and 'every cube has twelve edges'.

*Nothing Is Red and Green All Over.* Nearly everyone will concede that 'nothing is red and green all over (at the same time)' expresses a necessary truth that is known *a priori;* the question is whether it is synthetic.[28] Given the account of analyticity described above, the question comes down to this: is the statement true by virtue of definitions plus logic? Anyone who says yes must answer the question: true by *what* definitions and *what* logic?

For starters, we may consider a definition that looks in part like this:

x is red =Df . . . & x is not green & . . .

A definition containing the displayed conjunct would let us derive 'nothing is both red and green' from 'nothing is both green and not green', which is a truth of logic. But what would the rest of the definition look like? How are we to fill in the blanks? Sticking with the "definition by exclusion" strategy, we would have

x is red =Df x is not blue & x is not green & . . .,

with one conjunct for each color not overlapping redness.[29] A possible drawback of the resulting definition is that it would contain infinitely many conjuncts. Setting that problem aside, there is the following difficulty, which was raised by Arthur Pap: not all colors can be defined in this purely negative way, on pain of circularity in the total system of color definitions (for we would be defining 'x is green' as 'x is not red & . . .'). Enough of the color terms will have to be defined positively to give us some purchase on the negatives. A strong case can be made that the positive definitions will have to be *ostensive*—to be red is to be the color of *this object*. Now consider two colors F and G that have been defined in this ostensive way: it will be an *a priori* truth that nothing is both F and G, but nothing in the present strategy will show that such truths are analytic.

Let's try another tack. Why not define colors in terms of physical magnitudes, perhaps along the following lines:

x is red =Df x reflects light of wave length 1.

x is green =Df x reflects light of wave length m.

The incompatibility of colors would then simply be a consequence of the incompatibility of certain physical magnitudes.[30]

I leave aside the objection that we understand color terms perfectly well before we know any physics, and that definitions like those above are not true to our naive understanding. The objection I wish to press is that we have only relocated our difficulty. This was pointed out by F.P. Ramsey in his review of the *Tractatus,* in which Wittgenstein had tried a similar strategy: he sought to reduce color incompatibilities to the impossibility of a particle having two velocities at once. Ramsey commented:

But even supposing that the physicist thus provides an analysis of what we mean by 'red', Mr Wittgenstein is only reducing the difficulty to that of the *necessary* properties of space, time, and matter or the ether. He explicitly makes it depend on the *impossibility* of a particle being in two places at the same time.[31]

What we would need now is the basis in definitions and logic for saying that a particle cannot have two velocities, or that an object cannot have two different reflectance profiles, and so on. . . .

*Every Cube Has Twelve Edges.* This is a nice example for illustrating Kant's views on the epistemology of geometry.[32] Unlike many geometrical propositions; this one (which is actually a proposition of topology rather than of geometry proper) holds in Euclidean and non-Euclidean geometries alike, so there is no challenge to its apriority from non-Euclidean geometry. The question, as with the previous example, is whether it is analytic or synthetic. It is not immediately or obviously analytic, for the standard definition of 'cube' is 'regular solid (or polyhedron) with six square faces', in which there is no mention of the number of edges. How, then, do we know that the proposition is true? Most people verify it simply by visualizing a cube and counting its edges—an exercise in what Kant calls "pure intuition." If we are to exhibit the proposition as analytic, we must deduce the number of edges in a cube using just logic and any relevant definitions. Readers may wish to try their hands (or heads) at this.

Some will try to make the statement immediately analytic after all, saying that *their* definition of 'cube' *does* include the having of twelve edges. To them I say: very well, it is analytic that cubes as you define them have 12 edges. But consider now the following proposition: every cube as defined by me (in terms of six faces) is a cube as defined by you (in terms of twelve edges). That is, every regular solid with six square faces is a solid with twelve edges. I submit that this proposition may be seen to be true *a priori* as easily as the first, but it is nor true by definition. Or if it is, that has yet to be made out. So, we may as well expend our efforts on the original statement.[33]

Here is one good try at extracting twelve edges from the original definition of a cube:[34]

1. Every cube is a polyhedron with six square faces (by definition).
2. Six separate squares have twenty-four edges, since each square (by definition) has four edges and $6 \times 4 = 24$.
3. When six squares are assembled into a cube, each edge of a square coincides with the edge of another square to form one edge of the cube, and each edge of the cube is an edge of exactly two squares (no square edge

coinciding with more than one cube edge). Thus, the number of edges in the original group of squares decreases by one half,
4. Therefore, every cube has twelve edges (24 ÷ 2). Q.E.D.

That apparently does it—at least if we may correctly assume (in opposition to Kant) that arithmetic is analytic, and that for counting purposes coincidence is as good as identity.

Even granting these assumptions, however, there is a further hitch. Where does step 3 come from? I readily concede its *truth*, for I see that things work as step 3 says when I picture squares coming together to form a cube. But unless step 3 is itself true by definition, we have not yet shown that the conclusion of the argument is analytic.

Well, perhaps step 3 is true by virtue of the definition of a polyhedron. A topology textbook offers this:

> By a *polyhedron* we mean any system of polygons arranged in such a way that (1) exactly two polygons meet (at an angle) at every edge, and (2) it is possible to get from every polygon to every other polygon by crossing edges of the polyhedron.[35]

The first clause of this definition delivers the essential part of our step 3.

That may end the argument over 'every cube has twelve edges', but there are other apparent instances of the synthetic *a priori* in the vicinity. Let's turn our attention to 'every cube has eight corners (i.e., vertices)'. That proposition is also *a priori*, but its analyticity is not brought out by any of the definitions so far considered. We could make it analytic by adding to the definition of a polyhedron a clause from which we could deduce something analogous to step 3 above: each vertex of a square coincides with two other such vertices to form one vertex of the cube, and each vertex of the cube is a vertex of exactly three squares (no square vertex coinciding with more than one cube vertex).[36] Then we could conclude that every cube has eight vertices (since six squares have twenty-four, which divided by 3 is 8).[37]

My rejoinder is by now predictable: the foregoing strategy would make analytic a statement that was formerly synthetic and whose content we knew to be true *a priori* even when the statement was synthetic. That is, we knew *a priori* that cubes in the original "thinner" sense (i.e., polyhedra with six square faces, with polyhedra defined as in the textbook definition above) have eight vertices. We can, if we like, make analytic the statement that formerly expressed what we knew about cubes, but what would that show? The knowledge was there before the analyticity. Indeed, the analytic statement does not even express our old knowledge, but a more highly articulated proposition instead.

*Is It Analytic That All* A Priori *Truths Are Analytic?* The thesis that there are synthetic *a priori* truths need not be supported by examples alone. What is the status of the opposing thesis that all *a priori* truths are analytic? It is not an empirical thesis, so if true at all, it had better be analytic.[38] But is it? Defenders of the thesis have seldom risen to the challenge of demonstrating its own analyticity.[39]

## Notes

1. Gottlob Frege, *The Foundations of Arithmetic,* translated by J.L. Austin (Evanston, Ill.: Northwestern University Press, 1980), p. 3.
2. Alvin Plantinga, *The Nature of Necessity* (Oxford: Oxford University Press, 1974), pp. 1–2.
3. I do not discuss here Saul Kripke's suggestions that there are *a priori* truths that are not necessary and necessary truths that are not *a priori*. See his *Naming and Necessity* (Cambridge, Mass.: Harvard University Press, 1980), pp. 53–56 and 97–105.
4. For anticipations of the synthetic *a priori* in Kant's predecessors, however, see Lewis White Beck, "Analytic and Synthetic Judgments Before Kant," in *Essays on Kant and Hume* (New Haven, Conn.: Yale University Press, 1978), pp. 80–100.
5. In the *Prolegomena* Kant puts the point this way: "Analytical judgments express nothing in the predicate but what has been already actually thought in the concept of the subject, though not so distinctly or with the same (full) consciousness" (p. 14).
6. See Lewis White Beck, "Kant's Theory of Definition," in *Studies in the Philosophy of Kant* (Indianapolis, Ind.: Bobbs-Merrill, 1965); reprinted in *Kant: Disputed Questions,* edited by Moltke S. Gram (Chicago: Quadrangle Books, 1967), pp. 215–27.
7. For discussion of this, see Henry E. Allison, *The Kant-Eberhard Controversy* (Baltimore: Johns Hopkins University Press, 1973), pp. 42–43.
8. Quoted in Allison, The *Kant-Eberhard Controversy,* pp. 174–75.
9. To avoid this objection, one might try to unpack Kant's notion of "covert" containment in terms of latency or dispositionality: we say that property P is contained in concept S if anyone who thinks of something as S *and considers whether it is also P* must think that it is P. But this proposal will classify as analytic some propositions that Kant wants to count as synthetic—for example, a straight line is the shortest distance between two points.
10. In chapter 1 of *Kant's Analytic* (Cambridge: Cambridge University Press, 1966), Jonathan Bennett notes the narrowness of Kant's definition and complains that it makes the existence of synthetic *a priori* judgments too easy to establish. He therefore suggests a broader notion according to which a proposition should count as analytic if it may be verified by purely conceptual considerations. I think this threatens to make the nonexistence of synthetic *a priori* judgments too easy to establish: if 'purely conceptual' equals *a priori,* it is trivially true that everything *a priori* is analytic. On the other hand, if conceptual considerations are limited (as I propose below) to those mobilizing definitions or analyses and logic, there is still room for the synthetic *a priori.*
11. Ironically, those who criticize Kant's definition for being subjective or psychologistic often rely on a loose notion of contradiction that is at least as subjective as anything Kant offers. They call a statement contradictory not because it has the logical form of a contradiction, but because it has a contradictory ring to their ears.
12. Accurately speaking, this is a definition of what it is to be *analytically true.* We need also to recognize the category of the *analytically false:* A is analytically false iff from A itself, a formal contradiction may be derived, and so on. Synthetic statements then comprise all those that are neither analytically true nor analytically false.
13. Gottlob Frege, *The Foundations of Arithmetic,* sec. 3.

14. Rudolf Carnap, *The Logical Structure of the World*, translated by Rolf A. George (Berkeley: University of California Press, 1967), p. 176.

15. C.I. Lewis, *An Analysis of Knowledge and Valuation* (La Salle, Ill.: Open Court, 1946), p. 96.

16. W.V. Quine, "Two Dogmas of Empiricism," in *From a Logical Point of View* (New York: Harper Torchbooks, 1963), pp. 20–46, in sec. 1.

17. Question: why is there no analytic *a posteriori*? Answer: the definition of '*a posteriori* proposition' that complements our definition of '*a priori* proposition' is that p is such that no one *could* know it save through experience. Although there may be analytic propositions that a given person actually comes to know on the basis of experience (someone looks out the window, sees that it is raining, and deduces 'it is raining or it is not raining' by the law of addition), there are arguably no analytic propositions that could be known *only* through experience.

18. Note, however, that classifying logical principles as analytic does nothing to explain how we know them to be true. As we have defined 'analytic', logical principles are included within the sphere of the analytic simply by courtesy; it is analytic that they are analytic.

19. Compare Kant's letter to Schulz of November 25, 1788, in which he points out that one may form different concepts of the same number by many different additions and subtractions. If equations of arithmetic were analytic, he argues, then in thinking 3 + 4, one would also be thinking 2 + 5, which "does not jibe with my own awareness." See Arnulf Zweig, ed., *Kant: Philosophical Correspondence*, 1759–99 (Chicago: University of Chicago Press, 1967), pp. 128–30.

20. For a brief discussion of these two points and related matters, see Karel Lambert and Gordon Brittan, *An Introduction to the Philosophy of Science* (Englewood Cliffs, N.J.: Prentice-Hall, 1970), ch. 2.

21. Kant claims synthetic *a priori* status for geometry at large, making exception only for propositions such as 'a = a' that serve as "links in the chain of method" (B16–17). Other examples of synthetic *a priori* propositions in geometry he cites are the following: space has three dimensions (B41); two straight lines cannot enclose a space (A47/B65); the sum of the angles of a triangle is equal to two right angles (A716/B744).

22. David Hume, *A Treatise of Human Nature*, I.ii.4 (pp. 49–50 in Selby-Bigge's edition). This passage also gives the following reason for regarding the common maxim as synthetic: "A right line can be comprehended alone; but this definition [of a right line as the shortest] is unintelligible without a comparison with other lines. . . ."

23. Accurately speaking, what it makes analytic is 'any straight line between two points is shorter than any nonstraight line between the points'. The additional implication of the Hume-Kant proposition that there is only one such straight line is not a matter of definition, and is indeed not even true in Riemannian geometry.

24. Ludwig Wittgenstein, *Tractatus Logico-Philosophicus*, translated by D.F. Pears and B.F. McGuirmess (London: Routledge & Kegan Paul, 1961), proposition 6.36111. In my copy of the *Tractatus*, Wittgenstein's figure b unfortunately contains an erroneous extra hyphen, destroying the congruence of a and b.

25. For more on this point, see section XI of my "Right, Left, and the Fourth Dimension," *The Philosophical Review*, 96 (1987), 33–68, and also in *The Philosophy of Right and Left*, edited by James Van Cleve and Robert E. Frederick (Dordrecht: Kluwer, 1991), pp. 203–34.

26. Compare the following passage from II.xiii.3 of the *New Essays on Human Understanding* in which Leibniz distinguishes between an absolute and a relative sense of distance:

    To put it more clearly, the distance between two fixed things—whether points or extended objects—is the size of the shortest possible line that can be drawn from one to the other. This distance can be taken either absolutely or relative to some figure which contains the two distant things. For instance, a straight line is abolutely the distance between two points; but if these two points both lie on the same spherical surface, the distance between them *on that surface* will he the length of the smaller arc of the great circle that can be drawn from one to the other, [ *New Essays on Human Understanding*, translated by Peter Remnant and Jonathan Bennett (Cambridge: Cambridge University Press, 1981), p. 146; emphasis mine]

27. It must be confessed that this way of defending Kant affords no guarantee that absolutely straight lines are actually exemplified: they would not be if a curved space were the whole of space. But that is all right, since the synthetic *a priori* status of principles about lines or figures does not depend on whether the lines or figures are actually exemplified. For more on this point, see Gary Rosenkrantz, "The Nature of Geometry," *American Philosophical Quarterly,* 18 (1981), 101–10.

28. This is not one of Kant's own examples. What he says at B44 implies that there are no synthetic *a priori* truths about colors, but I think he was surely wrong about that.

29. Why not simply say 'for each color distinct from redness'? Because determinates of redness (e.g., scarlet) are distinct from it, as are its determinables (e.g., being red-or-orange), yet we do not want our definition to imply that red things cannot be scarlet or red-or-orange.

30. The physical definitions could be more sophisticated than this, perhaps making reference as well to effects on the human nervous system.

31. F.P. Ramsey, "Critical Notice of L. Wittgenstein's *Tractatus Logico-Philosophicus,*" *Mind,* 32 (1923), 465–78, at p. 473. In "Some Remarks on Logical Form" [*Proceedings of the Aristotelian Society,* 9 Suppl. (1929), 162–71], Wittgenstein in effect concedes Ramsey's point, allowing that atomic propositions may exclude one another even though they do not contradict one another.

32. It is also the chief supporting example used by C.H. Langford in "A Proof That Synthetic *A Priori* Propositions Exist," *The Journal of Philosophy,* 46 (1949), 20–24. Langford at first appears to make his task too easy by defining an analytic proposition as "one that can be certified solely by reference to logical principles" (p. 22). It emerges, however, that recourse to definitions is also permitted. It will become clear below that I agree with Langford on this point: "[I]t is sufficient for our purposes that there should be at least one adequate definition from which this consequence [having twelve edges] does not follow" (p. 22).

33. This paragraph gives my answer to the title question of Lewis White Beck's "Can Kant's Synthetic Judgments Be Made Analytic?" *Kant-Studien,* 46 (1955), 168–81; reprinted in *Kant: Disputed Questions,* edited by Moltke S. Gram (Chicago: Quadrangle Books, 1967), pp. 228–46. A synthetic sentence 'S is P' can always be made analytic by enriching the meanings of the subject term, but the sentence 'every S in the old sense is an S in the new sense' will be synthetic and *a priori* if the original sentence was. There is no banishing the synthetic *a priori* by this method.

34. Thanks to my former student Jeremy Bernstein.

35. D. Hilbert and S. Cohn-Vossen, *Geometry and the Imagination,* translated by P. Nemenyi from the 1932 German edition (New York: Chelsea, 1956). According to Imre Lakatos, *Proofs and Refutations* (Cambridge: Cambridge University Press, 1976), p. 15, this definition comes originally from Möbius, who used it to prevent two polyhedra with an edge or a vertex in common from counting as a single polyhedron.

36. I do not know what the formulation of this clause generalized to cover all polyhedrons should be.

37. Here is another strategy: if it is analytic that cubes have six faces and twelve edges, we may use Euler's formula ($V - E + F = 2$) to deduce that they have eight vertices. But now we must determine whether Euler's formula is analytic or synthetic. I invite the reader to consult Lakatos's discussion of the proof of this formula in *Proofs and Refutations,* asking himself whether the various lemmas that are needed are true by definition or simply seen to be true on the strength of their intuitive (*anschauliche*) evidence.

38. As pointed out by A.C. Ewing in *The Fundamental Questions of Philosophy* (London: Routledge and Kegan Paul, 1951), ch. 2.

39. A notable exception is Anthony Quinton, "The *A Priori* and the Analytic," *Proceedings of the Aristotelian Society,* 64 (1963–64), pp. 31–54; reprinted in *Philosophical Logic,* edited by P.F. Strawson (Oxford: Oxford University Press, 1967), pp. 107–28. Quinton's purported proof consists in the following chain of claimed implications: *a priori* => necessary => not contingent => not contingent on anything outside => true in virtue of factors internal to

itself => true in virtue of its meaning. I question the equation of 'contingent' with 'contingent on something'—'contingent' just means 'possibly false'. I also question the significance of the conclusion that necessary truths are true in virtue of meanings. It is by virtue of its meaning that a sentence expressing a necessary truth expresses the truth that it does; it is not by virtue of the meaning of the sentence expressing it that a given truth is necessary.

## CHAPTER 22

# Pure Intuition and Kant's Synthetic
## *A Priori*

### EMILY CARSON

In Chapter 21 James Van Cleve defends Kant's claim that geometry is synthetic *a priori*. This defense essentially involves Kant's notion of pure intuition: in the case of the proposition that every cube has twelve edges, Van Cleve explains that we verify its truth by visualizing a cube and counting its edges. We readily concede the truth of the proposition that when we assemble six squares into a cube, the number of edges in the cube is half the number of edges in the original group of six squares because we *see* that this is what happens when we 'picture' squares coming together to form a cube. Van Cleve calls this visualization "an exercise in what Kant calls 'pure intuition'" (see p. 301 above).

While this example nicely illustrates *one* epistemological aspect of Kant's appeal to intuition in mathematics, we'll see that Kant's conception of intuition is considerably richer and more sophisticated than Van Cleve's defense indicates. Considering the context in which Kant developed his philosophy of mathematics will give us a broader view of the role of intuition in mathematical cognition. We'll see that Kant had metaphysical as well as epistemological reasons for thinking that mathematical propositions are synthetic *a priori*.

First I'll consider a reading of Kant on which he introduces pure intuition into his account of geometrical knowledge because the limited resources of eighteenth-century logic were insufficient for carrying out mathematical inferences. Pure intuition, the argument goes, provided Kant with an extra-logical form of inference. On this view, the introduction of pure intuition stems from *logical* concerns about geometrical inference. Against this, in the second section, I trace the development of Kant's views about mathematical cognition in order to outline the broader *metaphysical* and *epistemological* issues about mathematics that also contributed to the development of Kant's Critical philosophy. In the third section, I explain how Kant addresses these issues by analyzing the conditions of possible experience. This analysis results in his conception of space and time as forms of intuition, which, in turn, explains the character of geometric and arithmetic cognition. Lastly, I explain how the resulting view of mathematical cognition complements and differs from that offered by Van Cleve.

## A Logical Role for Intuition

Kant tells us in the introduction to the *Critique of Pure Reason* (B16) that the propositions of geometry are synthetic. Take for example, the proposition that the straight line between two points is the shortest: "the concept of the shortest . . . cannot be extracted out of the concept of the straight line by any analysis," so the proposition is synthetic. This argument is essentially negative: geometrical propositions must be synthetic because they are not analytic. So Kant asserts that "help must be gotten from intuition" in order to synthesize the concepts of 'shortest' and 'straight line between two points.'

But is Kant's argument for the role of intuition in geometry just this negative one? Some commentators have suggested that Kant's claim that geometry is synthetic results from the limited logical resources available to him. Bertrand Russell, for instance, notoriously claimed in *Mysticism and Logic* that "the proof that all pure mathematics, including Geometry, is nothing but formal logic, is a fatal blow to the Kantian philosophy" and that "the whole doctrine of a priori intuitions, by which Kant explained the possibility of pure mathematics, is wholly inapplicable to mathematics in its present form" (Russell 1917, 74). Given modern polyadic logic, we *can* represent geometrical concepts in such a way that their properties can be 'extracted' from the concept. So the theorems of Euclidean geometry *do* follow logically from the postulates and definitions.[1] But does the development of modern logic really undermine Kant's view that geometrical truths are synthetic *a priori*?

Van Cleve suggests one reason why it does not. In many cases, modern logic enables us to "make analytic a statement that was formerly synthetic and whose content we knew to be true *a priori* even when the statement was synthetic" (see p. 302 above). As Van Cleve puts it: "the knowledge was there before the analyticity" (see p. 302 above). In what follows, I suggest that it is the special character of this 'pre-analytic' knowledge that Kant aims to explain with his doctrine of pure intuition. While pure intuition does fill logical gaps in Euclidean demonstrations, that is not its only—nor even its primary—role.

## Mathematics and Metaphysics

More than twenty-five years before the publication of the *Critique of Pure Reason*, Kant entered into a debate over the relative claims to truth of mathematics and metaphysics. The dispute revolved around an apparent conflict between the metaphysical doctrine of Leibnizean indivisible monads and the infinite divisibility of geometrical space. In his *Physical monadology*, Kant asked:

> how, in this business, can metaphysics be married to geometry, when it seems easier to mate griffins with horses than to unite transcendental philosophy with geometry? For the former peremptorily denies that space is infinitely divisible, while the latter, with its usual certainty, asserts that it is infinitely divisible.
>
> (Kant 1902–, 1:475)

The metaphysicians' response to this challenge—at least as Kant saw it—was to reduce knowledge of the sensible world, which included geometry, to confused sensible knowledge of things that are known more clearly by the intellect. On their view, geometrical concepts like infinite divisibility apply to sensible *appearances*, but not to the ultimate monadic *reality* that those appearances confusedly represent.

Kant objected that these metaphysicians turned the "reliably established data" of geometry "into subtle fictions, which have little truth to them outside the field of mathematics" (Kant 1902–, 2:167–168). Against this threat to geometry from metaphysics, he tried to explain the peculiar certainty of mathematical knowledge in his Prize Essay of 1763. One distinguishing feature of mathematics that Kant highlights is its use of synthetic definitions. Definitions in philosophy aim to capture and clarify antecedently-given concepts. But mathematicians first introduce their concepts by means of the arbitrary combination of a few "clear and certain" given concepts (Kant 1902–, 2:278). For example, in mathematics the concept of a square is the result of an arbitrary combination of the concepts *four-sided*, *equilateral*, and *rectangle*. That is all there is to being a square. The peculiar certainty of mathematics is partly due to the fact that mathematicians *create* concepts and so know what is and what is not contained in them.

But why should we think that any arbitrary combination of concepts gives us a legitimate object of mathematical study? Is the concept of a figure enclosed by two straight lines on a par with the concept of a square? The answer is no. Mathematics also contains a few "immediately certain" indemonstrable propositions that allow us to distinguish legitimate (or 'real') definitions from illegitimate definitions (Kant 1902–, 2:281). So, for example, the proposition that there can only be one straight line between two points rules out the concept of a figure enclosed by two straight lines. Mathematicians begin with a few given concepts and indemonstrable propositions, build up further concepts by combining the given concepts in accordance with those indemonstrable propositions, and then derive further propositions from the complex concepts and indemonstrable propositions.

In the Prize Essay, Kant says very little about how we know these indemonstrable propositions. He tells us that they are "presupposed as true" and "regarded as immediately certain" (Kant 1902–, 2:281). He likely did not see it as part of his task to explain how these propositions are known. He claims that he is just giving an empirical description of mathematical method and not trying to explain it philosophically (Kant 1902–, 2.275). But without some explanation of the status of those indemonstrable propositions, Kant seems to face the same objection that he himself leveled against the so-called 'metaphysicians.' If mathematicians proceed by arbitrarily combining concepts and then demonstrating claims about them on the basis of assumptions, then why aren't the concepts of mathematics "subtle fictions"? Kant's account of mathematical method needs a metaphysical grounding. We need to explain why arbitrarily combining mathematical concepts gives us legitimate objects of knowledge while arbitrarily combining philosophical concepts does not. In other words, we need to explain why the synthetic method is appropriate in mathematics but not in philosophy.

Kant identifies another distinctive feature of mathematical method that suggests that sensibility is involved in mathematical cognition. Mathematical inferences, he says, proceed by means of concrete "signs" rather than by abstract reflection. This feature is illustrated by the geometrical demonstration that space is infinitely divisible. The geometer, Kant says, takes a straight line standing vertically between two parallel lines, and from a point on one of these draws lines to intersect the other two. "*By means of this symbol*," Kant claims, the geometer "recognises with the greatest certainty that the division can be carried on *ad infinitum*" (Kant 1902–, 2:279). This appeal to "sensible signs" provides "a degree of assurance characteristic of seeing something with one's own eyes" (Kant 1902–, 2:291). Moreover, we can draw universal conclusions from these particular concrete signs. We can discover the properties of all circles, Kant says, by drawing just one circle.

So, the features of mathematical method that explain its peculiar certainty are its use of the synthetic method and the role of signs as sensible means to cognition. As we'll see below, this fits with Van Cleve's description of how we might verify the proposition that every cube has twelve edges by visualization. But it leaves a host of questions unanswered:

How do we know the indemonstrable propositions?
How can we draw universal conclusions from particular examples?
How can sensibility have a role in what is supposed to be a priori knowledge?

In the next section, we'll see that pure intuition is the key to Kant's metaphysical grounding of the Prize Essay explanation of mathematical certainty. But we'll also see that what makes Kant's account of mathematical cognition in the *Critique of Pure Reason* especially interesting is that he introduces pure intuition through arguments that don't have anything to do with mathematics. So Kant's explanation of the synthetic *a priori* status of mathematical propositions *follows from* his more general analysis of the conditions of possible experience. Because of this, Kant has an argument against the metaphysicians' account of mathematical truth, not just an alternative to it.

## Conditions of Possible Experience

Kant's general project in the *Critique of Pure Reason* is to explain the possibility of synthetic a *priori* cognition. Although he takes as given the existence of such cognition, he says "even without requiring such examples for the proof of the reality of pure *a priori* principles in our cognition, *one could establish their indispensability for the possibility of experience itself, thus establish it* a priori" (B5). This suggests that Kant thinks that we can establish the existence of synthetic *a priori* propositions by showing that they are necessary conditions of possible experience. Kant proceeds to do this by analyzing our cognition.

There are, according to Kant, two 'stems' of human cognition (A15/B29): sensibility, through which objects are given to us in intuition, and understanding, through which objects are thought by means of concepts. In the Transcendental Aesthetic, Kant considers the conditions under which objects of cognition are given to us in intuition. In the Transcendental Analytic he considers the conditions under which objects are thought through concepts. Kant wants to determine what the conditions of sensibility are. His proposal is to "isolate sensibility by separating off everything that the understanding thinks through its concepts," then "detach from [what remains] everything that belongs to sensation." We will then be left with "all that sensibility can make available *apriori*" (A22/B36). Kant will argue that we are left with two pure forms of sensible intuition, space and time, which serve as "principles of *a priori* cognition."

In the Metaphysical Exposition of the Concept of Space, Kant argues from the way we experience outer objects to the conclusion that the original representation of space is an *a priori* intuition. By means of outer sense, "we represent to ourselves objects as outside us, and all as in space" (A22/B37). Outer experience is of objects in space that have determinate shape, size, and position with respect to each other. But to represent objects as in spatial relations, Kant argues that we must represent them as occupying regions of an antecedently given space. It follows that "this outer experience is itself first possible only through this [representation of space]" (A23/B38). In other words, the original representation of space can't be acquired from outer experience because it is presupposed by that very experience. It must therefore be *a priori*.

From further features of our outer experience—that the space in which it takes place is essentially singular and infinite—Kant concludes that the representation of space is an intuition. What Kant means by space being singular is that "if one speaks of many spaces, one understands by that only parts of one and the same unique space" (A25/B39). And what he seems to mean by space being infinite is that any given space, no matter what size, is bounded by more space (see A32/B48 for a parallel claim about time). From the fact that we experience space as singular and infinite together with claims about the difference between intuitions and concepts,[2] Kant concludes that the original representation of space must be an intuition.

So on the basis of claims about the way we represent space and objects in space, Kant has argued that the original representation of space is an *a priori* intuition. As promised, he has isolated "what sensibility can make available *a priori*," and has identified "a condition of sensibility, under which alone outer intuition is possible for us" (A26/B43). He can now prove the Introduction's claim that we can establish the existence of synthetic *a priori* principles by showing "their indispensability for the possibility of experience itself." Since the *a priori* intuition of space is a condition of sensibility under which alone outer intuition is possible for us, and geometry is the science of space, geometry is therefore "a science that determines the properties of space synthetically and yet *a priori*" (B41). Because the representation of space is *a priori*, so are propositions about it. Because the representation of space is an intuition, cognitions of properties of space require "the help of an intuition added to the concept" and so are synthetic.

But this gives rise to another puzzle. Kant has argued that there *must be* an *a priori* intuition of space, but how is it possible to intuit something *a priori*? An intuition is a representation that depends on the presence of an object, but it seems that an *a priori* intuition would have to occur *prior to* the presence of any object, *without* the object being present. What could the object of such a representation be?

Kant thinks that the puzzle arises only if we take our intuition to represent things as they are in themselves (A26/B42). So he concludes that the spatial properties of objects are not objective properties of things in themselves, but rather reflect the subjective conditions of sensibility (A23/B37). This is Kant's doctrine that space is transcendentally ideal. Space is nothing but a form of intuition. Kant sums up the implications of this doctrine for geometry in his general remarks on the Transcendental Aesthetic:

> If, therefore, space (and time as well) were not a mere form of your intuition that contains *a priori* conditions under which alone things could be outer objects for you, which are nothing in themselves without these

subjective conditions, then you could make out absolutely nothing synthetic and *a priori* about outer objects.

(A48/B66)

I have argued that Kant does not simply *assume* that geometry is synthetic *a priori* cognition, nor does he argue *from* the synthetic *a priori* status of geometry *to* the claim that space is a mere form of intuition. Rather, he argues for these claims on the basis of what he takes to be necessary conditions of experience. Why does this matter?

The doctrine of pure intuition allows Kant to distinguish his claim that geometry is necessarily true and applicable to the world from the metaphysicians' claim that it is "an empty delusion of the imagination" (Kant 1902–, 1:476). If Kant's argument for the doctrine of pure intuition *depends on* the assumption that geometry is true, necessary, and applicable, then Kant is simply begging the question against the metaphysician. But if, on the other hand, Kant's argument for the doctrine of pure intuition is independent of such mathematical considerations, then Kant has an *argument against* the metaphysicians' claims against mathematics.

Having an argument against the metaphysicians was important to Kant. In the Second Antinomy, he considers some objections put forward by "monists." Instead of granting that mathematical proof gives us "insights into the constitution of space, insofar as it is in fact the formal condition of the possibility of all matter," they "regard these proofs only as inferences from abstract but arbitrary concepts which could not be related to real things" (A439/B467). Although we don't need experience of 'real things' for the synthetic *a priori* cognition of shapes drawn in space, "still this cognition would be nothing at all, but an occupation with a mere figment of the brain, if space were not to be regarded as the condition of the appearances which constitute the matter of outer experience" (A157/B196). This passage reveals a further metaphysical role for Kant's notion of pure intuition: to ensure the objective reality of geometrical concepts. It is not enough just to show that geometrical cognition is based on an *a priori* intuition; we also have to show that that intuition is not an arbitrary 'figment of the brain.'

In other words, even if Kant did begin by assuming the synthetic *a priori* status of geometry, there would be the further question of showing that the propositions of geometry are not "a mere play" of representations of the imagination:

Space has three dimensions, between two points there can be only one straight line, etc. Although all these principles, and the representation of the object with which this science occupies itself, are generated in the mind completely *a priori*, they would still not signify anything at all if we could not always exhibit their significance in appearances. Hence it is

> always requisite for one *to make* an abstract concept *sensible*, i.e., display the object that corresponds to it in intuition, since without this the concept would remain (as one says) without sense, i.e., without significance. Mathematics fulfills this requirement by means of the construction of the figure.
>
> (A239–40/B299)

This is the metaphysical role for the doctrine of pure intuition in Kant's philosophy of mathematics: by constructing our concepts in pure intuition, we exhibit their objective content, thereby showing that they are not "mere plays" of imagination. In the next section, I will discuss the account of construction in pure intuition that allows Kant to give a more detailed answer to the three open questions about mathematical knowledge from the Prize Essay.

## Van Cleve, Pure Intuition, and Construction

Van Cleve illustrates an epistemological role for pure intuition with his example of the proposition that every cube has twelve edges. We can verify this proposition "simply by visualizing a cube and counting its edges—an exercise in what Kant calls 'pure intuition'" (see p. 301 above). I've argued that there is also a metaphysical role for intuition in Kant's philosophy of mathematics, which only comes out when we consider the philosophical debate about mathematical knowledge in the background.

We lose sight of this metaphysical role if we read Kant as just *assuming* that geometry gives us synthetic *a priori* truth and then trying to show how this is possible. This is why I have tried to complement Van Cleve's discussion of the synthetic *a priori* with a fuller story about Kant's views. In the selection you've just read, Van Cleve defends the characterization of synthetic *a priori* cognition Kant gives in the *Critique*'s Introduction. This characterization does not refer to the doctrine of pure intuition, which is not developed until later. Van Cleve later goes on to discuss the ideality of space with an exclusive focus on the so-called 'argument from geometry': as Van Cleve sees it, Kant's argument for the ideality of space takes as "a crucial presupposition . . . that geometrical truths—some of them, at least—be both synthetic and *a priori*" (Van Cleve 1999, 36).

Van Cleve's presentation obscures the fact that I've tried to highlight here, that Kant had an independent argument for the synthetic *a priori* status of geometry. The synthetic *a priori* status of geometry is not a *presupposition* of Kant's argument for transcendental idealism. It is a *conclusion* from his analysis of conditions of experience. In this way, we can see Kant as supplying the metaphysical grounding that I argued his account of mathematical method in the Prize Essay needed. We can also see that there is a much richer epistemological role for intuition in Kant's account of mathematical cognition than

Van Cleve's example of visualization suggests. To bring this out, let's consider Kant's discussion of the method of mathematics in the Transcendental Doctrine of Method at the end of the first Critique.

The Transcendental Doctrine of Method again compares the mathematical method of attaining certainty to the method of attaining certainty in philosophy. The basic difference is that "philosophical cognition is rational cognition from concepts" whereas mathematical cognition is cognition "from the *construction* of concepts" (A713/B742). This time, though, Kant gives us not just a description but an *explanation* of the difference. The question of why synthetic definitions are admissible in mathematics but not in philosophy becomes the question of why mathematicians can construct their concepts and philosophers can't. The answer lies in the doctrine of pure intuition expounded in the Transcendental Aesthetic. To construct a concept means to exhibit *a priori* the intuition corresponding to it. But as we've seen, the only intuitions given *a priori* are space and time, so only concepts of space and time can be exhibited *a priori* in pure intuition (A715/B743). This is why only mathematical cognition involves construction of concepts.

We now see more clearly that the special character of mathematical cognition rests on Kant's argument from the nature of our experience of objects as in space to the claim that space and time are *a priori* intuitions. But how does this appeal to construction in pure intuition address the three open questions from the Prize Essay? Kant again identifies the same distinguishing features of mathematics: it is grounded on definitions, axioms, and demonstrations. All of these distinctive features can now be explained by appeal to the notion of construction in pure intuition.

As in the Prize Essay, Kant tells us that mathematics admits of definitions because the concepts are "arbitrarily thought." But now he acknowledges that this is not yet enough: "I cannot say that I have thereby defined a true object." There is no guarantee of an object corresponding to an arbitrarily thought concept *except* in the case of "those containing an arbitrary synthesis which can be constructed *a priori*,"

> . . . and thus only mathematics has definitions. For the object that it thinks it also exhibits *a priori* in intuition, and this can surely contain neither more nor less than the concept, since through the explanation of the concept the object is originally given.
>
> (A729–730/B757–758)

This is what I have called the metaphysical role for intuition in Kant's account of mathematical cognition. The notion of construction also explains the particular epistemological character of mathematics. Indemonstrable propositions, or axioms, for Kant, are immediately certain synthetic *a priori* principles. Because we can construct mathematical concepts in intuition, we can thereby connect predicates *a priori* and immediately and directly cognize that connection. For example, upon constructing a straight line between two points, we can cognize immediately and directly that the straight line is the shortest line between two points. But this construction is particular. So how does it tell us that *all* the shortest lines between two points are straight lines?

Kant explains this with reference to the construction of the concept of a triangle. Although the intuition is an individual object, it nonetheless "expresses universal validity for all possible intuitions that belong under the same concept" (A713/B741). To construct a concept, I exhibit an object corresponding to the concept

> either through mere imagination, in pure intuition, or on paper, in empirical intuition, but in both cases completely *a priori*, without having had to borrow the pattern for it from any experience. The individual drawn figure is empirical and nevertheless serves to express the concept without damage to its universality, for in the case of this empirical intuition we have taken account only of the action of constructing the concept, to which many determinations, e.g., those of the magnitude of the sides and the angles, are entirely indifferent, and thus we have abstracted from these differences, which do not alter the concept of the triangle.
>
> (A714/B742)

We can draw general conclusions from particular figures because we don't focus on the particular features of the individual figure but rather on the *act* of constructing the figure in accordance with the pure intuition of space. In this way, geometry and its axioms "express the conditions of sensible intuition *a priori*" (A163/B204).

Although this could also describe the kind of visual inspection of a cube that Van Cleve takes as an example of an exercise in pure intuition, Kant goes on to give a more detailed example that suggests that what he has in mind by 'construction' includes something more like a Euclidean proof. To discover how the sum of the angles of a triangle are related to a right angle, the geometer constructs a triangle:

> Since he knows that two right angles together are exactly equal to all of the adjacent angles that can be drawn at one point on a straight line, he extends one side of his triangle and obtains two adjacent angles that together are equal to two right ones. Now he divides the external one of these angles by drawing a line parallel to the opposite side of the triangle, and sees that here arises an external adjacent angle which is equal to an internal one, etc.
>
> (A716/B744)

This is just Euclid's proof that the sum of the angles of the triangle is equal to two right angles. (It's from Book 1, Proposition 32 of the *Elements*.) We don't cognize that the angles of a triangle are equal to two right angles by mere visual inspection of a triangle, but by a step-by-step demonstration appealing to previous theorems, axioms, and definitions. There is a role for pure intuition at each of these stages. Even the epistemological role for intuition is richer than Van Cleve's example of the cube suggests.

## Conclusion

Van Cleve's primary goal is to show that Kant is right that there are synthetic *a priori* propositions. I have tried to uncover the broader historical background to Kant's conception of the synthetic *a priori* by situating it in the philosophical and mathematical context of his time. This is not meant to imply that the interest of Kant's philosophy of mathematics is essentially tied to its historical context. On the contrary, it seems to me that by recognizing the broader philosophical issues that Kant's account of mathematical cognition was designed to address, we can also broaden our view of the philosophical interest of that account. Questions about the content of mathematical propositions, their claim to truth, and the relation between pure and applied mathematics persist in contemporary philosophy. Kant's philosophy of mathematics represents perhaps the most systematic attempt to address these questions and to incorporate them into a more general philosophical project.[3]

## Acknowledgement

I'm grateful to Lisa Shabel for comments on an earlier draft of this chapter. Work on this chapter was generously supported by a grant from the Social Sciences and Humanities Research Council of Canada.

## Notes

1. For example, the Euclidean proof that an equilateral triangle can be constructed from any given line segment appeals to the point of intersection of two circles. With only monadic logic, Euclid's axioms and definitions cannot be expressed in such a way that the existence of that point of intersection follows logically from those axioms and definitions. Instead, the existence of this point could only be guaranteed by actually constructing it: as Kant would say, "exhibiting it in pure intuition." With the development of polyadic logic in the nineteenth century, however, it became possible to express a continuity axiom that guaranteed the existence of the point of intersection, so the existence of such a point *can* be said to follow from axioms and definitions. This example is presented in detail in Friedman (1992, 59).
2. Concepts are inherently general, while intuitions are singular. A concept can contain within itself only finitely many concepts, but an intuition can contain an infinite set of representations within itself.

# What Is Transcendental Idealism?

# Editors' Introduction

Kant's *Critique of Pure Reason* is an extended argument for the view he calls 'Transcendental Idealism.' But what *is* transcendental idealism? Is it a metaphysical view about the nature of the world—or an epistemological view about how we *know* the world? Kant's readers from the eighteenth century on have disagreed about how transcendental idealism is best understood. Interpretations fall into two main categories:

1. 'One-world' interpretations hold that there aren't two sets of things, things in themselves and appearances, merely two different ways of *considering* things. We can consider things as they appear to us, or as they are in themselves. One-world interpretations often deny that transcendental idealism is a metaphysical theory, holding that it's purely epistemological.
2. Traditional 'two-world' interpretations hold that things in themselves and things as they appear to us are two genuinely distinct sets of things. Two-world interpretations often adopt an extreme Berkeleian idealism or phenomenalism about appearances, holding that tables, chairs, and human bodies are merely mental entities.

Both interpretations face serious problems. Major problems for typical, epistemological one-world interpretations are that Kant often does seem to say that transcendental idealism is a metaphysical view, that things as they appear to us really depend on our minds and that there is an aspect of reality that we cannot know. And a major problem for the traditional two-world interpretation is that there are overwhelming reasons to think that Kant is not a Berkeleian idealist about appearances. He explicitly denies that transcendental idealism is Berkeley's idealism, and if he *were* a Berkeleian idealist it would be hard to see how his talk of things in themselves was legitimate.

In her book *Kantian Humility*, Rae Langton proposes a third alternative that is supposed to capture the advantages of both one-world and two-world interpretations. It makes Transcendental Idealism a metaphysical view and at the same time explains what our connection with things in themselves consists in. The key ingredient is her claim that when Kant talks about appearances, he's really talking about the relational properties of things (and when he's talking about things in themselves, he's talking about their intrinsic properties).

Lucy Allais finds a great deal to admire in Langton's book—but also a great deal to criticize. She worries that although Langton's view is elegant and philosophically interesting, it's not really *Kant's* view. She thinks the attempt to find a one-world reading of Transcendental Idealism that makes it a metaphysical view is worth pursuing—but not in terms of Langton's distinction between intrinsic and relational properties. Thus, Allais' response to Langton is a nice example of how scholarly disagreement can be constructive.

## Note on References

The *Critique of Pure Reason* is typically referred to by page number in the original first, or 'A', and second, or 'B', editions. Hence (A84/B116) is a passage that appears on p. 84 in the first edition and p. 116 in the second edition, while (B19) is a passage that appears on p. 19 of the second edition and did not appear at all in the first edition. There are two standard English translations of the *Critique*—by Kemp Smith (1933) and Guyer and Wood (1988). We have not noted which translation an author is using, or whether they are using their own translation.

## Further Reading

- Henry Allison (2004). *Kant's Transcendental Idealism.*
- Sebastian Gardner (1999). *Routledge Philosophy Guidebook to Kant and the Critique of Pure Reason.*

## CHAPTER 23

# Excerpts from *Kantian Humility*

RAE LANGTON

## Introduction

> Many historians of philosophy, with all their intended praise, let the phi-
> losophers speak mere nonsense. They do not guess the purpose of the
> philosophers . . . They cannot see beyond what the philosophers actually
> said, to what they really meant to say.
>
> (Kant 1790/1973)

Kant is rather scathing of a certain kind of history of philosophy. Alert to the
possibility that interpretive charity and interpretive fidelity may sometimes
pull in different directions, he favorably contrasts the stance of intelligent and
charitable engagement with the stance of an uncritical devotee. If Kant is right
to value the former, then the history of philosophy since his time has been
fortunate, since there has been no lack of intelligent and charitable engagement. This is perhaps especially true with respect to interpretations of Kant
himself. What did Kant himself actually say, or mean to say? He said that there
is a distinction between appearances and things in themselves, that things in
themselves exist, and that we have no knowledge of things in themselves. This
has seemed to come dangerously close to nonsense, and there has accordingly
been no lack of charitable interpreters only too willing to suppose that he did
not mean quite what he said, and that a different purpose must be guessed.
Kant's purpose must be to say something else, something mild, and sane, and
wise. Kant gives some license, as we can see, for this kind of rational reconstruction: he gives license for seeing beyond what the philosopher actually
said, to what he really meant to say.

It seems unlikely, though, that a philosopher did not mean to say what he said, when he said it over and over again. And it is worth bearing in mind that Kant himself did not appear to think his philosophy was mild, and sane, and wise. Startling, yes; frustrating, yes; wise, perhaps; mild, no.[1] Faced with this stubborn fact, there is a choice. One can let the philosopher speak nonsense. One can turn an indulgent blind eye to the metaphysical lapses. Or, best of all, one can aim for an alternative which achieves both fidelity and charity, which accepts that this is what the philosopher actually said, and that it is what the philosopher meant to say, and that it is not nonsense after all.

Kant says that there is a distinction between things in themselves and phenomena. What he says is admittedly metaphysics, but none the worse, I think, for that. He says that things as we know them consist "wholly of relations" (A285/B341). He says that we have no insight into "the inner" of things (A277/B233). He has a distinction between substances, bearers of intrinsic properties, on the one hand; and relational properties of substances on the other. He says that we have no knowledge of the intrinsic properties of substances. This, as it stands, is not idealism, but a kind of epistemic humility. There are inevitable constraints on what we can know, inevitable limits on what we can become acquainted with. And while those limits could be correctly described, in Strawson's phrase, as 'the bounds of sense', such a description fails to capture Kant's thought that there is a particular sort of thing that is beyond the bounds of sense, something abstractly characterizable in metaphysical rather than epistemological terms: not simply as "that which is beyond the bounds of sense", but as "that which has an intrinsic nature" . . .

## Chapter 1

### 1. Introduction

Kant affirms the existence of things in themselves and speaks of them affecting our minds, and being the cause of appearances. Since the earliest days, this has been seen as the fundamental sticking point in Kant's philosophy.[2] If Kant's philosophy is right, then we have no knowledge of things in themselves: we cannot know that they exist, nor can we know that they are causes of appearances, and affect us . . . Kant's philosophy has been thought to imply two relations of affection, empirical and transcendental. We are affected by bodies; and we are affected by things in themselves. Both relations of affection seem illegitimate on the assumption of idealism, since the first requires causal agency of a mere representation, and the second is supposed to be unknown. Our concern here will be chiefly with the problem raised by things in themselves.

The problem, thus described, attributes to Kant two metaphysical theses.

K1 Things in themselves exist.
K2 Things in themselves are the causes of phenomenal appearances.

And it attributes to Kant an epistemological thesis.

K3  We can have no knowledge of things in themselves.

Trouble comes with the conjunction of the three. For the epistemological the-sis appears to imply these corollaries:

C1  We cannot know that things in themselves exist.
C2  We cannot know that things in themselves are the causes of phenom-enal appearances.

We cannot know K1 and K2. Kant's story makes itself untellable.

## 2. Allison's Deflationary Proposal

In Chapter 11 of *Kant's Transcendental Idealism*, Henry Allison confronts these problems. His response to the alleged problem of empirical causation is swift. It is a mistake, he says, to suppose that Kant cannot legitimately speak of affec-tion by empirical objects: "Kant *not only can but does* speak about the mind as affected by empirical objects."[3] He gives examples. But Allison cannot argue by equivocation—even if he not only can but does. Allison's 'can' is equivoca-tory. That Kant *does* something implies that he *can* do something in one sense, but not in the other. As Kant reminds us, should reminders be needed, doing and legitimately doing are not the same.[4] There is more, though, to Allison's defense. He says, and I think rightly, that a problem of empirical affection would arise only for a Berkeleian Kant, for whom appearances are just ideas, and he says that the Berkeleian Kant is a fiction. And he saves his most elegant solution for the most fundamental problem, the one that concerns us here: namely, the existence of, and affection by, unknowable things in themselves.

The mistake, says Allison, is to construe Kant's basic theses as metaphysical theses. Construed metaphysically, the contrast between phenomenal appear-ance and thing in itself lands us with 'two distinct entities' or 'two kinds of entity' (Allison 2004, 240 and 248). That is where the trouble starts, and that is where we can stop it in its tracks. Kant is not interested in making exist-ence claims, says Allison. He is interested in philosophical methodology. It is not that there exist two kinds of thing, phenomena and things in themselves. Rather, there are two ways of considering things. We can consider things, at the empirical level, in relation to our sensibility. And we can consider things, at the transcendental level, in abstraction from that relation. When doing science we sometimes consider a thing in abstraction from certain properties it has, such as weight; but this does not show that there are weightless things. When evalu-ating an applicant for a job, we sometimes consider the applicant in abstraction from certain properties she has, such as height; but this does not show that there are people who have no height. When doing philosophy, we sometimes consider things in abstraction from their relation to our sensibility, in abstraction from their spatial, temporal, properties; but this does not show that there are non-spatial, atemporal, non-causal things. Kant's distinction between phenomena and things in themselves is a distinction between two ways we have of considering things, and from that distinction no metaphysical theses follow. In the absence of metaphysical theses, no further problems arise.

In place of the metaphysical K1 and K2, we have the following anodyne theses:

A1  We can consider things 'in themselves', i.e. in abstraction from the conditions of our sensibility.

A2  Things considered in abstraction from the conditions of our sensibility can be considered only as something that affects the mind.

Allison's view makes it analytic that things in themselves are not describable spatiotemporally. Statements about things in themselves are, by definition, statements that abstract from any talk of space, time, and the categories. This kind of abstraction is just what constitutes the transcendental level of considering things. Since knowledge arises only with the concrete application of the forms and categories, Kant's thesis K3 about our ignorance of things in themselves becomes nothing more than this:

A3  Things considered in abstraction from their relation to our sensibility are things considered in abstraction from their relation to our sensibility.

On Allison's view, there are no unknowable entities in the picture. If we are asked to say more about the 'something' in A2 that is supposed to affect the mind, we must refuse. To say anything more at the transcendental level would be to make oneself guilty of a kind of methodological impurity. We can say nothing more until we stop abstracting, until we descend to the empirical level. Then, of course, our answer to the question 'What affects the mind?' must be an empirical answer. Light, air, elements, and all the familiar denizens of the globe are the things that affect our minds. There is no problem of affection. The 'something' in A2 is not something over and above the familiar phenomenal objects: it is identical with the class of phenomenal objects 'referred to collectively'. It is the class of those objects, considered in an abstract way.

## 3. Reasons for Suspicion

Allison's is an ingenious and attractive solution to an old and ugly problem. But I would like to suggest that there are reasons for suspicion. I have an ulterior motive. I have up my sleeve a solution that is, though less ingenious, more attractive.

First, there is a problem about analyticity. Allison's approach makes it analytic that we have no knowledge of things in themselves. To consider things in themselves is simply to consider things in abstraction from the conditions of our knowledge: K3 has become the tautological A3. From one point of view this is an advantage, but from another it is a grave defect, for it fails to do justice to an aspect of Kant that ought not to be ignored. What I have in mind is not exactly a Kantian philosophical thesis, in the sense that K1–K3 are philosophical theses. Rather, it is a Kantian attitude to these philosophical theses, and in particular to the third. When Kant tells us that we have no knowledge of things in themselves, he thinks he is telling us something new and important. The truth of K3 is a major philosophical discovery. Moreover, it is not just a discovery with a definite, non-trivial content. It is a depressing discovery. Kant thinks we are missing out on something in not knowing things as they are in themselves. Kant speaks of our yearning for something more, he speaks of doomed aspirations, he speaks of "our inextinguishable desire to find firm footing somewhere beyond the bounds of experience" (A796/B824). It is not easy to see how this inextinguishable desire could be for the falsity of A3.

It is not inconceivable, of course, that we might have a futile yearning for the falsity of an analytic truth. The proposition that 'All men are mortal' may be analytically true, and greatly mourned for all that . . . We can always cry for the moon, want the impossible—even the logically impossible. But I say that it *is* inconceivable that we could have a yearning for the falsity of A3—it is inconceivable that we could have an "inextinguishable desire" to consider things abstractly without considering things abstractly. I think this is reason enough to reject Allison's anodyne interpretation.

There is a further problem with the analyticity. If K3 were really just A3, then the question of how anyone or anything *could* have knowledge of things in themselves would be nonsense. If Allison were right, then Kant would not attempt to say what it could be to have knowledge of things as they are in themselves. He would not attempt to give any content to what is being denied by K3. But he does. He says, for example, that to have knowledge of a thing in itself would be to be able to ascribe to it "distinctive and inner predicates" (A565/B593).[5] The fact that Kant says anything at all about this question is hard to reconcile with Allison's interpretation. On Allison's view, to speak of a thing in itself is *ipso facto* to speak of a thing in *abstraction* from any distinctive predicates whatsoever.

Second, there is a problem about causality. Allison says that we render the causal claim about things in themselves innocuous by the simple assertion of A2, which does not commit us to non-spatial, atemporal, unknowable things. That is true. A2 does not require a causal relationship between our minds and some non-spatial, atemporal, unknowable existents. Allison avoids the traditional problem of affection. But there is a new problem in its place. A2 remains a causal claim: something affects the mind. And the question must be raised whether one is entitled to make any causal claims at all while 'considering things' at the transcendental level. If A2 is a causal claim, and causality is a category of things considered only in relation to our sensibility, then Allison seems to be failing by his own lights. In asserting A2, we fail to abstract completely from the relations things have to our sensibility. We fail to keep to the transcendental level. In ascending to the transcendental level, we are supposed to abstract from all the 'conditions of sensibility', namely space, time, and the categories. But in ascribing causality to things, we fail to abstract from the categories.

There is a further problem with the causal claim in A3. Allison's idea, if it worked, would make sense of the claim that things in themselves affect us. But it renders false the Kantian claim that things in themselves are the causes of phenomenal empirical objects. If a first thing is identical with a second thing, then it cannot be its cause.[6] And if the 'something' in A2 is *identical* with the class of phenomenal objects, referred to in an abstract collective way, then that 'something' cannot be their cause.

I have given grounds for suspicion, but they are not conclusive. They suggest that Allison is trying to see beyond what the philosopher actually said, to what he really meant to say: they suggest that Allison's project, like others before him, is rational reconstruction after all. But Allison does indeed have a solution, where others have failed. And he thinks that non-deflationary attempts are bound to fail. He thinks Kant's problems will go away only if we stop injecting him with the poison of metaphysics. Otherwise we are bound to be left with a philosophy that crudely divides the world into different entities, that supposes an incoherent double affection, that attempts to tell the untellable. If we abandon metaphysical interpretations, and accept Allison's deflationary proposal, we will be saved much philosophical embarrassment.

I have suggested that the price of acceptance is too high. If it is, we shall need to find an alternative. I have an alternative. It is not deflationary. It does not avoid metaphysics. But it does offer a solution to the old problem.

## 4. A Metaphysical Proposal, and an Acid Test Passed

Are there two worlds, or one world considered two ways? Are appearance and thing in itself the very same? Kant seems ambivalent. Consider the following passage.

> We call certain objects, as appearances, sensible entities (phenomena), thereby distinguishing the way that we intuit them from the nature they have in themselves, we place these (considered according to this latter nature) . . . in opposition to the former, and . . . call them intelligible entities (*noumena*).

(B306)

If we pursue the thread of Kant's anaphors we find one answer. When we call objects, as appearances, sensible entities (phenomena), we distinguish the way that we intuit *them* from the nature that belongs to *them* in themselves. The objects that have a nature that belongs to them in themselves are the same as the objects that we intuit. The labels 'noumena' and 'phenomena' refer to the same things. So it seems at first sight. However, one can find in the same passage a different answer. Phenomenal and noumenal 'entities' are described and put 'in opposition' to each other, as if they are two non-overlapping sets of things. One world or two? This ambivalence needs an explanation.

The explanation I would like to suggest draws on what Kant says elsewhere, and its defense is the topic of chapters to come. There is one world: there are simply, as Kant says with appropriate vagueness, objects, or things. But there are two, non-overlapping sets of properties. Kant speaks in this passage of the nature that things have in themselves, as he speaks elsewhere of the "distinctive and inner predicates" of things (A565/B593). The nature things have in themselves is different from what we encounter when we intuit them: the inner or *intrinsic* predicates are different from the predicates encountered by us. There is one world, one set of things, but two kinds of properties: intrinsic properties, and properties that are "in opposition" to the intrinsic, namely relational properties. The labels 'phenomena' and 'noumena' seem to label different entities, but really they label different classes of properties of the same set of entities. This helps to explain the ambivalence.

A distinction between two sets of properties is a metaphysical distinction, but this one has epistemological significance. To have knowledge of a thing in itself, Kant says, would be to be able to ascribe to it distinctive intrinsic predicates (A565/B593), which we cannot do. K1–K3 should be understood something like this:

M1 There exist things in themselves, i.e. things that have intrinsic properties.

M2 The things that have intrinsic properties also have relational properties: causal powers that constitute phenomenal appearances.

M3 We have no knowledge of the intrinsic properties of things.

Instead of an inconsistent triad, we have a consistent one. The old and ugly problem disappears. The third claim about knowledge does not undermine the first two. It has no unwelcome corollaries. Kant's story does not make itself untellable.

Kant's existence claim in K1 looked incompatible with the knowledge claim of K3: if we literally have no knowledge of things in themselves, then we do not even know that they exist. If K3 is true, then K1 is false. But interpreted as M3 and M1 there is no inconsistency. We can know *that* there are things that have intrinsic properties without knowing *what* those properties are. Knowledge of things *as* they are in themselves involves the ability to ascribe 'distinctive intrinsic predicates' to a thing. That involves more than simply knowing that there are things that have intrinsic properties.

Kant's causal claim in K2 looked incompatible with the knowledge claim of K3. The claim that things in themselves affect us, and that things in themselves are the cause of phenomena, conflicts with the claim that we have no knowledge of things as they are in themselves. If K3 is true, then K2 is false. Interpreted as M3 and M2, however, there is no inconsistency, at least on a certain assumption. On the assumption that causal powers are not intrinsic properties, we can know that a thing has certain causal powers without knowing what its intrinsic properties are. We can know that things are in certain causal relations with other things without being able to ascribe to them any 'distinctive and intrinsic predicates'. If this is so, there is no problem of affection here.

Finally, we do not need to ignore Kant's sense of loss. Kant's attitude to K3 is not the attitude of a man doing conceptual analysis. We have no knowledge of things in themselves despite having an 'inextinguishable desire' for such knowledge. This attitude makes more sense on the assumption that K3 is really M3. There is indeed an entire aspect of the world that remains hidden from us. We are indeed missing out on something. It may be a trivial, analytic thesis to say, with Allison, that we can have no knowledge of things in abstraction from the conditions of knowledge. It is by no means trivial, analytic, that we have 'no insight whatsoever into the intrinsic nature of things' (A277/B333). That is a substantial philosophical discovery, and, in Kant's eyes, a cause for mourning

## Notes

1. Kant says it is "startling" (A285/B341), and admits that it leaves unsatisfied an "inextinguishable yearing" (A796/B824). An example of a sane and mild interpretation [is] discussed in Chapter 1 [of Langton's *Kantian Humility*].
2. Jacobi (1815, 304) being one of the first to draw attention to it . . . See Allison (2004, 247–254)'s discussion of this problem . . . Guyer (1987, 338) shares my suspicion of what he calls Allison's 'anodyne conceptual analysis', though he does not give the same reasons for suspicion. He too thinks that Allison's attempted solution to the problem fails . . . My explanation of Allison's proposal draws partly on Guyer's helpful discussion, though he would disagree with my proposed solution.
3. Allison 2004, 249, emphasis added. My objection is not to the overall strategy of his defence of empirical affection, but to this particular punning argument.
4. Kant distinguishes the question of right (quid juris) from the question of fact (quid facti) at the beginning of the Transcendental Deduction (A84/B116).
5. To have knowledge of a thing in itself would be to know it as 'ein durch seine unterscheidenden und inneren Prädikate bestimmbares Ding' (A565/B593), a thing determinable through its distinctive and inner, or intrinsic, predicates.
6. This happens to be endorsed by Kant in a very early philosophical work. "It is inconsistent that anything should have the reason for its existence in itself", he says in Proposition VI of *A New Exposition of the First Principles of Metaphysical Knowledge* (Kant 1902-, 1.394). He there draws the implication that God is not his own cause.

## CHAPTER 24

# Langton, Kant, and Things in Themselves

LUCY ALLAIS

Rae Langton's book *Kantian Humility* (1998) addresses an old problem at the heart of understanding Kant's transcendental idealism: how to make sense of Kant's claim that we cannot have knowledge of things as they are in themselves, which Langton refers to as Kant's humility. The problem is central to Kant's critical philosophy, and there is no agreed solution. Langton's lively and stimulating account makes a fascinating contribution to this debate.

Kant sees transcendental idealism as a major philosophical revolution—one that will enable us to solve problems that have vexed philosophers for centuries and to establish both the possibility and the limits of metaphysics. At the center of transcendental idealism is a distinction between things as they are in themselves and things as they appear to us. Kant argues that things as they appear to us are in some sense "representations" (A30/B45), which would not exist without our minds (A42/B59; A370; A490–1/B518–9; A492/B520), and that we cannot have knowledge of things as they are in themselves. In the first *Critique* Kant develops and defends what can be called a metaphysics of experience: an account of synthetic *a priori* claims which are true of the spatio-temporal objects we experience, such as the claim that every event has a cause, or the claim that substance is conserved in all interactions. He also presents a critique of traditional metaphysics (which he calls transcendent metaphysics) that aims to have *a priori* knowledge of things that are not possible objects of experience, such as God, Cartesian souls, and Leibnizian monads. Kant argues that knowledge of such things is impossible for us. Finally, he presents a solution to the free will problem that is supposed to show that we cannot know we have free will, but also that empirical, scientific knowledge can never rule out free will and that free will is metaphysically possible. Transcendental idealism is at the center of all these projects in the *Critique*, and, in relation to his solution to the free will problem, it is also crucial to Kant's ethics.

Thus, understanding transcendental idealism is clearly crucial for understanding the first *Critique* and Kant's critical philosophy in general. However, in the more than two hundred years since the publication of the first *Critique*, there has been no agreement on how to interpret the position, and not even a tendency towards convergence. Commentators disagree about how to understand Kant's distinction between appearances and things as they are in themselves, and even about whether it is a metaphysical or an epistemological distinction.[1] They disagree about whether Kant is an idealist about things as they appear to us, i.e. whether he thinks that they depend on our minds in some sense.[2] They disagree about his reasons for thinking that we do not have cognition of things as they are in themselves, about what his notion of things as they are in themselves amounts to, and even about whether Kant is committed to there actually existing something corresponding to the notion of things as they are in themselves.[3]

Faced with so much disagreement amongst commentators, readers might be tempted simply to blame Kant for not being clearer, and might wonder why it is worth trying to understand transcendental idealism at all. But it seems to me that a central cause of the disagreement is also one of the most interesting features of Kant's thinking. Kant's philosophy constantly involves an attempt to mediate between and do justice to conflicting philosophical pulls, such as those towards realism and idealism. There are significant philosophical considerations that have driven philosophers to these competing positions, and rather than opting for one option, Kant frequently tries to do justice to both. This is a large part of what makes his work so fascinating, deep, and rewarding. Whether or not we think that there is one interpretation of transcendental idealism unambiguously supported in the *Critique* (I do), and whether or not we think the position achieves what Kant intends it to, following the twists of the argument gives us insight into a fascinating philosophical tightrope that Kant attempts to stay on.

Something similar can be said about following the different *interpretations* of Kant's thought that commentators have given. Although I will mainly present my disagreements with Langton's reading here, I hope also to show that even when we disagree with an interpretation, it may still give us great insights into the text—even change the terms of the debate. I see Langton's book as a fascinating and important contribution to understanding Kant.

Langton presents as one of her aims being faithful to what Kant actually says. She holds that Kant said "that things in themselves exist, and that we have no knowledge of things in themselves" (see p. 323 above). Lots of philosophers think this cannot be made sense of. They worry that if Kant is right that we cannot have knowledge of things in themselves, then "we cannot know that they exist, nor can we know that they are causes of appearances, and affect us" (see p. 324 above). Many commentators interpret Kant in a way which involves not attributing to him the claim that things in themselves exist.[4] Langton presents a way of reading Kant which shows that Kant's claims about things in themselves are consistent and are part of a philosophically interesting position which has relevance for contemporary philosophers.

She argues that Kant's distinction between things in themselves and appearances should be understood as a distinction between intrinsic and extrinsic properties of things. Thus, Kant's claim that we cannot know things as they are in themselves should be understood as saying that we cannot know the intrinsic properties of things. On Langton's reading, instead of the apparently inconsistent claims:

1. Things in themselves exist.
2. Things in themselves are the cause of phenomenal appearances.
3. We can have no knowledge of things in themselves.

we have:

1. M1 There exist things in themselves, i.e. things that have intrinsic properties.
2. M2 The things that have intrinsic properties also have relational properties: causal powers that constitute phenomenal appearances.
3. M3 We have no knowledge of the intrinsic properties of things.

Kant does not, on the surface, present the distinction between things in themselves and appearances as a distinction between intrinsic and relational (or extrinsic) properties of things, so Langton needs to show that this is a reasonable way of reading it. She also needs to show that Kant holds that intrinsic properties are causally inert, so that no property could be both an intrinsic property and a causal power. Finally, she needs to show that Kant holds that causal powers cannot be reduced to intrinsic properties.

In making this case, Langton uses a number of strategies. She places a lot of emphasis on two texts written much earlier than the first *Critique*, the *New Exposition* (1755) and *Thoughts on the True Estimation of Living Forces* (1757), which give us insight into the development of Kant's views. She spends some time examining Leibniz's views, in order to understand Kant's disagreement with him. And she engages to some extent in reconstruction. Kant's argument appears to have a missing premise, so what thought might we attribute to him to make the argument work?

I have a few worries about how faithful Langton is to what Kant actually says. I will discuss these in increasing order of seriousness. First, a more textually accurate way of setting up the initial three claims would be:

1. T1 Things exist that have a way they are as they are in themselves.
2. T2 The way things are in themselves causes or grounds the way they appear to us.
3. T3 We cannot have knowledge of the way things are as they are in themselves.

On this way of presenting Kant's position, there is much less obvious tension between the claims. Langton argues that on her reconstruction, the apparent inconsistency disappears, because "We can know *that* there are things that have intrinsic properties without knowing *what* those properties are" (see p. 329 above). But the same move could be used to say that we can know *that* there are things that have a way they are as they are in themselves, without knowing *what* things are like as they are in themselves. Neither reading involves saying something contradictory. And both readings require explaining why we should believe in these properties whose natures we cannot know.

This does not show that M1–M3 cannot be the way to understand 1–3. But it does show that Langton's presentation makes the problem she is trying to solve seem more serious than it is. And making the problem seem very serious is part of her strategy for motivating a radical solution that requires reconstructing the argument and adding unstated premises.

Second, Langton's account of Kantian appearances is questionable. Langton stresses Kant's claim that things as they appear to us consist "wholly of relations" (A285/B341), and says very little about his saying that things as they appear to us are mere representations.[5] The former is something Kant says seldom, and presents almost as an afterthought (A49/B66-7). The latter is something he repeats throughout the *Critique*, almost whenever he talks about transcendental idealism. He also frequently says that they depend on our minds, which he sometimes expresses by saying that they are "in us."[6] These claims are made in all the places where Kant directly presents and argues for transcendental idealism (see, for example A42/B59; A490–1/B518–9). Langton does acknowledge this problem, and discusses Kant's idealism in her final chapter. She suggests that the idealism may lie in the fact that his views about things in themselves might imply that ultimate reality is not physical in nature (Langton 1998, 207). The problem with this is that it cannot be the point of Kant's idealism about *appearances*.

However, this is not an objection to Langton's position as a whole. It is an objection to her presentation of that position. Although Langton says that she is not concerned with the idealist part of Kant's position, she sometimes presents her reading as if it were an interpretation of Kant's transcendental idealism as a whole, as opposed to an account of things in themselves and why we cannot know them, and a partial account of the status of appearances.

My third worry about Langton's textual evidence concerns the status of things in themselves and the distinction between intrinsic and extrinsic (or relational) properties. It is worth noting that there is nowhere in the *Critique* where we find Kant simply saying, as Langton says he does: "things in themselves exist" (see p. 323 above). Many philosophers question whether Kant is actually committed to the existence of an aspect of reality that we cannot know. Some argue that Kant's commitment to things in themselves is a commitment to the unavoidability of the *concept* of things as they are in themselves, and that it is a limiting concept, not one which has actually existing parts of reality falling under it.[7] I agree with Langton on this point. I think that seeing Kant as having a commitment to the existence of things in themselves is the most plausible way of reading almost all the texts in which he talks about them.[8] But this way of reading Kant is controversial, and the opposing arguments need to be dealt with.

The central part of Langton's interpretation is her account of intrinsic properties. She argues that

1. Things in themselves are things with intrinsic properties;
2. intrinsic properties are causally inert; and
3. the relevant extrinsic or relational properties—causal powers—cannot be reduced to intrinsic properties.

None of these claims feature obviously in the text of the first *Critique*. In Langton's summary of what she takes to be Kant's view, she says that Kant holds that things as we know them consist entirely of relations and that we have no insight into the inner nature of things (see p. 324 above). She then immediately claims that Kant "has a distinction between substances, bearers of intrinsic properties, on the one hand; and relational properties of substances on the other" (see p. 324 above).[9] Kant clearly says that appearances are relational, but he does not clearly assert that what we do not know of things is their intrinsic properties, much less that intrinsic properties are causally inert.

The claim that we know relations features in the Transcendental Aesthetic almost as an afterthought, and Kant does not explain it. Nor does he talk about things in themselves as things with inner natures. The section in which Kant discusses relations and intrinsic properties in most detail is the section called "On the amphiboly of the concepts of reflection through the confusion of the empirical use of the understanding with the transcendental" (A260–292/B316–349). This section is one of the most difficult parts of the *Critique*. It contains a detailed engagement with Leibniz, and it is often not clear whether claims Kant makes are his own view, or merely what he is attributing to Leibniz in order to reject. Many of Langton's interlocutors have argued that she attributes to Kant claims which are not his, but rather part of his presentation of the Leibnizian view he rejects, and that the case for her interpretation rests on taking claims out of context.[10] Langton makes frequent use of Kant's claim that "Substances in general must have some intrinsic nature, which is therefore free from all external relations" (A274/B330).[11] This is one of the few texts in support of her interpretation that actually come from the first *Critique*. The claim clearly occurs in Kant's reconstruction of the steps that lead Leibniz to his monadology—that is, in a series of claims which end with the conclusion that monads constitute the fundamental matter of the universe. This conclusion is emphatically not something Kant thinks we can establish, so we cannot assume that he endorses all the premises that lead up to it.

In the Amphiboly, Kant criticizes ways in which we might be tempted to take relations between concepts to give us insight into the objects of our knowledge. He says that since our cognition is limited to things that are given to us in intuition, we must consider conclusions we can draw from relations between concepts together with the forms of our sensible intuition (space and time). Otherwise, although our thoughts may lead to a conceptually consistent system (such as the Leibnizian monadology), it will not be one of which we can have knowledge, since one of the conditions of cognition will be missing. The important discussion for our purposes concerns Kant's discussion of the opposed concepts of "the *inner* and the *outer*" (A265/B321). Here Kant discusses the idea that we know only relations, and that relations require something non-relational. He says that:

> In an object of the pure understanding only that is internal that has no relation (as far as the existence is concerned) to anything that is different from it. The inner determinations of *substantia phaenomenon* in space, on the contrary, are nothing but relations, and it is itself entirely a sum total of mere relations. We know substance in space only through forces that are efficacious in it, whether in drawing others to it (attraction) or in preventing penetration of it (repulsion and impenetrability); we are not acquainted with other properties constituting the concept of the substance that appears to us in space and which we call matter. As object of the pure understanding, on the contrary, every substance must have inner determinations, and forces that pertain to its inner reality.
>
> (A265–266/B321–322)

In this passage, it is clear that Kant thinks that phenomena are purely relational, but it is less clear that he is committed to there existing something intrinsic. It might be that he is simply making a claim about what objects of the pure understanding would be like if there were any. In other words, he is arguing that *if* there were objects which could be known by the intellect alone, independent of the senses, these would be things with inner natures. But the objects *we* know, and the only objects we *can* know, are the spatiotemporal things that affect our senses, and these do not have inner natures.

On this reading, Kant is clearly arguing with Leibniz. But his disagreement does not concern the reducibility of relations. It concerns Leibniz's failure to see that cognition requires two distinct ingredients, intuitions and concepts, and the implications of this. It is worth looking at one of the texts in some detail. In discussing Leibniz's position, Kant says:

> According to mere concepts the inner is the substratum of all relation or outer determinations. If, therefore, I abstract from all conditions of intuition, and restrict myself solely to the concept of a thing in general, then I can abstract from every outer relation, and yet there must remain a concept of it, that signifies no relation but merely inner determinations. Now it seems as if it follows from this that in every thing (substance) there is something that is absolutely internal and precedes all outer determinations, first making them possible, thus that this substratum is something that contains no more outer relations in itself, consequently that it is *simple*. . . All this would be correct, were it not that something more than the concept of a thing in general belongs to the conditions under which alone objects of inner intuition can be given to us, and from which the pure concept abstracts. For these show that a persistent appearance in space (impenetrable extension) contains mere relations and nothing absolutely internal, and nevertheless can be the primary substratum of all outer perception. Through mere concepts, of course, I cannot think something external without something inner, for the very reason that relational concepts absolutely presuppose given things and are not possible without these. But since something is contained in the intuition that does not lie at all in the mere concept of a thing in general, and this yields the substratum that cannot be cognized through mere concepts, namely a space that, along with everything that it contains, consists of purely formal or also real relations, I cannot say that since without something absolutely inner no thing can be represented *through mere concepts*, there is also nothing outer that does not have something absolutely internal as ground in the things themselves that are contained under these concepts and in *their intuition*.
>
> (A284–285/B340–341)

Kant says that if we were thinking of objects independently of whether they are objects of our sensible intuition, then we would have to think of them as having absolutely inner natures. But in fact, objects of sensible intuition do not have anything that is absolutely inner, and the objects we cognize are only self-sufficient and persistent relations. Again, the passage is clear about Kant's view of appearances as relations, and it also tells us something about his *reason* for thinking that we can know only relations: he seems to think that this follows from the idea that we can cognize only spatiotemporal objects.

What is not clear from this passage, taken on its own, is whether Kant thinks there actually *is* anything with an absolutely inner nature. It might be that the idea of something that is absolutely inner is supposed to be a characterization of *noumena* in the positive sense (objects which could be given to a non-sensible intuition), in which case Kant is agnostic as to whether there actually are things with an absolutely inner nature. He is merely telling us what such objects would be like, if there were any.

Thus the Amphiboly passages, on their own, do not appear to conclusively support or deny a commitment to things in themselves. However, when read in the light of the rest of the *Critique*, it seems to me that Langton's view that Kant is committed to the actual existence of something that has an intrinsic nature can be defended. Kant says that the claims that what is relational requires something non-relational, and that what is outer requires something inner, are conceptual truths. If logic requires us to assert the existence of a way things are as they are in themselves, then surely we must assert this.[12] This reading is also supported by the way Kant initially presents his notion of things in themselves. He starts talking about things in themselves without introducing or explaining the terminology. This suggests that he does not take the notion of a thing in itself to be a technical or unusual notion that requires introduction and definition. It is simply the notion that things have a way they are which is independent of other things, and, in particular, independent of us.[13] This is not an unusual idea: Locke uses the expression in this way, saying of primary qualities "We have by these an idea of the thing as it is in itself" (*Essay* II.viii.23).

A serious problem with the idea that the notion of things in themselves is a limiting concept devoid of metaphysical commitment is that one of Kant's main concerns in his attack on transcendent metaphysics is giving a detailed account of those ideas that reason requires us to postulate but that correspond to things with respect to which we *cannot* even know that they exist, never mind know anything about their nature. If Kant's notion of things in themselves were supposed to function like the ideas of reason—as a notion we cannot avoid positing that does not correlate with any actual metaphysical commitment—it is extremely difficult to see why he does not draw attention to this. Thus, although the Amphiboly section on its own does not unambiguously support a commitment to the existence of things that have an intrinsic nature which we cannot know, there is sufficient basis elsewhere in the *Critique* for thinking that Kant is committed to the existence of things as they are in themselves, and for understanding this as saying that Kant is committed to the idea that there exist things that have a way they are independent of their relations to other things and to us. To this extent, Langton's reading can be defended.

What I question, in Langton's reading, is her claim that

i. Kant thinks that intrinsic properties are causally inert;
ii. Kant thinks that causal powers cannot be reduced to intrinsic properties; and
iii. (i) and (ii), together with the relatively obvious claim that we must be affected by things to know them, imply that we cannot have knowledge of things as they are in themselves.

In order to show that intrinsic properties are causally inert, Langton attributes a very specific account of intrinsic properties to Kant: they are properties objects could have independently of the existence of any other things and in the absence of laws. She says that Kant thinks that laws of nature are not necessary consequences of the intrinsic natures of substances, and that he takes this to show that facts about intrinsic properties place no constraints at all on facts about causal powers (Langton 1998, 118).

There are two general textual reasons for thinking that this cannot be Kant's position. First, it is inconsistent with Kant's views about the possibility of metaphysics. Although, with Langton, I disagree with those who think that there is no metaphysics in the *Critique*, Kant does very clearly argue that we cannot establish metaphysical claims beyond the bounds of experience. The claim that intrinsic properties are causally inert seems to be just such a claim. Langton's argument that laws don't follow logically from intrinsic natures ignores Kant's account of what kind of metaphysics *is* possible, since her arguments about what is logically possible and what is contingent ignore both Kant's account of real possibility (A244/B302, Bxxvi*n*) and his account of synthetic necessity. And while Kant disallows *knowledge* of things as they are in themselves, his solution to the free will problem is based on the *possibility* of some kind of noumenal causality.

Second, Langton's position implies that the way things are as they are in themselves has no implications for the way they appear to us. It is hard to see how this can be Kant's view. As we have seen, some interpretations deny that Kant is committed to there being a way things are in themselves. But almost all the passages that suggest that he has this commitment also suggest that the way things are in themselves is partly responsible for the way things appear to us as being. In the passage in which Kant first introduces the suggestion that appearances are relations, he says that "everything in our cognition that belongs to intuition . . . contains nothing but mere relations . . . But what is present in the place, or *what it produces* in the things themselves besides the alteration of place, is not given through these relations" (B66–67, my italics). Here he says that something in itself *produces* the alteration of place. Elsewhere he speaks of the "unknown ground" of appearances (A379, A360), and the "non-sensible cause" of representations (A494/B522).[14]

Moreover, there is almost no textual support for Langton's way of understanding Kant's views on intrinsic properties in the *Critique of Pure Reason*.

Langton bases her argument on an analysis of two earlier texts that predate his critique of metaphysics. She then argues that there are passages in the *Critique* that support her reading.

I will not discuss her interpretation of the early texts,[15] and do not have space here to engage with the texts she discusses from the *Critique* in detail, but it seems to me that her uses of the texts can be questioned. I will give one example, which draws attention to the difference that can be made by translation from the original German. Langton quotes Kant as saying that:

> Leibniz's monadology has its sole basis in the distinction between the intrinsic and the extrinsic, which he represented purely in relation to the understanding.
>
> (Langton 1998, 71; A274/B330)

The standard translation by Guyer and Wood (Kant 1781/1998) reads:

> Leibniz's monadology has no ground at all other than the fact that this philosopher represented the distinction of the inner and the outer merely in relation to the understanding.[16]

Leaving aside Langton's use of 'intrinsic' and 'extrinsic,' as opposed to the more literal 'inner' and 'outer,' Langton's translation suggests that the monadology is based simply on the distinction between intrinsic (inner) and extrinsic (outer). But the passage is clearly concerned with Leibniz's *representing the inner and the outer merely in relation to the understanding*—in other words, that he fails to consider them in relation to the spatial form of our intuition.

My final worry about Langton's radical reconstruction of Kant's argument is that it is partly motivated by the idea that Kant is missing an argument for humility. She says that Kant presents humility as following from receptivity, the fact that we must be affected by things to have knowledge of them (see p. 324 above; see also Langton 1998, 124 and 211), but that he does not say *why* it follows. She devotes much of her book to an ingenious and fascinating account of missing premises in this argument. But Kant does not present humility as following from receptivity, and he has a central argument for humility, which he presents right up front, when he first talks about transcendental idealism. Kant argues that cognition, or knowledge proper, requires both concepts and intuitions; that empirical intuition requires *a priori* intuition; and that *a priori* intuition cannot present us with something mind-independent.[17] Following this, he concludes that space is not a property of things as they are in themselves; that it is mind-dependent; that empirical (spatial) objects are appearances that do not present us with things as they are in themselves; and that appearances are mind-dependent. Since we need intuition for cognition, and the only things presented to us in intuition are not mind-independent, we cannot have knowledge of mind-independent reality.

There may be some premises missing in this argument. A Leibnizian might ask where the argument is for the most fundamental disagreement with Leibniz: the claim that cognition requires both concepts and intuitions. And we might wonder why Kant thinks something that is present to the mind *a priori* (*a priori* intuition) cannot represent something that is independent of us. However, the argument is not based on receptivity.

It is correct that Kant thinks that knowledge given through the senses does not give us knowledge of things as they are in themselves. He says, "The representation of a *body* in intuition . . . contains nothing at all that could pertain to an object in itself" (A44/B61; see also A44/B62). However, this is not merely because sensibility involves things affecting us, but rather because being presented with individual particulars in empirical intuition, through things affecting us, requires *a priori* intuition. Thus, it is true that Kant thinks that receptivity could not give us knowledge of things in themselves. However, this is not a premise in his argument. It is a consequence of his views about the need for, and nature of, *a priori* intuition.

Despite these disagreements, the importance of Langton's work to understanding Kant seems to me to be indisputable. Very little work on transcendental idealism has paid much attention to Kant's claims that appearances are purely relational.[18] She makes a valuable contribution to the project of showing that Kant's transcendental idealism is not an extreme, phenomenalist idealism. She forges interpretative space between the merely epistemological, anti-metaphysical interpretations, and the extreme idealist, phenomenalist interpretations (the traditional 'two-world' view), showing the possibility of an ontological one-world interpretation. The account leaves space for non-phenomenalist readings of Kant's idealism about appearances[19]—for ontological, one-world views which still incorporate a significant sense in which Kantian appearances are mind-dependent. Developing such an account and relating it to the important material Langton brings into focus concerning relations, would, it seems to me, give us an account that really is faithful to what Kant says.

## Notes

1. See Allison 2004.
2. For examples of idealist interpreters see Bennett (1966, 23 and 126), Guyer (1987, 334–335), Guyer (2007, 12), Strawson (1966), Turbayne (1955), and Van Cleve (1999). For non-idealist interpretations see Bird (1962, 50,148), Bird (2006), Collins (1999), and Dryer (1966, 500).
3. For a denial that Kant is committed to the existence of an aspect of reality which we cannot cognize see Allison 2004; Bird 1962, 2006; Grier 2001; Hanna 2006; and Senderowicz 2005.
4. See, for example, Bird (2006, 553).

5. See e.g. B45; A98; A101; A109; A113; B164; A190/B235; A197/B242; A369; A370; A372; A383A385; A386; A493/B521; A490/B518–A491/B519; A492/B520; A494/B522; A499/B527; A507/B535; A563/B591; A793/B821.

6. See e.g. A42/B59; A370; A490–491/B518–519; A492/B520.

7. See Bird (1962, 29, 74), Bird (2006, 553, 579), Grier (2001), Hanna (2006), Schrader (1968, 173, 181), Senderowicz (2005).

8. See Bxx; A26/B42; A30/B45; A44/B61; B164; A190/B235; A191/B236; A251–252; A276/B332; A288/B344; A379–380; A393; A494/B522; A496/B524. In addition, there are a number of philosophical reasons why Kant requires a commitment to things in themselves, as I argue in Allais (2010a).

9. Although Kant thinks that we can legitimately use the category of *substance* in knowledge claims only in relation to something that is given in experience, in space and time, we could restate Langton's account simply in terms of the idea that *things* have intrinsic natures: they have a way they are as they are apart from other things and apart from us.

10. See Bird (2000, 106) and Rosefeldt (2001, 267).

11. This is Langton's translation. The more literal translation by Guyer and Wood (Kant 1781/1998) is that "substances in general must have something inner, which is therefore free of all outer relations" (A274/B330).

12. But against this, see Hanna (2006, 197).

13. See Ameriks (2006, 74–75).

14. See also A44/B61; A190/B235; A251–252; A288/B344; A360; A393; A496/B524.

15. See Watkins (2005, chapter 2).

16. The original German reads, "Die Leibnizische Monadologie hat gar keinen andern Grund, als daß dieser Philosoph den Unterschied des Inneren und Äußeren bloß im Verhältnis auf den Verstand vorstellete."

17. I discuss this argument in detail in Allais (2010b).

18. Warren (2001) is an important exception.

19. I attempt to develop such account in Allais (2007). See also Rosefeldt (2001).

PART **XIII**
# Why Read the History of Philosophy?

# Editors' Introduction

Throughout this book, we have seen a variety of different answers to interpretive questions, and also different approaches to how to answer those questions. Some authors focus more narrowly on the text, while others pay more attention to the context in which it was written. Some authors are more concerned with the truth of the text they are interpreting, while others do not find this central or even relevant. Given this variety of approaches, it is not surprising that historians of philosophy sometimes explicitly discuss the methodology of their inquiry. In this section, Daniel Garber and Martin Lin present different views about how one should investigate the history of philosophy.

Daniel Garber's chapter begins by discussing Jonathan Bennett's approach to studying the history of philosophy, as exemplified by his book about Spinoza's *Ethics* (Bennett 1984). In that book, Bennett argues that we are more likely to make progress in understanding Spinoza by focusing closely on his text itself, rather than trying to learn more about the context in which it was written. Though he acknowledges there are some benefits to knowing about the context in which Spinoza wrote, Bennett thinks these are relatively small, and most of what is to be gained from knowledge of context can be gained from relatively little knowledge of it.

Garber raises several questions about that approach, both with regard to how much we ought to seek information about the context, and to how much one cares about the truth of the claims made in Spinoza's text. Garber then presents an alternative view of how to approach the history of philosophy, arguing for "an *historical* reconstruction" that tries to understand, e.g. Spinoza's, texts "in terms that he or a well-informed contemporary of his may have understood."

345

Lin discusses the approaches of both Bennett and Garber. He then argues that there is an important connection between views about methodology and views about why philosophy is valuable. He argues that much of the value of the history of philosophy is connected to the fact that philosophy's investigation of fundamental issues proceeds very slowly, and that many views from the history of philosophy, even if unfashionable, are still possible and unrefuted views.

## Further Reading

- Margaret Dauler Wilson (1992). "History of Philosophy in Philosophy Today; and the Case of the Sensible Qualities."
- Richard Rorty, Jerome B. Schneewind, and Quentin Skinner (1984). *Philosophy in History: Essays on the Historiography of Philosophy.*
- Quentin Skinner (1969). "Meaning and Understanding in the History of Ideas."

## CHAPTER 25

# Does History Have a Future? Some Reflections on Bennett and Doing Philosophy Historically

## DANIEL GARBER

The history of philosophy seems to play a very significant role in the actual practice of philosophy; historical figures come up again and again in the courses we had to take, both as undergraduates and as graduate students, and historical figures continue to come up again and again in the papers we read, the courses we teach, the conferences we attend. Philosophy seems to be a subject that is obsessed with its past, but it is more than just an obsession. Most, of us would agree that understanding the history of philosophy is somehow important to *doing* philosophy, that we are better philosophers for knowing the history of our subject. I think that this is true. As philosophers, we have an obligation to ourselves to reflect on this fact: *why* is history important to our enterprise, and *how* is history important to our enterprise?

This is what I would like to do in this short essay, make some observations about the ways in which history of philosophy can and does influence the practice of philosophy. I shall begin by discussing the view of history found in Jonathan Bennett's recent and already enormously influential book, *A Study of Spinoza's Ethics*. I have chosen to talk about that book in good part because it is, I think, the best representative of a certain genre of writing in the history of philosophy; Bennett nicely articulates a view of the history of philosophy that is widespread among writers on the subject, particularly those writing in English, Bennett's view, widely shared, is that history is important because studying historical figures can teach us philosophy; in the history of philosophy we have a storehouse of arguments and positions worth taking seriously as philosophy, worth discussing and debating in the same way the work of a very good contemporary philosopher is worth discussing and debating, I shall not really criticize Bennett's view of the matter. There is a sense in which he and the multitude of other philosophers and historians of philosophy who share his view are absolutely correct. But, I shall argue, Bennett makes use of only a portion of the riches that history has to offer. In the second part of this essay I shall try to sketch and illustrate a somewhat different conception of the use of history in philosophy that complements the conception Bennett offers.

## History as Storehouse

I would like to begin my discussion by outlining what I take to be Jonathan Bennett's attitude toward history in his recent book, *A Study of Spinoza's Ethics*. My interest in the book will be largely metaphilosophical (or, perhaps, metahistorical); though I have some disagreements with Bennett on matters of substance, I shall do my best not do drag them in here and muddy the waters.

Early in the book, Bennett gives the reader ample indication of the nature of his interest in Spinoza. "I am not writing biography," he notes. "I want to understand the pages of the *Ethics* in a way that will let me learn philosophy from them."[1] A bit later in the book, Bennett indicates that his interest is "not with Spinoza's mental biography but with getting his help in discovering philosophical truth."[2] At the end of the book Bennett writes:

> The courtly deference which pretends that Spinoza is always or usually right, under some rescuing interpretation, is one thing; it is quite another to look to him, as I have throughout this book, as a teacher, one who can help us to see things which we might not have seen for ourselves. That is showing him a deeper respect, but also holding him to a more demanding standard.[3]

Bennett's interest here is clear: it is finding philosophical truth and avoiding philosophical falsehood that he is after, and the study of Spinoza is supposed to help us in this search. What he says about Spinoza presumably holds more generally for the study of other figures in the history of philosophy. So conceived, the history of philosophy is a kind of storehouse of positions and arguments, positions and arguments that we can use as guides or inspirations to the positions we should take, or illustrations of dead ends that we should avoid.

This last provision is important. The point is *not* that Spinoza (or any other historical figure) will simply hand us philosophical truth on a platter, arguments or positions that we can immediately adopt without change. Bennett's Spinoza often makes mistakes, and bad ones; hardly an argument in the *Ethics* can stand without *some* correction. Yet we can learn from Spinoza even when he is wrong (or, at least we *usually* can; Bennett seems unsure about whether anything can be learned from the mistakes Spinoza makes when discussing the eternity of the mind).[4] Bennett writes:

I do say that Spinoza's total naturalistic program fails at both ends and in the middle; as though he undertook to build a sturdy mansion all out of wood, and achieved only a rickety shack using bricks, as well as wood. But his attempt was a work of genius; and a thorough, candid study of it can be wonderfully instructive. The failures have at least as much to teach as the successes, if one attends not only to *where* Spinoza fails but *why*.[5]

Bennett completes the thought a few pages later:

I spoke of how much we can learn from Spinoza's successes and, especially, his failures. It is his minimalism that makes his work so instructive. If you set a mechanical genius to build an automobile engine out of a Meccano set, you won't get a working engine from him, but as you watch him fail you will learn a lot about automobile engines.[6]

(In giving these quotations I don't mean to imply that they are transparently intelligible or true on their face, but 1 would like to postpone those questions for the moment.)

What does the history of philosophy look like from Bennett's point of view? We begin by trying to reconstruct the arguments the philosopher we are studying gave, trying to follow the train of thought he followed. But our ultimate goal is philosophical truth, and it is with that in mind that we must approach our reconstruction; we must carefully examine the truth of the premises, the validity of the inferential steps, and with a cold and unsentimental eye, judge the truth or falsity of the conclusion and the adequacy of the means by which the conclusion was reached. If appropriate, we might make *some* attempt to patch up the argument, adding new premises, substituting better premises for worse, trying a new path to the conclusion in question, or whatever. This is, I think, a fair representation of what Bennett is doing in the Spinoza book.

All of this is interesting and, in an important sense, valuable activity. But if we are to follow Bennett and hold that the history of philosophy is valuable primarily insofar as it helps us to find philosophical truth, in some more or less direct sense, then there are certain consequences we must accept.

First of all, if we insist on philosophical truth as the *only* motivation for studying history, then a great deal of the history of philosophy may turn out to be marginal to the philosopher. Bennett would agree that few historical figures have any large store of doctrines or arguments that we would now consider live candidates for truth or even approximate truth. There are those who study Aristotle or Saint Thomas, Kant or Marx, because they think that at least some of what they wrote is close to being true, and because they believe that attention to their writings can help lead us directly to insights we would not otherwise have. But how many study Descartes or Leibniz or Spinoza for this reason? The noble attempts of the past, one might argue, are instructive in their *failures*. But while failures *can* be instructive, a few can go a long way. The student architect can learn to fit the building to the available materials and know the strengths and weaknesses of both from the building that collapsed. But one learns to design successful buildings by studying *successful* buildings, not just failures. Having had a deprived childhood, I'm not sure l know exactly what a Meccano set is, but if it is what I think it is, I doubt that I could learn much about automobile engines by watching someone try to build one from a Meccano set, no matter how talented one might be. Similarly, the philosopher must learn to recognize a bad argument and must be trained to avoid the mistakes people make. This is only a small portion of one's philosophical education, which, I think, should focus on positions and arguments that people think are live candidates for the truth, at least insofar as one is being trained to seek philosophical truth, Bennett may overestimate what we can learn directly from failed arguments and programs. Insofar as the great majority of historical arguments, positions, and programs are failures when judged against the high standard of philosophical truth (as we see it), the study of the history of philosophy may have less to contribute to philosophy than Bennett seems to think, and less than we historians would like.

There is another feature of Bennett's position worth drawing out. Bennett's position has the danger of distorting the history of philosophy. First of all, insofar as we regard history of philosophy as contributing to the discovery of philosophical truth, we are led to emphasize those portions of a philosopher's work that speak to our interests, that address our conception of where philosophical truth is to be found, leaving other aspects of the work aside, thereby mutilating what may be a unified and systematic point of view. Bennett has *not* done any such thing to Spinoza, but one can call to mind the numerous commentaries on Descartes and anthologies of his writing that barely mention his work in mathematics, physics, or biology; the accounts of Pascal that focus on the wager argument without indicating its larger context; books like Anthony Kenny's little book *Aquinas,* in the Past Masters series, or John Mackie's *Problems from Locke,* which quite self-consciously use standards of contemporary relevance to choose what to discuss and what to ignore. In each case, the focus on philosophical *truth* distorts our *historical* understanding of the figure and his position. But there is another way in which historical distortions may enter. If our interest is philosophical truth, then the point of the historical enterprise is to capture whatever philosophical truth or interesting philosophical falsehood there may be in some philosopher's writings. What this has often meant, in practice is what has been dubbed *rational reconstruction,* taking the argument or position as given and making sense of it in terms that make sense of it to our philosophical sensibilities, whether or not the reformulation captures anything the philosopher himself would have acknowledged. Examples of this include Bernard Williams's reconstruction of the argument of Descartes' *Meditations* using modern epistemological concepts, or Benson Mates's reconstruction of Leibniz's doctrine of possible worlds using contemporary modal logic. Bennett is tempted in this direction as well. In a passage, part of which we have already quoted, he writes;

> I want to understand the pages of the *Ethics* in a way that will let me learn philosophy from them. For that, I need to consider what. Spinoza had in mind, for readings of the text which are faithful to his intentions are likely to teach me more than ones which are not—or so I believe, as I think him to be a great philosopher. And one can be helped to discover his intentions by knowing what he had been reading, whose problems he had been challenged by, and so on. But this delving into backgrounds is subject to a law of diminishing returns: while some fact about Maimonides or Averroes might provide the key to an obscure passage in Spinoza, we are more likely to get his text straight by wrestling with it directly, given just a fair grasp of his immediate background. I am sure to make mistakes because of my inattention to Spinoza's philosophical ancestry; but I will pay that price for the benefits which accrue from putting most of one's energies into philosophically interrogating Spinoza's own text.[7]

Indeed, many benefits come from directly interrogating a historical text, leaving aside nice worries about historical context, but there is a danger of misunderstanding. (In Bennett's Spinoza book this comes out most clearly in his discussion of space and his attribution of a "field metaphysic" to Spinoza in chapter 4, a lovely philosophical position, but one that I do not think occurred to Spinoza.)

This may sound like a criticism of the approach Bennett takes to history, but I assure him, it is not. If our only goal is philosophical truth, then history of philosophy may turn out to be marginal, if not altogether expendable; if our goal is simply philosophical truth, we must face up to the facts in an unsentimental way. And, if our goal is philosophical truth, then historical veracity can have only an instrumental value at best; it is of value only insofar as it helps us attain our principal goal. The point of interpretation, on this view, is to make the philosophy breathe, to make it available to us, and historical veracity is important only insofar as it serves this end.

In calling for us to focus on the truth and falsity of Spinoza's claims, the adequacy and inadequacies of his arguments, Bennett is implicitly contrasting the approach that he takes with other more disinterestedly historical and, in one sense, less philosophical approaches that one might take to the material. In one place Bennett contrasts his approach with that of "intellectual biography," with "mental biography" in another, and with that "which pretends that Spinoza is always or usually right, under some rescuing interpretation" in a third passage.[8] Now, it seems to me that the disinterested historian shouldn't always assume that Spinoza is *right*. But insofar as we agree with Bennett that

Spinoza was "a great philosopher," we should at very least subscribe to the working hypothesis that what Spinoza is up to is *sensible*, the sort of thing that a smart person might believe in a particular historical context, given what he had learned, what others around him believed, the assumptions taken for granted, and so on. (This is just a special case of what has been called the principle of charity or, in variant, the principle of humanity in the theory of interpretation in the philosophy of language.) This is not to say that we should not expect to find lapses of reasoning and judgment, even when the whole context is open to us, or that this kind of historical inquiry will clear up all our puzzlements. It is important to remember that Spinoza, for example, was a puzzle to his contemporaries as well, and they had more access to his context than any of us can ever hope to have. In its way, this kind of rationality is no less demanding a standard to hold Spinoza to than philosophical truth is.

Unlike philosophical truth, which judges Spinoza by what is true, or by what we have come to think is true, this standard is *internal*. The alternative to the sort of history Bennett advocates is an *historical* reconstruction of Spinoza's views, the attempt to understand Spinoza's positions and arguments in terms that he or a well-informed contemporary of his may have understood. It involves coming to understand what Spinoza or a contemporary of his would have considered unproblematic background beliefs, what they would have had trouble with, and in the light of that and other similar contexts, coming to understand what Spinoza's conception of his project was, how he thought he had established the conclusions he had reached, and what he thought was important about those conclusions, all under the assumption that by and large, Spinoza's project is the work of a smart person working within a particular historical context. This sort of investigation is not biography of any sort, neither intellectual nor mental; it is, quite simply, the history of philosophical ideas.

In practice, the kind of history I was sketching *may* come out looking very little different from the history Bennett prefers. As Bennett has pointed out, if it is the lessons of history for philosophical truth that interest us, then the lessons are likely to be more interesting the closer we come to a genuine representation of Spinoza's (or whoever's) thought. The only conspicuous difference may be the relative lack of judgments of truth and falsity in the sort of disinterested history I propose. If our interest is in historical reconstruction, the question of the ultimate truth or falsity of the doctrines is simply not at issue; the only thing that is important is whether or not our account has made the beliefs intelligible. Sometimes this will call for a judgment that *on his own terms*, some premise or inference a philosopher uses may not be available to him, properly speaking. If we are interested in historical reconstruction, then, for example, the falsity of a premise then universally accepted is not a relevant part of the story.

Bennett would certainly have to agree that there is a real project here, whether or not he himself is interested in carrying it out. I think that he would also have to agree that there is no reason why one must choose one conception of the history of philosophy over the other. While in practice a single scholar may find it difficult to pull off both sorts of history at the same time, within the confines of a single essay or book, they are not competing programs in the sense in which, say, deontological programs for ethics compete with teleological programs. One can find the history of philosophy richer for having both approaches represented in the literature, one can find both interesting and never be put into the position of having to choose one over the other. In this sense the two approaches to history of philosophy are complementary) rather than competing.

A question remains, a central question. On Bennett's view, the history of philosophy is important to philosophy in an obvious way; on his conception, history of philosophy actually contributes to the unearthing of philosophical truths. Now, as I noted, the sort of disinterested historical reconstruction I have sketched can *contribute* to Bennett's enterprise, but taken by itself, does it have any philosophical interest at all? Leaving aside the question of the philosophical truth it may help to uncover, is the purely historical study of philosophical ideas of more than antiquarian interest? Is there any reason for philosophers qua philosophers to take an interest in such disinterested history?

## In Defense of Disinterested History

In arguing for the philosophical significance of disinterested history, I would like to proceed historically and begin with a consideration of the views of a philosopher whose opinion on the matter is in many ways attractive to me. The philosopher I have in mind here is Descartes. As Bennett proposes we learn from Spinoza, I propose that there is much we can learn from Descartes.

Descartes may seem at first glance an odd character to turn to in this connection. Descartes was conspicuously unsympathetic to the study of books, old *or* new. In the *Discours,* Descartes wrote:

[A]s soon as I was old enough to emerge from the control of my teachers, I entirely abandoned the study of letters. Resolving to seek no knowledge other than that which could be found in myself or else in the great book of the world, I spent the rest of my youth in traveling. . . . For it seemed to me that much more truth could be found in the reasoning which a man makes concerning matters that concern him than in those which some scholar makes in his study about speculative matters. For the consequences of the former will soon punish the man if he judges wrongly, whereas the latter have no practical consequences and no importance for the scholar except that perhaps the further they are from common sense the more pride he will take in them, since he will have had to use so much more skill and ingenuity in trying to render them plausible.[9]

This attitude also comes out nicely in a letter from 1638. Unfortunately, the recipient of the letter is unknown, as is the book Descartes is commenting on in the letter, but his point is clear:

> [The author's] plan of collecting into a single book all that is useful in every other book would be a very good one if it were practicable; but I think that it is not. It is often very difficult to judge accurately what others have written, and to draw the good out of them without taking the bad too. Moreover, the particular truths which are scattered in books are so detached and so independent of each other, that I think one would need more talent and energy to assemble them into a well-proportioned and ordered collection . . . than to make up such a collection out of one's own discoveries. I do not mean that one should neglect other people's discoveries when one encounters useful ones; but I do not think one should spend the greater part of one's time in collecting them. If a man were capable of finding the foundation of the sciences, he would be wrong to waste his life in finding scraps of knowledge hidden in the corners of libraries; and if he were no good for anything else but that, he would not be capable of choosing and ordering what he found.[10]

Descartes does not mince words here. If it is truth we are after, books will not help us to find it. He does not seem to think that we can learn much from other people's mistakes, unlike Bennett; mistakes just engender other mistakes. The truths we find in books are so rare and so scattered that anyone who has the ability to recognize them and seek them out would be better off simply looking for them on his own, directly, without the help of these paper-and-ink teachers. If it is philosophical truth you are after, Descartes tells Bennett (and anyone else who will listen), then don't look to the philosophers of the past. (It is somewhat disquieting to the historian when one of his or her subjects talks back in such a rude way.)

Descartes, in general, has little truck with scholarship, with the study of the past, but Descartes was not altogether dismissive of history. Though he thought it inappropriate to look for philosophical truth in history, he did not think that reading the authors of the past is *altogether* without value. In the *Discours* he wrote:

> I knew . . . that reading good books is like having a conversation with the most distinguished men of past ages—indeed, a rehearsed conversation in which these authors reveal to us only the best of their thoughts.

This conversation is valuable to us for an interesting reason. According to Descartes:

[C]onversing with those of past centuries is much the same as traveling. It is good to know something of the customs of various peoples, so that we may judge our own more soundly and not think that everything contrary to our own ways is irrational, as those who have seen nothing of the world ordinarily do.[12]

Through such experience in books and in the world Descartes claims that he learned that there are "many things which, although seeming very extravagant and ridiculous to us, are nevertheless commonly accepted and approved in other great nations; and so I learned not to believe too firmly anything of which I had been persuaded only by example and custom."[13]

The idea is an interesting one. We can learn from the past in something of the same way we can learn from travel. By traveling we can get a certain kind of perspective on our lives and the way we lead them, the things we do and the things we believe. We go to other countries, learn their languages, observe their customs, eat their foods (or, at least, observe the kinds of foods they eat), discuss their beliefs about the world. This, Descartes thinks, can give us a certain perspective on our own lives. It can, among other things, free us of the belief that the way *we* see things is the way things *have* to be, that X is fit for human consumption but Y is not, that weeks must have seven days, that children must be raised by their own parents, etc. Descartes' point is not relativistic here; he would be among the last to say that anything goes. Even though we observe others eating a certain food we do not, we may still shun it and continue to hold the belief that it is unhealthy or improper for us to eat. Seeing what others do may at least get us to raise the question for ourselves *why* we have the beliefs and customs we do and, perhaps, lead us to see what is arbitrary and what is well grounded in our beliefs and behavior.

A similar case can be made with respect to the study of the past in general, and the study of past philosophy in particular, Descartes suggests. Many of the philosophical beliefs we now take for granted are not shared by figures in the past. By studying the past, taking the past seriously, we are led to reflect on our beliefs, in just the same way as we are led by travel to reflect upon our customs. Such reflection need not lead to a change in our beliefs. The fact that some past geographers thought the earth flat, or past physicists thought that there is such a thing as elemental fire that by its nature rises, these historical observations should not move us to give up our present conceptions of geography or combustion. Reflection on some of the things people have believed should at least cause us to ask ourselves *why* we believe the things we do, and *whether* our grounds are sufficient to support the explicit or implicit beliefs we have and assumptions we make.

Is such reflection important for us as philosophers? It does not *directly* contribute to the discovery of philosophical truth in the way in which discovering a good argument (or an interesting false one) in the work of a historical figure perhaps might, in the way in which Bennett conceives of history contributing to the practice of philosophy. The sort of contribution Descartes saw was of a different, and more subtle, though no less important kind. Historical investigation conceived in this alternative way gives us a kind of perspective on the beliefs we have and the assumptions we make. It helps us sort the good from the bad, the arbitrary from the well grounded, insofar as it challenges us to reflect on why we believe what we do. While it may not help lead us directly to new arguments and new philosophical truths, it leads us directly to something just as valuable: *philosophical questions.*

All of this is very abstract and cries out for some concrete examples, specific assumptions and beliefs we make that are illuminated by such historical reflection. Before I present such an example, I would like to continue a bit longer in this abstract vein.

Descartes has suggested a philosophical use for the history of philosophy different from the one Bennett suggests; the suggestion, as I have developed it, is that the history of philosophy can be important not because it leads to philosophical *truths,* but because it leads to philosophical *questions.* But what sort of history is relevant here? To learn from history in the way Descartes suggests we can involves trying to understand historical figures on *their own terms.* If I travel to Tokyo or Nairobi, look for what is familiar to me in the alien setting, and seek it out, I may acquire a nice camera cheaply, or learn one way *not* to make a pizza. I may indeed have a lovely vacation, but I will not learn what I might. Similarly, if what I am looking for in history is a guide to philosophical truth, if I look for things recognizable to *me* as interesting philosophical problems and promising (if possibly flawed) philosophical arguments, as Bennett seems to suggest we should, then I may miss features of philosophy as it has been that might raise interesting questions about philosophy as it is. To learn from history in the way Descartes suggests, we should—we must, I think—undertake the kind of disinterested historical investigation I suggested earlier as an alternative to the sort to which Bennett's views lead him. If it is an historical *perspective* on our beliefs and assumptions we are interested in, then the truth *or* the falsity of past views is *simply irrelevant.* It matters not at all whether Descartes' or Aristotle's or Kant's views are true or false for this use of history. What is important is that we understand *what* their views were, and that we understand *how* it is that smart people could have *regarded* them as true. It is not their truth, much less their falsity, that causes us to reflect on our own beliefs; it is the fact that smart people took seriously views often very different from ours that is important here.

This, I think, answers the question posed at the end of the last section. The sort of disinterested historical reconstruction I proposed as a complement to Bennett's philosophically informed investigation of the history of philosophy *is* philosophically significant, a worthwhile activity for philosophers to engage in, though for a reason somewhat different from what Bennett suggests for his program. Bennett's history seeks philosophical truth, *answers* to philosophical questions; mine seeks the *questions themselves*.

## Raising Questions; Science and Philosophy

I have been sketching out a way of doing philosophy historically, using a disinterested historical reconstruction of past thought as a way of raising important philosophical questions that might otherwise escape our notice. A brief example illustrates the approach I have been advocating.

Bennett makes an interesting statement in the course of his commentary on Spinoza. He writes: "Much of the *Ethics* is philosophical rather than scientific, i.e., is answerable to conceptual analysis rather than to empirical observation."[14] The claim is *not* central to Bennett's reading of Spinoza, and in raising questions about it I don't mean to cast doubt on Bennett's larger interpretation (though I do think that on at least one occasion it does lead him a bit astray). The quotation appeals to a certain widely held conception of philosophy; that it is an activity pretty largely distinct from scientific activity, and that philosophy makes use of conceptual analysis, whereas science makes use of observation and experience. This conception of philosophy and its relation to science is worth some historical examination.

We might begin by noting that in Spinoza's day, things were not so neatly partitioned. It is now generally recognized that the words "philosophy" and "science" didn't have distinct and separate meanings in the seventeenth century. Whereas "philosophy" was sometimes used narrowly, in perhaps something of the way we use it now,[15] it was also used more broadly to include knowledge in general, including what we now call science, as in the title to Descartes' *Principia Philosophies,* three-fourths of which is scientific by our standards. Similarly, whereas "science" was sometimes used as we do now,[16] it often took on a meaning derived from its Latin origin, *scientia,* knowledge. This, of course, is only a matter of terminology. The important question is not what things were called, but whether Spinoza and his contemporaries drew an interesting distinction between what *we* call philosophy and what *we* are inclined to call science, between a certain collection of foundational questions, investigated through argument and conceptual analysis, and a different set of questions about the natural world, investigated through observation and experience.

Here, I think we can say that while we can certainly find different questions studied by different thinkers using different modes of investigation, there is no radical distinction between what we call philosophical and what we call scientific.

It is quite widely known that arguments that are in general terms philosophical play a major role in seventeenth-century science. A nice example is the derivation Descartes gave for his laws of motion. Descartes started from two main premises. The first was an analysis of the "nature of time," which, Descartes claims, is "such that its parts are not mutually dependent," and from which he argued that God is required to keep everything in existence at every moment.[17] The second premise was that God is immutable by his nature and operates "in a manner that is always constant and immutable."[18] From these premises Descartes argued that a constant quantity of motion is maintained in the world, and that bodies in uniform rectilinear motion will tend to remain in uniform rectilinear motion.[19] These conclusions, conclusions that spring from Descartes' metaphysical foundations, were enormously influential on later seventeenth-century physicists. Though not altogether correct in detail, Descartes' conclusions constituted the first published statement of a conservation principle and the first clear version of what Newton was later to call the principle of inertia. When Newton presented his version of these laws in his *Principia* almost fifty years later, the metaphysical argument was gone. But it wasn't dead. Leibniz, Newton's great and greatly maligned contemporary, a physicist and mathematician whose only clear better was Newton himself, made free use of metaphysical arguments in his physics. Like Descartes, Leibniz chose to derive the laws of motion from God, though in a different way: from God the creator of the best (and so, most orderly) of all possible worlds, not God the moment-by-moment sustainer of all. God, Leibniz reasoned, would want to create the world in such a way that whatever power, whatever ability there is to do work in a complete cause, must be found intact in its full effect. Using this as his main premise, Leibniz established two of the main principles of classical mechanics, the law of conservation of what we call kinetic energy ($mv^2$, *vis viva*), and the conservation of what we call momentum ($mv$).[20]

These arguments establish what we would call scientific conclusions by way of what we would call philosophical premises. There are also instances in which what we would call (and Bennett has called) conceptual analysis taken more narrowly is used in the service of science. What I have in mind is Descartes' celebrated arguments for the identification of space and body, and his conclusion that there is no empty space, no vacuum. In one representative version, noted by Spinoza in his *Principles of Descartes' Philosophy*, quoted and discussed by Bennett in his commentary, the claim reads:

> Space and body do not really differ [because] body and extension do not really differ, and space and extension do not really differ. It involves a contradiction that there should be a vacuum [i.e.] extension without bodily substance.[21]

Bennett claims that this position is a purely philosophical one, and that neither Descartes nor, following him, Spinoza should confuse this with doing science.

He writes: "[W]hen he [Descartes] says that there is no vacuum, he is not predicting what you will find if you ransack the physical universe. His point is a conceptual one."[22] Bennett furthermore regrets "that he words this possible philosophical truth so that it sounds like a scientific falsehood" and goes on to chastise Descartes and Spinoza for their occasional lapses into thinking that this philosophical argument has empirical consequences for physics.[23] Bennett is too charitable here, and in his charity, he misses the point of the argument, both in Descartes and in Spinoza. Descartes' point was *precisely* to establish that there is no vacuum in the physical world, and I know of no reason to believe that Spinoza read the argument any differently. Whether or not there is a philosophical truth in the claim, it was what we have come to recognize as a scientific falsehood that interested Descartes and his contemporaries; the denial of a vacuum not only in philosophy but also *in rerum natura* was an important feature of Cartesian physics, one that grounds Cartesian cosmology, the vortex theory of planetary motion.[24]

The examples so far are of cases in. which philosophical argument, conceptual, analysis, leads to what we would consider scientific conclusions. There are a few interesting and, to the modern mind, very strange instances in which seventeenth-century philosophers used empirical claims to support conclusions that we would consider philosophical. The case is strange, and I'm not entirely sure I have it right, but Leibniz seems to have taken such a position. Leibniz held (or, at least, he *often* held) that animals are genuine substances, corporeal substances. As substances, Leibniz argued, they cannot arise through natural means, nor can they perish by natural means. This is a conclusion Leibniz often establishes by pure philosophical argument; it is a conclusion of the celebrated predicate-in-notion argument, of *Discourse on Metaphysics,* §8,[25] and, Leibniz sometimes argues, of the no-less-philosophical principle of continuity.[26] Leibniz also called on the exciting discoveries of microscopists like Leeuwenhoek and Malpighi for support. For example, he wrote to Queen Sophie Charlotte in May 1704 concerning an important consequence of his view of corporeal substance:

> Speaking with metaphysical rigor, there is neither generation nor death, but only the development and enfolding of the same animal. . . . Experience confirms these transformations in some animals, where nature herself has given us a small glimpse of what it hides elsewhere. Observations made by the most industrious observers also lead us to judge that the generation of animals is nothing but growth joined with transformation.[27]

Microscopic examiners are being called upon to support one of the basic propositions of Leibniz's metaphysics, the natural ungenerability and incorruptibility of substance.

If this strikes us as being a bit strange, stranger still is Henry More, who calls upon the world of ghosts and goblins as *empirical* support for his belief in the existence of incorporeal souls. In his *Immortality of the Soul* (1662 edition) More calls our attention to

> such extraordinary Effects as we cannot well imagine any natural, but must needs conceive some free or spontaneous Agent to be the Cause thereof, whereas yet it is clear that they are from neither Man nor Beast. Such are speakings, knockings, opening of doors when they were fast shut, . . . shapes of Men and several sorts of Brutes, that after speech and converse have suddenly disappeared.[28]

That there are such happenings is, for More if not for us, an empirical fact. For More these apparitions speak strongly in favor of souls distinct from body: "Those and like extraordinary Effects . . . seem to me to be an undeniable Argument that there be such things as *Spirits* or *Incorporeal Substances* in the world."[29] More may have been deluded in thinking that there are ghosts and obscure about how the phenomenon in question is supposed to support his conclusion, but he certainly seemed to think that the question of the existence of incorporeal substance, a metaphysical question par excellence, could be settled by a trip to a haunted house. In this he was not alone. Hobbes, no advocate of immaterial substance, made a special point of denying the reality of ghosts as part of his case against incorporeal souls.[30] Although he did not support the view More was pressing, Hobbes certainly seemed to think that empirical evidence was germane to the question.

Why are these historical observations interesting? For one, they do pertain to the proper interpretation of Spinoza and his contemporaries; they suggest that we should be careful about attributing *our* distinction between philosophy and science to earlier thinkers. There is a philosophical lesson to be learned as well. My point is *not* that we should look for philosophical truth in the sorts of arguments I was discussing; the laws of motion shouldn't be derived from God, nor should the question of the vacuum be settled by an appeal to our intuitions about space and extension. Nor do I think that metaphysical issues about the nature of substance can be settled by looking into microscopes, nor should we consider seriously the ontological status of ghosts and goblins. Much that was live in seventeenth-century thought is now dead, and I don't intend to revive it. The examples I have given do raise an interesting question: Why is it that *we* tend to see such a radical break between philosophy and science, and, more important, *should we?* The question can be raised directly, without the need for history, as Quine has done. But history brings the point home in an especially clear way: It shows us an assumption we take for granted by pointing out that it is not an assumption everyone makes.

## Conclusion

Some years ago, an anthropologist friend told me something of what it is like to do field work. When one enters a new community, she said, it is all very alien, an alien language, alien customs, alien traditions. After a while things change; the language and customs become familiar, and one is inclined to think that the differences are only superficial, that the once-alien community is just like home. The final stage comes when the similarities and differences come into focus, when one recognizes what one's subjects share with us, while at the same time appreciating the genuine differences there are between them and us. The case is similar for the history of philosophy. We cannot ignore the ways in which past thinkers are involved in projects similar to ours, and the ways in which we can learn from what they have written, how it can contribute to our search for philosophical enlightenment. At the same time, we cannot ignore the ways in which they differ from us, the way in which their programs differ from ours, the way in which they ask different questions and make different assumptions. Both are important to a genuine historical understanding of the philosophical past, but just as important, we as philosophers can learn from both.

## Notes

1. Jonathan Bennett, A *Study of Spinoza's Ethics* (Indianapolis, Ind.: Hackett Publishing Company, 1984), p. 15.
2. Ibid., p. 35.
3. Ibid., p. 372.
4. Ibid., pp. 372, 357.
5. Ibid., p. 38.
6. Ibid., p. 41.
7. Ibid., pp. 15–16.
8. Ibid., pp. 15, 35, 372.
9. Descartes, *Discours de la methode*, I, AT VI 9–10; CSM I 115.
10. AT II 346–47; CSMK 119.
11. *Discours* I, AT VI 5: CSM I 113.
12. *Discours* I, AT VI 6; CSM I 113–14
13. *Discours* I, AT VI 10; CSM I 115–16.
14. Benneu, *Spinoza*, P. 24.
15. See, e.g.. *Discours* I, AT VI 6, 8–9; CSM I 113, 114–15.
16. See, e.g., the preface to the French translation of the *Principia Philosophiae;* AT IXB 14, CSM I 186.
17. *Principia* I 21, AT' VIIIA 13; CSM I 200.
18. *Principia* II 36, AT VIIIA 6; CSM I 240.
19. *Principia* II 36–59, AT VlIIA 61–65; CSM. I 240–42.
20. For an account of Leibniz's work here, see, e.g., Martial Gueroult, *Leibniz: dynamique et metaphysique* (Paris: Aubier-Montaigne, 1967), chapter 3.
21. C. Gebhardt, ed., *Spinoza Opera* (Heidelberg: Carl Winter, 1925), I: 187–88, as paraphrased in Bennett, *Spinoza*, p. 100. Spinoza refers the reader here to Descartes' *Principia* II 17–18, AT VIIIA 49–50; CSM I 230–31.
22. Bennett, *Spinoza*, p. 101, 23 Ibid.

24. Descartes' view was that the present state of the world can be explained if we imagine an initial state of disorder, which sorts itself out into swirls of fluid by way of the laws of motion alone. These swirls of fluid, vortices, are what Descartes identifies with planetary systems, a sun at the center of each, and planets circling about the sun. Essential to this account is the assumption that all motion produces circular motion, which Descartes derives from the doctrine of the plenum. It is because all space is full, he argues, that all motion must ultimately be circular, one hunk of material substance moving to make room for a given moving body, a third hunk moving to make room for the second, and so on until a final hunk moves to take the place left by the original moving body. In this way, Descartes' whole cosmology depends on the denial of the vacuum. For the account of motion as circular, see *Principia* II 33 (AT VIIIA 58–59; CSM I 237–39) and for the derivation of the cosmos from an initial state, see *Principia* III 46ff. (AT VIIIA 100ff.; CSM I 256ff.).

25. Sec C. I. Gerhardt, ed., *Leibniz: Philosophische Schriflen* (Berlin: Weidmannsche Buchhandlung, 1875–1890), 4:432–33, translated in Leroy Loemker, ed. and trans., *Leibniz: Philosophical Papers and Letters* (Dordrecht: D. Reidel, 1969), pp. 307–8. See also the letter to Arnauld, 28 November/8 December 1686. Gerhardt 2:76.

26. See Leibniz's letter to Queen Sophie Charlotte, 8 May 1704, Gerhardt 3:345.

27. Ibid. See the discussion of this and the references cited in Michel Serres, *Le systeme de Leibniz* (Paris: Presses Universitaires de France, 1968), 1:354ff.

28. Henry More, *The Immortality of the Soul*, p. 50, in *A Collection of Several Philosophical Writings of Dr Henry More* (London: William Morden, 1662).

29. Ibid.

30. Hobbes, *Leviathan,* chapter 46; cf. chapter 2.

## CHAPTER 26

# Philosophy and Its History

## MARTIN LIN

Philosophy, perhaps more than any other discipline, is fascinated by its own history. Introductory philosophy courses for undergraduates often focus on great works from the distant past by authors such as Plato and Descartes. Conferences, journals, and graduate seminars are devoted to the discussion of the history of philosophy. Philosophy departments normally include specialists on the history of philosophy. Philosophers conducting cutting edge research often take the trouble to situate their work with respect to long dead predecessors.

In all of these respects, philosophy is vastly different from, for example, physics. Undergraduates are not taught physics by reading and discussing the works of Archimedes or Newton. Of course, students are taught Newtonian mechanics, but they don't read and discuss the *Principia* in the way that philosophy students might study the *Republic* or the *Meditations*. Conferences, journals, and graduate seminars on the history of physics abound. But they are not normally considered part of the disciplinary activity of physics itself.

It is striking that philosophy as a discipline takes ownership of the study of its history in a way that physics does not. And physics does not appear to be, in this regard, unusual. I have just checked the undergraduate teaching schedules for several leading departments of economics, mathematics, and psychology.[1] None of them are offering a single course on the history of their discipline. Most philosophy departments, by contrast, are offering multiple courses on the history of philosophy. None of these departments of mathematics, psychology, or economics, with one exception, employ researchers who specialize in the history of their disciplines. (The one exception is an economics department that lists a faulty member who specializes on the history and, interestingly enough, the *philosophy* of economics.) Why is philosophy so different from other disciplines in regard to its relationship to its history?

I believe that reflecting on the answer to this question can help illuminate the issue of method in the history of philosophy. There is debate among historians of philosophy about the sorts of things that are important in the study of the history of philosophy—the sorts of questions and issues that should be emphasized and the sorts of benefits we should expect to receive from the study of the history of philosophy. The debate about method is ultimately, I believe, a debate about value. Different methods will be better and worse suited to the realization of different values. One way of describing the distinctive relation that philosophy has to its history is to say that philosophy values its history more than other disciplines. But why? Sorting out the debate among historians of philosophy about what is valuable about the study of history might help explain why philosophy values its history more than do other disciplines. The ability of one account of the value of history to explain this better than another might be one criterion that we can use to adjudicate the debate about method.

We could divide recent history of philosophy into two main approaches. One approach focuses mainly on arguments and positions. The other approach emphasizes historical contexts. Jonathan Bennett is a prominent exponent of the first approach. He describes his approach as one "in which one studies the texts in the spirit of a colleague, an antagonist, a student, and a teacher—aiming to learn as much philosophy as one can from them" (Bennett 2001, 1). Bennett is motivated to study the history of philosophy by a desire for philosophical truth. He wants to learn philosophy from the great philosophers of the past. He wants their help in discovering philosophical truth. We can, Bennett believes, learn philosophy from historical figures in much the same way that we can learn philosophy from any intelligent philosopher: by considering their views and evaluating their arguments. In essence, on this view, what we do when we study a historical figure is little different from what we do with our philosophical colleagues. We argue and discuss philosophy with them. This being so, when we reconstruct a historical figure's arguments, we should attend to the plausibility of its premises, the strength of its inferences and plausibility of its conclusion. If appropriate we can suggest emendations that would strengthen the argument. These are the sort of things that help us work toward the solution of a philosophical problem.

Daniel Garber, in his important and influential paper "Does History Have a Future?" advocates for a rather different approach to the history of philosophy. I will explain Garber's positive program presently, but first I would like to explain Garber's dissatisfaction with Bennett's. Garber agrees that we can, at least sometimes, learn philosophy from historical figures. But if we think that the only legitimate motivation for the study of the history of philosophy is philosophical truth then, Garber reminds us, we must be prepared to reach some clear-eyed unsentimental conclusions about the history of philosophy. If philosophical truth is the only motivation for studying the history of philosophy, then, he claims, much of that history will turn out to be marginal. Many of the great philosophers of the past argue for conclusions that do not appear plausible by contemporary standards, and their arguments for these conclusions are based on assumptions that are equally implausible. Aquinas' arguments for the existence of God or Spinoza's argument for the claim that there is only one substance are unlikely to be accepted by contemporary philosophers. Sometimes they make errors of reasoning that would not go undetected by contemporary philosophers given current standards of clarity and precision. How then are we to learn philosophy from them?

But learning philosophy from the work of a historical figure need not presuppose that the figure is right. Indeed, more often, Bennett suggests, we can learn from the mistakes made in the course of the arguments of such figures. Bennett compares studying the impressive failures of our philosophical ancestors to observing a mechanical genius try to build an automobile engine out of a Meccano set. We won't get a working engine but, Bennett claims, we may very well learn a great deal about engineering (Bennett 1984, 41).

It is possible, Garber allows, to learn from failures, but a little, he insists, can go a long way. An architecture student may learn a lot from studying a failed building or two, but the bulk of her studies will surely be devoted to studying successful buildings and the principles behind them. Why should philosophy be any different? In the end, Garber suggests, if what one wants is philosophical truth, then only a small portion of one's philosophical education should be spent studying the heroic failures of the past. The bulk of one's efforts should be spent studying positions and arguments that remain live candidates for truth (see p. 350 above).

Returning to our original question, if Garber is right, then the desire for philosophical truth cannot justify the vast resources that the discipline of philosophy devotes to the study of its history. That is, Bennett's view of what is valuable about the history of philosophy should lead us to conclude that the history of philosophy should have only a marginal role in the practice of philosophy.

Not only may the history of philosophy provide only arid soil for the cultivation of the kind of value that Bennett seeks, but the focus on philosophical truth, Garber warns, can lead us to distort the philosophical content of a thinker's work by tempting the interpreter to attempt to explicate a thinker's ideas in terms that, while congenial to our contemporary sensibilities, do not accurately represent the actual ideas of the thinker. The very act of translating a philosopher's ideas into a contemporary idiom risks historical misrepresentation. Garber is not entirely explicit about why he thinks that the attempt to explicate a philosopher's theory in terms alien to the thinker's own puts the interpreter at risk of misinterpretation. After all, every act of interpretation involves taking ideas expressed in one set of terms and translating them into others. That is just what interpretation is. But perhaps what worries Garber is that if the vocabulary of the interpretation is sufficiently alien to the philosopher being interpreted, it is unlikely that the interpretation actually expresses the intentions of that philosopher. There is perhaps some merit to this worry, but one of the examples that Garber gives to illustrate the method of rational reconstruction raises questions. He cites Benson Mates' (1994) work on Leibniz's conception of possible worlds where Mates formalizes certain aspects of Leibniz's philosophy within a system very different from any system in which Leibniz might have worked. In general, it's hard to see anything wrong with that. If, for example, a historical figure's argument contains scope ambiguity[2] and translating her argument into first-order logic reveals the ambiguity, this fact seems to be of undeniable interest, even if the figure in question was ignorant of first-order logic. Pointing out this fact runs no risk of historical distortion. No doubt an Abelard or a Leibniz would be unable to grasp the point without a little tutoring (but probably not much), and yet that doesn't mean that the observation introduces historical misrepresentation. It is true and historically accurate to say of our imagined example that the text as written by the historical figure contains a scope ambiguity. Nothing has been misrepresented by revealing this.

What is more, if we look at how Mates himself presents his project, it doesn't raise concerns of this nature. Here is Mates describing his project:

When defining logical truth in terms of interpretations or models, logicians frequently make reference to the Leibnizian idea that a proposition is a necessary truth if and only if it is true of all possible worlds. The same idea is usually mentioned in discussions of the semantics of modal logics. As soon as one looks a bit further into the matter, however, it becomes apparent that the concepts of 'possible world' employed by modern investigators are quite different from that of Leibniz himself; and although perhaps this is all to the good, there maybe some interest in considering what the effect would be if a more strictly Leibnizian approach were followed . . . It also should be mentioned at the outset that clearly the formalized language toward which Leibniz was moving would have been more like that of Lesniewski than like the Fregean system employed by most logicians today, and inevitably a certain amount of distortion is involved in attempting to apply his ideas to a type of language he never considered. Nevertheless I believe that such application is not without interest.

(Mates 1994, 208–209)

Mates' intent here is to consider how the incorporation of certain features of Leibniz's conception of a possible world would affect modern model-theoretic approaches to the semantics of modal logic. Certainly such questions are not out of bounds. And asking them does not invite historical misunderstandings.

Mates allows that applying Leibniz's ideas to a formalized language that Leibniz never considered involves some inevitable distortion. But Mates is not saying that formalizing a thinker's informal writings in a formal system of which she was ignorant inevitably involves distortions. If the expressive power of the formal system is at least equal to the expressive power of the natural language in which the original text was written, then no distortions are inevitable. What Mates is talking about is applying some of Leibniz's *ideas about logic* to a logical system very different from the one that he had in mind or was working toward. In this case, the application will not always be perfectly smooth without some distortion or adjustment of the ideas. But such distortions are not a species of misunderstanding. Indeed, noting where such distortions are necessary in order to apply Leibniz's ideas to a particular formal language *promotes* understanding. We understand Leibniz much better if we are aware of what modifications or adjustments to his ideas are need to apply his ideas to a particular language. Of course, Garber might legitimately worry that the same method of rational reconstruction could prove disastrous in the hands of a philosopher less scrupulous and attentive to these issues than Mates. But every method results in misunderstanding if applied in a careless or irresponsible way.

Having characterized Bennett's method of doing the history of philosophy and introduced several worries about it, Garber characterizes his own preferred method, which he calls "disinterested historical reconstruction." Taking Spinoza as an example, Garber urges us to:

> attempt to understand Spinoza's positions and arguments in terms that he or a well-informed contemporary of his may have understood. It involves coming to understand what Spinoza or a contemporary of his would have considered unproblematic background beliefs, what they would have had trouble with, and in the light of that and other similar contexts, coming to understand what Spinoza's conception of his project was, how he thought he had established the conclusions he had reached, and what he thought was important about those conclusions, all under the assumption that, by and large, Spinoza's project is the work of a smart person working within a particular historical context.
>
> (see p. 352 above)

How is this method different from the one preferred by Bennett? After all, if Bennett didn't think that Spinoza was an excellent philosopher and that therefore there was much to learn from him, he wouldn't bother to study him. This being so, we are much more likely to learn philosophy from Spinoza if we take the trouble to get him right, that is, to understand his ideas as he understood them. The main point of disagreement that Garber sees between himself and Bennett is that Bennett, in seeking to learn philosophical truth from Spinoza, spends a lot effort in assessing the truth of Spinoza's doctrines and the acceptability of the arguments for them. This assessment takes place from Bennett's own perspective as a late twentieth-century philosopher. Garber is less interested in what appears true or false from our own perspective. He is interested in what would have been reasonable to Spinoza given his historical context.

This introduces the provocative notion that what is reasonable is relative to a historical content. Could reasonability be historically relative? That is, could it be relative to the wider intellectual, cultural, and material environment? Garber suggests that it is. In the above-cited passage he says that assessing reasonability involves identifying claims that a thinker's contemporaries would have regarded as unproblematic background beliefs. The idea is, presumably, that if one's contemporaries believe that some proposition is unproblematic then it is reasonable to believe that proposition. This is controversial. One might object, for example, that widespread irrationality is still irrationality and agreeing with it is not reasonable. But certainly that a belief is widespread can help *explain* (although perhaps not *justify*) why someone believes it. Noting that a belief was widespread during a philosopher's era can help forestall wild goose chases for other kinds of explanation. So investigation of historical context can contribute in this way to making intelligible that a certain thinker held some doctrine.

Of course, Bennett acknowledges that insight can be gained by familiarity with historical context. But he also notes that there is a diminishing marginal return on it and the finite attention of an historian of philosophy might well be better spent in direct contact with the historical figure's own texts. He suggests that just a fair grasp of the historical context is often sufficient.

I think that all parties to the debate would have to concede that there are no hard and fast rules about the correct ratio of the study of context to the study of the texts themselves. And, presumably, different ratios will conduce to different insights. The rational reconstructor and the historical reconstructor may well, Garber concedes, both arrive at the same ratio. What will differ in the end is the lack of concern for truth on the part of the practitioner of historical reconstruction.

At this point, I'd like to raise some questions about Garber's idea that we can assess a doctrine's reasonability (relative to a historical context) without attempting to assess its truth. This may be so, but assessing truth and assessing reasonability are not always, in practice, independent matters. Assessing a philosophical doctrine for truth is often part of an effective procedure for making it intelligible or showing how it was reasonable by a thinker's own lights. Suppose that a figure from the history of philosophy believes that $p$. The question that ultimately concerns the disinterested historian is, why did this philosopher believe that $p$? Or alternatively, why was the philosopher reasonable in believing that $p$? You might begin to try to answer this question by first asking yourself if you believe that $p$. If you do, then why? Would the grounds for your belief be available to the philosopher being interpreted? If you don't believe that $p$, then why not? Which of your background beliefs could you alter so that $p$ would become reasonable? And so forth. By working backwards from what is reasonable by her own lights, the historian can arrive at what would be reasonable by the lights of the historical figure being interpreted. Such a procedure does not uniquely determine an interpretation. It serves, however, to set us off on the right track or, at the very least, to give us some starting points from which to work. Of course, this procedure will be more effective the closer our beliefs are to the beliefs of the target of interpretation. But it should come as no surprise to anyone that it is easier to interpret a thinker who is more like us than someone who is less like us.

If our inquiry is not guided by assessment of truth, as Garber's ideal of disinterested historical reconstruction is not, what alternative methods are there? I think Garber's emphasis on historical context provides some indication of a possible answer. In our search for the basis of the reasonability of the doctrines of a philosopher we might attempt to immerse ourselves deeply enough in the thinker's historical context that we acquire the ability to see the world from the perspective of a philosophically well-informed contemporary. Once we acquire this ability, judgments of what is reasonable and what is not from within that historical context will become like second nature to us. At one point in Chapter 25, Garber compares the historian of philosophy to an anthropologist in the field (see p. 361 above). And although Garber doesn't make this point explicitly, perhaps the anthropologist exemplifies this approach in a particularly pure form. The anthropologist completely immerses herself in the culture that she studies. She lives among the members of that culture and participates in their way of life. Over time, familiarity is achieved and, with familiarity, insight. Obviously the historian of philosophy is at a distinct disadvantage compared to the anthropologist. The historian cannot literally participate in the life of the culture that she studies. But it is not unreasonable to suppose that immersion in the materials that are available to the contemporary historian—the texts, art, artifacts, and the like—can help the historian achieve the kind of familiarity sought by the anthropologist, albeit to a lesser degree. Once she is suitably familiar with the context, she can reliably make judgments of reasonability.

Previously we noted that starting from judgments of truth or reasonability by the lights to the historian becomes less effective the greater the gulf separating the perspective of the historian from the perspective of the target of interpretation. The method of immersion in historical context also faces limitations. Immersion is a time consuming process. It is difficult to know in advance which contexts are most important for understanding a given issue. When dealing with historical figures the opportunities for immersion are much poorer than those open to, for example, the anthropologist in the field and the degree of familiarity sought is, in the normal case, a far from perfectly realized ideal. Moreover, contexts are broad and diffuse things. So immersion in a context requires a breadth of learning that can be disproportionate to the narrowness of the questions that might interest the historian of philosophy. It is also difficult to practice historical immersion and philosophical reflection from one's own point of view simultaneously.

What is there to choose between assessing reasonability by working backwards from assessments of truth and the method of immersion in historical context? They each have strengths and weaknesses. I believe all parties would have to admit that both methods can be effective. Their relative effectiveness will depend on a host of factors: the intellectual disposition of the historian; the kinds of doctrines under consideration; the forms of reasonability being assessed, etc. Perhaps the only judicious conclusion to be drawn is that the history of philosophy is best served by using both approaches. No single method, it is reasonable to think, is equal to the task of rendering intelligible the entire history of philosophy. It does, however, bear repeating that the method that involves assessing truth is useful even if the primary goal pursued by the historian isn't philosophical truth but rather historical insight instead.

As discussed above, Garber characterizes his method in contrast to Bennett's in terms of the values pursued. Bennett seeks philosophical truth whereas Garber seeks to show how a thinker's views were reasonable given her historical context. Understanding why a thinker's views were reasonable given her historical context is a historical goal; it is a form of historical understanding. The historian of philosophy who has such understanding as her ultimate goal is arguably more a historian than a philosopher. But showing that a thinker's views were reasonable given her historical context isn't the ultimate goal for Garber. He thinks that it has specifically philosophical benefits as well. To make this point, he discusses Descartes' view that reading the work of long dead authors is intellectually beneficial in much the same way that travel is. Descartes thinks that by traveling we can get a certain perspective on our own lives by learning about the way of life of people in distant places. In particular, it can free us from the belief that the way that we see things is the only way to see them. That, for example, by exposing ourselves to the ways of life of people in distant lands, we may come to questions believes such as "X is fit for human consumption but Y is not, that weeks must have seven days, that children must be raised by their own parents, etc." (see p. 355 above). At the very least, such a perspective can lead us to question why we have the beliefs and customs that we do and lead us to see what is arbitrary in our beliefs and customs and what is not.

In reading the work of historical figures, just as we do when we travel, we expose ourselves to very different perspectives and presuppositions. We broaden our horizons and gain perspective on our own views. The philosopher who reads none of the greats from the philosophical past is like the parochial person who has never traveled outside of her own region. Just as she is liable to have an overly narrow and provincial perspective on the world and is less likely to question the way of life of the people who surround her, so too will the philosopher who reads no history of philosophy be liable to have a narrow and provincial perspective on philosophy.

This is a very deep and important insight into one way that studying history can be valuable. I have no doubt that studying the history of philosophy has just the sorts of benefits that Garber describes and that those benefits are important and valuable. And yet I find it somewhat dissatisfying as an account of why the history of philosophy is important to philosophy. Recall that we began this discussion by observing that philosophy has a very unusual relationship to its history in that studying the history of philosophy appears to be regarded by many philosophers as important to doing philosophy. The intellectual benefits of studying history that Garber describes seem to be benefits that any area of inquiry could receive from studying its own history. Physicists could obtain historical perspective on their own beliefs by studying phlogiston theory or the Aristotelian theory of the elements. Psychologists could gain perspective by studying phrenology or behaviorism. Why should philosophers value having their horizons broadened through the study of history any more than researchers in any other discipline?

I think both Bennett and Garber make an unwarranted assumption about philosophy and its history that colors their views on method. By challenging this assumption I hope to shed light on the special relationship between philosophy and its history. Bennett thinks we can learn philosophy from studying its history but that we are just as likely (if not more likely) to learn from the mistakes of historical figures than their successes. Garber justifiably points out that there is a limit to how much we can learn from mistakes and suggests that we do not directly learn much philosophy from studying its history. A greater source of value of the study of the history is that it allows us to gain a new perspective on our own philosophical practices and assumptions by exposing ourselves to unfamiliar ideas. The assumption that Bennett and Garber both appear to make is that philosophy is making relatively rapid progress. The philosophical present has superseded its past rendering it obsolete as a direct source of philosophical knowledge. This confidence in the progress that philosophy is making leads Bennett to emphasize the ways that we can learn from the mistakes of the past and leads Garber to emphasize the indirect philosophical benefits of studying the history of philosophy.

This assumption does not survive scrutiny. Philosophy has not made rapid progress. There is no large body of established philosophical fact. The ideas of historical figures have not been, by and large, definitively refuted. I do not deny that philosophy has made some progress over the course of its long history. No doubt standards of rigor and argumentation have risen. Innovations in logic, decision theory, and other technical disciplines have allowed us to pose questions and evaluate answers to them with greater and greater precision. But even a cursory comparison to, for example, the natural sciences reveals that, in substantive matters, the rate at which philosophy has been making progress is painfully slow. What important philosophical doctrine has been definitely refuted? Perhaps one might be tempted to cite mind-body dualism, the description theory of names, or Leibniz's theory of monads. But these doctrines are merely unfashionable; they have not been refuted. (Indeed, some of them appear to be on the brink of a revival.) Perhaps some doctrines have been refuted but that does not undermine my point. It is rare that an important philosophical position has been definitely refuted.

What does this have to do with the special relationship between philosophy and its history? It means that, given the rate of progress in philosophy, the time scale relevant to philosophical progress is massively longer than the time scale relevant to progress in, for example, the natural sciences. Philosophical time passes slowly. In fact, it passes so slowly that, from the perspective of philosophical time, even our ancient predecessors like Plato and Aristotle are near contemporaries of ours. For this reason, studying their works is just part of the normal process of literature review in which any intellectually responsible researcher must engage. A contemporary philosopher who ignores the history of philosophy is not dissimilar to the philosopher who only reads the work of her departmental colleagues or old grad school friends. A comprehensive view of the state of the discussion of a particular philosophical problem requires engagement with the history of philosophy. Alternatively, the history of philosophy is just philosophy. No doubt the study of long dead philosophers poses special problems that the study of our more recent contemporaries does not. Languages must be learned. Archives must be navigated. Unfamiliar ideas must be grasped. Historical contexts must be investigated. But none of these relate to the viability of the ideas from which these difficulties can separate us.

This helps explain the special relationship between philosophy and its history. Physics, for example, makes progress at a much faster rate than philosophy. Phlogiston theory is a dead letter. The value of studying it for the physicist can only take the form of learning from past failures or giving her historical perspective. This is not so with, for example, mind-body dualism. Although currently unfashionable, it remains a live candidate for truth. Since Descartes offers one of the most worked out and sophisticated accounts of mind-body dualism, his work on the topic is still required reading for anyone thinking about the metaphysics of mind.

So where does this leave us with respect to methodology? How does the claim that the history of philosophy contains our near contemporaries change how to approach the study of the history of philosophy? There appear to me two main methodological consequences. The first is that we should not assume that a large portion of the philosophical lessons that we can learn from the history of philosophy will come from, as Bennett sometimes suggests, learning from mistakes. This means approaching the ideas of historical figures with the humility appropriate to someone whose epistemic situation with respect to the issues under discussion is not much better, if at all, than that of the historical figure being studied. This is not the "courtly deference" that pretends the historical figure is always right that Bennett correctly decries. But neither is it the high-handedness that pretends that the orthodoxies and presumptions of the present age are always more respectable and better justified than the ideas of our predecessors. The second is that we need not eschew judgments of truth and falsity. Garber rightly thinks that there is only so much we can learn from the failures of our predecessors and so searches for other ways that we can benefit philosophically from the study of the history of philosophy. But this presumes that if there is philosophy to be directly learned from the history of philosophy at all, then it must come mostly from studying failed theories. And this presumes that most of the theories of historical figures are failed. Until philosophy makes substantial sustained progress, we are in no position to dismiss our predecessors' theories as failures. To learn from them does not require us, therefore, to learn from failures.

It is difficult to have a debate about methodology without turning one's interlocutors into straw men. This is because there is only a small range of issues about which reasonable people might disagree. The real differences between different methodologies are generally more a matter of emphasis and nuance than sharp differences. There is broad consensus about method with real disagreement only at the margins. I find this observation comforting because perhaps it is not too much to hope that this widely shared sense of what is reasonable in historical method is explained by the fact the we are all, together, on the right road.

## Notes

1. The departments were the economics departments of Chicago, MIT, Berkeley, and Harvard; the psychology departments of Harvard, Stanford, and Berkeley; and the mathematics departments of Princeton, Harvard, and the University of Michigan for the Spring semester of 2010. This list is somewhat arbitrary, but no similarly arbitrary list of philosophy departments would yield even somewhat similar results.
2. Editors' note: An example of a sentence with scope ambiguity is 'Everyone loves somebody', which could mean either 'for each person, there's someone that person loves' or 'there's some person that everybody loves.'

# Bibliography

## Abbreviations

The following abbreviations are used in giving references.

*Berkeley*

| | |
|---|---|
| Alciphron | *Alciphron, or The Minute Philosopher* |
| Dialogues | *Three Dialogues between Hylas and Philonous* |
| PHK | *Principles* |
| NTV | *New Theory of Vision* |
| TVV | *Theory of Vision Vindicated* |

The authors in Part 8 use the edition of Luce and Jessop (Berkeley 1948–57) while the authors in Part 9 use the edition of Ayers (Berkeley 1975).

*Descartes*

AT    Charles Adam and Paul Tannery, ed. 1996. *Oeuvres de Descartes.* 11 vols. Paris: J. Vrin.
CSM   John Cottingham, Robert Stoothoff, and Dugald Murdoch, trans. 1984. *The Philosophical Writings of Descartes.* Cambridge: Cambridge University Press.

*Hume*

E   *Enquiry Concerning Human Understanding*
T   *Treatise of Human Nature*

*Leibniz*

AG    Roger Ariew and Daniel Garber, trans. 1989. *Philosophical Essays.* Indianapolis: Hackett.
Couturat   Louis Couturat, ed. 1988. *Opuscules et fragments inédits.* Hildesheim: Olms.
Dutens   Louis Dutens, ed. 1768. *Opera Omnia.* Geneva: Fratres De Tournes.

G                 C. I. Gerhardt, ed. 1965. *Die philosophischen Schriften*. 7 vols. Hildesheim: Olms.

Leibniz-Des Bosses     Brandon C. Look and Donald Rutherford, trans. 2007. *The Leibniz–Des Bosses Correspondence*. New Haven, CT: Yale University Press.

Loemker       Leroy E. Loemker, trans. 1969. *Philosophical Papers and Letters*. Second edition. Dordrecht: D. Reidel.

MP           M. Morris and G. H. R. Parkinson, ed. 1975. *Leibniz: Philosophical Writings*. Totowa: Rowman and Littlefield.

NE           Peter Remnant and Jonathan Bennett, trans. 1981. *New Essays on Human Understanding*. Cambridge: Cambridge University Press.

*Locke*

Essay    *Essay Concerning Human Understanding*

*Malebranche*

SAT    T. M. Lennon and P. J. Olscamp, trans. 1997. *The Search after Truth*. Cambridge: Cambridge University Press.

**Pre-1900 Works**

Annet, P. 1744a. *The Resurrection of Jesus Considered. In Answer to the Tryal of the Witnesses. By a Moral Philosopher*. Third edition. London: Printed for M. Cooper.

——1744b. *The Resurrection Reconsidered. Being an Answer to Clearer and Others*. London: Printed for the author by M. Cooper.

Anonymous (George Hooper?). 1699. "A Calculation of the Credibility of Human Testimony." *Philosophical Transactions of the Royal Society* 21: 359–365.

Aquinas, T. 1945. *Summa Contra Gentiles*. In *Basic Writings of Saint Thomas Aquinas*, vol. 2, ed. A. Pegis. New York: Random House.

Babbage, C. 1838. *The Ninth Bridgewater Treatise*. Second edition. London: Frank Cass, 1967.

Bayes, T. 1763. "An Essay towards Solving a Problem in the Doctrine of Chances." *Philosophical Transactions of the Royal Society* 53: 370–418. Reprinted in *Biometrika* 45 (1958): 296–315.

Bayle, Pierre. 1991. *Historical and Critical Dictionary*. Edited by Richard H. Popkin. Indianapolis: Hackett.

Berkeley, George. 1948–1951. *The Works of George Berkeley*. Edited by T. Jessop and A. Luce. London: Thomas Nelson.

——1975. *Philosophical Works*. Edited by M. R. Ayers. London: Dent.

Boyle, Robert. 1772. *Works*. London: Printed for W. Johnston *et al*.

——1979. *Selected Philosophical Papers of Robert Boyle*. Edited by M. A. Stewart. Manchester: Manchester University Press.

——1996. *A Free Enquiry into the Vulgarly Received Notion of Nature*. Edited by Edward B. Davis and Michael Hunter. Cambridge: Cambridge University Press.

Butler, Joseph. 1736/1896. *The Analogy of Religion, Natural and Revealed, to the Constitution and Course of Nature*. Edited by W. E. Gladstone. Oxford: Clarendon Press.

Campbell, George. 1762. *A Dissertation on Miracles*. Edinburgh: A. Kincaid and J. Bell.

Chandler, S. 1744. *Witnesses of the Resurrection of Jesus Christ Reexamined: And Their Testimony Proved Entirely Consistent*. London: Printed for J. Noon and R. Hett.

Charleton, Walter. 1654. *Physiologia Epicuro-Gassendo-Charletoniana, or a Fabric of Philosophy Natural/founded upon the Hypothesis of Atomes*. London: Printed by Tho. Newcomb for Thomas Heath.

Collier, Arthur. 1713. *Clavis Universalis*. London: Printed for Robert Gosling.

Erdmann, J. E. 1891. *History of Philosophy*. Translated by W. S. Hough. Second edition, 3 vols. London: Sonnenschein.

Euler, Leonhard. 2009. *Letters to a German Princess*. In *Kant's Critique of Pure Reason: Background Source Materials*, ed. Eric Watkins. Cambridge: Cambridge University Press.

Galilei, Galileo. 2008. *The Essential Galileo*. Edited by Maurice A. Finocchiaro. Indianapolis: Hackett.

Hegel, G. W. F. 1969. *The Science of Logic*. Translated by A. V. Miller. London: Allen and Unwin.

——1991. *The Encyclopedia Logic*. Translated and edited by T. F. Geraets, W. A. Suchtig, and H. S. Harris. Indianapolis: Hackett.

Hobbes, T. 1839. *Elements of Philosophy: The First Section, Concerning Body*. In *The English Works of Thomas Hobbes*, vol. 1, ed. Sir W. Molesworth. London: John Bohn.

——1994. *The Elements of Law: Human Nature and De Corpore Politico*. Edited by J. C. A. Gaskin. Oxford: Oxford University Press.

Hume, D. 1932. *The Letters of David Hume*. Edited by J. Y. T. Greig. Oxford: Clarendon Press.

——1954. *New Letters of David Hume*. Edited by R. Klibansky and E. C. Mossner. Oxford: Clarendon Press.

——1999. *An Enquiry Concerning Human Understanding*. Edited by T. Beauchamp. Oxford: Oxford University Press.

——2001. *A Treatise of Human Nature*. Edited by D. F. Norton and M. J. Norton. Oxford: Oxford University Press.

——2007. *An Enquiry Concerning Human Understanding*. Edited by Peter Millican. Oxford: Oxford University Press.

Jackson, J. 1744. *An Address to Deists*. London: Printed for J. and P. Knapton.

Jacobi, F. H. 1815. *Werke*, vol. 2. Leipzig: Gerhard Fleischer.

Kant, Immanuel. 1781/1933. *Critique of Pure Reason*. Translated by Norman Kemp Smith. London: Macmillan.

——1781/1998. *The Critique of Pure Reason*. Edited and translated by Paul Guyer and Allen Wood. Cambridge: Cambridge University Press.

——1790/1973. "On a Discovery." In *The Kant-Eberhard Controversy*, trans. H. Allison. Baltimore, MD: Johns Hopkins University Press.

——1902–. *Gesammelte Schriften*. 29 vols. Berlin and Leipzig: de Gruyter.

——1997. *Prolegomena to Any Future Metaphysics*. Translated by Gary Hatfield. Cambridge: Cambridge University Press.

Laplace, P. S. 1812. *Théorie analytique des probabilités*. Page references to the third edition (1820), reprinted in *Oeuvres complètes de Laplace*, vol. 7, 1886. Paris: Gauthier-Villars.

——1814. *Essai philosophique sur les probabilités*. Page references to F. W. Truscott and F. L. Emory, trans., *A Philosophical Essay on Probabilities* (New York: Dover, 1951).

Locke, John. 1823. *Works*. London: Thomas Davison, Whitefriars.

——1975. *An Essay Concerning Human Understanding*. Edited by P. H. Nidditch. Oxford: Clarendon Press.

Malebranche, N. 1992. *Philosophical Selections*. Edited by S. Nadler. Indianapolis: Hackett.

Mill, J. S. 1843. *A System of Logic*. Page references to the eighth edition (New York: Harper and Bros, 1874).

Patrides, C. A., ed. 1970. *The Cambridge Platonists*. Cambridge, MA: Harvard University Press.

Price, R. 1768. *Four Dissertations*. Second edition. London: A. Millar and T. Cadell.

Reid, Thomas. 1969. *Essays on the Intellectual Powers of Man*. Edited by B. Brody. Cambridge, MA: MIT Press.

Shapiro, Lisa. 2007. *The Correspondence between Princess Elisabeth of Bohemia and René Descartes*. Chicago, IL: The University of Chicago Press.

Sherlock, T. 1728. *Tryal of the Witnesses of the Resurrection of Jesus*. London: J. Roberts. Page references to the eleventh edition (London: J. and H. Pembert, 1743).

Spinoza, Benedict. 1925. *Opera*. Edited by Carl Gebhardt. 4 vols. Heidelberg: Carl Winter.
——1985. *The Collected Works of Spinoza*, vol. 1. Edited and translated by Edwin Curley. Princeton, NJ: Princeton University Press.
Suárez, F. 1994. *On Efficient Causality*. Translated by A. J. Freddoso. New Haven: Yale University Press.
West, G. 1747. *Observations on the History and Evidence of the Resurrection of Jesus Christ*. London: Printed for R. Dodsley.
Woolston, T. 1727–1729. *Six Discourses on the Miracles of Our Saviour*. London. Reprinted New York: Garland Publishing, 1979.


**Post-1900 Works**

Adams, Robert Merrihew. 1983. "Phenomenalism and Corporeal Substance in Leibniz." *Midwest Studies in Philosophy* 8: 217–257
——1994. *Leibniz: Determinist, Theist, Idealist*. Oxford: Oxford University Press.
——1997. "Things in Themselves." *Philosophy and Phenomenological Research* 57 (4): 801–825.
Alanen, Lilli. 2003. *Descartes's Concept of Mind*. Cambridge, MA: Harvard University Press.
Alexander, Peter. 1985. *Ideas, Qualities, and Corpuscles: Locke and Boyle on the External World*. Cambridge: Cambridge University Press.
Allais, Lucy. 2007. "Kant's Idealism and the Secondary Quality Analogy." *Journal of the History of Philosophy* 45 (3): 459–484.
——2010a. "Transcendental Idealism and Metaphysics." *Kantian Yearbook* 2: 1–31.
——2010b. "Kant's Argument for Transcendental Idealism in the Transcendental Aesthetic." *Proceedings of the Aristotelian Society* 110 (1): 47–75.
Allison, Henry. 2004. *Kant's Transcendental Idealism, Revised and Enlarged Edition*. New Haven, CT and London: Yale University Press.
Ameriks, Karl. 2006. *Kant and the Historical Turn*. Oxford: Clarendon Press.
Anstey, Peter. 2011. *John Locke and Natural Philosophy*. Oxford: Oxford University Press.
Antognazza, Maria Rosa. 2009. *Leibniz: An Intellectual Biography*. Cambridge: Cambridge University Press.
Ariew, Roger. 1983. "Mind–Body Interaction in Cartesian Philosophy: A Reply to Garber." *Southern Journal of Philosophy* 21 (supp.): 33–37.
Atherton, Margaret. 1984. "Knowledge of Substance and Knowledge of Science in Locke's *Essay*." *History of Philosophy Quarterly* 1 (4): 413–427.
——1990. *Berkeley's Revolution in Vision*. Ithaca, NY: Cornell University Press.
Ayer, A. J. 1973. *The Central Questions of Philosophy*. London: Penguin.
Ayers, M. R. 1981. "Mechanism, Superaddition, and the Proof of God's Existence in Locke's *Essay*." *Philosophical Review* 90: 210–251.
——1991. *Locke*. 2 vols. London: Routledge.
Barnard, G. A. 1958. "Thomas Bayes: A Biographical Note." *Biometrika* 45: 293–295.
Beebee, Helen. 2006. *Hume on Causation*. London: Routledge.
Bennett, Jonathan. 1966. *Kant's Analytic*. Cambridge: Cambridge University Press.
——1984. A *Study of Spinoza's Ethics*. Indianapolis: Hackett.
——2001. *Learning from Six Philosophers*. Oxford: Oxford University Press.
Bird, Graham. 1962. *Kant's Theory of Knowledge*. London: Routledge and Kegan Paul.
——2000. "Review of Kantian Humility." *Philosophical Quarterly* 50: 105–108.
——2006. *The Revolutionary Kant*. Chicago, IL: Open Court.
Blackburn, Simon. 1990. "Hume and Thick Connexions." *Philosophy and Phenomenological Research* 50 (supp.): 237–250.
Boas (Hall), Marie. 1952. "The Establishment of the Mechanical Philosophy." *Osiris* 10: 412–541.
Boulter, S. 2002. "Hume on Induction: A Genuine Problem or Theology's Trojan Horse?" *Philosophy* 77: 67–86.

Broad, C. D. 1916–1917. "Hume's Theory of the Credibility of Miracles." *Proceedings of the Aristotelian Society* 17: 77–94.
——1975. *Leibniz: An Introduction*. Edited by C. Lewy. Cambridge: Cambridge University Press.
Broughton, Janet and Ruth Mattern. 1978. "Reinterpreting Descartes on the Notion of the Union of Mind and Body." *Journal of the History of Philosophy* 16 (1): 23–32.
Brown, D. J. 2006. *Descartes and the Passionate Mind*. Cambridge: Cambridge University Press.
Brown, Stuart. 1984. *Leibniz*. Minneapolis: University of Minnesota Press.
Burns, R. M. 1981. *The Great Debate on Miracles. From Joseph Glanville to David Hume*. East Brunswick, NJ: Associated University Presses.
Chappell, Vere. 1989. "Locke and Relative Identity." *History of Philosophy Quarterly* 6 (1): 69–83.
Collins, Arthur. 1999. *Possible Experience*. Berkeley and Los Angeles: University of California Press.
Cover, J. A. and John Hawthorne. 1999. *Substance and Individuation in Leibniz*. Cambridge: Cambridge University Press.
Della Rocca, Michael. 1996a. *Representation and the Mind–Body Problem in Spinoza*. New York: Oxford University Press.
——2003. "A Rationalist Manifesto: Spinoza and the Principle of Sufficient Reason." *Philosophical Topics* 31: 75–94.
——2008a. *Spinoza*. New York: Routledge.
——2008b. "Rationalism Run Amok: Representation and the Reality of the Affects in Spinoza." In *Interpreting Spinoza*, ed. Charles Heunemann. Cambridge: Cambridge University Press.
——2010. "PSR." *Philosophers' Imprint* 10: 1–13.
——forthcoming. "Rationalism, Idealism, Monism, and Beyond." In *Spinoza and German Idealism*, ed. Eckart Förster and Yitzhak Y. Melamed. Cambridge: Cambridge University Press.
Des Chene, Dennis. 1996. *Physiologia*. Ithaca, NY: Cornell University Press.
Dijksterhuis, E. J. 1961. *The Mechanization of the World-Picture*. Oxford: Oxford University Press.
Downing, Lisa. 1998. "The Status of Mechanism in Locke's *Essay*." *Philosophical Review* 107: 381–414.
——2007. "Locke's Ontology." In *The Cambridge Companion to Locke's Essay*, ed. L. Newman. Cambridge, Cambridge University Press.
——2009. "Locke: The Primary and Secondary Quality Distinction." In *The Routledge Companion to Metaphysics*, ed. R. L. Poidevin, P. Simons, A. McGonigal, and R. P. Cameron. London, Routledge.
Dryer, D. P. 1966. *Kant's Solution for Verification in Metaphysics*. London: George Allen and Unwin.
Earman, John. 2000. *Hume's Abject Failure: The Argument against Miracles*. New York: Oxford University Press.
Fogelin, Robert J. 2001. *Routledge Philosophy Guidebook to Berkeley and the Principles of Human Knowledge*. London: Routledge.
——2003. *A Defense of Hume on Miracles*. Princeton, NJ: Princeton University Press.
Frankfurt, Harry G. 1970. *Demons, Dreamers, and Madmen: The Defense of Reason in Descartes's Meditations*. Indianapolis: Bobbs-Merrill.
——1978. "Descartes on the Consistency of Reason." In *Descartes: Critical and Interpretive Essays*, ed. M. Hooker. Baltimore: Johns Hopkins University Press.
Friedman, Michael. 1992. *Kant and the Exact Sciences*. Cambridge, MA: Harvard University Press.
Garber, Daniel. 1985. "Leibniz and the Foundations of Physics: The Middle Years." In *The Natural Philosophy of Leibniz*, ed. Kathleen Okruhlik and R. Brown. Dordrecht: Springer.
——2009. *Leibniz: Body, Substance, Monad*. Oxford: Oxford University Press.

Garrett, Don. 1979. "Spinoza's 'Ontological' Argument." *Philosophical Review* 88 (2): 198–223.

Geach, Peter. 1968. *Reference and Generality*. Second edition. Ithaca, NY: Cornell University Press.

Gewirth, Alan. 1941. "The Cartesian Circle." *Philosophical Review* 50: 368–395.

Grandy, Richard. 1979. "Stuff and Things." In *Mass Terms: Some Philosophical Problems*, ed. F. J. Pelletier. Dordrecht: Reidel.

Grice, H. P. 1941. "Personal Identity." *Mind* 50 (200): 330–350.

Grier, Michelle. 2001. *Kant's Doctrine of Transcendental Illusion*. Cambridge: Cambridge University Press.

Griffin, Nicholas. 1977. *Relative Identity*. Oxford: Clarendon Press.

Guyer, Paul. 1987. *Kant and the Claims of Knowledge*. Cambridge: Cambridge University Press.

——2007. "Debating Allison on Transcendental Idealism." *Kantian Review* 12 (2): 10–14.

Hanna, Robert. 2006. *Kant, Science and Human Nature*. Oxford: Clarendon Press.

Hartz, Glenn. 1998. "Why Corporeal Substances Keep Popping Up in Leibniz's Later Philosophy." *British Journal for the History of Philosophy* 6: 193–207.

Heilbron, J. L. 1979. *Electricity in the 17th and 18th Centuries*. Berkeley: University of California Press.

Hilbert, D. and S. Cohn-Vossen. 1956. *Geometry and the Imagination*. Translated by P. Nemenyi. New York: Chelsea.

Hirsch, Eli. 1976. "Physical Identity." *Philosophical Review* 85: 357–389.

Jacovides, Michael. 2002. "The Epistemology under Locke's Corpuscularianism." *Archiv für Geschichte der Philosophie* 84: 161–189.

——2008. "Lockean Fluids." In *Contemporary Perspectives on Early Modern Philosophy*, ed. Paul Hoffman, David Owen and Gideon Yaffe. Peterborough, ON: Broadview Press.

Jolley, Nicholas. 1990. "Berkeley and Malebranche on Causation." In *Central Themes in Early Modern Philosophy*, ed. Jan Cover and Mark Kulstadt. Indianapolis: Hackett.

Kargon, Robert. 1966. *Atomism in England from Hariot to Newton*. Oxford: Clarendon Press.

Kaufman, Dan. 2007. "Locke on Individuation and the Corpuscular Basis of Kinds." *Philosophy and Phenomenological Research* 75 (3): 499–534.

Kemp Smith, Norman. 1941. *The Philosophy of David Hume*. London: Macmillan.

Kenny, Anthony. 1968. *Descartes: A Study of his Philosophy*. New York: Random House.

——1970. "The Cartesian Circle and the Eternal Truths." *Journal of Philosophy* 67: 685–700.

——1984. *Aquinas*. Oxford: Oxford University Press.

Kuhn, Thomas. 1952. "Robert Boyle and Structural Chemistry in the Seventeenth Century." *Isis* 43: 12–36

Lakatos, Imre. 1976. *Proofs and Refutations*. Cambridge: Cambridge University Press.

Lambert, Karel and Gordon Brittan. 1970. *An Introduction to the Philosophy of Science*. Englewood Cliffs, NJ: Prentice-Hall.

Langton, Rae. 1998. *Kantian Humility: Our Ignorance of Things in Themselves*. Oxford: Oxford University Press.

Lee, Sukjae. 2008. "Necessary Connections and Continuous Creation: Malebranche's Two Arguments for Occasionalism." *Journal of the History of Philosophy* 46 (4): 539–565.

Loeb, Louis. 1981. *From Descartes to Hume*. Ithaca, NY: Cornell University Press.

——1992. "The Cartesian Circle." In *The Cambridge Companion to Descartes*, ed. John Cottingham. Cambridge: Cambridge University Press.

LoLordo, Antonia. 2011. "Person, Substance, Mode and 'the Moral Man' in Locke's Philosophy." *Canadian Journal of Philosophy* 40 (4): 643–688.

Look, Brandon C. 1999. *Leibniz and the "Vinculum Substantiale."* Stuttgart: Steiner Verlag.

——2010. "Leibniz's Metaphysics and Metametaphysics: Idealism, Realism, and the Nature of Substance." *Philosophy Compass* 5 (11): 871–879.

Loptson, Peter. 1999. "Was Leibniz an Idealist?" *Philosophy* 74: 361–385.

Loptson, Peter and Richard Arthur. 2006. "Leibniz's Body Realism: Two Interpretations." *The Leibniz Review* 16: 1–42.

Lowe, E. J. 2009. *More Kinds of Being*. Oxford: Wiley-Blackwell.

McCann, Edwin. 1994. "Locke's Philosophy of Body." In *The Cambridge Companion to Locke*, ed. V. Chappell. Cambridge: Cambridge University Press.

McCracken, Charles. 1983. *Malebranche and British Philosophy*. Oxford: Oxford University Press.

Mackie, John. 1976. *Problems from Locke*. Oxford: Oxford University Press.

Mandelbaum, Maurice. 1964. *Philosophy, Science, and Sense Perception: Historical and Critical Studies*. Baltimore: Johns Hopkins University Press.

Mates, Benson. 1986. *The Philosophy of Leibniz: Metaphysics and Language*. New York: Oxford University Press.

——1994. "Leibniz on Possible Worlds." In *Leibniz: Critical Assessments*, ed. R. S. Woolhouse. London: Routledge.

Mattern, Ruth. 1980. "Moral Science and the Concept of Persons in Locke." *Philosophical Review* 89 (1): 24–45.

Melamed, Yitzhak. 2010. "Acosmism or Weak Individuals? Hegel, Spinoza, and the Reality of the Finite." *Journal of the History of Philosophy* 48: 77–92.

——2012a. "Why is Spinoza NOT an Eleatic Monist? (Or Why Diversity Exists?)" In *Spinoza on Monism*, ed. Philip Goff. Houndmills, Basingstoke, UK: Palgrave.

——2012b. "Inherence, Causation, and Conceivability in Spinoza." *Journal of the History of Philosophy* 50 (3): 365–386.

Melamed, Yitzhak and Martin Lin. "The Principle of Sufficient Reason." *The Stanford Online Encyclopedia of Philosophy* (summer 2010 edition), ed. Edward N. Zalta, available at http://plato.stanford.edu/entries/sufficient-reason/.

Mercer, Christia. 2001. *Leibniz's Metaphysics: Its Origins and Development*. Cambridge: Cambridge University Press.

Millican, Peter. 1993. "'Hume's Theorem' Concerning Miracles." *Philosophical Quarterly* 43: 489–495.

——2011. "Twenty Questions about Hume's 'Of Miracles.'" In *Philosophy and Religion*, ed. Anthony O'Hear. Royal Institute of Philosophy Supplement 68.

Monk, Ray. 1996. *Bertrand Russell: The Spirit of Solitude, 1872–1921*. New York: Simon and Schuster.

——2000. *Bertrand Russell, 1921–1970: The Ghost of Madness*. New York: Simon and Schuster.

Nadler, Steven. 1996. "'No Necessary Connection': The Medieval Roots of the Occasionalist Roots of Hume." *The Monist* 79: 448–466.

——2000. "Malebranche on Causation." In *The Cambridge Companion to Malebranche*, ed. Steven Nadler. Cambridge: Cambridge University Press.

Nelson, Alan and Lex Newman. 1999. "Circumventing Cartesian Circles." *Noûs* 33: 370–404.

Newman, Lex. 1999. "The Fourth Meditation." *Philosophy and Phenomenological Research* 59 (3): 559–591.

——2010. "Descartes' Epistemology." In *Stanford Encyclopedia of Philosophy* (summer 2010 edition), ed. Edward N. Zalta, available at http://plato.stanford.edu/archives/fall2010/entries/descartes-epistemology/.

Noonan, Harold. 1978. "Locke on Personal Identity." *Philosophy* 53 (205): 343–351.

O'Neill, Eileen. 1998. "Disappearing Ink: Early Modern Women Philosophers and their Fate in History." In *Philosophy in a Feminist Voice*, ed. Janet Kourany. Princeton, NJ: Princeton University Press.

Ott, Walter. 2009. *Causation and Laws of Nature in Early Modern Philosophy*. Oxford: Oxford University Press.

Pappas, George. 1987. "Berkeley and Immediate Perception." In *Essays on the Philosophy of George Berkeley*, ed. Ernest Sosa. Boston: Reidel.

Parsons, Charles. 1967. *Mathematics in Philosophy: Selected Essays*. Ithaca, NY: Cornell University Press.

——1992. "The Transcendental Aesthetic." In *The Cambridge Companion to Kant*, ed. Paul Guyer. Cambridge: Cambridge University Press.

Phemister, Pauline. 2005. *Leibniz and the Natural World: Activity, Passivity, and Corporeal Substances in Leibniz's Philosophy*. Dordrecht: Springer.

Radner, Daisie. 1971. "Descartes' Notion of the Union of Mind and Body." *Journal of the History of Philosophy* 9: 159–170.

Read, Rupert and Kenneth A. Richman, ed. 2000. *The New Hume Debate*. London: Routledge.

Redwood, John. 1976. *Reason, Ridicule, and Religion*. Cambridge, MA: Harvard University Press.

Rorty, Richard, Jerome B. Schneewind, and Quentin Skinner, ed. 1984. *Philosophy in History: Essays on the Historiography of Philosophy*. Cambridge: Cambridge University Press.

Rosefeldt, Tobias. 2001. Review of J. Van Cleve, *Problems from Kant*; A. Collins, *Possible Experience*; R. Langton, *Kantian Humility*. *European Journal of Philosophy* 9 (2): 263–269.

Russell, Bertrand. 1900/1937. *A Critical Exposition of the Philosophy of Leibniz*. London: Routledge.

——1917. *Mysticism and Logic*. London: George Allen and Unwin.

——1945. *The History of Western Philosophy*. New York: Simon and Schuster.

Rutherford, Donald. 1995. *Leibniz and the Rational Order of Nature*. Cambridge: Cambridge University Press.

——2008. "Leibniz as Idealist." *Oxford Studies in Early Modern Philosophy* 4: 141–190.

Ryle, Gilbert. 1949. *The Concept of Mind*. London: Hutchinson.

Schaffer, Jonathan. 2009. "On What Grounds What." In *Metametaphysics*, ed. David J. Chalmers, David Manley, and Ryan Wasserman. Oxford: Oxford University Press.

Schmaltz, Tad. 2007. *Descartes on Causation*. Oxford: Oxford University Press.

——2009. "Nicolas Malebranche." In *Stanford Encyclopedia of Philosophy* (winter 2009 edition), ed. Edward N. Zalta, available at http://plato.stanford.edu/archives/win2009/entries/malebranche/.

Schrader, George. 1968. "The Thing in Itself in Kantian Philosophy." In *Kant: A Collection of Critical Essays*, ed. Robert Paul Wolff. London: Macmillan.

Senderowicz, Yaron. 2005. *The Coherence of Kant's Transcendental Idealism*. Dordrecht: Springer.

Shabel, Lisa. 2006 "Kant's Philosophy of Mathematics." In *The Cambridge Companion to Kant*, ed. Paul Guyer. Second edition. Cambridge: Cambridge University Press.

Shapiro, Lisa. 1999. "Princess Elisabeth and Descartes: The Union of Soul and Body and the Practice of Philosophy." *British Journal for the History of Philosophy* 7 (3): 503–520.

Shoemaker, Sidney. 1963. *Self-Knowledge and Self-Identity*. Ithaca, NY: Cornell University Press.

Skinner, Quentin. 1969. "Meaning and Understanding in the History of Ideas." *History and Theory* 8 (1): 3–53.

Sleigh, Robert C., Jr. 1990. *Leibniz and Arnauld: A Commentary on their Correspondence*. New Haven, CT: Yale University Press.

Smith, Justin E. H. 2011. *Divine Machines: Leibniz's Philosophy of Biology*. Princeton, NJ: Princeton University Press.

Stoneham, Tom. 2002. *Berkeley's World*. Oxford: Oxford University Press.

Strawson, Galen. 1989. *The Secret Connexion*. Oxford: Clarendon Press.

Strawson, Peter. 1959. *Individuals*. London: Methuen.

——1966. *The Bounds of Sense*. London: Methuen.

Stuart, Matthew. 1996. "Locke's Geometrical Analogy." *History of Philosophy Quarterly* 13 (4): 451–467.

——1998. "Locke on Superaddition and Mechanism." *British Journal for the History of Philosophy* 6 (3): 351–379.

Swinburne, Richard. 1970. *The Concept of Miracle*. New York: St. Martin's Press.

——1979. *The Existence of God*. Oxford: Clarendon Press.

Talbott, William. 2011. "Bayesian Epistemology." In *Stanford Encyclopedia of Philosophy* (summer 2011 edition), ed. Edward N. Zalta, available athttp://plato.stanford.edu/archives/sum2011/entries/epistemology-bayesian/.

Thomas, Roland. 1924. *Richard Price: Philosopher and Apostle of Liberty*. London: Humphrey Milford.

Turbayne, Colin. 1955. "Kant's Refutation of Dogmatic Idealism." *Philosophical Quarterly* 5 (20): 225–240.

Tversky, Amos and Daniel Kahneman. 1974. "Judgment under Uncertainty: Heuristics and Biases." *Science* 185: 1124–1131.

Van Cleve, James. 1999. *Problems from Kant*. New York and Oxford: Oxford University Press.

Van Inwagen, Peter. 1990. *Material Beings*. Ithaca, NY: Cornell University Press.

Warren, Daniel. 2001. *Reality and Impenetrability in Kant's Philosophy of Nature*. New York: Routledge.

Watkins, Eric. 2005. *Kant and the Metaphysics of Causality*. Cambridge: Cambridge University Press.

Westfall, Richard. 1966. *Science and Religion in Seventeenth Century England*. Ann Arbor: University of Michigan Press.

——1971. *The Construction of Modern Science*. New York: John Wiley and Sons.

Wilson, Catherine. 1989. *Leibniz's Metaphysics: A Historical and Comparative Study*. Princeton, NJ: Princeton University Press.

——1994. "Reply to Cover's 1993 Review *of Leibniz's Metaphysics.*" *Leibniz Society Review* 4: 5–8.

Wilson, Margaret D. 1979. "Superadded Properties: The Limits of Mechanism in Locke." *American Philosophical Quarterly* 16: 143–150.

——1982. "Superadded Properties: A Reply to M. R. Ayers." *Philosophical Review* 91 (2): 247–252.

——1992. "History of Philosophy in Philosophy Today; and the Case of the Sensible Qualities." *Philosophical Review* 101 (1): 191–243.

——1999. *Ideas and Mechanism*. Princeton, NJ: Princeton University Press.

Winkler, Kenneth. 1991. "Locke on Personal Identity." *Journal of the History of Philosophy* 29 (2): 201–226.

——1994. *Berkeley: An Interpretation*. Oxford: Clarendon Press.

Wittgenstein, Ludwig. 1958. *Philosophical Investigations*. Translated by G. E. M. Anscombe. New York: Macmillan.

Woolhouse, Roger. 1988. *The Empiricists*. Oxford: Oxford University Press.

——2007. *John Locke: A Biography*. Cambridge: Cambridge University Press.

Wright, John P. 1983. *The Sceptical Realism of David Hume*. Manchester: Manchester University Press.

Xu, Fei. 1997. "From Lot's Wife to a Pillar of Salt: Evidence that *Physical Object* is a Sortal Concept." *Mind and Language* 12: 365–392.

# Index